Spiritual Merchants

Spiritual Merchants

religion, magic, and commerce

Carolyn Morrow Long

The University of Tennessee Press / Knoxville

Quotation from the lyrics of "Hoochie Coochie Man," written
by Willie Dixon, copyright 1957, 1964, 1992 Hoochie Coochie
Music (BMI), administered by Bug Music. All rights reserved.
Used by permission.

Extensive quotations from Harry Middleton Hyatt's *Hoodoo-
Conjure-Witchcraft-Rootwork*, vols. 1–5 (Hannibal, Mo.: Western Publishing Co., 1970–78), used by permission of the estate
of Harry M. Hyatt.

All products and catalogs, unless otherwise noted, are from the
collection of the author and were photographed by Hugh
Talman. The owners of candle shops, *botánicas*, and *yerberías*,
and the manufacturers of spiritual products were photographed
by the author, unless otherwise noted. All photographs are used
by permission of the subject.

The paper used in this book meets the minimum requirements of
ANSI/NISO Z39.48-1992 (R 1997) (Permanence of Paper). The
binding materials have been chosen for strength and durability.

Library of Congress Cataloging-in-Publication Data

Long, Carolyn Morrow.
   Spiritual merchants : religion, magic, and commerce / Carolyn
Morrow Long.
      p. cm.
Includes bibliographical references and index.

ISBN 1-57233-109-7: (cl.: alk. paper)
ISBN 1-57233-110-0 (pbk.: alk. paper)
1. Charms—United States. 2. Talismans—United States.
3. Medicine, Magic, mystic, and spagiric—United States.
4. Afro-Americans—Religion. 5. Afro-Caribbean cults—
United States. 6. Religious articles—United States.
7. Religious supplies industry—United States. I. Title.
GR105 .L58 2001
299'.64—dc21   00-009886

for
Mister Doug
. . .

Contents

Illustrations

Acknowledgments

This book could never have happened without the encouragement of the University of Tennessee Press, the cooperation of the retailers and manufacturers of spiritual products who were willing to share information, and the many friends and colleagues who helped in various ways.

Meredith Morris-Babb, former acquisitions editor at University of Tennessee Press, believed that I could do this, and her successor, Joyce Harrison, continued to have faith in me.

I am eternally grateful to Martin Mayer, owner of Indio Products in Los Angeles, who not only gave a fascinating account of his own entry into the spiritual products business and allowed me to tour his factory and showroom, but also put me in touch with a network of other pioneers in the industry. I also thank Ann Epstein and Samuel Rosen of the Charleston Cut-Rate Drugstore, Doc and Richard Miller of Millers' Rexall Drug, Joseph Gerache of the Corner Drugstore, Nettie Seligmann of Harry's Occult Shop, Deloris Kay of the Keystone Lucky Store, Dale Silverberg of Lady Dale's Curio Shop, Thomas "Pop" Williams of Eye of the Cat, Ray Minton and Albert Hampton of Ray's New Age Curios, Otto Chicas of Botánica Chicas-Rendón, Ray Pizzarro of the Seven Powers Garden Temple, Frank Rodriguez of Botánica Solano, Catalina de Guzman of Botánica San Miguel, Luz Vara of House of Power, Rosario Garcia and Eloy Nañez of Rosario's Mistic, Catherine Yronwode of Lucky Mojo Products, Elliot Schwab of Schwab's Beale Street Department Store, Melinda Menke Burns and Lista Wayman of Keystone Laboratories, Gary Young of Lucky Heart, xii

Si Rosenstein of Lama Temple, Ed Kay of Dorene Publishing and Mysteria Products, Robert and Steve Amateau of M & A Amateau, and Milton Benezra of Original Products.

My friend Erin Loftus gave me the can of Uncrossing Power Incense that started me on my quest; later, she transported me around the South Carolina and Georgia Low Country in search of root doctors and hoodoo stores. She also read the entire manuscript and helped hammer out difficult points of interpretation and organization. Nancy Ochsenschlager provided me with a home in New Orleans, and, through her work with the Jazz and Heritage Festival, has given me an entrée into the community that I otherwise would not have had. Brooklyn friends Lucia McCreery and Eileen Lynch also gave me shelter and went "spiritual shopping" with me. Eddie Rodriguez was my Spanish language interpreter and guide to the *botánicas* of Spanish Harlem. My sister Kay Kunzler provided transportation and accompanied me to the spiritual stores of Jacksonville, Florida. Kelley Loftus did the same for the *yerberías* of Houston. Stanford Pritchard gave valuable advice on writing style. Hugh Talman devoted an entire Saturday afternoon to photographing all the bottles, tins, packets, labels, and catalog advertisements that illustrate these chapters.

Wyatt MacGaffey, expert on the religion of the Kongo people, read the section on African influences. Haitian *oungan* Max Beauvoir read the section on Vodou, and Michael Atwood Mason, anthropologist and *oloricha*, read the Santería section. I had intense and beneficial conversations with Ina Fandrich regarding her Ph.D. dissertation, "The Mysterious Voodoo Queen Marie Laveaux." Susheel Bibbs, who is currently researching the connection between Marie Laveau and the early civil rights advocate Mary Ellen Pleasant, also shared her discoveries. Roger Pinckney, author of *Blue Roots: African-American Folk Magic of the Gullah People*, provided inside information on Georgia/South Carolina Low Country root doctors and gave me a tour of Doctor Buzzard's old stomping grounds on St. Helena Island. Michael E. Bell, who wrote his Ph.D. dissertation on "Pattern, Structure, and Logic in Afro-American Hoodoo Performance," offered insights on the theory of charm formulation.

I benefited from the advice of several of my colleagues at the National Museum of American History, Smithsonian Institution, even though this project was not sponsored or funded by the Smithsonian. Michael Harris, formerly of the Medical Sciences Collection, helped me explore the relationship between charm beliefs, spiritual products, medicine, and pharmacy. I had an interesting exchange of ideas with Charlie McGovern—a curator in the Department of Cultural History who is investigating the commodification of blues music and the evolution of the recording industry—on the similarities between his research topic and mine. Archivist Scott Schwartz, who has documented the serpent-handling churches, also helped me deal with the problem of presenting a culture that is often sensationalized. Cynthia Vidaurri, Latino project coordinator at the Smithsonian's Center for Folklife Programs and Cultural Studies, offered insights on Mexican-American religion and magic.

David Estes, Claude Jacobs, Virginia Meacham Gould, and Roger Abrahams were my academic readers for University of Tennessee Press. All made useful suggestions, and Estes and Jacobs have become valued friends as a result of this process. David Estes also reviewed the completed manuscript prior to final submission. Nevertheless, I am responsible for any errors of content and interpretation.

I found material at many libraries and research institutions, but special thanks are due to the staffs of the Louisiana Collection at the New Orleans Public Library, the Historic New Orleans Collection, and the New Orleans Archdiocesan Archives; to Mary Linn Wernet, archivist at the Cammie G. Henry Research Center, Northwestern State University Library in Natchitoches, Louisiana, who provided hundreds of photocopies from the Louisiana Writers' Project Collection; and to Montrose Waters at the Local History and Genealogy section of the Library of Congress, who hauled out dozens of city directories. My greatest debt is to the staff of the Smithsonian Institution Libraries, who made it possible, through interlibrary loan, for me to have access to hundreds of books and journal articles.

Most of all, heartfelt gratitude to my husband, Douglas Wonderlic, who has lived with this project for six years, accompanied me on many research trips, read every word of every draft, and been my best friend always.

Introduction

An outsider, passing through certain African American and Latino neighborhoods, begins to notice shops with names like Fulton Religious Supply, Seven Archangels Candle Shop, Botánica San Lazaro, Botánica Hijo de Changó, House of Power, or Yerbería Pancho Villa. Curious, the stranger enters. The interior is crammed from floor to ceiling with a bewildering array of merchandise, some recognizably Christian and some decidedly not. Statues of the saints come in every description, from life-sized images to plastic dashboard icons. The shelves are lined with bottles of bath-and-floor wash, soaps, oils, perfumes, lotions, bath crystals, sachets, sprinkling powders, floor sweeping compound, incense, aerosol sprays, and candles. Their colorful and evocative labels offer Strong Love, Domination, Peaceful Home, Money Jackpot, Get Away Evil, Court Case, High John the Conqueror, or Death unto My Enemy; they solicit the aid of St. Michael the Archangel, the Seven African Powers, or the Virgin of Guadalupe. Behind the counter are glass jars of dried leaves and flowers, sticks and twigs, brownish powders, twisted black tubers, and pale roots like tiny, shriveled human hands. The display case contains religious medals and holy cards, charm packets and animal bones. Racks exhibit books of prayers and psalms, dream interpretation, and magical formulae. Festoons of necklaces hang from hooks—red and white, red and black, green and black, blue and clear, yellow and amber, all white, and multicolored. There are conical cement heads with cowrie-shell mouths and eyes, chains adorned with miniature tools, wooden machetes, iron horseshoes, seashells, and silver and brass crowns. And among these seemingly exotic goods, one finds mundane items like laundry bluing, saltpeter, sulfur, lye, ammonia, turpentine, cleaning fluid, and rubbing alcohol. A hand-lettered sign announces that consultations are available.[1]

■ ■ ■

This is the domain of the spiritual merchants, purveyors of health, attraction, control, success, protection, revenge, luck, the power of the saints, and the authority of the African gods. Their packaged wares, known in the trade as "spiritual products," are mass-produced renditions of the traditional spirit-embodying and spirit-directing charms used in the African-based New World belief systems. The businesses called religious stores or candle shops sell charm ingredients, occult books, and various manufactured potions oriented toward African American Voodoo and hoodoo. In the context of this book, Voodoo refers to the organized religion, closely related to Haitian Vodou, that flourished in New Orleans during the colonial period and into the nineteenth century and is now experiencing a revival. Hoodoo (called rootwork in the Georgia and South Carolina Low Country) denotes the magical practices of "workers" or "doctors" who serve individual clients. As many black Americans abandon such beliefs, hoodoo-oriented religious stores and candle shops are becoming rare. More common are the businesses known as *botánicas*, offering plants, products, and ritual paraphernalia to the followers of Santería, an Afro-Cuban religion practiced primarily by immigrants from Latin America and the Caribbean. In the Southwest, similar stores called *yerberías* stock the herbs and charms used in the Mexican systems of healing and sorcery called *curanderismo* and *brujería*, as well as Santería-oriented products that have been adopted by Mexican Americans.[2]

Although *charm* is strictly a European term and is seldom used in the African-based belief systems, I have employed it as a generic designation for the many names by which these powerful artifacts are called. A charm is any object, substance, or combination thereof believed to be capable of influencing physical, mental, and spiritual health; manipulating personal relationships and the actions of others; and invoking the aid of the deities, the dead, and the abstract concept of "luck." While a charm may consist of a single bone, a root, or a stone, charms are most often made from symbolic components that together accomplish a specific goal, taking the form of baths and washes, anointing substances, powders and sweeping compounds, fumigants, things to be ingested, and ingredients contained in bags, bottles, or other receptacles.

The preparation of charms is based upon an underlying structure that allows for considerable variation and innovation on the part of the individual practitioner. This concept is discussed in depth by Michael E. Bell in his 1980 Ph.D. dissertation, "Pattern, Structure, and Logic in Afro-American Hoodoo Performance."[3] The magical aspect of charm belief is governed by the principles of "sympathetic magic." Charms and their attendant rituals are believed to produce results because of a sympathetic connection between the charm and the person or events that the charm user desires to influence. This is accomplished by a combination of imitation and contact.

Imitative charms, operating according to the concept that like produces like, include symbolic ingredients whose properties, appearance, or name is suggestive of the purpose for which the charm was created. Thus salt, a preservative, is used for protection against evil. High John the Conqueror, a phallus-shaped root with a name that connotes power, is used to conquer enemies, bring good luck, and achieve sexual mastery over women. Images that represent the intended target of the charm—a photograph, drawing, or doll in the likeness of the person whom the charm user wishes to influence—are also examples of imitative magic.

Contagious charms operate according to the concept that things that have once been in contact continue to act on each other. Human remains and dirt from a grave invoke, by contagious magic, the power of the dead. Animal parts embody the characteristics of that animal. The possession of bodily products and intimately associated articles from a living person, or even the writing or speaking of the person's name, allows the maker of the charm to control the individual from whom they are derived. The introduction of one's own hair, fingernails, sweat, blood, or urine into the food or even into the presence of another person is also a means of control.[4]

More important than the magical principles of imitation and contact is the spiritual presence that governs the charm. In the African traditional religions, European folk Christianity and popular magic, and the African-based New World belief systems, charms are often believed either to be endowed with an indwelling spirit or to enable the user to contact and direct an external spirit. An African deity, God the Father, Jesus, the Holy Ghost, one of the saints, a folk hero, or the dead might be summoned through the ritual use of charms. In African American hoodoo practice, the religious concept of an indwelling spirit has sometimes been lost, and the user may believe that the charm itself performs the desired act. The principles of imitative and contagious magic, plus the spiritual presence behind the charm, work to achieve the intention of the charm user through choice of ingredients, charm type, and related ritual actions.

Charms and spiritual products become meaningless when they are removed from the context of belief. The person who has faith indeed feels that these agents are effective. The believer who wears a magical powder to attract a lover, sprays the house to draw money, carries a charm when applying for a job, takes a special bath to cleanse herself of evil influences, or anoints his hands with lucky oil before gambling may be endowed with the self-confidence that can produce successful results. When both the charm user and the target are believers, spouses can be controlled, undesirable neighbors can be made to move, couples can be broken up, and sickness or even death can result from the use of malefic charms. American medical journals occasionally report cases of what is referred to as "voodoo death," the inexplicable demise of a person who is convinced that he or she is the victim of sorcery.[5] Belief is reinforced when the charm user's intention is realized. A charm's failure to perform is rationalized by saying that it was used improperly, that an enemy was using something stronger, that the user's faith was insufficient, or that the desired outcome was against God's will.[6]

Traditional practitioners, through divination or consultation, diagnose the client's problem, prescribe the appropriate charms and rituals, and give advice for future action. These services are usually referred to as "work"—and there is literally work to be done. Ingredients must be sought out and prepared and ritual actions must be performed, often over an extended period. "Work" gives the client a sense that he or she is doing something about the situation and that life is no longer out of control.

Like the retailers and manufacturers of spiritual products, these traditional practitioners are also "spiritual merchants." In the ritual economy of religion and magic,[7] the devotee/client must exchange services, goods, or money for charms, healing, and empowerment. That for which one pays nothing is considered to be worth nothing. The deities and the ancestors are "paid" with ceremonies and offerings, the indwelling spirit of the charm is "fed" with various substances, and a fee is rendered to the practitioner. In the United States, some spiritual professionals charge hundreds of dollars to devise a charm and conduct the ritual necessary for treating personal problems or illness. Even when there is no fee as such, the client is usually expected to buy the requisite supplies or give a "free will love offering" to the practitioner. It is therefore not surprising that customers are willing to pay what may seem like greatly inflated prices for spiritual products purchased from a store or mail-order company.

■ ■ ■

I am often asked how I became involved in research on the charm beliefs of people of African descent in the Americas and the evolution of the spiritual products industry.

Growing up in Florida and South Georgia in the 1940s, I was surrounded by people of color who were, to a white girl in the segregated South, both familiar and unknowable. In the mid-1950s I became a teenaged rhythm-and-blues fan. Late at night, ear to the radio, parents ordering me to "shut that stuff off and go to sleep," I listened to the powerful radio signal of WLAC/Nashville, one of the few stations to play R&B at the time. Raised on the Hit Parade and the Grand Ole Opry, this music offered me a glimpse into a different world. I was especially intrigued by the mysterious references in song lyrics such as Willie Dixon's "Hoochie Coochie Man," recorded by Muddy Waters in 1954:

> I got a black cat bone,
> I got a mojo too,
> I got John de Conquer root,
> I'm gonna mess wit' you;
> I'm gonna make all you girls
> Lead me by my hand
> Then the world will know
> That I'm a Hoochie Coochie man.

Thus began a lifelong interest in a subject about which most white people, and even many African Americans, have little knowledge.

■ ■ ■

My first trip to New Orleans in the late 1970s was akin to my discovery of rhythm-and-blues. Seduced by the music, the parades, the manifestations of folk Catholicism, and the pervasive Voodoo atmosphere, I have returned again and again.

I began to explore the connection between New Orleans Voodoo and Haitian Vodou when the 1989 Smithsonian Institution Festival of American Folklife presented "The Caribbean: Cultural Encounters in the New World," including the Vodou Society of Madame Nerva from Haiti. Two museum exhibitions brought to my attention the direct relationship between African culture and African American folk traditions. *The Four*

Introduction

Moments of the Sun (National Gallery of Art, 1981), curated by Robert Farris Thompson, made me aware that the bottle-trees, grassless "swept" yards, and seashell-decorated gravesites remembered from my southern childhood were of African origin. *Astonishment and Power: Kongo Minkisi and the Art of Reneé Stout* (National Museum of African Art, Smithsonian Institution, 1993), curated by Wyatt MacGaffey and Michael D. Harris, was even more relevant in its comparison of the *minkisi* charms of the Kongo people to the mojo bags and lucky "hands" of African American hoodoo.

It was at about this time that I became aware of commercially pro-duced spiritual products. A friend had brought me a can of Sonny Boy's Uncrossing Power Incense, purchased at a neighborhood "hoodoo drug-store" in Charleston, South Carolina. Intrigued, I sought more of these artifacts. Visiting another friend's Flatbush Avenue neighborhood in Brook-lyn, I began to discover the religious stores and botánicas, with their dis-plays of beautiful, compelling, and (to me) utterly mysterious merchandise. In the fall of 1993 I found the spiritual section at A. Schwab's venerable Beale Street department store in Memphis and the F & F Candle Shop in New Orleans. I was hooked.

On these first timid incursions into the world of the spiritual mer-chants, I was embarrassingly aware of my lack of knowledge and under-standing. As my interest and curiosity evolved into a serious research project, I realized that, although mainstream Americans view charms, spiritual prod-ucts, and the beliefs that they embody as exotic, threatening, or absurd, when considered within their cultural context, these things are simply part of everyday life. The participants in the belief system, who use traditional homemade charms and buy spiritual products, do not consider them un-usual or mysterious. For them, attendance at a ceremony or consultation with a spiritual professional is as normal as going to church or to the doc-tor, and a visit to the candle shop, the botánica, or the yerbería is as ordi-nary as a trip to the drugstore or the supermarket. Likewise, the retailers and manufacturers of the products do not consider their wares bizarre or comical. For them, this is a means to earn a livelihood and provide a prod-uct to eager customers. Whether the believer serves the spirits with offer-ings and ritual actions, pays for advice and homemade charms from a traditional practitioner, or purchases spiritual products from a store or mail-order company, the required exchange must occur between the seeker and holder of spiritual power.

■ ■ ■

My educational background in studio art and art history prompted my initial aesthetic response to the world of the spiritual merchants. Entering a spiritual store was like visiting a museum filled with wondrous things. I have since adopted the methodology of the cultural historian in looking at charms and spiritual products as artifacts within a cultural context. This is aptly stated in Jules David Prown's introductory article in *History from Things: Essays on Material Culture:* "The study of material culture is the [attempt] to understand culture, to discover the beliefs—the values, ideas, attitudes, and assumptions—of a particular community or society at a given time. The underlying premise is that human-made objects reflect . . . the beliefs of the individuals who commissioned, fabricated, purchased, or used them and, by extension, the beliefs of the larger society to which these individuals belonged."[8]

I began with the artifacts themselves, from traditional charms handmade for an individual client to manufactured spiritual products mass marketed to the public. My study was supplemented by my own interviews and fieldwork and by library/archival research. I have maintained an objective viewpoint throughout this project. It has never been my intention to pass judgment on the logic of charm use or on the morality of selling and manufacturing spiritual products. The spiritual merchants presented in this book range from those who are genuine spiritual professionals, to those who sincerely desire to help people even though they are not themselves believers, to those who are outright charlatans. I leave it to the reader to judge where various individuals fall on this continuum.

Fieldwork consisted of visiting stores, collecting spiritual products, contacting manufacturers, and, when possible, gathering information from participants in the culture. Conducting research on the spiritual products industry presents difficulties not encountered when investigating the history of other American commodities. For a number of reasons, some spiritual merchants are highly secretive. Articles in the popular press, with flippant titles like "Goods for What Ails You," "Deep Voodoo," or "The Superstition Trade," have ridiculed the retailers and manufacturers of spiritual products and made them wary of talking to outsiders. Some merchants report verbal attacks by fundamentalist Christians who believe them to be selling the accoutrements of the Devil. Old-timers in the business remember the era when the sellers and makers of spiritual products were fined, jailed, or shut down for violation of various licensing and anti-swindling laws. The owners of mail-order companies worry about charges of fraud by federal postal authorities. Manufacturers fear surveillance by the Food and Drug Administration. One person cited the possibility that inclusion in my book might attract unfavorable attention from the Internal Revenue Service.

In the course of my collecting I went to approximately sixty spiritual stores in New Orleans; Memphis; Vicksburg; Miami; Jacksonville, Florida; Savannah; Charleston; Columbia, South Carolina; the Washington, D.C., area; Baltimore; Philadelphia; New York; Houston; Phoenix; and Los Angeles. When visiting a store I would chat with the personnel and observe and interact with the other customers. I always bought something. A few stores had a deliberately forbidding atmosphere; the lights were dim and the owner or sales clerk was uncommunicative. Most of the stores that I visited, however, were cheerful and friendly. If the circumstances seemed right, I explained my research project and asked permission to do a tape-recorded interview and to photograph the owner and the interior of the store. In some cases I returned for further conversations or followed up with long-distance telephone calls. A typed copy of the interview was sent to the informant and comments and corrections were invited.

From my growing collection of spiritual products I ascertained the names and locations of the manufacturers and called to request a catalog. I collected catalogs from thirty manufacturers and mail-order retail companies, including some vintage issues purchased from dealers in advertising ephemera. The older catalogs, dating from the late 1920s through the early 1950s, are filled with wonderfully exuberant illustrations and advertising copy. Recent catalogs range from glossy, four-color productions illustrated with photographs of the merchandise, to modest efforts that are typewritten, hand-illustrated, and reproduced on an office copier. All furnish a list of products, prices, and ordering information, and some offer advice on use of the products.

Through the catalogs, by telephone, or by referring to city directories, I learned the name of the company's owner and sent a letter explaining my project and assuring that any information provided would be treated seriously and respectfully. I included a questionnaire asking when the company was founded and by whom, how the owner entered the spiritual products business, whether the company was family owned, the race and religion of the owner, and the race and religion of the users of their products. A stamped, self-addressed envelope was provided for the return of the completed form. Only a few company owners responded to my initial questionnaire. If my letter of inquiry was not answered, a follow-up telephone call sometimes had good results, but some flatly refused to be interviewed, taking the perfectly understandable point of view that it is unwise to talk to strangers. Altogether, I contacted twenty manufacturers and actually interviewed fourteen by telephone or in person. During these conversations I not only sought the information solicited in my questionnaire but also explored the more sensitive issues of how the manufacturers regard the spiritual products business and to what degree they understand and accept the beliefs of their customers. With permission, these in-depth interviews were tape recorded. As with the store owners with whom I spoke, a draft of the relevant manuscript section was sent to the informant.

Insofar as possible, I tried to gain personal experience of the traditional African-based New World belief systems rather than mere "book knowledge." I attended several Vodou, Santería, and New Orleans Voodoo ceremonies as an invited guest. African American hoodoo was much less accessible. Because of the stigma attached to hoodoo, many African Americans deny any knowledge of such matters. I tried my black co-workers—scholars and professionals, clerks, security guards, and custodians—people with whom I have been friends for years, but they would skitter around the topic in embarrassment. All claimed to have no personal experience with hoodoo, although some said they knew someone who did—a great aunt in South Carolina; a mother who grew up in New Orleans; a man who used to be a janitor in the building. "And would that person be willing to share some information with me?" I would ask eagerly. "No, she died last year"; "No, she would act like she didn't know what you were talking about"; "No, he moved away and I don't know what happened to him."

I also broached the subject while serving on a mostly black, mostly female jury in Washington, D.C. My fellow jurors were more forthcoming than my colleagues, possibly because they knew they would never see me again. Women ranging in age from their twenties to their late seventies all knew of charm beliefs, although none admitted to using these things themselves. They spoke of love powders and the inclusion of one's bodily fluids in a man's food as a control charm, and were so worried about specks floating in our pitcher of ice water that they sent it back, fearing that it might be a "court-case" charm to influence the jury. One middle-aged woman was obviously uncomfortable with this conversation and busied herself reading her Bible. She took me aside at lunch to tell me that *her* family didn't believe in such things. "My father taught me that God made the African slaves suffer so terribly because they worshiped idols and believed in Voodoo." At the conclusion of our jury service the oldest of the women gave me a goodbye hug. "Don't you get too involved in this stuff, honey. It can be dangerous."

■ ■ ■

My inquiry into the charm beliefs of Africans, Europeans, and African Americans continues a tradition of scholarly research by anthropologists, folklorists, and historians. I read widely in the areas of West and Central African culture and religion, European folk Christianity and magic, and the religions of the African Diaspora. I felt that a thorough knowledge of traditional beliefs, rituals, and charms was absolutely necessary for an understanding of the products that are sold and used today.

African American magico-religious beliefs in the United States from about 1830 until the early 1940s are well documented. Many nineteenth- and early-twentieth-century writers, both white and black, viewed the retention of African language, customs, and beliefs as evidence of "savagery," which had to be overcome in order to achieve the "civilization" exemplified by European culture. Others were free of such biases and simply presented their data as interesting folklore. Some of the nineteenth-century material was written or collected by African Americans themselves. It includes the narratives of former slaves, such as Frederick Douglass and Henry Bibb, and the articles published in *The Southern Workman*, the newsletter of the Hampton Institute. White folklorists and "local color" writers also published articles on African American Voodoo and hoodoo. Newbell Niles Puckett's *Folk Beliefs of the Southern Negro* (1926) contains worthwhile information, but Puckett's work is flawed by the attitude of amused condescension that was typical of white southerners of his time. Zora Neale Hurston's "Hoodoo in America," published in the *Journal of American Folklore* in 1931 and later included in her book *Mules and Men* (1935), is the first study of twentieth-century hoodoo by an African American who became a participant in the culture. Unfortunately for the researcher, Hurston did not use the real names of the practitioners with whom she apprenticed or record the names of the stores where she shopped for spiritual products.

My two most valuable sources are the interviews with African Americans conducted by the Federal Writers' Project of the Works Projects Administration between 1935 and 1942, and Harry Middleton Hyatt's *Hoodoo-Conjuration-Witchcraft-Rootwork*, a five-volume collection of interviews recorded between 1936 and 1941.

The Federal Writers' Project was part of a government effort to provide employment for white-collar workers during the Great Depression. Through interviews and by searching newspaper files and public records, fieldworkers from the state offices undertook the documentation of existing folk culture. The Writers' Project is best known for its series of state and city guide books and for the interviews with former slaves, many of which have now been published, but the American Guides and the ex-slave narratives represent only a fraction of this remarkable endeavor.[9]

The work of the Louisiana, Florida, and Georgia (Savannah Unit) Writers' Projects is particularly valuable for the hoodoo researcher, and I have used it extensively. The Louisiana Writers' Project (LWP) material is especially rich in Voodoo and hoodoo. Fieldworkers interviewed Louisianians of every ethnic group, including many people of color. They made typed copies of a number of newspaper articles on Voodoo and compiled a bibliography of hundreds of others. They also located and transcribed civil and ecclesiastical records relating to New Orleans' most famous Voodoo priestess, Marie Laveau. In 1940 LWP staff writer Catherine Dillon drew upon these interviews, newspaper articles, and official documents to produce a 700-page manuscript entitled "Voodoo." Marcus Christian, director of the Negro Project at Dillard University, compiled a history of African Americans in Louisiana, including a chapter called "Voodooism and Mumbo Jumbo."[10] The LWP folklore collection is now housed at the Cammie G. Henry Research Center, Northwestern State University Library in Natchitoches, Louisiana, and carbon copies of some of the reports are also included in the Robert Tallant Papers at the New Orleans Public Library. The Marcus Christian papers are at the University of New Orleans Library. The majority of this documentation, including Dillon's "Voodoo" manuscript and Christian's "History of the Negro in Louisiana," remains unpublished, although some of the material, greatly altered, appears in *Gumbo Ya-Ya* (1945) and in Robert Tallant's racist and sensationalistic *Voodoo in New Orleans* (1946). Tallant changed the names of the informants, recombining bits and pieces of the interviews to make the material more "interesting," and in some cases invented informants and interviews in order to prove some point.

Some of the Florida Writers' Project material was published, with little alteration, as *Palmetto Country* (1942), but much has not been published. The files are located at the Bureau of Florida Folklife Programs in White Springs, Florida. I used the original, unpublished interviews from both the Louisiana and Florida Writers' Projects. The work of the Savannah Unit of the Georgia Writers' Project was published, in edited form, as *Drums and Shadows: Survival Studies among the Georgia Coastal Negroes* (1940). I have been unable to locate the original interviews. I also consulted the South Carolina Writers' Project collection at the University of

South Carolina Library, but found the few reports on Low Country rootwork to be disappointing.

Many of the Federal Writers' Project interviews are rendered in the stereotypical Negro dialect frequently used in the 1930s and 1940s to represent African American speech. This is not only difficult to read, it is also offensive to present-day readers because of its racist connotations. In this work, I have therefore edited passages quoted from the interviews, retaining the idioms and grammatical structure of the original, but using standard English spelling.

At the same time that Federal Writers' Project interviewers were collecting folklore all over the country, Harry Middleton Hyatt, an Episcopal priest from Quincy, Illinois, undertook a study of African American hoodoo beliefs. Using personal funds, he made several trips, traveling from New York City down the Atlantic seaboard, over to the Gulf Coast of Florida, proceeding to New Orleans, and then up through the Mississippi Delta as far as Memphis. Hyatt's method was to have a "contact man" in the black community who would seek out potential informants and bring them to the place where he was working—always a hotel, social hall, or private home owned by African Americans. The interviews were recorded on wax Telediphone cylinders. Hyatt considered his informants to be professionals who should be paid for their time. He believed he had developed the ability to spot those who were concocting an imaginary story just to collect the money. He never asked their names or addresses, feeling that such questions were likely to frighten and inhibit the informants, and sometimes he did not even note the gender of an interviewee. Each is identified only by a number and a descriptive nickname. Hyatt offered his informants no explanation of his motive for soliciting hoodoo material; many assumed that he intended to become a hoodoo doctor himself. During his five-year odyssey, Hyatt recorded interviews with 1,606 informants. In the 1970s, he finally was able to hire typists to transcribe the interviews from the wax cylinders. The transcriptions were published in five massive volumes (4,754 pages altogether) entitled *Hoodoo-Conjuration-Witchcraft-Rootwork*. The speakers' pronunciation is rendered phonetically, resulting in some very peculiar spellings that are even more difficult to decipher than the Federal Writers' Project reports. I have also converted these to standard English spellings while retaining the style of the informants' speech.

Many subsequent works on African American magical and spiritual practices have drawn upon the nineteenth-century narratives of former slaves; the *Southern Workman* articles; the material collected by Puckett, Hurston, the Federal Writers' Project, and Harry Middleton Hyatt; and other published sources. Essays include Elliot Gorn's "Black Magic: Folk Beliefs of the Slave Community" (1989) and David H. Brown's "Conjure/Doctors: An Exploration of a Black Discourse in America, Antebellum to 1940" (1990). Several Ph.D. dissertations also address nineteenth- and early-twentieth-century practices. Ina Fandrich's "The Mysterious Voodoo Queen Marie Laveaux" (Temple University, 1994) is a study of spiritual power and female leadership in nineteenth-century New Orleans. Fandrich's research in civil and archdiocesan records uncovered concrete historical documentation of Marie Laveau, but most of the oral histories quoted in her dissertation were gleaned from Robert Tallant's *Voodoo in New Orleans* rather than from the original Louisiana Writers' Project interviews. Yvonne Chireau's "Conjuring" (Princeton, 1994) deals primarily with the role of conjure as a "strategy of explanation, prediction, and control" in the community of slaves and freedmen. Michael E. Bell's "Pattern, Structure, and Logic in Afro-American Hoodoo Performance" (Indiana University, 1980) is a very useful analysis of the data recorded by Harry Middleton Hyatt.

Beginning with Melville Herskovits's *The Myth of the Negro Past* (1941), and continuing with Albert Raboteau's *Slave Religion: The "Invisible Institution" in the Antebellum South* (1978) and Robert Farris Thompson's *Flash of the Spirit: African and Afro-American Art and Philosophy* (1983), writers have drawn parallels between religious and magical beliefs, music, dance, and the visual arts in Africa and the Americas. Much attention has been given to the recent involvement of black Americans in African-based religions such as Vodou, Santería, and New Orleans Voodoo, but there has been little documentation of present-day hoodoo and rootwork. Anthony Pinn, in *Varieties of African American Religious Experience*, emphasizes the validity of non-Christian religions within the African American community. In *American Voudou: Journey into a Hidden World* (1998), Rod Davis seeks the connection between African religion and magic and the practices of African Americans in the United States. Davis found many who were willing to discuss the adoption of Vodou and Santería by black Americans and the revival of New Orleans Voodoo, but few who would talk about hoodoo.

Little has been published on the subject of hoodoo practice in the later twentieth century. *Voodoo and Hoodoo* (1978) was written by Jim Haskins, an African American who grew up in a small Alabama town where he was aware of hoodoo from childhood. The introductory chapters, "Roots in Africa" and "Culture Clash and Accommodation," are especially useful. Roger Pinckney's *Blue Roots: African-American Folk Magic of the Gullah People* (1998) deals with rootwork in the South Carolina Low Country. Neither of these books are intended as scholarly works, and sources of information are not cited. Loudell Snow, an anthropologist who has done extensive documentation of the medical folklore of African Americans, focuses on faith healers, psychic readers, and small-scale entrepreneurs who promote charms and services through newspaper advertisements and flyers. Snow is the author of "Sorcerers, Saints, and Charlatans: Black Folk Healers in Urban America" (1978) and "Mail Order Magic: The Commercial Exploitation of Folk Belief" (1979). Her book *Walkin' over Medicine* (1993) gives an overall view of African American attitudes toward health and includes some hoodoo-related material.

None of these writers has fully explored the commercial exchange between believers/clients and spiritual professionals or the commodification of traditional charms by outsiders. For information about the spiritual products industry, I had to rely almost entirely on archival research in city directories, census records, mail fraud investigations, and newspaper files, in addition to my interviews with retailers and manufacturers. Very little has been published about manufactured spiritual products, as opposed to charms formulated from natural and household substances, because most writers on African-based religions view manufactured products as a corruption of the traditional belief system. Although Puckett, Hurston, Tallant, and Snow mention spiritual products, only Haskins and Davis give the actual names and addresses of stores. Manufacturers and wholesalers are not discussed at all.

There is, at this time, no single publication that deals with both the history and current practice of the African-based belief systems in the United States and the resulting evolution of the spiritual products industry. *Spiritual Merchants* is intended for the reader who, like myself, has been intrigued by the world of charms and practitioners, candle shops, botánicas, and yerberías, and the manufacturers of spiritual products. I hope my work will be useful to scholars from a wide variety of disciplines, including folklore, ethnography, history, and religious studies, as well as to the general reader who will find in this book an introduction to a vibrant aspect of contemporary culture.

Part I will explore the role of charms in Africa and Europe, the confluence of African and European religion and culture in the Americas, and the traditional practitioners and charm beliefs of Haitian Vodou, Cuban Santería, New Orleans Voodoo, and southern hoodoo. I provide previously unpublished information on the legendary Voodoo queens and hoodoo workers Marie Laveau, Doctor John, and Doctor Buzzard. Emphasis is given to the common themes that run throughout these various cultures: the principles by which charms operate and ingredients are chosen, the intentions for which charms are used, and the exchange between clients and practitioners in the spiritual marketplace. In part II, I will trace the development of the spiritual products industry out of those traditional cultures, from early twentieth-century mail-order "doctors" and "hoodoo drugstores" to contemporary retailers and manufacturers, demonstrating how merchants who are not members of the culture entered the business. In these chapters I will address issues of race, religion, class, and economic motivation, and the complex relationships between the users, sellers, and makers of spiritual products. The final chapter is a case study of John the Conqueror root and its metamorphosis from spirit-embodying charm to commercial spiritual product.

PART I

Historical Antecedents and Traditional Practices

CHAPTER 1

African Origins and European Influences

African Origins

The charms used by New World people of African descent are derived from religious and magical traditions brought from West and Central Africa, and from European elements incorporated into the rituals and charm beliefs of the enslaved Africans. The Atlantic slave trade began in 1517. The first Africans were imported to the island of Hispaniola (now Haiti and the Dominican Republic) to replace the Arawak and Taino Indians whom the Spanish had initially attempted to enslave. Native peoples, unable to withstand enforced labor and European diseases, died in appalling numbers, and the use of European indentured servants proved to be uneconomical. The same scenario occurred in all the New World colonies. As a result, African slavery spread from Hispaniola to the other Caribbean islands, then to the mainland of North and South America, and became fully developed when the plantation system began to require a large labor force in the eighteenth and nineteenth centuries. The French, Spanish, Portuguese, English, Dutch, and Danish imported slaves from a large area of the west coast of Africa, occupied by the present-day countries of Gambia, Senegal, Mali, Sierra Leone, Liberia, Ghana, Togo, Benin, and Nigeria; and from an area of central Africa now occupied by the countries of the Democratic Republic of Congo, Cameroon, Congo-Brazzaville, Gabon, Cabinda, and Angola.

Denmark, in 1792, was the first to cease participation in the slave trade. The importation of slaves from Africa to the English colonies and the United States was outlawed in 1808, and Great Britain attempted to negotiate agreements with the other slave-trading countries to stop this evil. The Dutch complied in 1814. Cuba outlawed the importation of Africans in 1820, and Brazil in 1830. Men and women continued to be smuggled from Africa to the New World by virtually all of the slave-trading nations, including the United States, until 1862. The institution of slavery was still legal in some colonies and former colonies until almost the end of the nineteenth century. Cuba finally abolished slavery in 1886 and Brazil in 1888.[1]

Many African nations, speaking diverse languages and holding disparate religious beliefs, comprised the slave population whose descendants now inhabit the Caribbean, South America, and the United States. Those who most influenced the African-based New World religions were the Fon of the ancient West African kingdom of Dahomey, now Benin and Togo; the neighboring Yoruba of what is now Nigeria and parts of Benin; and the BaKongo from what is now the Central African nations of Angola and the Democratic Republic of Congo (the region and the culture are called Kongo, the people are BaKongo, and the language is KiKongo). The Fon, the Yoruba, and the BaKongo were imported to almost every colony in the New World, although their numbers varied according to trade agreements made between each slave-trading country and the various African nations.[2] Haitian Vodou and Louisiana Voodoo have Fon, Yoruba, and Kongo elements; Cuban Santería and Brazilian Candomblé are primarily of Yoruba origin; Cuban Palo and African American hoodoo are predominately Kongo influenced.

At the time of the slave trade, the traditional nature-centered religions of West and Central Africa were characterized by the concept that human well-being is governed by spiritual balance, by devotion to a supreme creator and a pantheon of lesser deities, by veneration and propitiation of the ancestors, and by the use of charms to embody spiritual power. Modern Africa is dominated by Islam and Christianity, and the extent to which magical and religious traditions and healing techniques are still practiced varies from country to country. In some, they are officially recognized; in others they have been forced underground, and some elements have been lost altogether.

In traditional African thought, the goal of all human endeavor was to achieve balance. Human beings were believed to come into the world pure and good and to defile themselves by acts that offended the community, the natural environment, the deities, or the ancestors, thereby upsetting spiritual balance. Physical and mental illness, injuries, and bad luck in general were thought to be the result of strife, greed, aggression, irresponsibility, and neglect. This is borne out by present-day beliefs about healing. Although modern Africans are well aware that disease is caused by microbes, parasites, and physical abnormalities, they still seek a spiritual explanation for why one individual becomes sick and another, under the same circumstances, remains healthy. Traditional African healing employed medicines derived from plants and animals, techniques for raising or lowering body temperature, fumigation, massage, dance, prayer, and sacrificial offerings, all intended to restore balance.[3]

Many African religions recognized a supreme creator who was neither good nor evil, male nor female, and was far removed from the affairs of human beings. The Fon and the Yoruba believed that below the Supreme Being were lesser deities, called *vodu* by the Fon and *orisha* by the Yoruba, who acted as intermediaries between men and the Supreme Being. The vodu and the orisha manifested themselves as the spirits of plants, animals, stones, and natural phenomena like rivers, oceans, lightning, and wind. They had control over human creativity, sexuality and reproduction, warfare, commerce, agriculture, disease, healing, and death. The divine trickster, ruler of the crossroads, controlled access to the spirit world and served as a messenger between human beings and the other deities; he also governed chance and could be persuaded to alter a person's fate. The deities could be benevolent or vengeful, depending on how well they were served by their devotees. They offered advice, foretold the future, and healed sickness, but they also could cause disease and bad luck.[4]

The Kongo people recognized a supreme being called Nzambi Mpungu and believed the universe to be inhabited with spirits that were personified by objects called *minkisi* (the singular is *nkisi*). Minkisi worked for the BaKongo just as the vodu and the orisha aided the Fon and the Yoruba. These spirit-embodying artifacts were used for healing, divination, acquiring wealth, protection, judgment, and punishment. The following explanation of minkisi was written in 1915 by Kavuna Simon, a Kongo convert to Christianity:

> [Minkisi have] the power to afflict and to heal. They receive these powers by composition, conjuration, and consecration. They are composed of earths, ashes, herbs, and leaves, and of relics of the dead . . . in order to relieve and benefit people, and to make a profit . . . to visit consequences upon thieves, witches, those who steal by sorcery, and those who harbor witchcraft

powers . . . to oppress people . . . to cause sickness in a man, and also to remove it. To destroy, to kill . . . to look after their own-ers and to visit retribution on them. . . . When you have com-posed [an *nkisi*], observe its rules lest it be annoyed and punish you. It shows no mercy.

The minkisi with which most people are familiar are the carved hu-man figures—embellished with beads, strips of cloth, animal skins, snail or cowrie shells, mirrors, and raffia—that are now displayed in museums. Pack-ets of magical ingredients were located in the head, belly, back, or genital area. Many of the male figures have been driven full of nails, spear points, knives, and bits of iron to arouse the indwelling spirit to action against an enemy—to "nail" a wrong-doer or "hammer a curse." The large figures were originally owned by priests called *nganga*, who had either made them or purchased them for a considerable sum, and had undergone initiation in order to use them. The nganga expected to derive a profit from the use of his nkisi, just as any professional requires payment for his or her services.[5]

In addition to serving the deities, most Africans had great reverence for the spirits of departed ancestors who had lived a wise and virtuous life. The ancestral spirits were remembered with offerings and praise songs; in return, they served as guides and advisors to the living. Like the deities, they would turn away, withhold their assistance, or even cause harm if they were not properly honored. Special care was taken during funerals to ensure that the ghost of the deceased did not return to haunt the living. Graveyard dirt and the bones of the dead were believed to embody the spiritual power of the ancestors.[6]

The deities and the ancestors together constituted the world of the spirits. The living served and fed the spirits, and the spirits reciprocated by helping the living. Both the deities and the ancestors manifested themselves to the faithful through spirit possession. The spirits were honored and summoned through elaborate communal ceremonies, which included drumming, chanting, and sacrificial offerings. It was believed that when possession occurred, the deity or ancestor actually displaced the devotee's own spirit, and used his or her body to act and speak.

Traditional African charms were created according to the principles of imitative and contagious magic and the premise that everything in the natural world is endowed with an indwelling spirit, or can direct the power of an external spirit, which may be used for benefit or harm.

The Fon called such charms *gbo*. Herskovits, in *Dahomey: An Ancient West African Kingdom*, defines *gbo* as "cures or supernatural aids, as well as their anti-social counterparts." They were created and sold by ritual specialists.[7] Suzanne Preston Blier discusses these charms in her essay "Vodun: West African Roots of Vodou."

> [Gbo] take the shape of special soaps, drinks, pendants, rings, hipcords, bound packets . . . [and] bottles or gourds filled with various materials—the latter being used to hold a range of powerful solutions that can be consumed or secured to trees in the field in order to protect the crops. . . . Added to the surface . . . are a wealth of materials, among them cords, leaves, iron, skeletal matter, locks, pegs, beads, cloth, gourds, earth, fur, and feathers, which individually or in combination activate the [assemblage] and convey key concerns addressed within. Most objects also emphasize attributes of binding, knotting, or piercing as a means of promoting their larger empowerment and protection roles.[8]

Gbo were "fed" with liquor, palm oil, blood, or various preparations of millet, corn flour, or hot peppers.

The Yoruba believed that plants, animals, and minerals, as well as certain man-made artifacts, had their own life force and spiritual power, called *ashé*. Within the temple, ordinary objects like cowrie shells, pieces of iron, stones, tree limbs, clay pots, and gourd bowls became representations of the deities.[9]

Among the BaKongo we find nonfigural minkisi, similar to the gbo of the Fon, which could be owned by ordinary people at small expense. These were worn on the body, hung up in the house, buried in the yard, or placed in the garden to protect the owner and his goods. Like the spirit-embodying figures, these charm assemblages contained an indwelling spirit called *mooyo*. Like gbo, they consisted of symbolic ingredients contained in snail shells, gourds, boxes, clay pots, or little cloth bags. Some types of small minkisi were wrapped in red flannel and tied with black thread. Some required "feeding" with palm wine, saliva, or blood.[10]

The contents of an nkisi were called *bilongo*. The word *bilongo*, translated by Europeans as "medicine," was not used by the BaKongo to denote only bodily remedies. What we would call "bad luck"—lack of success, loss of property, and crop failure—as well as physical illness, was treated by the bilongo contained in an nkisi. The ingredients were chosen for symbolic and linguistic reasons; they were not pharmacologically active. Graveyard dirt evoked the power of the dead. The personal attributes of the deceased— virtue, strength, virility, or malice—were thought to permeate the dust from his or her grave, and the use of that dust endowed a charm with those qualities. The head of a poisonous snake, animal teeth, the talons of a bird of prey, and knotted nets and cords symbolized the ability to attack or trap wrongdoers. Swollen, twisted, or phallus-shaped roots represented Funza, the embodiment of power and masculinity. The name of the plant, mineral, or animal part used in an nkisi was often a pun on some desired action. For example, the *mbidi* fruit was a pun on the word *bila* (praise); *matadi* (stones) was a pun on *tala* (look); *nsimba* (a bat claw) was a pun on *simba* (seize).[11]

Central to Kongo belief was the concept of the progression of human beings through the realms of the living and the dead. This was envisioned as a sacred cosmogram, the "four moments of the sun," represented by a cross within a circle. The right-hand arm of the cross represented dawn—the birth of the individual. The summit connoted noon—the peak of that person's strength on earth. The left-hand arm was evening—physical death. The bottom symbolized midnight—the power of the dead. The spirit was believed to make this journey in an everlasting cycle. The intersection of the two crossed lines symbolized the point of concentrated power where the realm of the living intersects with the realm of the spirits. The cosmogram was incorporated into minkisi and was drawn on the ground where one stood to swear an oath.[12]

The BaKongo and related peoples of Central Africa chewed and spat the juice of a magical root to ward off enemies and detect sorcerers. This was the bitter rhizome of *munkwiza*, a member of the ginger family (*Costus lucanusianus*), also called *disisa* or *nsanga-lavu*. Munkwiza was associated with chiefly power—the chief's soul, in fact, was said to reside in it. It was believed that the chief could "chew [the root] and spit at serpents to control their attack," and that if he "pointed *munkwiza* at [a person suspected of sorcery], that person would swell up and die." Many ceremonial artifacts from the Congo region, now in museum collections, depict the use of munkwiza root. A wooden nkisi shows a figure chewing munkwiza and sitting on a two-headed dog. An ivory scepter and a wooden staff both depict a chief holding a magical horn in his left hand and an elongated munkwiza root, which he chews, in his right.[13]

European Influences

As a result of contact with Europeans, enslaved Africans became aware of, and to some extent assimilated, the religious and magical beliefs held by French, Spanish, Portuguese, and English masters and indentured servants.

Of greatest importance was the folk Christianity and popular magic practiced by many Europeans of the sixteenth through the nineteenth centuries. Characterized by veneration of the saints as minor deities, belief in spirits, and the use of sacramental objects as charms, folk Christianity was remarkably similar to the traditional religions of Africa. European popular magic and healing were also compatible with African magical and medicinal practices. The theories of European intellectuals who dabbled in "ceremonial" magic and the Jewish kabbalah appear in the magical spell books that are still popular among people of African descent in the Americas.

■ ■ ■

Christianity began as a radical movement within Judaism and gradually spread throughout the Roman world. This monotheistic doctrine— primarily concerned with the subjugation of man's "animal" nature, with sin and redemption, and with the afterlife—was directly at odds with the polytheistic nature-centered religion of the Romanized Celtic peoples of Western Europe and the British Isles. The church and its missionaries, convinced that theirs was the one true religion, sought—with limited success—to eliminate pagan practices. The process of Christianization was not complete until about the ninth century, and there was a considerable blending of official Christianity with traditions and practices that were pagan in origin.

Converts were attracted to Christianity by the concept that all Christians are valued by God, by the promise of Heaven, the threat of Hell, and by the notion that they were acquiring a new and more powerful magic. Their practice of Christianity was essentially polytheistic, recognizing God the Father as supreme creator; a pantheon consisting of Jesus Christ, the Virgin Mary, and the saints; and a trickster in the persona of the Devil. Indigenous nature spirits and Roman deities who had governed springs and wells, the fertility and sexuality of human beings, disease and healing, the fruitfulness of crops and animals, metalworking, hunting, and warfare were equated with the Christian saints. Veneration of the pagan mother-goddesses was transferred to the Virgin Mary. The animal-horned gods of sexuality and fecundity became the representation of the Christian devil, who is depicted with horns, a tail, and cloven hooves.[14] The saints took on the status of minor deities who could intercede between human beings and God the Father. They were thought to have miraculous powers to heal and protect if properly honored, or to harm if they were neglected. The springs and wells that had been sacred to pagan water goddesses became the holy wells and baptisteries of Christian saints, at which even today offerings of coins and flowers are left and strips of cloth are tied to surrounding trees. Pagan fire and water festivals evolved into Christian holy days and secular celebrations, marked by bonfires and visits to holy wells and lakes. The most important of these was held on the eve of the summer solstice, which became conflated with the Feast of St. John the Baptist. St. John's Eve was celebrated with bonfires in France and Spain until the end of the nineteenth century.

European Christians believed in the reality of ghosts and spirits. The church taught that ghosts were souls caught in purgatory, unable to enter Heaven without the aid of expensive prayers and masses. Most people had a more practical notion of ghosts; they were thought to appear in order to comfort and counsel family members, warn of danger, enforce the terms of a will or deathbed promise, expose a murderer, or return stolen goods. Good and evil spirits—angels and demons—were thought to be in regular communication with human beings. A person who awoke exhausted from a sleepless night might say that he or she was "hag-ridden" by a malevolent spirit.[15]

■ ■ ■

Traditions of magic and folk medicine were preserved into the nineteenth century by men and women called wizards, cunning folk, wise men/women, or witches. Some practiced beneficial magic and healing, and others were thought to cause human illness, impotence, infertility, and abortion, to harm livestock, precipitate crop failure, and raise storms. Witches were often said to have been born with a caul (the amniotic membrane that sometimes covers the face of a newborn baby), to be the seventh child of a seventh child, and to be accompanied by an animal "familiar," often a black cat.[16] The word *witchcraft* derives from the Old English *wiccecraeft*, meaning "knowledge," and originally signified proficiency in the magical and medicinal arts, rather than diabolism. During the infamous trials of the thirteenth through the seventeenth centuries, these traditional practitioners, along with other innocent people, were accused of entering a pact with the Devil, denying the Christian faith, desecrating the sacraments, and participating in sexual orgies, human sacrifice, and ritual cannibalism.

Europeans held strong beliefs in the efficacy of charms, some of which survive until the present. Sacramental objects, the sign of the cross, and other religious artifacts were thought to be especially powerful. Holy water was imbibed as a cure for sickness and was sprinkled on people, houses, and ships to protect them from harm, and on livestock and fields to ensure fertility. The consecrated host was thought to have the power to put out fires, cure swine fever, and fertilize fields, and could also be used as a love charm. The sign of the cross was employed to ward off ghosts and evil spirits. A small wax cake bearing the image of the Lamb of God was worn as a defense against the Devil and a preservative from thunder and lightning, fire, drowning, and death in childbirth. Similar powers were ascribed to printed verses from the Gospel of St. John, which were to be worn on one's person. Christian prayers, or the names of the Father, Son, and Holy Ghost, were used to heal illness, stop bleeding, and relieve the pain of burns.[17] The alleged body or bones of a saint, a handkerchief soaked with the blood of a holy martyr, a sliver of the cross upon which Jesus was crucified, or a thorn from the crown which was pressed upon his brow, were thought to work miracles and cures, ensure good harvests, and protect the owner from harm.[18] Ex votos and milagros, in the shape of arms, legs, hands, eyes, breasts, lungs, hearts, babies, animals, food crops, or praying figures, are still placed on Christian altars and affixed to the statues of saints as petitions for a remedy.

Nonsacramental objects also served as charms. Plants were used for both magical and medicinal purposes. Some of the most common magical herbs were mandrake, garlic, basil, fennel, rosemary, rue, and yarrow to guard against supernatural attack; St. John's wort, mistletoe, and valerian for protection against lightning, ghostly visitations, and malign witchcraft; sage for wisdom and longevity; roses, daisies, and orris root for love; mugwort for prophetic dreams; and henbane and yew to conjure up the spirits of the dead. Medicinal herbs included asafetida, worn around the neck to keep away colds and fevers; mint for stomach disorders; and foxglove for heart ailments.[19] Salt, the universal preservative, was used for protection from evil; iron horseshoes, a symbol of strength, were hung over the door to prevent evil spirits from entering; graveyard dirt invoked the powerful spirits of the dead.

The image of an individual, made of wax, wood, or rags, might be pierced, burned, buried, or thrown into running water to achieve a desired outcome. Magical control was thought to be achieved by introduction of one's own body parts or by-products into the food of another, or by possession of the target's bodily products or unwashed clothing. It was believed that the preserved hand of a hanged man, called the "hand of glory," could render the person who carried it invisible and enable him to commit crimes without detection. A bag buried under the threshold, containing hair and fingernail parings from a corpse, was believed to cause chills and fever. From the records of the Inquisition comes the report of a charm made of "iron nails, needles and thread . . . fingernails, bones, and long strands of hair" found in the bed of a woman who believed she had been made sick by sorcery. The "witches' ladder," a string with nine knots, was used as a death charm, and knots were also used to "tie up" the sexuality of men and women and to prevent procreation. Reversal of the normal order, such as the inversion of the crucifix or the recitation of the Lord's Prayer backward, were used to invoke evil spirits.[20]

One finds in European magic the "law of return," which holds that an evil spell can be made to rebound against the spell caster. A farmer, believing that his cattle were dying from unnatural causes, might take the heart from one of the dead animals, stick it full of pins, and hang it in the chimney to direct the charm back against the sorcerer. Persons who believed they were the target of black magic could punish the evildoer by means of a "witch-bottle." A bottle containing urine, hair, fingernail parings, pins, iron nails, and sometimes heart shapes cut from felt and pierced with pins, was tightly sealed and buried to cause the slow demise of the enemy by urinary stoppage. The bottle might also be heated until it exploded, causing the sudden death of the evildoer. The earliest known witch-bottles were seventeenth-century stoneware "bellarmines"; glass medicine bottles were used later. Examples of witch-bottles have been found under house foundations, in chimneys, in churchyards, and in riverbeds.[21]

The Protestant Reformation, begun by Martin Luther in 1517, attempted to eliminate from Christianity those practices considered to be more magical than religious. In areas dominated by the Protestant church, the veneration of the saints and the use of sacramental objects and relics as charms was banned. Such things were considered both wicked and ineffectual—a cheap solution to difficulties that had been sent by God as punishment for sin or to test the faith of the believer. The Protestant exhorters taught that problems could only be solved by righteous living, hard work, and prayer. Ordinary people found little comfort in this theological remedy for misfortune, and they continued to turn to magic and the services of the witch for help with practical matters such as human fertility and health, love and marriage, the increase of animals and crops, protection and revenge against human enemies, and preservation from natural disasters and supernatural evils. In the Latin-Catholic countries of France, Spain, and Portugal, reliance on the intercession of the saints and the use of magical sacramental objects and relics continued unabated.[22]

While the common folk held to their tradition of popular magic, the study of ceremonial magic was taken up by intellectuals. Magicians, alchemists, astrologers, philosophers, and some medical doctors visualized the natural and spirit world as a vast, interconnected universe, where every element was capable of influencing the whole. They studied the occult properties of plants, animals, minerals, letters, colors, numbers, the influence of the stars, and the power of the spiritual beings with whom they believed the universe to be populated. They were particularly attracted to the Jewish system of mysticism and magic called the kabbalah. The theories of ceremonial magic were disseminated through the writings of the Swiss physician and alchemist known as Paracelsus and the German occult philosopher Cornelius Agrippa. Allegedly ancient works such as the *Greater Key of Solomon*, the *Lemegeton*, the *Grimorium Verum* of Alibeck the Egyptian, and the *Corpus Hermeticum* of Hermes Trismegistus were "rediscovered"— the actual antiquity of some of these texts is questionable. Other formulae for invoking spirits were circulated in manuscript form.[23]

Preoccupation with the occult continued among certain French and English intellectuals in the nineteenth and early twentieth centuries. Eliphas Levi, whose name was really Alphonse Louis Constant, was a French Catholic who studied for the priesthood before becoming involved in occultism. His works were based on earlier occult texts and were particularly influential among English magicians such as Arthur Edward Waite, MacGregor Mathers, and Aleister Crowley. Waite, Mathers, and Crowley translated Levi's writings and also produced their own works on magic, alchemy, the tarot, and the kabbalah.[24]

African-based New World Cultures

Elements of European folk Christianity and popular and ceremonial magic converged with African medical, magical, and religious traditions in the New World. The medicinal and spiritual practices of Native Americans were also added to the mix. Some of these diverse elements were incompatible and others were easily accepted by all. The Africans and Indians, as subjugated peoples, initially had to do most of the accepting, but the African and Native American influence on people of European descent has also been great. The Americas are neither European, African, nor Indian, but a cultural *mélange*.

The African concept of physical and mental health, equated with balance of the body, mind, and spirit, and harmony with the human community and the dead, is essential to the belief systems of people of African descent in the New World. Some aspects of European herbal medicine and magico-religious healing practices were also adopted. The strong-smelling herb asafetida, for example, is worn around the neck by African Americans to keep away colds and fevers, just as it was in Europe.

Africans were adept at incorporating the deities and practices of others into their own belief systems. When neighboring African kingdoms engaged in warfare, the deities of the victor would be accepted by the conquered people without replacing their existing gods and goddesses. When the slaves were "conquered" by Christian masters and missionaries, they absorbed God the Father, his son Jesus, the Virgin Mary, and the saints into their pantheon and equated them with their own deities. In the countries colonized by the French, Spanish, and Portuguese, organized Afro-Catholic religions evolved. In areas dominated by the English, Africans blended their own form of worship with Protestant Christianity and continued their magical practices outside the confines of the church.

In both Catholic and Protestant New World societies, the Christian Church attempted to eradicate African traditions. Like the practitioners of pre-Christian religious, magical, and medicinal traditions in Europe, practitioners of the African-based New World religions were called devil worshipers, their dancing and drumming ceremonies were perceived as sexual orgies, and their practice of animal sacrifice was assumed to include human victims. Like the horned gods of the pagans, the African trickster-gods became associated with the Devil, and the African snake deity—spirit of wisdom and creativity—was interpreted by Christians as a manifestation of evil. But like the Christianized Europeans, Christianized Africans in the New World were able to retain elements of their own religion.

In their respect for the spirits of departed ancestors, African and European beliefs were somewhat similar. Both cultures honored their forebears, and the ghosts of the dead were of concern to slaves and masters alike. Tales of "hags," malevolent beings who leave their bodies at night to torment and exhaust sleepers, are heard among both blacks and whites in the New World and come from the European belief that an evil spirit can "ride" a sleeping person.

The focus of this study is, of course, on magical rituals and charm beliefs, and in this area there was also a great deal of similarity between African and European traditions. The Fon had their gbo charms; the Yoruba had sacred plants, animals, and minerals; the BaKongo had their minkisi and their magical munkwiza roots; and the Europeans had their sacramental objects, relics, magical herbs, waxen images, and witch-bottles.

We can safely conclude that African American charms are primarily of African origin with considerable influence from European folk

Christianity and popular magic. Charm beliefs were a vibrant, living tradition at the time that slaves were being taken from Africa to the New World, and African magical and medicinal baths, anointing substances, fumigants, and charm assemblages are strikingly analogous to magical and medicinal substances and objects used by people of African descent in the Americas. The Kongo cosmogram turns up in charms and rituals in Latin America, the Caribbean, and the United States in the use of crossed elements in charm preparation, the drawing of cross-marks on the tombs of those believed to possess spiritual power, and the significance of the crossroads. The African American practice of chewing and spitting a magical root would certainly appear to have African antecedents.

It is more difficult to identify the European influences. Only the Christian components—candles, incense, oils, holy water, the crucifix, images of the saints, the names of the Trinity, spoken or printed prayers, psalms, and Bible verses—are unquestionably European. Among the English Protestant colonizers of North America, magical substances and objects were certainly used by the common folk who came as indentured servants, and probably by educated people of the slave-owning class as well. In Louisiana, Haiti, Cuba, and elsewhere in the Caribbean and South and Central America, charm beliefs were still inextricably entwined with folk Catholicism.

There are indeed parallels between European and African American charm beliefs. Plants, animal parts, salt, iron horseshoes, graveyard dirt, images, and human bodily products have analogous uses in Africa and Europe. Like the "hand of glory," the "lucky black cat bone" is thought to make a person invisible and allow him to commit crimes with impunity. As with practitioners of European folk magic, people of African descent use a string with nine knots to "tie up" the sexuality of a lover; the resulting selective impotence is called "loss of nature." Europeans inverted the crucifix or said the Lord's Prayer backward to invoke evil spirits; people of African descent invert a charm container or turn the image of a saint upside down to make it "work." The European concept of the "law of return" is the same as the African American belief in "turning the trick" against the maker of a harmful charm. European "witch-bottles" filled with pins, nails, and bodily products are remarkably similar to African American bottle charms. Europeans and African Americans both used a beef heart stuck with pins as a death charm. And like European witches, many African American hoodoo workers attributed their abilities to having been born with a "veil" (caul) or to being a seventh child of a seventh child.

African Origins and European Influences

European magic was not only introduced into the New World as oral tradition. Such beliefs were also circulated in the form of handwritten manuscripts and printed volumes, which were later reissued in various languages, plagiarized, altered, and scrambled, and are still distributed as magical spell books. Occult texts called *grimoires* were used by people of African descent in the French Caribbean colonies. Two such books, *La Poule Noire* (The Black Pullet) and *Les Secrets Merveilleux de la Magie Naturelle du Petit Albert* (Little Albert's Marvelous Secrets of Natural Magic), commonly called the *'Tit Albert*, were favored by French-speaking blacks in Louisiana. Occult books were also popular among African Americans. Two works of German origin, *The Egyptian Secrets of Albertus Magnus*, a collection of folk medicine and charms, and *The Sixth and Seventh Books of Moses*, based on the kabbalah and other Hebrew texts, were translated into English in the nineteenth century. L. W. DeLaurence's *Great Book of Magical Art*, a mishmash of ideas culled from European and English texts on ceremonial magic, the kabbalah, Hinduism, and Spiritualism, was published in Chicago in 1902. These books, and others like them, were used by hoodoo workers in the United States and are still sold today, adding elements of European folk and ceremonial magic to the African American belief system.

Native American beliefs were incorporated into the African-based belief systems in South and Central America, but were negligible in most of the Caribbean islands, where the native population had been virtually exterminated before the arrival of large numbers of enslaved Africans. In the southeastern United States, Native Americans and people of African descent mingled and intermarried, and blacks undoubtedly gained a knowledge of sacred and medicinal plants from their Indian associates. But the concept of "luck" and the idea that people and events can be influenced by means of charms is alien to the indigenous peoples of North America. While Indian herbalism may have been incorporated into African American practice, little else of Indian origin can be identified in Voodoo, hoodoo, and rootwork.[25]

CHAPTER 2

African—Based Religions in the Latin—Catholic Colonies

The retention of African beliefs in the New World was influenced by the ratio of blacks to whites, the number of slaves born in Africa relative to those born in the colonies, and the degree of supervision by masters and overseers. The evolution of the African-based New World religions depended on the national origin of the slave population of each colony, as well as the compatibility of the religion of the Europeans with that of the Africans. In the French, Spanish, and Portuguese colonies of South America and the Caribbean, we find a vibrant combination of Catholicism with the Fon, Yoruba, and Kongo religions. In the English North American colonies, Protestantism was paired with the Kongo belief system.[1]

In the Latin-Catholic colonies, labor-intensive agricultural and mining economies required a huge slave population. Slavery on the sugar plantations of Cuba and Saint-Domingue (now Haiti) and in the mines of Brazil was so brutal that slaves survived only an average of ten years, and the workforce had to be continually replenished by new arrivals from Africa. Hundreds of blacks were managed by a few whites, whose influence on their culture was minimal. Urban slaves experienced better circumstances. Many were skilled artisans who were able to earn money for the purchase of their freedom, resulting in a sizable population of free people of color.

The rulers of France, Spain, and Portugal answered to the Roman Catholic Church, which recognized African slaves as human beings and felt obligated to convert them to Christianity. A body of law, known as the

Black Codes, spelled out the treatment of slaves and stipulated that all must be baptized and instructed in the Catholic faith.[2] But the Catholicism to which the Africans were exposed was not exactly orthodox. Although most of the white colonists thought of themselves as devout Christians, priests were few, religious education was almost nonexistent, and people who were unable to comprehend the more complex points of theological doctrine practiced a kind of folk Catholicism that adhered even less to official church doctrine than that of Europe. In the French, Spanish, and Portuguese colonies of South America, the Caribbean, and Louisiana, the saints, rather than serving as Christian role models as intended by the Catholic Church, were treated as minor deities and venerated at home altars; sacramental objects were commonly used as charms.[3]

The identification between the African deities and the saints is based less on a similarity of characteristics than on visual details found in the chromolithographed images given to the slaves by Catholic missionaries and still reproduced as holy cards. The Vodou snake-deity Dambala has nothing in common with St. Patrick; the unifying element is the serpents that, in the chromolithograph of St. Patrick, are being driven over the edge of a cliff. The voluptuous Ezili-Freda, the Vodou spirit of love and femininity, shares no characteristics with the Mater Dolorosa except that both are beautiful, light-skinned women. Changó, who in Santería personifies thunder, lightning, and masculinity, is identified with a female saint, St. Barbara, because her persecutors were destroyed by lightning. Babalú Ayé, ruler of disease and healing, is represented by St. Lazarus because his chromolithograph depicts him as a leper.

We will concentrate here on Vodou and Santería in order to understand their influence on beliefs and practices in the United States and to identify and explain some of the ritual objects, plants, images of saints, and spiritual products sold in American botánicas. Because many devotees of Santería are also involved to some degree with Palo and Espiritismo, these belief systems will also be discussed.

What evolved into Vodou and Santería originated in the coastal West African nation-states now occupied by Benin, Togo, and Nigeria, known collectively as the Bight of Benin. Vodou is primarily based on the religion of the Fon people, who were present in large numbers in the slave population of Saint-Domingue. Santería originated with the Yoruba, who constituted a large percentage of the population in Cuba. The Fon kingdom of Dahomey and the city-states of the Yoruba were ruled by priestly monarchs and possessed highly developed cultures. Their complex and sophisticated religions followed the previously described model of a supreme being and a pantheon of lesser deities. During the late-eighteenth and early-nineteenth centuries, these neighboring nations engaged in warfare with each other, selling their prisoners of war into slavery. Neighboring Muslim peoples also sold Fon and Yoruba captives to slave traders. Among the prisoners were rulers, priests, healers, musicians, and artists, as well as more ordinary folk, all of whom helped to transmit the culture to the Americas.[4]

The years of interaction between the Fon and the Yoruba resulted in a great deal of cultural interchange, and Vodou and Santería are therefore analogous in many ways. Both are characterized by recognition of a supreme being and a pantheon of deities and ancestors that manifest themselves through spirit possession. Some of the deities of Vodou and Santería have similar names and attributes, and all are paired with Catholic saints. The deities are honored with spectacular altars, and their symbols are kept in special lidded jars. Religious ceremonies serve the spirits with music, dance, and offerings, and seek to resolve difficulties within the community. Some aspects of initiation into Vodou and Santería are similar, requiring the candidate to return to a state of infancy and be reborn into the religion.

Vodou

The colonial period in Saint-Domingue came to an abrupt end in 1791 with the bloody slave revolt that triggered the Haitian Revolution. Under the leadership of the black generals Toussaint L'Ouverture, Jean-Jacques Dessalines, and Henri Christophe, the French forces were defeated, and in 1804 Saint-Domingue became the Republic of Haiti, the first independent black nation in the Americas. All of the whites and many of the wealthy free people of color fled to France, Cuba, or Louisiana. The original constitution of Haiti prohibited any white person from becoming a citizen or owning property. The French Catholic priesthood was expelled and did not return until an 1860 concordat with Rome. Few foreign governments recognized the Republic of Haiti, and the country was left in near isolation for most of the nineteenth century. Although Vodou was not officially sanctioned by the Haitian government during this period, worshipers were not persecuted and the religion evolved and grew strong without interference.

Gradually, outsiders returned to Haiti. Vodou was severely repressed during the occupation by the U.S. Marines from 1915 to 1934. The Catholic

Church has initiated periodic "antisuperstition campaigns," destroying Vodou temples and ceremonial objects. Evangelical American Protestant missionaries have been totally uncompromising, equating Vodou with Satanism. During the Duvalier years, 1957 to 1986, foreign tourism was promoted, and spurious "tourist voodoo" shows flourished in Port-au-Prince, degrading the religion to mere entertainment. With the coming of a fragile democracy in Haiti, Vodou may be entering a new phase of acceptance and appreciation as a serious religion. The Constitution of 1987 guarantees the protection of all religious practices, including Vodou.[5]

The name Vodou comes from *vodu*, which in the language of the Fon means "mysterious forces or powers that govern the world and those who reside within it."[6] In the Fon religion, the Supreme Being, an androgynous deity called Mawu-Lisa, created the vodu to act as intermediaries between itself and human beings. In Haiti the Supreme Being is called Bondye (Bon Dieu), and is the equivalent of the Christian God the Father. The lesser deities are called *lwa*.[7]

The lwa number in the hundreds, and new manifestations are constantly evolving. They are often divided into two major categories, Rada and Petwo. The Rada deities are those who came from Africa; the name derives from the ancient Dahomean city of Arada. They are gentle, wise, and "cool." The Petwo deities are usually said to have originated in Haiti, born out of the struggle against slavery, oppression, and poverty. They are aggressive and "hot"; they get the job done in a hurry and can be dangerous. Petwo is also heavily influenced by Kongo religious practices. Many of the lwa have both a Rada and a Petwo manifestation, and some, such as Ogou and Ezili, have many names and personalities, ranging from benign to terrifying. It is not true, as is sometimes stated, that Rada is "white magic" and Petwo is "black magic."

The following is a very brief summary of the most important lwa and their corresponding saints: Legba, derived from the trickster-god Eshu (recognized by both the Fon and the Yoruba), is the aged guardian of the crossroads who opens the gate between the human and the spirit world; he is associated with the image of St. Peter holding the keys of heaven. Dambala, the wise and gentle snake god, is associated with the image of St. Patrick banishing the serpents. The spirit of iron and warfare, Ogou, is identified with St. James the Great, and sometimes with St. Michael the Archangel, because both are warriors who brandish an iron weapon. Agwe, the master of the ocean, is represented by St. Ulrich, who holds a fish. The Rada lwa Ezili-Freda personifies femininity, love, and beauty, a gorgeous light-skinned courtesan dressed in silk and lace; she is associated with the Mater Dolorosa. In her Petwo aspect she is Ezili-Dantò, a tough, hardworking black peasant woman who is a fiercely protective mother. Dantò is represented by the Mater Salvatoris—the Black Madonna. The Gèdès are a group of spirits who govern death, the cemetery, and sex. Their chief is Bawon Samedi (Baron Saturday), who is associated with St. Gerome, a monk depicted with a human skull on his desk. Bawon dresses in a black tuxedo and top hat, smokes cigars, wears dark glasses, tells obscene jokes in a peculiar nasal voice, and dances the lascivious, pelvis-thrusting *banda*. The sacred twins, the Marasa, are represented by the twin saints Cosmas and Damian. Azaka is the patron of agriculture, represented by St. Isidore the Farmer. Gran Bwa is the spirit of the forest, represented by the image of the martyred St. Sebastian tied to a tree.

Participants in the religion do not refer to themselves as "Vodouists"; they simply say that they "serve the lwa." All consider themselves good Catholics. The members of a Vodou congregation are called *la société* (the society) and are expected to help and support each other. No initiation is required to become a member of a société, but the initiation rites for *ounsi* (the female assistants of the Vodou temple) are rigorous and expensive. After the candidates are instructed in the ritual chants, salutations, and dance steps, they participate in prayers and ritual baths and undergo a seven-day period of seclusion. Each candidate receives the lwa who will be her spiritual protector. At the end of the seven days, the initiates are "reborn." Each receives a necklace in the symbolic colors of her lwa, is dressed in new white clothing, and is presented to the société in an elaborate celebration.[8]

Vodou priests are called *oungan*, and priestesses are *mambo*. When an oungan or mambo is initiated, he or she is said to "take the *ason*"—the gourd rattle that is the symbol of priestly authority. These religious professionals are supported by the Vodou society, and usually need not have outside jobs. Fees are charged for services, consultations, preparation of charms, and healing. Some priests are also skilled artists who supplement their income through the sale of paintings, ironwork, and sequined Vodou flags.

The complex of buildings that constitutes a Vodou temple includes an open courtyard where large ceremonies are held, and the sanctuary called the *ounfo*. Inside the ounfo are altars of great beauty and complexity. They display statues and chromolithographs of the saints, food offerings, bottles of liquor, candles, dolls dressed to represent the lwa, cigarettes and cigars, perfume, native Indian ax-heads believed to be sacred thunder stones, and various kinds of charms. There are also the *govi*—lidded jars where the lwa reside. The govi are "dressed" in the symbolic colors of the lwa that they house.

The purpose of a Vodou service is always to honor the lwa and to bring the congregation together for the resolution of problems. The ceremony begins with ritual salutations between the presiding oungan or mambo and the ounsi. The sword and the beaded and sequined flags are carried in a procession around the ounfo. Libations are poured on the ground. There are songs and prayers. Symbols called *vèvè* are drawn on the ground with cornmeal to summon the spirits: a pair of serpents for Dambala, a boat for Agwe, a heart for Ezili, and more abstract symbols for the other lwa. The lwa for whom the service is intended determines the selection of songs, drum rhythms, and offerings of prepared food, fruit, and sacrificial animals. The animal designated for sacrifice is most often a chicken, but sometimes a pig, a goat, or a bull is required. It is killed quickly and neatly by a trained ritual specialist. When the desired spirit has arrived, he or she possesses, or "mounts," the body of one of the worshipers, and the possessed person becomes the deity, takes on the voice and manner of the lwa, and is dressed in the appropriate attire regardless of gender. A man possessed by Ezili-Freda may put on a gown, behave seductively, and be offered sweets; a woman possessed by Ogou may don a military uniform, speak in a gruff voice, drink strong cane liquor, and swing a machete. The lwa addresses the congregation through the possessed devotee. The ceremony usually ends with a community feast; the elaborate meal has been given to the spirits, who in turn give it back to the people.

In addition to the large services, in which the whole congregation participates, an oungan or mambo may perform consultations, readings, or healing ceremonies for an individual. The goal is to use the energies of the client to solve problems, usually related to personal relationships, money, employment, or health. This is referred to as *travay*, meaning "work." The role of the priest as healer is especially important in rural Haiti, where access to medical doctors is almost nonexistent. As in Africa, the Vodou definition of health is equilibrium and harmony between body, mind, and spirit. The presence of pathogens is acknowledged, but it is disharmony that causes illness.[9]

When a client comes for a consultation, the oungan or mambo evokes a particular lwa to deal with the problem. The lwa, speaking through the priest, prescribes certain magical and medicinal rituals—usually a combination of offerings, prayers, candles, powders, baths, massage, or herbal teas. A written petition or a photograph may be placed on the altar for the lwa. Sometimes the image of a saint is turned upside down to arouse the spirit to action. A charm may be fabricated and blessed by the priest so that it can "work" for the client.[10]

There are also practitioners called *bòkò*, whose purpose is less benevolent. Unlike the oungan or mambo, who is concerned with the welfare of the congregation, the *bòkò* is interested in personal power. He is what would traditionally be called a sorcerer. His altar is filled with skulls and whips; ritual objects that are tied, knotted, and crossed; bottles and dolls wrapped with cord and hung upside down; and vessels and mirrors tied to chairs. In her article on a Port-au-Prince bòkò, "A Sorcerer's Bottle: The Visual Art of Magic in Haiti," Elizabeth McAlister defines him as "a man out for himself, a freelancer . . . an entrepreneur . . . a man who will 'work with both hands,' that is, for [both] healing and revenge."[11]

Some of the charms used in Haitian Vodou are directly related to the gbo of the Fon and the minkisi of the BaKongo. Like the African and European charms discussed in the last chapter, they consist of symbolic ingredients and operate according to the principles of imitative and contagious magic. All Vodou charms could be categorized as *pwen*, meaning a point of concentrated energy intended to control people and events. The Kongo influence is evident in the presence of many crossed or tied elements. Pwen are often incorporated into some sort of container. Karen McCarthy Brown, in her 1991 study of Haitian Vodou priestess Mama Lola (*Mama Lola: A Vodou Priestess in Brooklyn*), gives several examples of pwen: To dissolve a relationship, two dolls are bound back to back and hung up in the cemetery. A pwen intended to bring back a lover is made by writing the man's name eleven times on both sides of a piece of paper; the paper is folded, put in a bottle of honey water, and sealed with wax drippings from a candle. The bottle is bound round and round, top to bottom, until it is completely covered with white string. A *gad* (bodyguard) is a type of pwen intended for protection. In Brown's book, Mama Lola expresses shock at the carelessness of one of her clients: "Look at her . . . she got no *gad* on herself. She got no *gad* on the house. She got those little children. They got nothing on them!" After her house was broken into, Mama Lola made a gad from a doll with a mirror bound to its chest, which was submerged in a bottle of water and positioned in the window where the thief had entered.[12] *Wanga* are charms, provided by a bókó, intended to cause the downfall of an enemy. Their symbolic ingredients often include human remains and dirt from the crossroads. They can also take the form of powder sprinkled on the ground in the shape of a cross where the intended victim will walk.

The charms called *pakèts kongo* (Kongo packets for protection and healing) are directly descended from Kongo minkisi. Pakèts kongo have a gourdlike shape with a globular body and a slender "stem"; some have "arms" that give them an anthropomorphic look. The herbs and other ingredients inside the body are wrapped in silk, bound with ribbons secured with pins, and adorned with sequins, beads, metallic cloth, and feathers. Some are topped with a crucifix or other crossed elements.[13] Many Kongo minkisi also display this gourdlike shape, although they are more crudely made.[14]

Santería

After the revolution put an end to Haitian sugar production, Cuba became the major producer of sugar in the Caribbean, and huge numbers of slaves were imported to Cuba to work in the sugar mills. Some 20 to 50 percent of the Africans entering Cuba between the late eighteenth and mid-nineteenth centuries were Yoruba. Fon and BaKongo were also represented in large numbers.[15] Africans were legally imported into Cuba until 1820, but smuggling continued until 1862. Slavery was finally abolished in 1886. While arrivals from the African homeland kept the religion and culture strong, there has been a continuous European presence in Cuba, and the population is much more racially mixed than that of Haiti. The island remained a colony of Spain until 1898. Cuba was occupied by the United States in 1898–1902 and again in 1906–9. Afro-Cuban religious celebrations were banned by the U.S. military government and continued to be prohibited by Cuban authorities until the mid-twentieth century. Since the revolution of 1959, Cuba has had a Communist government that views all religion as folklore. People are free to practice any religion so long as it is not perceived as politically or ideologically incompatible with Communism.[16]

The Yoruba slaves in Cuba called themselves Lucumí—a contraction of the Yoruba phrase meaning "my friend." Just as Africans in Haiti masked their beliefs behind a veneer of Catholicism, the Lucumí associated their deities with God the Father, Jesus, the Virgin Mary, and the saints. The Catholic Church encouraged urban slaves and free blacks to organize social clubs and mutual aid societies, called *cabildos*, which were based on national origin. The cabildos afforded the means to preserve the worship traditions of the various African nations. After emancipation, the cabildos were disbanded and reemerged as Afro-Cuban religious houses called *reglas*.

The Lucumí cabildo became known as La Regla de Ocha, and other Afro-Cubans and some whites eventually became members. Although the religion is commonly referred to as Santería (way of the saints), believers prefer Ocha or Lucumí, emphasizing its African aspect.[17] I use Santería in this work with no intention to offend, but because the name is more familiar to readers than Ocha and Lucumí.

Santería, like other African traditional religions, recognizes a supreme being, Olodumare, the remote, genderless creator of the universe; the *orisha* (*orichas* or *ochas* in Cuban Spanish),[18] who serve as intermediaries between Olodumare and human beings; and the deified ancestors, called *egun*. The entire universe, including Olodumare, the orichas, the ancestors, human beings, plants, animals, minerals, fire, water, earth, and wind, is thought to be endowed with *aché*, the primal force.

Some of the orichas have counterparts among the Vodou lwa, with similar names and attributes. This brief summary lists the most important orichas: Eleguá, like Legba, is a trickster-god who delights in confusing people. He is also a guardian spirit, and he acts as a messenger between the orichas and humankind. One of his representations is a small, conical cement or clay head with eyes, mouth, nose, and ears made of cowrie shells, with a nail protruding from the top. His Catholic counterpart is the child El Niño de Atocha. Obatalá, the oricha of wisdom, peace, purity, and creativity, is represented by an aspect of the Virgin, Our Lady of Mercy. Ogún, like Ogou in Haiti, governs iron, physical labor, and warfare; he is associated with the warrior saints James the Great and Michael the Archangel. Yemayá is the oricha of the ocean and of motherhood, associated with Our Lady of Regla, a black virgin. She is analogous to Ezili-Dantò. Ochún, the oricha of rivers, is, like Ezili-Freda, a lovely woman of mixed race who symbolizes feminine beauty and sensuality. She is represented by Our Lady of Charity (La Virgen de la Caridad de Cobre). Changó is the lord of thunder and lightning, the epitome of masculinity, who is very attractive to women. He is identified with St. Barbara. In his manifestation as Changó Macho, he is depicted as a powerfully built African. Oyá is the oricha of storms and winds. She governs the marketplace, masquerades, and the cemetery, and is the personification of female leadership. Oyá is represented by the Virgin of Candelaria, a rather militant-looking virgin who carries a sword. Orula, represented by St. Francis of Assisi, is the lord of divination. The Ibeyi, like the Marasa, are twin children associated with St. Cosmas and St. Damian. Ochosi is the divine hunter and patron of prisoners. He and Osun, another warrior spirit, are the companions of Ogún. Babalú Ayé governs disease and healing. He is associated with St. Lazarus, the patron saint of lepers

A person who wishes to join the religion undergoes progressive initiations. The priests who officiate at initiation become the *madrina* (godmother) and *padrino* (godfather) of the devotee. At the first initiation, *los collares* (the necklaces) are conferred by the madrina. The necklaces, which have been soaked in an herbal bath, represent Eleguá, Obatalá, Yemayá, Ochún, Changó, and sometimes Oyá. The necklaces are composed of beads in the symbolic colors of the orichas: red and black for Eleguá, all white for Obatalá, blue and clear for Yemayá, yellow and transparent amber for Ochún, red and white for Changó, and nine colors for Oyá.

In the second initiation, *los guerreros*, the devotee is invested with the warrior spirits Eleguá, Ogún, Ochosi, and Osun, who protect him or her from physical and spiritual harm. During the ceremony, the padrino presents the symbols of these deities to the candidate: the cement head of Eleguá, an iron cauldron filled with eight miniature tools for Ogún, a small iron bow and arrow for Ochosi, and a metal rooster with four bells for Osun. Eleguá, Ogún, and Ochosi are kept as guardians just inside the door. Osun's rooster is placed high on a shelf, to warn the initiate by falling over when danger threatens.

The next order of initiation is undertaken by those who desire to become a priest of the religion. Believers prefer the title *oloricha* (*babaloricha* for a man and *iyaloricha* for a woman), but *santero* and *santera* are more commonly used by outsiders. This extremely complex and expensive seven-day process is called *kariocha* (crowning the oricha on the head) or *asiento* (making the saint). A person must take on the character of a baby in the womb in order to be reborn. Afterward, the candidate is presented to the community, seated within an altar space and dressed in a splendid consecration garment and crown especially designed to portray the characteristics of the ruling oricha.[19] A celebration takes place, and the fruits, vegetables, and animals that were offered to the oricha become a communal feast. For one year following initiation, the new priest must observe certain restrictions and always dress in white.[20] Divination may determine that a man should become a *babalawo*, a priest of Orula, the highest order of the Santería hierarchy. This path is not open to women.

The Santería temple is called a *casa de ocha* (house of the orichas) or an *ilé*. Within the ilé, objects sacred to the orichas are kept in a special cabinet; if space permits, a shrine room is set aside for this purpose. The stones that contain the spiritual essence of the orichas are kept in *soperas* (lidded porcelain tureens) or in earthenware or iron pots. The soperas and other vessels are decorated according to the oricha contained within. They are draped with elaborate, multistranded necklaces in the symbolic colors of the orichas. The soperas for the female deities are topped by beautiful metal crowns—brass for Ochún and Oyá, silver for Yemayá. Ogún's iron cauldron, sometimes containing horseshoes, railroad spikes, and other iron objects, is draped with a chain to which are affixed miniature iron tools. Offerings to the orichas are placed on top of their containers, and the stones must be periodically anointed with substances appropriate to the particular oricha.

Ceremonies are held not only for initiation of new candidates, but also to commemorate the initiation anniversary of a priest, to celebrate the birthday of an oricha, to bring in the new year, or to resolve problems within the community. Services are also conducted for individual clients. Cleansings involve the passing of an animal (usually a fowl) or a bunch of herbs over the body of the worshiper to pick up evil influences.

Because every major and even minor decision is based upon the consultation of oracles, many people resort to a priest of Santería for readings. *Obi* involves casting four pieces of coconut; positive, negative, or uncertain answers are obtained according to the number of pieces that fall with the white flesh or the brown shell facing up. Even noninitiates may use this system. The cowrie shell divination, the *caracoles*, must be performed by an oloricha. The objective is for an oricha, speaking through the priest, to enable the devotee to solve problems by guiding him or her toward a more balanced life. For each question asked, sixteen shells are thrown. There are 256 possible configurations of the shells, falling with either their "mouth" side or their back side up. Each configuration represents a body of proverbs, myths, and recommended sacrifices, which must be interpreted by the priest. A skilled reader can answer extremely complicated questions about personal relationships, career, money, and health problems. The client is advised to take certain actions and is told to offer a small sacrifice to the oricha. The highest form of divination is the oracle of Ifá, which may only be consulted by a babalawo, a priest of Orula. The babalawo uses a divining chain, to which are attached eight pieces of coconut shell.

As in Vodou, every religious act, whether it is a large ceremony involving hundreds of worshipers or a private ritual performed by an individual, requires some sort of offering (*ebó*) to the orichas. This may be flowers, fruit, liquor, cooked foods, or the sacrifice of living animals, determined by the purpose of the ritual, the traditional preference of the oricha, and the instructions received through divination. Animals are killed instantly by a ritual specialist. Sometimes the offerings are eaten by the participants and sometimes they must not be eaten. When the purpose of the ceremony is thanksgiving to the orichas for favors granted, or when a member of the community is being initiated, all of the foods, both vegetable and animal, are cooked and eaten by the participants. It would be considered inappropriate to consume offerings that are made to propitiate an angry oricha, animals that are killed to save the life of a devotee, and animals that have been used in spiritual cleansings. The desire of the oricha in regard to disposal of the offering is determined by divination.

We have already noted the use of many ritual objects in Santería. With a few exceptions, charm assemblages of the type found in Vodou, which are related to Fon and Kongo charms, do not occur in Santería. Recall that the Yoruba recognized the spiritual power (ashé) in plants, animals, minerals, and man-made artifacts, but did not construct charms analogous to gbo or minkisi. *Resguardos* (defenses, similar to Haitian gad) are charm packets containing herbs, powders, sticks, and stones to impart good luck and protection to the owner; they must be periodically given offerings of rum and tobacco smoke. David H. Brown, in *Garden in the Machine: Afro-Cuban Sacred Art and Performance in Urban New Jersey and New York*, described a particularly evocative charm against gossip, a beef tongue pierced by two knives and a number of pins, hanging in the window of an ilé. Printed images of the "Divine Eye and Tongue Passed through with Dagger" have the same significance.[21] Much more common is the use of fresh plants. Each oricha has his or her preferred plants, which may be used for cleansings, for *despojos* (healing and purifying baths), and for medicinal teas.

■ ■ ■

In addition to serving the orichas, some people also practice the Cuban belief system known as Palo Monte, Palo Mayombe, or La Regla de Kongo. A person may be both an oricha priest and a *palero*, but the two practices must be strictly separated. Palo, which is roughly analogous to Haitian Petwo, evolved out of the Kongo *cabildo*. The *palero* works with the dead and with Kongo spirits, perceived as hot, aggressive, quick, and potentially dangerous, like the rebellious Kongo slaves who fled the plantations to form "maroon" enclaves in the forests. (*Maroon* comes from the Spanish word *cimarrón*, meaning a runaway slave.) Palo is there-fore sometimes associated with sorcery. The spirits reside in three-legged iron cauldrons called *prendas*. The name Palo, in fact, derives from the Spanish word for "stick," and refers to the lengths of various magical woods (*palos*) that are incorporated into the prenda. Like Kongo minkisi, prendas are formulated from plant material, animal parts, stones, and other objects that embody spiritual power. Some contain graveyard dirt and human remains, which symbolically harness the powers of the dead. A Kongo cosmogram in the shape of a cross is often chalked in the bottom of the cauldron. Because of its explosive energy, the prenda must be kept as far as possible from the shrine of the orichas, in a separate room or even outside the house.[22]

■ ■ ■

Many followers of Santería also participate in Spiritist services based upon the philosophy of the nineteenth-century French scholar Hypolite Léon Denizard Rivail, better known as "Allan Kardec." Kardec's Spiritist doc-trine grew out of the Spiritualist movement that spread throughout the United States and Europe in the 1850s, when upper-class people became fascinated with the idea of communication with the dead or with spirit guides through a human medium. Spiritism, as set forth in the writings of Allan Kardec, found many adherents in South America and the Carib-bean. Kardec's books were extremely popular in Brazil, Puerto Rico, and Cuba, where his theories were incorporated into African-based religious systems. In Cuba and Puerto Rico this tradition is called Espiritismo. Espiritismo is a means of honoring and communicating with the ancestors by means of the *bóveda espiritual*, an altar table covered with a white cloth on which are placed glasses of water to attract the spirits, photographs of the dead, candles, and flowers. Spirit guides represent ethnic archetypes: *La Madama*, an ample-bodied black woman who is an herbal healer and fortune teller; *El Indio*, representing independence; and *El Congo*, a strong African. Prayers from Kardec's books are read, and the spirits possess the medium and give advice.[23]

Vodou and Santería in the United States

In the United States, the African-based New World religions have been continually reinforced by waves of immigration from Haiti, Cuba, Puerto

Rico, and other Caribbean and South America countries. Vodou and Santería have evolved differently owing to demographics and the prejudices of both Americans and the immigrant community.

In the early nineteenth century, shortly after the purchase of Louisiana by the United States, the Haitian Revolution drove thousands of refugees into Louisiana (and some into Charleston) and generated an increase in Vodou activity. American authorities, fearing a similar slave insurrection in this country, sought to control the new arrivals and to suppress Vodou. The government of Haiti was not recognized by the United States until 1862; even into the twentieth century, white Americans were uncomfortable with the idea of a nation administered by blacks. Negative stereotypes of Haitians in general and Vodou in particular reached new heights during the 1915–34 occupation of Haiti by U.S. Marines. Haitians were considered to be hopelessly mired in superstition and barbarism, a people incapable of governing themselves. A series of racist and sensationalistic novels and films emerged during this period: *The Magic Island, The White King of La Gonave, Cannibal Cousins, Voodoo Fire in Haiti, Black Bagdad,* and *I Walked with a Zombie.*[24]

Old prejudices resurfaced when large numbers of Haitians, fleeing desperate political and economic conditions in their own country, arrived in the United States in the mid-1980s. These immigrants, many of whom entered the country illegally, were stereotyped by Americans as poor, illiterate, carriers of the AIDS virus, and practitioners of sorcery. They were also looked down upon by other Spanish-speaking immigrants from Latin America and the Caribbean, from whom they, as Kreyól speakers, were isolated because of language.[25] Most of the Haitian immigrants have settled in Miami and New York, although there are small Haitian communities in other cities. For the reasons cited above, Haitians prefer to keep a low profile, and little Vodou activity is visible to the outsider. Vodou communities certainly exist in the United States, and some black and white Americans have become initiates, as documented in Karen McCarthy Brown's *Mama Lola,* but they remain underground.

In contrast, Santería is one of the fastest-growing religions in the United States, and evidence of oricha worship is encountered in every American city with a large Latino population. There has, of course, been a certain amount of prejudice against Cubans as well, especially Afro-Cubans, and Santería has certainly received its share of bad publicity. The bizarre ritual murders that occurred in Matamoros, Mexico, in 1989 were mistakenly attributed to Santería. Hollywood films and the popular press often convey a stereotypical portrayal of oricha worship as black magic and grisly animal sacrifice. Nevertheless, Santería has never generated quite the same fear and revulsion as Vodou, and its practice is therefore more open.

Cubans of African descent began to enter South Florida in the early nineteenth century as cigar makers, settling in Key West and the Tampa neighborhood called Ybor City. We have several accounts from the 1930s of the practices of Afro-Cubans in Tampa. These reports are racist, sensationalistic, and undoubtedly inaccurate, but it appears that both the followers of the orichas and the secret ñañigo societies were active in Florida. The ñañigos are Afro-Cuban descendants of Efik-speaking peoples from the Calabar region of West Africa. The files of the Florida Writers' Project contain descriptions of ñañigos, said to be dedicated to "crime, witchcraft, devil worship, and voodooism."[26] An article based on Florida Writers' Project reports was published in the 1939 *Southern Folklore Quarterly*, citing the practices of "Cuban Negroes who . . . prey on the gullibility of the ignorant for mercenary purposes, using the lore, the deities, potions, amulets, and the rest of their paraphernalia as scenery and mumbo-jumbo to impress their clients." The author never uses the terms *Santería* or *Lucumí* in describing the religion of the Afro-Cubans, but refers to "their chief deity" as Obatalá, assisted by "Shangó the God of Thunder and Elegbá the Evil-Doer." He describes twin dolls, evidently the Ibeyi, dressed in red and decorated with bead necklaces, coins, and keys. According to the article, a "witchdoctor's" house is recognized by the sign of three corncobs tied together and hung on the front door. Inside is an altar, on which are placed "gourds, coconuts, bouquets of flowers, wax candles, broken bits of china, and a few articles used in Catholic worship: rosaries, crosses, and the like." The practitioner used herbs for healing, offered help with love problems, and could place and remove curses.[27]

Santería was introduced into New York City in the 1930s and 1940s by Cuban immigrants. The first babalawo in New York was Pancho Mora, who arrived in 1946 and lived there until his death in 1986. Many of the popular Cuban musicians who settled in New York at that time, such as Mario Bauzá, Chano Pozo, and Frank "Machito" Grillo, were followers of the orichas. A community of Latin American, Caribbean, and black American worshipers eventually developed in multiethnic neighborhoods like Spanish Harlem and the South Bronx.[28]

Following the 1959 revolution, many Cubans, mostly white professionals, arrived in the United States, settling in South Florida. Later immigrants, especially those who came by way of Mariel in 1980, were primarily black working-class people. They tended to settle in the New York/New Jersey area. In *Santería from Africa to the New World*, George Brandon states that many of these émigrés became followers of the orichas after leaving Cuba, as a reaction to the sense of displacement that they experienced in the United States.[29] Afro-Cuban religious practices reached the West Coast in the 1980s, centering in Los Angeles.[30] Although Cubans and Puerto Ricans form the majority of the Santería community, they have been joined by Dominicans, Guatemalans, Salvadorans, Mexicans, Colombians, Venezuelans, and others.

In recent years, some well-educated, middle-class Americans have been attracted to Santería. Like those who have joined Vodou congregations, these new adherents avidly study the history and theology of the religion, attend seminars and workshops, and seek out mentors and spiritual communities. Some undergo initiation and are even more zealous in their devotion than those who were born into the religion. The folklore and anthropology programs at some universities have become centers for the study of the African-based religions. The internet has also become a venue for the dissemination of information. There are web sites, discussion lists, and newsgroups for both Vodou and Santería.

For people of African descent, the African-based religions are an affirmation of their cultural heritage. Walter King, the first African American to become an oloricha, was initiated in Cuba in 1959. Under the name Oba Osejiman Adefunmi, he founded the African Theological Archministry with the idea of uniting all the African Diaspora religions, purifying them of European/Christian influences, and making them more accessible to the public. This manifestation of the religion is sometimes called "Orisha-Vodu." In 1970, after a growing rift with the Cuban and Puerto Rican ocha community in New York, he founded the Oyotunji Yoruba Village in South Carolina.[31]

■ ■ ■

Vodou and Santería have, out of necessity, undergone changes in the United States in the late twentieth century. Most Americans are extremely uncomfortable with the idea of animal sacrifice. They overlook the fact that, in Haiti and Cuba, domestic animals are routinely killed in preparation for the family meal (just as they were in the United States before meat came neatly wrapped in plastic from the supermarket) and that many Americans still hunt and kill animals for sport. Officials in Miami are particularly troubled by the appearance of dead chickens and goats on the courthouse steps, and the discovery in the courtroom of such things as dead lizards with their mouths tied shut with twine or a beef tongue wrapped with black thread. A special "Voodoo Squad" of janitors has been appointed to remove the animal remains.[32] David H. Brown reports that, in the mid-1980s, New York/New Jersey ilés were regularly raided by the police and the ASPCA looking for evidence of animal sacrifice, and that worshipers attempting to leave offerings for the orichas in public places—the crossroads, the park, the church, the cemetery, the jail, the courthouse, the ocean, the river, the market, or the subway tracks—were subject to arrest for "littering."[33] The 1988 statement of a California animal-rights activist has racist and chauvinistic overtones: "We're a civilized society. . . . I can't condone the senseless . . . butchering and torture of these animals for a primitive religious belief. . . . If they want to practice [animal sacrifice], let them go back to where they came from."[34]

In 1987 the Miami suburb of Hialeah passed ordinances against animal sacrifice and shut down the temple of babalawo Ernesto Pichardo, declaring that "this community will not tolerate religious practices that are abhorrent to its citizens." Pichardo, assisted by the American Civil Liberties Union, took the case to the Supreme Court, where it was decided that animal sacrifice for religious purposes is permissible if the animals are killed without suffering; if only domestic fowl, pigs, cattle, sheep, and goats are used; if the meat is used for food; and if the dead animals are disposed of in an "acceptable" manner.[35] The first of these conditions is easily met—sacrificial animals are never tortured. The second also poses little difficulty—the orichas seldom ask for animals that are not normally consumed as food. But, as we have seen from the above discussion, some offerings are not to be eaten, and the orichas may require that sacrificed animals be left at places considered inappropriate by most Americans.

Other changes in Vodou and Santería are due to the monetary demands, increased mobility, and shortage of time and space engendered by the urban American lifestyle. Some priests and priestesses are unable to support themselves through their religious work and must have full-time outside jobs, leaving less time to attend to spiritual duties. People move often due to the exigencies of the job market, meaning that initiates will not be affiliated with the same community for a lifetime. The ceremonial headquarters of a Vodou or Santería congregation is usually located in an urban row house or a large apartment building, meaning that the size of the gathering is limited, libations must be poured into a basin instead of on the ground, and music, drumming, dancing, and spirit possession must be kept quiet so as not to attract unfavorable attention from the neighbors.[36] The internationally famous Haitian oungan Max Beauvoir now lives in an upscale apartment complex in Washington, D.C., where strict rules prohibit pets (one wonders how the management reacts to sacrificial animals) and social gatherings must end at midnight.[37] When I attended a Santería ceremony at a Washington, D.C., ilé, all offerings—fruit, cooked foods, and decapitated chickens—were neatly bundled up and whisked away to the building's dumpster.

Vodou and Santería have also generated a whole economy of artisans and merchants in the United States: seamstresses who specialize in initiation garments and other clothing, designers and builders of altars, makers of necklaces and bead-covered ritual objects, purveyors of live animals for sacrifice, importers of fresh herbs, and, of course, botánica owners.

In any city where the African-based religions are practiced, one will find botánicas that sell ritual items and spiritual products. The yellow pages of the Miami, New York, and Los Angeles telephone directories list column after column of botánicas under "religious goods." Botánicas provide everything necessary for Santería, Palo, and Espiritismo. There are necklaces in the colors of the orichas, cowrie shells for divination, porcelain soup tureens, clay pots, iron cauldrons, crowns, paper cups of *cascarilla* (powdered egg shell), palm oil, dried herbs, palos (sticks), plaster replicas and prints of the "tongue passed through with dagger," and images of the saints. One can find the attributes of the orichas: cement Eleguá heads; iron spikes, horseshoes, miniature tools, and full-sized wooden machetes for Ogún; Changó's double-headed ax; handcuffs for Ochosi, as well as his bow and arrow; Osun's rooster; seashells for Yemayá. Some stores have fresh plants flown in weekly from the Caribbean. Statues representing the spirit guides of Espiritismo are also sold in botánicas. La Madama, the black herbal healer and fortune teller, is represented by a figure adopted from the stereotypical Aunt Jemima–type "mammy." El Indio is portrayed as a North American plains warrior in a feathered headdress, and El Congo is depicted as an old black man wearing a straw hat, work clothes, and a red scarf. Many botánicas are owned by olorichas, paleros, or espiritistas who offer divination and consultations; those that are owned by noninitiates often have a reader on the premises. Outside of Miami, it is difficult to identify much that is specifically associated with Vodou, even in Haitian-owned stores.[38] In 1994 I visited two Haitian-owned botánicas in Brooklyn—Feraille and Botanique St. Jacques

Majeur—and found only generic spiritual products. Island of Salvation in New Orleans, run by a white couple who are initiates of Vodou, sells ritual items such as sequined Vodou flags and pakèts kongo.

The manufacturers of spiritual products have, of course, observed that there is a ready market for items incorporating the imagery of Santería and Espiritismo. According to one oloricha with whom I spoke, those who follow the most pure and orthodox forms of the African-based religions do not use commercial products. But many of those who buy are noninitiates with little understanding of these complex theologies, who are reinterpreting and adapting the products for their own uses. The iconography of Vodou is conspicuously absent, nor have I seen titles or images based on Palo. The names and images of the orichas, their corresponding saints, and the spirit guides of Espiritismo (and even its founder, Allan Kardec) are found on baths and washes, soaps, powders, perfumes, incense, aerosol sprays, and candles. Especially popular is the image of the Seven African Powers, which depicts the saints identified with the names of the major orichas.

The extent to which the accouterments of Santería are being commodified by those with no understanding of the religion is illustrated by an advertising flyer I received in late 1998. This piece of junk mail announces that "Santería is the most powerful force ever harnessed by man, and the Seven African Powers are the most potent force in all of Santería." For twenty-five dollars plus shipping, says the advertisement with my name mechanically inserted, I can possess the Jeweled Talisman of the Seven African Powers, set with seven semiprecious stones representing Our Lady of Mercy, St. Anthony, St. Barbara, St. Peter, St. Francis, Our Lady of Regla, and Our Lady of Charity—the orichas are never mentioned. This artifact will allegedly empower me to "amass huge fortunes, dispel all debts, win lottery millions, find true love, achieve every form of success, and enjoy happiness."[39]

African-Based Religions

CHAPTER 3

New Orleans Voodoo

The conditions that allowed African-based religions to develop in South America and the Caribbean generally did not exist in North America. But in Louisiana, originally a Latin-Catholic colony with a relatively high ratio of Africans and people of African descent to Europeans, Voodoo evolved in the eighteenth and nineteenth centuries as an organized religion with a pantheon of deities, a structured theology, and an initiated priesthood and congregation of believers. Most of this activity centered in New Orleans and the surrounding countryside. Although the practice was suppressed during much of the twentieth century, elements of the belief system survived in various altered and submerged forms, and there has been a recent upsurge of interest in Voodoo as a legitimate religion.

The name *Voodoo*, like Vodou in Haiti, comes from *vodu*, meaning "spiritual forces" in the Fon language. Until the early twentieth century the name was spelled "Voudou" by most Louisiana writers. "Voodoo" is an Americanized spelling that began to appear during the occupation of Haiti by American Marines, and was applied to the practice in both Haiti and Louisiana. The word has acquired the negative connotation of black magic. I do not use it here in this derogatory and racist context, but to distinguish the New Orleans tradition from Haitian Vodou. Many practitioners simply call it "the work" and refer to themselves as "workers."

Louisiana was colonized by the French in 1699, and the first African slaves were introduced in 1719. Although the colony was transferred to the Spanish in 1763 and governed by Spain until 1803, it remained French and African in culture. In 1803 Louisiana was returned to France; twenty days later it was sold to the United States. The inhabitants of Louisiana practiced the same sort of folk Catholicism, characterized by veneration of the saints as minor deities and the use of sacramental objects for magical purposes, as those in the other French, Spanish, and Portuguese colonies of South America and the Caribbean, including Saint-Domingue and Cuba.[1] As in other Latin-Catholic colonies, the Black Code stipulated that slaves, who were recognized as human beings, be baptized and instructed in the Catholic religion. The church, although it certainly did not condone Voodoo practice, made no official attempt to suppress it.

For several reasons, New Orleans Voodoo did not survive as a highly developed Afro-Catholic religion like Haitian Vodou and Cuban Santería. The ratio of blacks to whites was considerably lower in Louisiana than in the Caribbean, and fewer slaves were imported directly from Africa. Although Louisiana had a higher concentration of Africans than most other parts of the American South, their numbers were small compared to the African populations of Haiti and Cuba. The total number of Africans brought into Louisiana was approximately 28,000, while Saint-Domingue received approximately 864,000 and Cuba received approximately 702,000. Both these island nations are roughly the size of the state of Louisiana.[2] After Louisiana came under American control, the evolution of New Orleans Voodoo was cut short by increasingly repressive laws and police interference and by the disapproval of the Protestant churches that were winning many black converts. By the end of the nineteenth century, organized Voodoo had been virtually eradicated due to police harassment and religious intolerance.

New Orleans Voodoo before 1900

The elements that would become Voodoo arrived with the first Africans. Between 1719 and 1743 the Company of the Indies, licensed by the French government to control the slave trade between Africa and Louisiana, imported Wolofs, Fulbes, Mandingas, and Bambaras from the Senegambia region on the upper West Coast of Africa, now the countries of Senegal, Gambia, Sierra Leone, Ghana, and Mali. Some were Muslim, and the others practiced various forms of African traditional religion. A small number of slaves from the French Caribbean colonies of Saint-Domingue, Martinique, and Guadeloupe also entered Louisiana.[3] Antoine Le Page du Pratz, a French planter and employee of the Company of the Indies in Louisiana in the 1730s, published the first history of the colony, *Histoire de la*

Louisiane, in 1758. Le Page wrote in his chapter on the treatment of slaves: "Nothing is more to be dreaded than to see the negroes assemble together on Sundays, since, under pretext of the Calinda [a dance], they sometimes get together to the number of three or four hundred, and make a kind of Sabbath. . . . They are very superstitious and attached . . . to little toys which they call *gris-gris* . . . [and] they would believe themselves undone if they were stripped of these trinkets."[4] The word *gris-gris*, connoting a charm of any kind, is derived from the Mende language spoken by the Mandingas and Bambaras and is still part of the New Orleans Voodoo lexicon.[5]

Under Spanish rule, slaves were imported from many areas of West Africa, including Fon and Yoruba from the Bight of Benin and Kongo peoples from Central Africa. As we have seen, the religious beliefs of these nations were also the basis of Vodou, Santería, and Palo. In *Africans in Colonial Louisiana*, Gwendolyn Midlo Hall states that "Fon and Yoruba religious practices . . . account for the emergence and resilience of Voodoo in Louisiana. Fon and Yoruba women were present in significant numbers, and they tended to be clustered together on certain estates. . . . Kongo influence is discernible in . . . the use of the term *wanga* for a [harmful] charm."[6] Recall that *wanga* has the same meaning in Haitian Vodou. The first prosecution of Voodoo activity, the 1773 "Gri-Gri Case" in which several slaves were tried for conspiring to kill their master and the plantation overseer by means of a "poisonous" charm, is recorded in the Spanish Judicial Archives of Louisiana.[7]

During the French and Spanish colonial period, slaves were granted an unusual degree of autonomy and had many opportunities to gain their freedom. Some were manumitted by their owners for good and faithful service. Women who became the consorts of white men and bore their children were often freed, along with their offspring. Men could gain their liberty by serving in the militia. Many slaves became skilled artisans and were hired out by their masters; they were allowed to keep a portion of their earnings and used this money to purchase their freedom. Plantation slaves also escaped into the cypress swamps and bayous to form maroon communities with local Indians.

Because of the relative ease with which a Louisiana slave could become free, and because of the unusual degree of racial intermingling in colonial Louisiana, there existed a strong community of free people of color who were of mixed African and European heritage. These *gens de couleur libre* were a separate caste, neither white nor black. Some were wealthy and well educated, controlling extensive property in New Orleans or plantations in the countryside, and were themselves slaveholders. The majority owned their own homes and earned a modest living as artisans, militiamen, shop-keepers, street vendors, laundresses, boardinghouse managers, hairdressers, and seamstresses.[8]

Africans and people of African descent were able to mingle freely with their countrymen and preserve their cultural traditions. Sunday was set aside as a day of recreation for the slaves, and at several sites around New Orleans they were allowed to assemble for religious and secular cel-ebrations. By about 1740 an area behind the original city called the *Place des Negres* was being used as a public market by blacks. After 1800 slaves and free Negroes also met there to dance on Sunday afternoons, and the site came to be known as Congo Square. These gatherings drew many white spectators and became a tourist attraction for American and European visi-tors. In 1807 a traveler noted that the dancers were "ornamented with . . . [the] tails of the smaller wild beasts, [with] fringes, ribbons, little bells, and shells and balls, jingling . . . about the performers' legs and arms."[9] The English-born architect and engineer Benjamin Latrobe, in New Orleans to oversee the building of the municipal waterworks, saw the dances in 1819. While walking about the city on a Sunday afternoon, he heard "a most ex-traordinary noise," and, following the sound, found between five and six hun-dred blacks assembled in Congo Square. They were "formed into circular groups," in the center of which women were dancing, accompanied by Afri-can drums and stringed instruments.[10] Riverboat travelers reported see-ing hundreds of blacks "drumming, fifing, and dancing in large rings" on the river levees. In 1831 a French visitor saw slaves dancing on the banks of Lake Pontchartrain. They were, he said, gathered in "distinct groups, each with its own flag floating atop a very tall mast."[11] The circles de-scribed in these accounts probably represent societies based on national origin, somewhat resembling the cabildos of colonial Cuba.

There is no reliable firsthand report of an early Voodoo service. What is often cited as the description of a ceremony held in the swamp near New Orleans during the colonial period turns out not to have occurred in Loui-siana at all, but was lifted verbatim from a history of colonial Saint-Domingue, Medric Louis Moreau de Saint-Méry's *Description Topographique, Physic, Civile, et Historique de la Partie Francaise de l'Isle Saint-Domingue* (1797). Moreau describes a Vodou service for a serpent deity, undoubtedly Dambala, represented by a snake in a cage adorned with little bells. A "king" and "queen," possessed by the deity, counseled and instructed the assembled community; a goat was sacrificed, new initiates were received and given a

Historical Antecedents and Traditional Practices

protective charm, and the ceremony ended with drumming and dancing. Like subsequent writers on Vodou, Moreau felt compelled to describe this as a sexual orgy:

> The delirium keeps rising. . . . Faintings and raptures take over some of them and a sort of fury [takes] . . . the others, but for all there is a nervous trembling which they cannot master. They spin around ceaselessly. And there are some in this species of bacchanal who tear their clothing and even bite their flesh. Others, who are deprived of their senses and fall in their tracks, are taken . . . into the darkness of a neighboring room, where a disgusting prostitution exercises a most hideous empire.[12]

In 1883 Moreau's narrative reappeared in a travel journal called *Souvenirs d'Amérique et de France par une Créole,* published anonymously by a New Orleans resident, Hélène d'Aquin Allain. It has since been translated into English, paraphrased, and repeated by writers from the 1880s until the present.[13] Its origin has been forgotten. The description is now, unfortunately, accepted as the classic New Orleans Voodoo ceremony, complete with queen, snake, gris-gris, bloody animal sacrifice, and sexual debauchery.

At the time of the Louisiana Purchase in 1803, the population of New Orleans was French-speaking, Catholic, and a majority had some degree of African blood. The people, regardless of color, realized that *les Americains* would eventually destroy their way of life. The new Anglo-Protestant American citizens viewed Catholicism as idolatry and looked upon the white Creoles as indolent, uneducated, and lacking in business sense. They were horrified by the free-and-easy character and racial mixing of local society, the permissiveness of Louisiana slavery, and by the autonomy of the free people of color. Under the Americans, slavery became much more harsh and the rights of the colored Creoles were eroded.

Within a few years of the Louisiana Purchase, the Afro-French population further increased as a result of the revolution in Saint-Domingue (1791–1804) that ended with the creation of the Republic of Haiti. Thousands of free people of color and French planters, with their African (mostly Fon, Yoruba, and Kongo) slaves, fled the fighting and political upheaval. Some of the refugees escaped directly to Louisiana. Others sought shelter in Cuba, but after Napoleon's invasion of Spain in 1809 they were forced out by the Spanish government and made their way to Louisiana. In that year an estimated ten thousand newcomers arrived in New Orleans, outnumbering the local residents. The immigrants were more or less equally divided among whites, slaves, and free people of color.[14] The Haitians of African descent, both slave and free, brought their Vodou beliefs with them and found ready acceptance among those who already practiced the traditional African religions. According to historian Gwendolyn Midlo Hall, "Slaves from the Bight of Benin [including Fon and Yoruba imported during the Spanish colonial period] probably account for the emergence of Voodoo in Louisiana, which was reinforced by the massive immigration of Haitians in 1809."[15]

The Americans who moved into Louisiana following the Purchase of 1803 considered Voodoo both comical and frightening, and by 1820 the growing influence of the religion began to engender newspaper articles denouncing Voodoo. Journalists either adopted a jocular tone (implying that nobody with good sense would take it seriously) or attempted to demonize the practice by describing it as savage and orgiastic. The first such account, entitled "Idolatry and Quackery," reported the arrest of several persons of color and one white man on a charge of holding illegal nighttime meetings. "A house in the suburb Tremé has been used as a kind of temple for certain occult practices and the idolatrous worship of an African deity called *Vaudoo*. It is said that many slaves and some free people repaired there of nights to practice superstitious, idolatrous rites, to dance, carouse, &c."[16] The white citizens of Louisiana were well aware of the role of Vodou in the Haitian revolution. Attempted slave insurrections in Louisiana and elsewhere in the South, plus agitation by northern abolitionists, made authorities nervous about any mixed gathering of slaves, free people of color, and whites. Voodoo seemed like a particularly dangerous activity. These fears accelerated in the 1850s, and police regularly raided Voodoo services and arrested the participants for "unlawful assembly."[17] An article in the *Daily Picayune* stated that:

> This kind of meeting appears to be rapidly on the increase. . . . Carried on in secret, they bring the slaves into contact with disorderly free negroes and mischievous whites, and the effect cannot be otherwise than to promote discontent, inflame passions, teach them vicious practices, and indispose them to the performance of their duty to their masters. . . . The public may have learned from the [recent] Voudou disclosures what takes place at such meetings—the mystic ceremonies, wild orgies, dancing, singing, etc. . . . The police should have their attention continually alive to the importance of breaking up such unlawful practices.[18]

The Civil War period was particularly disruptive to the Voodoo community. New Orleans was occupied by Union troops, who were even less accepting of Voodoo activity than the local authorities had been. Congo Square was fenced and landscaped and the Sunday afternoon dances were abolished. During Reconstruction, according to Tulane University historian Blake Touchstone, "the conservative white press was quick to exploit . . . Voodoo, making it appear that blacks were ill prepared to vote and hold office. . . . Voodoo might be used to buttress white arguments of Negro inferiority and the need for legalized segregation.[19]

Late nineteenth-century writers denigrated Voodoo. James William Buel, in *Metropolitan Life Unveiled* (1882), included a chapter called "New Orleans—Negro Superstitions," in which he traced New Orleans Voodoo to its origins in "the heathenish atrocities perpetrated in Africa."

> Instead of recognizing a merciful spirit, which we call God, these barbarians call upon and labor with the devil. . . . All good, as well as all evil, is attributed to this demon, consequently sacrifices are made to appease [his] wrath or to invite his kind offices . . . in earlier years human sacrifices were undoubtedly rendered up with great ceremony. The reason why they are not still continued will be found in the civilizing influence of Christianity, and particularly in the deterrent effects of a stringent law that refuses to exempt priest or layman.[20]

Henry Castellanos, in *New Orleans As It Was* (1895), wrote of the "mysterious sect of fanatics imported from the jungles of Africa . . . with its stupid creed and bestial rites."[21] Even George Washington Cable, who usually was sympathetic to New Orleans' people of color, had no kind words for Voodoo. In his *Century Magazine* article, "Creole Slave Songs" (1886), he spoke of "worship [that was] as dark and horrid as bestialized savagery could make the adoration of serpents. So revolting was it, and so morally hideous, that even in the West Indian French possessions a hundred years ago . . . the orgies of the Voodoos were forbidden."[22]

Despite these prejudices and restrictions, Voodoo priests and priestesses served the congregation of believers throughout the nineteenth century. In Haiti or Cuba these spiritual leaders would have held the title of oungan or mambo, santero or santera; in Louisiana they were called "doctors" and "queens." There must have been many such practitioners in Louisiana, but only a few names—some of which may have been fictional—have been preserved through the work of journalists and local-color writers. One reads of Sanité Dédé, Marie Saloppé, Marie Comtesse, Doctor Jim Alexander, Malvina Latour, Doctor John, and, of course, Marie Laveau.[23] All but Doctor John and Marie Laveau have been forgotten.

Doctor John is remembered primarily because his title has been adopted by the popular New Orleans musician Mac Rebennack. Most of what we know about Doctor John comes from an 1885 *Harper's Weekly* article, "The Last of the Voudous," by Lafcadio Hearn, a journalist who worked in New Orleans from 1877 to 1887. According to Hearn, Doctor John was a native of Senegal who went by the name Jean Montane, a former slave who had made his way from Cuba to New Orleans as a ship's cook, worked as an overseer on the docks, and eventually became known as a fortune-teller and practitioner of herbal medicine. He is described as being "very strongly built, with . . . inky black skin, retreating forehead, small bright eyes, a flat nose, and a woolly beard, gray only during the last few years of his long life. He had a resonant voice and a very authoritative manner." His appearance was distinguished by a series of parallel scars on his cheeks, which he claimed were marks of royalty. Hearn tells us that Doctor John became wealthy from his Voodoo practice, owned a large tract of land on the Bayou Road between Prieur and Roman Streets, that he had numerous wives, one of whom was white, and many children. In his later years he lost his property and fortune due to gambling and bad investments and died penniless at the home of his daughter.[24]

Hearn's article is supported by the appearance in city directories of a physician named John Montane, free man of color, living at the corner of Bayou Road and Prieur. John Montane (also spelled Montanet and Montancé) appeared in the United States census for 1850, 1860, 1870, and 1880. He is easily identifiable because he was one of the few African-born New Orleanians still living by the last half of the nineteenth century. In 1850 he was listed as Jean Montanet, the owner of a coffeehouse; the only member of his household was a three-year-old boy. His real estate was valued at $4,000. In 1860 John Montane was living with a woman named Mathilde; their seven children ranged in age from fourteen to three years. His real estate was valued at $12,000 and his personal property at $500, comparable to the holdings of many well-to-do white New Orleanians. "Physician" was recorded as his occupation, although the census enumerator could not resist inserting "quack" in parenthesis. In 1870 and 1880, the woman listed as his wife was named Armantine. Montane's age was given as seventy-nine in 1880; five sons and daughters, the youngest of whom was only a year old, were living at the family home at 232 Prieur Street. The 1880 census calls Montane an "Indian doctor." His 1885 death certificate records him as John Montancé, a native of Africa, who died of Bright's disease on August 23. The death was reported by Alicia Montancé (a daughter named Alicia is listed in the census of 1870).[25] Curiously, there was no obituary in the local newspapers.

Marie Laveau is perhaps more famous today than she was during her own lifetime. Although volumes of nonsense have been written about her, she was an actual person about whom there exists a good deal of concrete documentation. Ina Fandrich's Ph.D. dissertation, "Mysterious Voodoo Queen Marie Laveaux: A Study of Spiritual Power and Female Leadership in Nineteenth Century New Orleans" (Department of Religious Studies, Temple University, 1994), is the first published history of Marie Laveau based on archival research. My own investigation of civil and ecclesiastical records verifies most, but not all, of Fandrich's assertions.

Marie Laveau was in some ways a perfectly ordinary free woman of color—a wife, a mother, and a devout Catholic, living in a modest home in the old section of New Orleans now known as the French Quarter. She was also extraordinary—a Voodoo professional and a highly successful spiritual merchant who, through a combination of physical beauty, charisma, showmanship, and shrewd business sense, made money and captured the imagination of people of all classes.

Marie Laveau was a woman of mixed African and European ancestry born in New Orleans around the turn of the nineteenth century. The years 1783 and 1794 have been suggested as possible birth dates, but archival evidence leads me to favor 1801.[26] The first official record of her existence documents her 1819 marriage in St. Louis Cathedral to Jacques Paris, a free man of color from Saint-Domingue. The sacramental register states that Marie was the natural daughter of Marguerite D'Arcantel and Charles Laveaux. Little is known about Marguerite D'Arcantel, but archival records indicate that she was the daughter of Catherine Pomet/Henry, a free woman of color.[27] We have substantially more information about Charles Laveaux. Although popular legend maintains that he was a wealthy white planter, Laveaux was actually a prosperous free man of color who owned several businesses and a considerable amount of real estate. When Marie married Jacques Paris she received from her father a lot on Rampart Street that later passed to one of her daughters.[28]

There is some indication that Marie gave birth to her first child a few months after her marriage to Paris. In a 1930 interview, Liga Foley, who claimed to be Marie Laveau's granddaughter, stated that her mother was born to Marie in late 1819. Paris was not the father, and this child, named Delphine, was raised in another household.[29] I was unable to find any documentation of a daughter named Delphine being born to Marie Laveau, or of the supposed granddaughter, Liga Foley.

Jacques Paris died or disappeared a few years later, and Marie became known as "the Widow Paris." She subsequently entered into a relationship with Louis Christophe Dominic Duminy de Glapion, which lasted until his death in 1855. Although later accounts assert that Glapion was a man of color from Saint-Domingue, his death certificate and property succession records indicate that he was born in Louisiana and was the legitimate son of white parents. His paternal grandfather was a French nobleman, the Chevalier Christophe de Glapion, Seigneur du Mesnil-Gauche (later shortened to Duminil or Duminy). The Chevalier de Glapion served as collector of royal fines under the Spanish government.[30] Christophe Glapion and Marie Laveau are said to have had fifteen children, but only Marie Heloïse (born in 1827, probably the same person as Eloise Euchariste, who died in 1862), Marie Louise Caroline (died in infancy 1829), François (1833–1834), Marie Philomene (1836–1896), and Archange (1838–1845) can be accounted for through civil and church records.[31] Only Philomene outlived her mother.

Between 1846 and her death in 1881, Marie—the Widow Paris—appeared regularly in the New Orleans city directories, usually as Mrs. Laveau (or Lavan) Paris, although she was sometimes listed as Marie Laveau or Marie Glapion. The family also appeared in the United States census. In 1850 the Widow Paris is listed as the head of household, along with Christophe Glapion, their daughters Heloïse and Philomene, and two young girls, Malvina and Henieta, who were probably the children of Heloïse. No occupation is given for Marie or Christophe. By the time the 1860 census was taken, Glapion had died and Philomene was still living with her mother, along with an unidentified person named Jean Phillipe and what are probably the same two girls, although they are called Alzonia and Amazone Crocker. Heloïse was not listed in the 1860 census. I was unable to locate the Laveau-Glapion family in the 1870 census, but Marie, Philomene, and Philomene's teenaged children appeared in the 1880 census.[32] Unlike Doctor John, Marie Laveau claimed ownership of no real estate or personal wealth.

The notion that Marie Laveau learned the intimate secrets of New Orleans' wealthy families through employment as a hairdresser first appeared in Henry Castellanos's New Orleans As It Was (1895), and is repeated in

Newbell Niles Puckett's *Folk Beliefs of the Southern Negro*. It is also corroborated in two interviews by the Louisiana Writers' Project.[33] Civil records, city directories, and newspaper stories published during Marie's lifetime never mention her having worked at this occupation.

The Laveau-Glapion family lived in a wooden Creole cottage at 152 St. Ann Street between Rampart and Burgundy. Contrary to the often-repeated story of Marie's having received this house from a grateful client, the records indicate that it was purchased by Christophe Glapion in 1832 from the estate of Catherine Pomet/Henry, Marie's maternal grandmother. Many people lived in this small house: Marie, Christophe, their children, grandchildren, and other relatives and friends. The cottage was demolished in 1903, and the site is now occupied by a double shotgun house, 1020–1022 St. Ann.[34]

Marie Laveau was recognized as the leader of the New Orleans Voodoo community around 1850. At her cottage on St. Ann Street, Marie held services, gave consultations, and dispensed gris-gris. She also presided over the annual St. John's Eve celebrations on Lake Pontchartrain, which were attended by hundreds of worshipers. She is believed to have retired as the reigning Voodoo queen in 1869 because of infirmity and old age, and, cared for by her daughter Philomene, devoted her remaining years to charitable works. Newspaper accounts tell of her building altars in the cells of condemned prisoners and administering to the religious needs of those awaiting execution at the parish prison.[35]

Marie Laveau died on June 15, 1881; she was said to be ninety-eight years old, but she may have been only about eighty. Every newspaper in New Orleans ran a lengthy obituary, all of which contained more fantasy than fact. Cemetery records show that she was interred, under the name Dame Christophe Glapion, in the family tomb in St. Louis Cemetery Number One.[36]

After Marie's retirement and subsequent death, newspaper reports cited various women as her successor: Eliza Nicaux, Mamma Caroline, Madame Euphrasie, Estelle, and Malvina Latour. George Washington Cable, in his 1886 *Century Magazine* article "Creole Slave Songs," also stated that Malvina Latour replaced Marie Laveau.[37] I have been unable to find Latour in city or church records.

The notion that one of Marie's daughters became the "second" Marie Laveau seems to have been conceived by Lyle Saxon in the 1920s. In *Fabulous New Orleans*, Saxon says that Marie Glapion, born to Marie Laveau and Christophe Glapion in 1827, was, "as a very young woman, known to the police as a worker of black magic. She became officially known as the Voodoo Queen." The designations "Marie I" and "Marie II" were first used by Louisiana Writers' Project staff member Catherine Dillon in her unpublished book-length "Voodoo" manuscript (1940). Robert Tallant, in *Voodoo in New Orleans*, elaborated on the theory that, as the first Marie grew older, she was secretly replaced by her daughter.[38] The oldest daughter of Marie Laveau and Christophe Glapion, Marie Heloïse (Eloise Euchariste), was indeed born February 2, 1827. She may have been the "Marie Clarisse [Euchariste?] Laveau," referred to in an 1859 *Daily Picayune* article about a "Voudoux house" on Rampart Street.[39] Marie Heloïse is documented to have had at least five children. She died in 1862 at the age of thirty-five.[40] Her early death rules out the possibility of her being the successor to Marie Laveau, although she certainly may have been involved in her mother's work.[41]

The idea of a "second" Marie Laveau is reinforced by the reports of the Louisiana Writers' Project. Many of the LWP informants had grown up within a few blocks of Marie Laveau's home. While a few of the older people remembered the elderly Widow Paris as "an old shriveled-up lady with snow white hair,"[42] those who would have been children and young adults in the 1870s and 1880s described a handsome and vigorous middle-aged woman, known to them as Marie Laveau, who lived in the St. Ann Street cottage and was active in Voodoo until the 1890s. Tallant theorized that this was Marie Philomene Glapion. According to the census and the city directories, Philomene spent most of her life at 152 St. Ann. During the late 1860s and early 1870s she may have established a household with her white consort, Emile Alexandre Legendre, but Philomene and her children are documented to have lived at 152 St. Ann from 1876 until her death in 1897. She is buried in the middle vault of the Laveau-Glapion tomb in St. Louis Cemetery Number One. The *Picayune Guide to New Orleans* stated that Philomene maintained the family home as a shrine: "In every room . . . [she] keeps an altar to the memory of her mother, with dozens of lighted candles burning for the repose of her soul. . . . To all outward appearances she is good and pious and devoted to the service of God. But somehow the whole place, with its lights, its altars . . . and superstitious memories, is so full of weird mystery that you are glad to emerge from it into the glorious sunlight."[43]

The LWP informants distinctly remembered Philomene and described her as tall, stately, beautiful, and a very strict Roman Catholic. Most denied that she had any dealings with Voodoo, although one woman said that "Madame Legendre was a sister of Marie Laveau . . . [and] practiced the same trade . . . her specialty was making novenas for those in trouble."[44] The identity of the "second" Marie Laveau—Marie Heloïse Euchariste, Marie Philomene, Malvina Latour, all of the above, or someone else entirely—remains a puzzle.

The Louisiana Writers' Project informants provided a wealth of detail about Marie Laveau's family, the house on St. Ann Street, and her religious and business practices. It must be kept in mind that these elderly people were recalling events forty to sixty years past and sometimes may have confused the practices of Marie Laveau with those of later spiritual workers. Most of those interviewed were born too late to remember the Widow Paris, and one assumes that they were referring to the second Marie. While the original Marie Laveau appears to have been a spiritual leader analogous to a Haitian mambo, under her successor Voodoo was already undergoing the transition from religion to magic.

Louisiana Writers' Project interviewee Marie Dédé grew up in the St. Ann Street neighborhood and was the playmate of Marie Philomene's children, Fidelia, Memie (Noémie), and Glapion (Alexandre).

> Marie Laveau used her front room for services and the second to sleep in. She would not let us children go in her front room . . . but we used to peep in there all the time. She had so many candles burning . . . I don't see how that house never caught on fire. . . . She had all kinds of saints pictures and flowers on the altar. In the front room by the door she had a big St. Anthony . . . and she would turn him upside down on his head in her yard when she had work to perform. . . . Memie would come get me and say, "Come see my grandma got St. Anthony on his head" . . . then [Marie Laveau] would . . . put us out and lock the gate.[45]

Charles Raphael, Raymond Rivaros, and Oscar Felix had been members of the second Marie Laveau's congregation between 1880 and 1884. They elaborated on the description of the altars, saying that the one in the front room was for "good luck charms, money-making charms, husband-holding charms . . . on this altar she had a statue of St. Peter and . . . St. Marron, a colored saint." (The name St. Marron, an unofficial saint who is unique to Louisiana, has the same derivation as *maroon*.) In the back of the house, they said, Marie had an altar for "bad work," surmounted by statues of a bear, a lion, a tiger, and a wolf.[46]

Raphael, Rivaros, and Felix described Marie Laveau's weekly services, which resemble Haitian Vodou ceremonies in some of their details. Charles Raphael related: "These meetings were called *parterres* (on the ground). A feast was spread for the spirits on a white tablecloth laid on the floor . . . certain foods were always present . . . *congris* [rice and peas], apples, oranges, and red peppers. Candles were lighted and placed in the four corners of the room." According to Raymond Rivaros:

> There was a big chair, like they use in church for the bishop, and Marie sat in it at the opening of the meeting. Then she would tell the people to ask for what they want, sprinkle them with rum, and start the dances. . . . I have seen those men turn the women over like a top. They had large handkerchiefs that they would put around the women's waist, and would they shake! There were more white people at the meetings than colored. The meeting lasted from 7:00 to 9:00 and they would have things to eat and drink.

Oscar Felix added that "the ceremonies all started out and ended . . . with Catholic prayers."[47]

The most important of the Voodoo ceremonies was held annually at Lake Pontchartrain or on Bayou St. John on June 23, St. John's Eve, which coincides with the summer solstice. These celebrations consisted of bonfires, ritual bathing, drumming, singing, dancing, and a communal meal. The custom of bathing in Lake Pontchartrain and Bayou St. John on St. John's Eve is probably derived from both European and African practices. Europeans built bonfires on St. John's Eve; Africans used ritual baths for healing and spiritual cleansing, and black New Orleanians may have associated immersion in the waters of Lake Pontchartrain, which they called St. John's Lake, with the baptism of Jesus by St. John the Baptist.[48]

It is not known exactly when the St. John's Eve Voodoo ceremonies began. In 1831 the newly opened Pontchartrain Railroad began running special cars to the lake for the festivities. Newspaper coverage of the event began in 1869, although it was noted that "in ante-bellum times, the St. John's Eve celebrations were things of interest which attracted large crowds of witnesses."[49] The custom might have been brought to Louisiana by the Haitian immigrants who arrived in the first decade of the nineteenth century. In Haiti, the feast day of John the Baptist, the patron of Freemasonry who is treated as a minor lwa, is observed with bonfires and ceremonies by both Freemasons and Vodou societies.[50]

Like the earlier Congo Square dances, the New Orleans St. John's Eve Voodoo celebrations became one of the "sights to see," and hundreds of white tourists and locals went to the lake seeking the "Voodoos." Historian Blake Touchstone made an exhaustive study of newspaper descriptions of the St. John's Eve Voodoo celebrations from the 1870s and 1880s, when the *Times* and the *Daily Picayune* usually sent a reporter out to cover the event. The woman referred to as "Marie Laveau" in these articles could not have been the Widow Paris. It was Touchstone's conclusion that the St. John's Eve activities, or at least those that were accessible to the press and the public, had become a sham. Some alleged "queens" and "doctors" staged phony ceremonies for which they charged admission—an early example of "tourist voodoo."[51]

Oscar Felix, when interviewed by the Louisiana Writers' Project, provided a very different account:

> We would go out to the old lake once every year. Oh, it was a big day for those who believed in [Marie Laveau's] work. . . . They would celebrate, eating and drinking; there was chicken, red beans and rice, cakes, and liquor. There was an altar on the ground with a big cross in the back, then right in front of the cross was a picture of St. Peter . . . [and] three large candles that were lit. . . . Then the leader would bring the picture of St. John and place it on the altar. They celebrated St. John's Day because they wanted to be like him. He was a great man and always did what was right.
>
> When they were ready to open the meeting, everybody would kneel before the altar and rap on the ground three times . . . for faith, hope, and charity, in the name of the Father, Son, and Holy Ghost. After that we would sing in Creole. . . . [It] was just like a Mass in a regular church. When this part of the ceremony was over they would do the "Creole Dance." One man would have two women on each side of him and they would put metal rings on their knees that would ring and rattle. He would first turn one [woman] around and then he would turn the other . . . then he would dance with one and then the other. [After the dance] everybody would bow down . . . and say the "Our Father." Of course we all would stay afterwards and eat and drink and have a good time.[52]

In addition to presiding at these ceremonies, both private and public, both of the Marie Laveaus gave consultations and prepared charms for clients.

The person referred to in most of the LWP interviews is probably the second Marie, but it is impossible to say this with certainty. Marie Laveau was particularly renowned for court cases, not so much because of her powerful gris-gris, but because of her influence with the police, the sheriff, and the judge. Marie Laveau was said to have become fabulously wealthy through her Voodoo work, and to have owned extensive real estate, but this is not substantiated by city records or the federal census.[53]

Marie Dédé, the childhood friend of the first Marie Laveau's granddaughter Noémie, recalled that "Memie used to tell me that white people paid her grandma plenty of money to get husbands for them or to win cases in the courts . . . she got a hundred dollars for getting a man for a white woman. . . . The colored people could not afford her high price. . . . Memie said her grandma was the first one to do that hoodoo work . . . there was plenty of people around her house all the time asking for special favors."[54]

None of the Louisiana Writers' Project interviewees remembered the composition of Marie Laveau's gris-gris, but the journalist Lafcadio Hearn published some charm formulae in his article "New Orleans Superstitions" in *Harper's Weekly Magazine* (1886). Although this piece is alleged to have been based on interviews with the second Marie Laveau, Hearn himself did not make this claim. He described some of the more common gris-gris:

> Fetishes—consisting of bones, hair, feathers, rags, or some fantastic combination of these and other trifling objects— [are put] into a pillow used by the party whom it is desired to injure . . . placed before the entrance of a house . . . or thrown over a wall into a yard. . . . Scattering dirt before a door, or making certain figures on the wall of a house with chalk, or crumbling dry leaves . . . and scattering them before a residence are also forms of maleficent conjuring. . . . The counter-charm . . . is to fling salt upon them and to sweep them away [with a broom].[55]

By the late 1890s all of the legendary Voodoo queens and doctors were dead. Private ceremonies and the St. John's Eve celebrations at Lake Pontchartrain were routinely broken up by the police.[56] The terms *Voudou* or *Voodoo* were being replaced by *hoodoo*, referring to a system of magic by which individual "workers" serve their clients. New Orleans Voodoo, as an organized religion, was going underground.

Voodoo Survivals and the Transition to Hoodoo: 1900—1940s

Voodoo was forced into more acceptable disguises by the increasing Anglo-American presence in Louisiana. The legal system, public opinion, and the Christian church were united in their crusade against African-based religion and magic.

Beginning in 1909, federal mail fraud laws were invoked against practitioners who conducted business by mail; conviction of mail fraud carried a penitentiary sentence. The Louisiana Board of Health, under the 1894 Medical Practice Act, prosecuted persons accused of practicing medicine without a license. A 1929 revision imposed a fifty- to one-hundred-dollar fine or a sentence of ten to ninety days in the parish prison. In 1897, 1916, and 1924, the city of New Orleans instituted statutes against fortune-telling and obtaining money under false pretenses.[57] These regulations were used to harass, fine, and jail many black spiritual workers.

The Catholic Creoles of color were influenced by the prevailing opinion of white Americans that Voodoo exemplified the ignorance and superstition of blacks and made them unfit for full citizenship. In an attempt to maintain their superior position, the colored Creoles distanced themselves from any association with Voodoo. Black Protestants, also desiring to appear respectable, pronounced that Voodoo was the Devil's work. These attitudes caused many people to fear and deny their former beliefs.[58] Some of the Louisiana Writers' Project informants who had previously been involved in Voodoo stated that they had "gotten religion"—meaning that they had joined the Baptist or Methodist Church—and given it up. One former "worker," who claimed to have been trained by Marie Laveau, was pressured by her family to renounce the practice: "I was one of the best in the work, could do wonders, but my son asked me to stop and make a vow never to do no more hoodoo. Boy, I used to make money."[59]

Spiritualism swept the United States during the 1850s and enjoyed great popularity in New Orleans among upper-class whites and the elite French-speaking free people of color. It was later taken up by working-class blacks.[60] By the early twentieth century, people who previously would have been called Voodoo queens or hoodoo doctors began to refer to themselves as "spiritual advisors" to avoid trouble with the authorities. Many who were interviewed by the LWP and Harry Middleton Hyatt spoke of having a certificate or a license that protected them from police interference.

Despite attempts at eradication by outsiders, and the alterations and disguises adopted by insiders, both the Voodoo religion and the magical practices of hoodoo have survived in the fertile ground of New Orleans. Some elements were preserved; some were modified or lost altogether.

Many of the religious aspects of New Orleans Voodoo were incorporated into the Spiritual churches, founded in 1920 by Mother Leafy Anderson, a black minister from Chicago who combined elements of Spiritualism, Pentecostalism, Catholicism, and Voodoo. The Spiritual churches have much in common with nineteenth-century New Orleans Voodoo. When one disregards the sensationalized depictions of Voodoo "orgies" written by outsiders, concentrating on accounts by actual participants, the parallels are clear. The Spiritual churches honor God the Father, Jesus, and an array of saints, ancestors, and spirit guides—particularly the Native American chief Black Hawk—by whom worshipers become possessed and through whose power they heal and prophesy. The interior of a Spiritual church is dominated by elaborate altars dedicated to the saints and the spirits, on which are placed offerings of food, liquor, and tobacco. Services are characterized by ecstatic music and dancing, and spiritual "work" may include the use of candles, incense, oils, baths, roots and herbs, and other charms. The predominately female priesthood are called reverend mothers.[61] Marie Laveau is respected as a "spiritual woman." A Louisiana Writers' Project fieldworker was told by one of Mother Anderson's pupils, Mother Dora Tyson, that "before Mother Anderson there was another great leader, Mother Laveau. The French people downtown still use her spirit." A present-day church leader, Bishop Edmonia Caldwell of the St. Daniel Spiritual Church, concurred that Marie Laveau is not considered an "evil" person.[62] Church members are not adverse to the idea that their faith has African elements, but they emphatically deny any association with hoodoo, by which they mean manipulation of spiritual powers to control or harm other people.

■ ■ ■

Between 1928 and 1940, Zora Neale Hurston, the Louisiana Writers' Project fieldworkers, and Harry Middleton Hyatt documented the practices of New Orleans spiritual workers. These narratives and interviews with traditional practitioners demonstrate the continuity between the Voodoo rituals and charm beliefs of the Marie Laveau era and the hoodoo practices of the early twentieth century.

While Haitian Vodou and New Orleans Voodoo are concerned with serving the deities and the ancestors, hoodoo is directed toward enhancing one's own personal well-being, influencing the actions of other people, and controlling external forces like luck. Hoodoo, as it was practiced in New Orleans in the first decades of the twentieth century, in many ways resembles the magical practices recorded elsewhere in the South. Adhering to the principles of imitative and contagious magic, charm ingredients were chosen because their physical appearance, their names, or their everyday functions symbolized the desired attribute or action. Among the natural ingredients used in charm formulation were plants, minerals, and animal parts and products. Possession of the bodily products or unwashed clothing of the target was a means of control, as was the writing of his or her name on a slip of paper. The spiritual potency of the dead was solicited through the incorporation of graveyard dirt into charms and by "planting" charms in the cemetery. Man-made objects and substances were also used in charms. Iron horseshoes, nails, and files represented strength. Thread and string "tied up" wrongdoers or secured a lover. Sharp pins, needles, and tacks were used to "pin down" the target. Perfume, honey, sugar, essences, and flavorings attracted lovers, friends, and customers. Hot elements, such as red or black pepper, dry mustard, gunpowder, and matches, "heated up" a situation for quick results. Strong-smelling substances like sulfur, ammonia, and asafetida were protective charms. Sour or bitter ingredients, such as lemon, beef gall, strong coffee, and vinegar, were employed for "bad work." Many magical ingredients were common preservatives, cleansers, and other household products. Salt was the most often-cited ingredient in protective charms. Other formulae called for baking soda, alum, saltpeter, sulfur, laundry bluing, ammonia, borax, or lye. Urine was also a frequent ingredient in cleansing and protective charms. In this context, urine was not considered unclean or disgusting. In the 1920s through the 1940s, when these charm formulae were collected, few homes had indoor toilets; people used chamber pots, and urine was referred to as "chamber lye."

Charm preparation involved ritual actions imitative of the desired result—bathing upward or downward, sweeping into or out of the house, folding toward or away from the user, turning upside-down or inside-out, crossing, tying, knotting, pinning, nailing, shaking, bottling up, treading underfoot, casting away, burying, or burning. The maker or user of the charm was sometimes required to perform the ritual at the "four moments of the sun"—sunrise, noon, sunset, or midnight. The number *three* (for the Father, Son, and Holy Ghost) had magical significance, and *nine* (three times three) was even more important. Rituals often called for the repetition of an action nine times or on nine successive days, or required the use of nine items.

The intention of these charms and their attendant rituals was to influence the physical, mental, and spiritual health of the charm user or the target; to manipulate relationships with lovers, family, friends, neighbors, customers, employers, authority figures, and adversaries; and to control external forces like luck, the saints, and the dead. The maker defined the target and intention of the charm by mental concentration or by speaking or writing the name of the target and the desired outcome. Some of the people interviewed by Hurston, the LWP fieldworkers, and Hyatt indicated that the charm was inhabited by an indwelling spirit who "worked" for the user; others spoke as though the charm itself performed the desired action.

New Orleans hoodoo differs from the conjure and rootwork practiced in the Anglo-Protestant South in its incorporation of Catholic-influenced altars, candles, incense, oils, holy water, and images of the saints, and the employment of certain other unique components like hot peppers, coconuts, beef hearts and tongues, dolls, and the miniature coffin.

In New Orleans, the use of altars, candles, and the power of the saints was ubiquitous, and many practitioners wore special attire inspired by the priestly vestments of the Roman Catholic Church. The altar could be a private shrine consisting of a few candles and holy cards, or an elaborate structure in the practitioner's place of business. Candles were employed to solicit the aid of a saint for beneficent purposes—referred to as "setting a light," or for "bad work"—when one was said to be "burning a candle on" the person one wished to harm. The color symbolism of candles was fairly consistent among all the interviewees: white for peace, red or purple for victory, pink for love, blue for protection, yellow or green for money, and black or brown for evil.

It is not known to what extent the vodu of the Fon and the lwa of Haitian Vodou made the transition to New Orleans. Presumably their names were familiar and their powers were invoked in eighteenth- and nineteenth-century Voodoo. By the time Voodoo survivals were being documented in the early twentieth century, the names of the lwa had almost disappeared. A spirit called "Joe Feraille" (Joe Iron) was probably a manifestation of Ogou. St. Michael was called Blanc Dani or Daniel Blanc, possibly a manifestation of Dambala, whose color is white. Liba, La Bas, and Limba were the Louisiana names for Legba; as in Haiti, he was associated with St. Peter. One former Voodooist, interviewed by the

Louisiana Writers' Project, stated that St. Peter was called La Bas. She remembered a song, originally sung in Louisiana Creole: "St. Peter, St. Peter open the door, I am calling you, come to me." Another woman, before embarking on some "work," used the invocation "*La Bas ouvre la port*. . . . Go spirits, open the way for us." These examples are reminiscent of the song for Legba that opens all Haitian Vodou ceremonies, in which the keeper of the gate to the spirit world is entreated to "remove the barrier for me, so that I may pass through" (*l'uvri bayè pu mwê pu mwê pasé*).[63]

The saints replaced the lwa as a sort of hoodoo pantheon called upon to solve everyday problems and aid in magical works. St. Peter, who holds the keys of heaven, was believed to open the door to the spirit world, guard the home against intruders, invite customers into one's place of business, and remove barriers to success. The Virgin Mary was called upon in matters of love and healing. St. Michael the Archangel, an Old Testament warrior spirit, conquered enemies. St. Expedite, called "the minute saint," was employed when results were needed in a hurry. St. Joseph was the patron of laborers because he was a carpenter; he was also considered the protector of the family and the home because he was the husband of the Virgin Mary and foster father of Jesus. St. Joseph was solicited to get a job, to find or keep a home, or to bring about a marriage. St. Raymond was called "the money saint" and was used for gambling and financial endeavors. St. Rita of Cascia protected women against abusive men. St. Anthony of Padua was enlisted to find lost articles and to bring back strayed lovers.[64]

Traditional New Orleans charms of the 1920s through the 1940s took the form of bath-and-floor wash to attract desirable individuals and influences and to keep undesirable people and evil spirits away; powders with which to "dress" the clothing or throw in the pathway of an enemy; oils and perfumes for anointing the body, "feeding" charm assemblages, and "dressing" candles; preparations with which to fumigate the home or business; and substances to be ingested. Gris-gris and wanga were formulated in glass bottles, jars, tin cans, inside a coconut or a lemon, or in a cloth bag. "Hands" or "tobies" were packets made of silk, red flannel, or chamois. The charm had to be "fed" periodically with whiskey, perfume, oil, or urine, and aroused to action by rubbing, striking, shaking, or turning it upside down. Many Louisiana informants gave variations of the beef-heart and miniature-coffin death charms, as well as the beef-tongue charm to confuse and silence one's adversaries in court. Dolls were sometimes used to represent the target of the charm; these were ordinary manufactured dolls, not homemade "voodoo dolls." A photograph, preferably a tintype, served the same purpose.

The documentation of New Orleans Voodoo and hoodoo practice by Hurston, the Louisiana Writers' Project, and Hyatt was undertaken at the very time that "workers" were beginning to abandon the use of natural and household charm ingredients in favor of manufactured products. It is particularly interesting that some old-fashioned "workers" were still making their own magical floor wash, "hot foot powder," and "war powder" and collecting "goofer dust" from the graveyard, while others combined traditional ingredients with commercially produced baths, floor wash, powders, oils, and perfumes. The transition from traditional charms to commercial spiritual products was accelerated, and perhaps even initiated, by the availability of these wares at New Orleans' hoodoo drugstores, especially the Cracker Jack. These businesses will be discussed in chapter 6.

■ ■ ■

The first serious study of New Orleans magico-religious practices was done by the black southern novelist and anthropologist Zora Neale Hurston. Hurston was in New Orleans, which she called the "Hoodoo Capital of America," from September 1928 to March 1929 and from November 1929 to March 1930.[65] There she sought out hoodoo workers and asked to be taken as an apprentice. Her findings were published in the October–December 1931 *Journal of American Folklore* as "Hoodoo in America," and a shorter version appeared in her 1935 book *Mules and Men*. Hurston stated that she had not used the real names of her mentors.[66] The spiritual professionals represented in her published works may have been composites of many individuals with whom she studied. The man she called "Luke Turner" bears some resemblance to Oscar Felix, the Louisiana Writers' Project informant cited elsewhere in this chapter, and "Father Watson" might have been Rockford Lewis, a minister and hoodoo worker who will be discussed in chapter 6. These intriguing possibilities invite further research. I have been unable to locate Hurston's New Orleans field notes, and presume they are lost.

By becoming a participant in New Orleans hoodoo culture, Hurston went further in her investigation than other early twentieth-century writers and had experiences that most of the others only learned about through interviews. Hurston reports that she was initiated three times, by "Luke Turner," "Father Watson," and "Anatol Pierre," for which she was stripped of her clothes and required to undergo a period of isolation, contemplation, and fasting, followed by an herbal bath, candle burning, and animal sacrifice. The ceremonies concluded with a festive meal for all the participants. Although much simplified, these initiations somewhat resemble those of Vodou and Santería.[67]

Hurston collected a number of typical Louisiana rituals and charm formulae. One of her mentors, called "Kitty Brown," specialized in affairs of the heart. A client who was unsure of her man's fidelity was told to make a controlling charm consisting of a silver dime to pay the indwelling spirit, some hair from the target's head, and his name written three times on a slip of paper to capture his essence. These ingredients were to be put in his unwashed sock, along with a piece of lodestone sprinkled with steel dust to draw the man to the woman. The sock was to be folded toward the charm maker, pinned with two crossed needles to keep the lover situated, "fed" with whiskey, and set up over a door.

"Father Watson" was a charismatic minister who conducted services, attired in a purple satin robe tied at the waist with a gold cord, at an auditorium called the "Myrtle Wreath Hall." He was also a hoodoo worker. Father Watson kept a jar of sugar and honey for "sweet" intentions, and a "break-up" jar, filled with vinegar and bitter coffee, for "bad work." Names and desires were written on paper and put in the appropriate jars. To keep a man in jail, Father Watson told Hurston to write the target's name on a slip of paper and put it in a deep bowl with red and black pepper, one eightpenny nail, and some ammonia. "Drop a key down in the bowl and leave another one against the side . . . every time you turn the key, add a little vinegar." The symbolism is obvious: sweet things for beneficent charms, and hot, strong, and bitter substances for antisocial purposes. The nail and the key secured the target.

Father Watson also introduced Hurston to the ritual for obtaining the black cat bone, which would enable her to "walk invisible." She was sent out after dark to catch a black cat. Then, accompanied by Father Watson and his wife, she went to the woods, where the live cat was thrown into an iron pot of boiling water "protected" by a circle of nine horseshoes. "Great beast-like creatures thundered up to the circle. . . . Death was at hand!" At midnight, after the flesh had boiled from the bones, Hurston selected the "lucky" bone, distinguished by its bitter taste.

"Doctor Duke" specialized in court cases. To help a client awaiting trial for attempted murder, Doctor Duke used dirt from the graves of nine children, soliciting the power of their innocent spirits; three teaspoons of sugar to "sweeten" the judge; and three of sulfur to speed the process. A new set of socks and underclothes was turned wrong side out and "dressed" with this powder. The doctor took the clothes to the jail and personally put them on his client just before he was escorted into the courtroom.

To silence opposing witnesses, Doctor Duke used the well-known beef-tongue charm. He "took a beef tongue, nine pins, nine needles, and split the tongue . . . wrote the names of those against our man, cut the names out and crossed them up in the slit with red pepper and beef gall, pinned up the slit with crossed needles and pins, hung it in the chimney and smoked it for thirty-six hours . . . then put it on ice and lit on it three black candles." Possession of the names of the witnesses placed them under the control of the charm maker; hot and bitter ingredients accelerated the process and made the targets uncomfortable; pins, needles, and thread held them fast. The slips of paper bearing their names were crossed inside the tongue and the pins and needles were also crossed, forming sites of concentrated power. Smoking and freezing the tongue rendered the witnesses unable to speak. Note the similarity to the Santería beef-tongue charm against gossip cited in chapter 2.

"Anatol Pierre" conducted an elaborate death ritual for a client who wanted to eliminate his sweetheart's husband. The fee was $250. The rival's name was written nine times on a slip of paper, placed inside a beef heart, pinned up with eighteen steel needles, and dropped into a jar of vinegar. A beef brain was set on a plate surrounded by nine hot peppers to cause insanity. A doll was named for the man and placed in a miniature coffin. A black cat and a black chicken were buried alive. The coffin and a beef tongue, into which the man's name had been inserted, were later buried upon their remains. Black candles were burned on the altar for ninety days, and Anatol Pierre slept in a black-draped coffin. According to Hurston, the victim died.

In the section called "Paraphernalia of Conjure," Hurston discussed ingredients commonly used for charm formulation. Some were common household items. Others were purchased at the hoodoo drugstore, probably the Cracker Jack. Hurston mentions magical herbs, lodestone, steel dust, gold and silver "magnetic sand," and commercially produced items like Lucky Dog, Essence of Bend-Over, War Water, Has-No-Harra, Fast Luck Oil, Three Kings and a Jack, Jockey Club Perfume, and Four Thieves Vinegar. According to Hurston, New Orleans' most popular hoodoo preparation, Van-Van, was made from alcohol and oil of lemon grass. She emphasized that the ingredients were less important than the intention: "Everything may be conjure and nothing may be conjure, according to the doctor, the time, and the use of the article."[68]

■ ■ ■

The Louisiana Writers' Project fieldworkers lacked Hurston's academic training in folklore and anthropology. Most of the fieldworkers were white, although there were several African American staff members.[69] Realizing that they would get little cooperation if they presented themselves as agents of a government program, the LWP fieldworkers often assumed the role of clients or individuals wishing to enter "the work." Some of the most interesting reports were submitted by Robert McKinney, a black journalist, and Hazel Breaux, a white woman. They often operated as a team, interviewing hoodoo workers, spiritual advisors, healers, card readers, and various other entrepreneurs. The Louisiana Writers' Project recorded the names and addresses of all interviewees.

During October, November, and December of 1936, McKinney and Breaux made repeated visits to the home of two elderly "workers," Mrs. Dereco and Madame Ducoyielle, and posed as persons desiring to enter the hoodoo business. Madame Ducoyielle, known as "Grandma" by her friends, drank gin mixed with beer and swore constantly. McKinney describes her as "a decrepit old lady nearly bent to the ground when she walks, who seems to say 'son of a bitch' every second." They were assisted in their ceremonies by Oscar Felix, called "Nom" by Mrs. Dereco and Madame Ducoyielle. This was the same Oscar Felix who had participated in the second Marie Laveau's services as a young man. He was listed in the city directory as a driver and furniture mover.

Madame Ducoyielle insisted that before embarking upon a career in hoodoo, McKinney and Breaux must participate in an "opening" ceremony, the purpose of which was to provide a feast for the spirits and solicit their help. Felix prepared an altar, placing the offerings on a clean white tablecloth in a manner similar to Marie Laveau's *parterres*. McKinney and Breaux gave a detailed description, accompanied by a sketch showing how the articles were positioned. The image of St. Peter, of course, represents Papa Legba, who opens the gate to the spirit world.

> A picture of St. Peter was placed in a leaning position against the wall. One white and one green candle were lighted and placed on each side of the altar . . . quart bottles of cider and raspberry pop . . . [and] a bunch of various colored candles were placed about midway . . . a plate of steel dust to the right of the picture, a plate of orris root to the left, a plate of dried basil in front. In the center . . . a plate of "stage planks" [ginger cakes] and a box of ginger snaps; to the left . . . was a plate of mixed

bird seed and some bananas, to the right, plates of powdered cloves, cinnamon, and some small apples. Two . . . pans of *congris*, a small bottle of olive oil, a bag of sugar, and a bottle of Jax beer were also used. . . . A camphor branch . . . was leaned against the picture, and a tall glass containing gin, sugar, water, and a spray of basil was placed in front of the picture.

The description of the ceremony is consistent with reports of earlier New Orleans Voodoo rituals and with services for Legba held in Haiti today. Oscar Felix stripped to the waist, removed his shoes, and rolled up his trousers. He commanded McKinney and Breaux to take off their shoes and stockings and not to cross their legs, fingers, or hands because the spirits would be unable to work. All knelt and knocked three times on the floor to invoke the aid of the spirits, then recited the Lord's Prayer. Felix became possessed, danced, chanted in Creole, twirled the participants and lifted them on his back. The liquid offerings on the altar were poured into a tub and used to anoint the bodies, hair, and clothing of the participants. The other articles were given to them to take home, including the mixture from the tub, which Felix said could be sold for five dollars a bottle as Luck Water. At the end, Felix came out of his trance with no difficulty, seeming perfectly sober even though he had consumed a whole bottle of gin. He charged two dollars for conducting the service, plus fifteen cents to pay the spirits, and offered to help McKinney and Breaux with their supposed "hoodoo practice" free of charge.[70]

Madame Ducoyielle took McKinney and Breaux to a church, pointing out the statues of various saints and demonstrating how they could be summoned by knocking three times on the statue. They also visited the St. Louis Cemetery, where she taught them to use the spirits of the dead by leaving offerings of congris, apples, or whiskey, or burning a candle—"Give them what they like after they do a favor for you." They made cross-marks on the tombs of people thought to possess spiritual power, a custom related to Haitian Vodou and derived from the Kongo cosmogram—either a cross-mark or an X—symbolizing a point of concentrated power where the world of the living meets the world of the spirits. This may have been introduced into New Orleans by the thousands of Haitian immigrants who arrived in the early nineteenth century. According to Haitian Vodou priest Max Beauvoir, "the practice is called *kwasiyen*, meaning to sign with a cross, and is used to establish contact with the lwa and on tombs when one wishes to be remembered by the dead."[71]

■ ■ ■

At approximately the same time that the Louisiana Writers' Project fieldworkers were documenting New Orleans practitioners, Harry Middleton Hyatt also visited New Orleans, which, like Hurston, he considered the most important hoodoo site in the United States. Hyatt began his Louisiana fieldwork in March of 1938. On this trip he conducted interviews at the Paterson Hotel on South Rampart Street, just three blocks from the Cracker Jack Drug Store. He returned in 1940, working across the Mississippi River in Algiers—locally known as "Hoodoos' Town"—and used a room in the Eagle Eye Hall. Hyatt interviewed more than two hundred people on his two visits to Louisiana. Of the twenty-nine complete interviews included in *Hoodoo-Conjure-Witchcraft-Rootwork*, ten are with men and nineteen with women. Judging from this small sample, it seems that the male practitioners regarded hoodoo as a moneymaking enterprise, while the women, more in the tradition of the reverend mothers of the Spiritual churches, appeared to be sincere believers.

The practitioner that Hyatt called "Hoodoo Book Man" generalized about the methods of New Orleans "workers":

> Most of them dress in a gown . . . if you go there for . . . hurtin'
> somebody, they puts on a black gown. If you go there for gamblin'
> they puts on . . . a green one. . . . He sets in front of that altar. The
> hoodoo people they got a altar made just like in a Catholic church.
> . . . Got all kind of candles and saints [on it] . . . and you tell him
> what you want him to do . . . and he set the candle to that saint.
> . . . But that is goin' to cost you money. . . . If you want a "hand" to
> gamble, it cost you maybe twenty-five or thirty dollars.[72]

"Gifted Medium" emphasized that she was a spiritualist, not a hoodoo, and that she did no "bad work," although she had "heard of it" from other people. On her altar she had a statue of the Sacred Heart of Jesus, St. Anthony, and the Blessed Mother, as well as a mirror used for contacting the spirits. She explained an attraction ritual similar to Father Watson's jar for "sweet" works, described by Hurston. "Gifted Medium" employed a can filled with syrup. Notice that the color of the syrup symbolized the race of the person to be influenced: "If they are white, it would be light syrup; if they are dark-complected, it can be dark syrup. Place the names wrote three times together [over top of each other], and put in the can and keep in a quiet or a dark place. That will sweeten the persons together."[73]

New Orleans Voodoo

Many of the charms collected by Hyatt were for good luck. The woman identified as "Custodian of a Shrine" gave Hyatt instructions for some "hands" that combine natural ingredients—cinnamon and sugar for attraction, John the Conqueror for success, and lodestone to draw money—with commercial spiritual products purchased at the Cracker Jack—Hot Foot Powder, Three Kings Oil, Essence of Van-Van, John the Conqueror powder, New Orleans Fast Luck Powder, lodestone, and parchment paper. To help a client get a job, "Custodian of a Shrine" instructed Hyatt to

> Get . . . a piece of John the Conker [Conqueror] root and . . . some cinnamon . . . and you get a piece of shammy [chamois] and you make a little . . . bag and sew [the root and the cinnamon] up [inside] very careful. . . . Give [the client] a little vial of this Three Kings [perfume] and bury [the bag and the vial] in one of those little ten-cent pocketbooks. . . . Every mornin' before he go look for a job, drop a few drops of this Three Kings on there. . . . He supposed to get a job 'tween nine mornin's.

A gambling "hand" was also made in a chamois bag, with pulverized white lodestone, John the Conqueror root, a pinch of sugar, and a pinch of cinnamon. This was to be carried in one's wallet and "fed" with essence of geranium. "You can sell that to any man . . . you can ask fifty dollars for it and you can guarantee it."[74]

Many of Hyatt's interviewees described charms and rituals for success in financial matters. "Custodian of a Shrine" gave a recipe for floor wash to draw customers into one's place of business. Laundry bluing, because of its color, protected the user from enemies; Van-Van was for luck: "You get you . . . ten cents bluing, ten cents of cinnamon, and ten cents of John the Conker powder . . . and mix [in] a tub of water . . . you boil . . . codfish balls . . . and you use the water offa that and put in that tub . . . get a bottle of Van-Van . . . and one quart of beer, and stir it all aroun' good." The user was supposed to start by scrubbing the sidewalk, then the steps, the porch, and finally inside the house, beginning in the four corners and ending in the center of the room. "That keeps your business there."[75]

Community and domestic squabbles led to the use of malevolent charms made from graveyard dirt; hot, strong, or bitter substances; or the by-products of contentious creatures. "Beer for St. Peter" gave a formula for homemade "hot foot powder," a banishing charm to make troublesome neighbors move out of a house: "You get you some cayenne pepper . . .

graveyard dirt . . . dirt from underneath their steps where they stay at . . . some filé . . . ground coffee . . . nine of them dirt daubers [nests] . . . an mix it up good . . . an then you throw that underneath their step. In three days' time when the rain fall, they'll move at twelve o'clock at night."[76]

Madam Lindsey of Algiers called herself "one of them old-time conjures." She made her own powders from natural and purchased materials. "I make it myself, but I get the ingredients from a druggist around here . . . and then I mix it." Madam Lindsey's interview demonstrates how a charm can absorb the characteristics of a person, dead or living, simply by proximity. She gave this formula for "war powder," which could be used to break up a couple or cause dissension in the home of one's enemies. In this case, the red color of the beans and peanut skins, plus hot cayenne pepper, served to heat up the process. These ingredients were combined with the excreta of a bulldog, symbolizing aggression.

> You take red beans and you parch 'em until you can beat 'em up into a fine powder. You take the [red] skin from peanuts and you mash that up as fine as you can. Then you parch peanut shells and make a powder out of that. Then you get graveyard dust, dog manure . . . try to get a bulldog, . . . and then bluestone, . . . cayenne pepper, black pepper, sulfur, and salt . . . put that all together and you mix it good . . . and put it in a tin can. And you get someone that's real mean . . . and you put it under their house . . . leave it . . . for three nights. Then . . . you got somethin' that'll raise hell anywhere—absolutely.[77]

From a woman named Minta Owens, Hyatt heard a version of the miniature-coffin death charm: "You make a little coffin [from a cigar box] . . . and put a doll baby in it, and name that doll baby 'Mary' [or whomever you want to die] . . . you lights a [black] candle and you wish, in the name of the Father, Son, and Holy Ghost, for Mary to die in nine days . . . and one day 'for long something happens."[78]

"I Come to Tell You 'bout My Father," the interview with Liza Moore, is a chilling story of hoodoo death and revenge instigated by a neighbor who envied the happy home and financial security enjoyed by the Moore family. "My mother . . . she didn't have to get out and work or look for nothin'. Dad made his money [from a successful carting business] and brought it home on Saturday." The neighbor, a single mother who "had to dig for a livin'," attempted to form a sexual liaison with Mr. Moore in exchange for payment, but he refused to get involved. Liza's mother learned of this and "runned her from St. Charles [Avenue] clean to Crowlett [Carondelet?]. . . . So to get even with Mama, I guess she thought she'd get one of us."

First Liza's little sister, Florence, died mysteriously; she foamed at the mouth and "her lips got blue and her li'l fingernails turnt blue . . . and her urinate was yellow just [like] . . . a egg [yolk]. . . . Then next come papa." Liza was preparing lunch when the undertaker's buggy came to the house and a man asked for her mother. "Cold chills runned over me, and my hair stood. . . . He say, 'Tell you mother that your daddy done got kilt.'" Mr. Moore had been dragged under the wheels of his wagon by a runaway mule.

After the funeral the "true" cause of death was disclosed. The envious neighbor had "took a fresh egg . . . and wrote papa's name on it," and had her son break it under the steps, saying, "Look Miz Moore, your husband goin' cross that egg under your steps . . . and he ain't goin' come home till they bring him back here a cold box of meat . . . and you'll have to get out and skuttle for a livin'." When the family searched under the front steps, there indeed was the broken egg with Alex Moore's name written on it. Mrs. Moore subsequently turned the curse back on the one who placed it by throwing the egg into the Mississippi River. The troublemaking neighbor "died in the detention house." Her son fell off a derrick into the river "and his face was all picked by the crabs."[79]

Hyatt finished his documentation of New Orleans Voodoo in 1940. The Federal Writers' Project, including the Louisiana office, was discontinued in 1943. Some of the Louisiana Writers' Project material was published in 1945 as *Gumbo Ya-Ya*. Robert Tallant's lurid *Voodoo in New Orleans*, loosely based on the LWP interviews, newspaper articles, and other printed sources, appeared in 1946. Voodoo survivals and hoodoo practices undoubtedly continued to exist, but they had ceased to be of interest to most researchers. With the exception of a short book, *Voodoo Past and Present*, published by Ron Bodin of the Center for Louisiana Studies, later twentieth-century Voodoo and hoodoo have not been documented.

New Orleans Voodoo Today

As we enter the next century, the city of New Orleans retains much of its European and African culture. The influence of both folk Catholicism and Voodoo remains strong.

Riders on the city bus cross themselves when the vehicle passes a Catholic church. Many New Orleanians address prayers to Our Lady of Prompt Succor when a hurricane threatens the city. At the Church of Our Lady of

Guadalupe, the faithful appeal to St. Expedite, whose statue is located just inside the door, and light candles and pray before the life-sized image of St. Jude (the Saint of Impossible Causes) while touching his extended foot—the paint and even the toes of the statue are worn away by the hands of petitioners. In the chapel at St. Roch's Cemetery, offerings of crutches, braces, plaster replicas of body parts, and devotional plaques are left in thanks for favors granted. At the St. Anne's Shrine, an eccentrically shaped pink cement grotto, devotees climb the staircase on their knees and bathe their faces with holy water from the basin. On Good Friday, people "make the nine churches," walking from one place of worship to another. The Sicilian custom of constructing altars in honor of St. Joseph on his feast day, March 19, has spread to people of many ethnic backgrounds. Visitors to the altars are given lucky fava beans to ensure wealth, special St. Joseph's bread to guard the home against storms, and are invited to write their petitions and promises to St. Joseph on slips of paper for consecration by the archbishop. On November 1 the cemeteries are filled with the living as family tombs are cleaned and decorated for All Saints' Day. Shrines to the Virgin Mary proliferate in front yards.

Voodoo is also pervasive in New Orleans, where one finds a combination of tourist hype and deliberate eccentricity with genuine African-based practices. The casual visitor to New Orleans sees only "tourist voodoo." French Quarter shops specialize in "voodoo dolls" made in China, alligator teeth and claws, "blessed" chicken feet, Marie Laveau's Magic Mojo Beans, and plastic New Orleans Voodoo Cockroaches. The adventurous tourist can take a guided tour of Voodoo landmarks such as the site of Marie Laveau's home on St. Ann Street and her tomb in St. Louis Cemetery; for a higher fee, the sightseer can witness a staged Voodoo ceremony and snake dance in the swamp. During the 1980s and 1990s, visitors to the French Quarter would have encountered Fred Staten, a local character and self-styled Voodoo practitioner better known as Chicken Man. Arrayed in a costume of bones, teeth, and feathers, Chicken Man would pose for photographs, provide lottery numbers, and formulate gris-gris bags bearing his "Blessed by Chicken Man" seal of approval. When Chicken Man died in December 1998, a French Quarter nightclub owner paid for a Voodoo jazz funeral that was a perfect example of entrepreneurial showmanship and authentic practice. The service was conducted by two of New Orleans' best-known Voodoo priestesses, Ava Kay Jones and Miriam Chamani. Chicken Man's ashes were placed in a horse-drawn hearse and given a traditional brass band parade through the French Quarter.[80]

An undetermined amount of old-fashioned hoodoo is still practiced by working-class New Orleanians. Cari Roy, a serious, full-time psychic reader at the venerable New Orleans fortune-telling salon called the Bottom of the Cup, told me that some of her clients are elderly black ladies from the housing projects who use her services to determine whether an enemy has "put something on them." This was verified by Jane "Miss Sister" Jones, a seventy-three-year-old resident of the St. Bernard Projects, who said that "a lot of people do things to harm others," although "it's not as bad as it used to be."[81]

There has also been a revival of interest in Voodoo among young, well-educated people of all races. In 1996 the New Orleans Jazz and Heritage Festival featured the crafts, music, and religion of Haiti, and in 1998 the traveling exhibition "Sacred Arts of Haitian Vodou" (organized by the Fowler Museum of Cultural History at UCLA) opened at the New Orleans Museum of Art, contributing to public understanding of the connection between Haitian Vodou and New Orleans Voodoo. Contemporary Voodoo priests and priestesses lead a middle-class, multiracial community of believers who are serious students of the religion. These leaders, in various ways, serve sincere believers and attempt to inform the public about Voodoo through workshops, newsletters, and web sites. Motivated by the necessity of earning a living, they also give performances for tourists and conventioneers and have appeared on national television. Like Marie Laveau, they are both spiritual professionals and entrepreneurs.

Ava Kay Jones, originally from Thibodaux, Louisiana, comes from a family of traditional Catholic Creoles of color; her mother and grandmother both had spiritual powers. She holds a bachelor's degree in French and Spanish and a law degree from Loyola University. She traveled to Haiti in 1985 to be initiated as a Vodou mambo; a few years later she was initiated as a priestess of Oyá in Orisha-Vodu, the African American variant of Santería. She works from her home, by appointment only, and heads a performance group of drummers and dancers called Voodoo Macumba. She is sometimes assisted in her work by Elmer Glover, a spiritual professional who doubles as a karate instructor. An energetic advocate for the legitimacy of Voodoo, Jones appears every year at the New Orleans Jazz and Heritage Festival, where she speaks with visitors, sells charms, and dispels misconceptions about the religion. In 1997 she was featured in a documentary video, "New Orleans Voodoo from the Inside."[82]

Sallie Ann Glassman, a white woman from Maine who was raised in the Jewish faith, with her partner Shane Norris, a former engineer, operate the botánica Island of Salvation in the Bywater neighborhood. Glassman's training is in studio art. She is the designer of the New Orleans Voodoo Tarot and also created the large, colorful murals that adorn the outside of the botánica and the painted vèvè that cover the floor. Glassman and Norris were initiated in Haiti in 1995. Authentic, Haitian-style services are held at their home near the botánica—in no way are these tourist events. A few nights before the 1998 St. Patrick's holiday, I was invited to a ceremony for Dambala, attended by several drummers and a handful of other participants. Glassman and Norris also host an annual celebration for Gèdè, the lwa of death, the cemetery, and sex, on All Saints' night. Following a communal feast, the congregation makes a procession to the nearby Louisa Street Cemetery. In previous years, participants entered the cemetery by scaling the walls, for which they were arrested. The 1998 service was conducted outside the locked gates. At both the ceremony for Dambala and the Gèdè celebration, most of the attendees were middle-class whites.

Glassman and Norris drew national attention in 1995 when they performed a ceremony at the crossroads of Piety and North Rampart Streets, calling upon the warrior spirit Ogou to rid their racially and economically mixed neighborhood of drugs and crime. Approximately one hundred people attended the ceremony, many of them white. The more notorious drug dealers turned up to disrupt the ritual; one pulled his car into the intersection and tried to drown out the drumming and chanting with a blast of "gangsta rap" from his radio. Neighborhood blacks were uncomfortable; some young people and children laughed and jeered, and the older people seemed afraid. One lady told Norris that it was "dangerous to play around with magic." In the summer of 1998 Glassman and Norris again performed a public ceremony, this time asking Ezili-Dantò to avert the damaging wind and rain predicted for Louisiana during the fall hurricane season.[83]

Priestess Miriam Williams Chamani comes from the black Spiritual church tradition. Originally from Mississippi, she traveled to New York City to work as a domestic, then to Chicago, where she became an operating-room technician. There she first entered the ministry. In 1982 she was ordained bishop of the Angel Angel All Nations Spiritual Church and later founded the Miriam Williams Healing Ministry. In 1990, with her Belizian husband Oswan Chamani (now deceased), she moved to New Orleans to establish the Voodoo Spiritual Temple. The temple, on North Rampart Street on the fringe of the French Quarter, includes altars dedicated to the lwa, the orichas, and Black Hawk, plus a small retail shop. Unlike the establishments of Jones and Glassman, the Voodoo Spiritual

Temple is easily accessible to outsiders and is often visited by tour groups. Weekly drumming ceremonies are held in the back courtyard. Priestess Miriam does readings, telephone consultations, and travels to clients' homes, sometimes even out of state, to perform spiritual work. In 1999 she was invited to Rybinsk, Russia, to instruct a group of students and establish a Voodoo community.[84]

Two purveyors of herbs, spiritual products, and ritual paraphernalia, the F & F (founded by a Cuban oloricha, Enrique Cortez, and now owned by Puerto Rican–born Felix Figueroa) and Botánica Solano (owned by the late Frank Rodriguez, originally from Cuba), cater to a multiracial clientele who practice the myriad spiritual traditions represented in New Orleans. Both botánicas also offer consultations. Another spiritual store, Divine Light, is owned by a white man whose background is in European occultism.

Pseudo voodoo intersects with genuine faith at the tomb of Marie Laveau in St. Louis Cemetery Number One. Tour guides, who have no idea of the significance of this ritual, instruct visitors to draw an X-mark on the tomb with a piece of red brick, rap three times, and make a wish. They spin fantasies about the "kind-hearted" Widow Paris and her "evil" daughter Marie II, identified as Philomene Glapion, who "used poison instead of spiritual power, performed abortions, and ran a house of prostitution."[85] Adherents of what I call "New Orleans Voodoo-Gothic Weirdness," pale young people with purple hair, tattoos, and multiple body piercings, perform various rituals and leave offerings.

The tomb is also a shrine for serious believers who wish to venerate the memory of the Voodoo queen, obtain power, or ask a favor. I once observed a young woman of color, obviously not a tourist, draw an X and stand with her open palm on the tomb, seemingly deep in prayer. On All Saints' Day in 1993 I documented the offerings left at Marie Laveau's tomb: fresh and artificial flowers, candles for the Virgin Mary, a tiny plastic skull, a black felt hat, cigarettes, match books, sticks of gum, coins, peppermint candies, Mardi Gras beads, white seashells, a pumpkin, the photograph of a black woman, two bottles of rum and a bottle of whiskey, three apples, and a jar of honey. Drawn on the pavement like a vèvè was a star made of dried red beans within a circle of green peas on a background of white rice.

Who left these artifacts? Were they true devotees, motivated by faith, or Voodoo imitators who thought it was a "cool" thing to do? I would suggest that, like much of today's eclectic New Orleans Voodoo, they probably represented a little of both.

CHAPTER 4

Conjure, Hoodoo, and Rootwork in the Anglo-Protestant South

T he rest of the American South, settled primarily by English and Scottish Protestants, was (and still is) very different from Latin-Catholic Louisiana. With some exceptions, the ratio of blacks to whites was lower, fewer slaves were imported directly from Africa, and Protestant Christianity was initially less compatible than Roman Catholicism with African religious traditions. These factors worked against the development of an organized African-based religion. Nevertheless, Africans and people of African descent were able to retain elements of their traditional culture, including the magical beliefs that were the basis of conjure, hoodoo, and rootwork.[1]

The first slaves were brought to the English colony of Virginia in 1619. Africans were introduced into Maryland and South Carolina in 1671 and into Georgia after that colony lifted the ban on African slavery in 1747. Gradually, slavery spread to the rest of the English North American colonies. Recent research has established that approximately one-third of those imported to the United States were Kongo-related peoples from Central Africa. On the rice plantations of the Georgia and South Carolina Low Country, Wolofs, Fulbes, and Mende peoples from Senegal and Gambia, and Akan and Ashante from what is now Sierra Leone, Liberia, and Ghana were preferred because of their experience with rice production, although here, as elsewhere, the majority of slaves were from the Kongo-Angola region.[2]

The typical eighteenth- and nineteenth-century plantation in the American South had about twenty slaves, resulting in more supervision by masters and overseers and considerable contact between blacks and whites. There were, however, exceptions. Some Virginia and Maryland tobacco plantations were enormous; the largest cotton plantations in Georgia, Alabama, and Mississippi used hundreds of field hands; and large numbers of slaves worked with relative independence on the vast rice, indigo, and cotton plantations of the Low Country.[3]

Compared to Brazil, Saint-Domingue, Cuba, and even Louisiana, the English North American colonies received proportionately fewer slaves directly from Africa. Importation of Africans into the United States was outlawed after 1808. Some slaves were legally imported from the English Caribbean islands and, after the first few generations, most were native born. There was less reinforcement of African cultural and religious traditions than in the South American and Caribbean colonies.[4]

Manumission was rare in the Anglo-Protestant South. Few slaves had the opportunity to purchase their freedom, and the black consorts and mixed-race children of plantation owners usually remained slaves. Although some free blacks were quite prosperous, there was no elite community of free people of color comparable to that of New Orleans. Free Negroes were feared and distrusted and often forced to live at the margins of society. Some states required them to have white guardians; some forced newly emancipated slaves to leave the state and forbade free blacks to enter.

English Common Law, unlike the black codes of the Catholic slave-trading countries of France, Spain, and Portugal, did not acknowledge the rights of slaves as human beings; they were viewed strictly as property. There was no legal requirement to Christianize the slaves, and the Church of England and other Protestant denominations made minimal efforts to convert them. Missionary work was limited to baptism, teaching of the Creed, the Lord's Prayer, and the Ten Commandments, and simple sermons on the themes of obedience and honesty. Protestant Christianity, with its emphasis on one God and the austerity of its ritual, had little appeal for Africans or people of African descent. The Reverend Charles Colcock Jones, a white Presbyterian minister who also owned three rice plantations and over a hundred slaves in the Georgia Low Country, blamed this resistance to Christianity on their "ignorance." In his 1842 treatise, *The Religious Instruction of the Negroes in the United States*, he noted their belief in "second-sight, in apparitions, charms, and witchcraft," lamenting that, "the superstitions brought from Africa have not been wholly laid aside."[5]

The English colonists and, later, the Anglo-Americans were hostile to missionary attempts to Christianize their slaves. They resented the time taken away from plantation work for religious instruction and church-going. Of particular concern was the idea that slaves who attained the status of Christians would thereby become equal with their masters and could no longer be held as chattel. Church authorities assured the planters that "the freedom which Christianity gives is a freedom from the bondage of sin . . . but being baptized . . . makes no change in . . . their outward condition [as slaves]."[6] It was also feared that any gathering of slaves, even for religious instruction and worship, could lead to rebellious plots. The objections of plantation owners were gradually overcome as they became persuaded that Christianization would make the slaves more docile.

During the Great Awakening of the late eighteenth and early nineteenth centuries, Baptist and Methodist evangelists, emphasizing the Bible stories, baptism by full immersion, and the ecstatic conversion experience, had much greater success among the slaves. A distinctive form of Afro-Protestant worship developed, characterized by a rhythmic preaching style, lively music accompanied by hand-clapping and foot-stomping, and possession by the Holy Spirit, called "shouting."[7]

The English and Scottish people who settled the American South brought with them not only their Protestant Christianity, but also the belief in magic and charms. Despite the attempts of the Protestant Church to eliminate these practices, the use of witch-bottles, bed-charms, and the consultation of wizards, cunning men and women, and sorcerers was widespread, especially among the common people. These beliefs were held by those who came to the colonies as indentured servants, as well as some members of the wealthy and educated classes. There were charges of witchcraft against whites, not only in Salem, Massachusetts, but also in colonial Virginia. Bottles filled with pins, resembling the witch-bottles of England and Europe, have been discovered at archeological sites in Virginia and Pennsylvania; these were assumed by the research team to have been made by white people. Books on the occult were included in the libraries of several plantation owners.[8] English popular and ceremonial magic could thus have been introduced into the African American belief system through association with whites.

Southern Conjure before 1900

As was the case in South America, the Caribbean, and Louisiana, the newly arrived African slaves brought their magico-religious practices to the English colonies. Even after most African Americans had converted to Christianity, there existed a parallel African-based tradition referred to in nineteenth-century accounts as conjure, tricking, or goofer, or, less often, by the English terms *witchcraft* or *cunning*.[9] *Hoodoo* and *rootwork* did not appear as designations for this practice until the twentieth century.

Because fewer among the slave population of the American South were African born, because blacks were more acculturated to white ways and were more closely supervised, and because African religious traditions were so denigrated by Anglo-Protestant Christians, conjure became distanced from its sacred origins and lacked the African religious element found in Vodou, Santería, and New Orleans Voodoo. The concern is not with the relationship of human beings to the universe, maintaining spiritual balance, and serving and honoring the deities and the ancestors. There are no priests and priestesses; no community of believers; no ceremonies involving music and drumming, sacrificial offerings, and spirit possession. Personal misfortune is thought to result from the ill will of one's fellow man, not from neglect of the deities, the saints, or the dead. Conjure is strictly pragmatic.[10]

Specialists, each serving his or her own clientele, were usually known as conjurers, trick doctors, or two-headed doctors. This last term recalls the Haitian expression for a Vodou priest who also dabbles in sorcery and is said to "work with both hands." In the Georgia and South Carolina Low Country practitioners were sometimes called wise men or wise women, as they were in England. In coastal Maryland and Virginia the term *high man* was common.[11] Several early nineteenth-century accounts specify that the plantation conjurer was African born. These solitary professionals were more related to the nganga of the Kongo people than to the vodu and orisha priests of the Fon and Yoruba, the oungan and mambo of Vodou, the olorichas of Santería, or the queens and doctors of New Orleans Voodoo. The occult practitioner not only prepared charms for positive and negative intentions, he or she also prescribed herbal remedies for physical ills. The medical role of the conjurer became even more important after emancipation, when freedmen were responsible for their own health care.

Although conjure incorporated Christian elements, the practice was usually devoid of the altars, candles, incense, oils, holy water, and images of the saints that prevail in the Afro-Catholic religions of South America, the Caribbean, and Louisiana. Charm rituals in the Anglo-Protestant South often called for recitation of the Psalms or the Lord's Prayer. We commonly find the invocation of the "three highest names"—Father, Son, and Holy Ghost, but the saints were mentioned only in the common phrase, "by St.

Peter, by St. Paul, by the Lord who saved us all." The aid of the Devil might be solicited for "bad work." Many practitioners attributed the greatest power to the spirits of the dead, reflecting an African (particularly Kongo) tradition with no Christian precedent.

In the nineteenth century, baths, salves, powders, and teas were made from natural and household ingredients, and many people carried or chewed a magical root. Charm assemblages bore a strong resemblance to Kongo minkisi in their use of symbolic ingredients. They were made from roots and herbs, reptiles and insects, human bodily products, unwashed clothing, salt, pepper, sulfur, pins, needles, iron nails, and graveyard dirt contained in glass bottles, jars, snuff cans, and cloth bags.

Black Americans held an essentially African concept of health, equating physical and mental well-being with balance of the body, mind, and spirit, and harmony with the human community and the dead. The prudent person took care to guard his or her body and surroundings from harmful influences through sensible living habits and preventive charms. Should sickness occur despite such precautions, consultation with a traditional practitioner would reveal whether the malady was "natural" (a common ailment caused by one's own negligence) or "unnatural" (caused by a human enemy). Diagnosis was sometimes accomplished by means of a silver dime, which was thought to turn black because it had absorbed evil conjure directed at the wearer. Another indication of unnatural sickness was its failure to respond to the usual treatments; a visit to a medical doctor was thought to make the condition even worse. The most extreme manifestation of unnatural sickness was "live things in the body," the ubiquitous belief (possibly of Kongo origin) that loathsome creatures have hatched and multiplied in one's insides due to a conjurer's having slipped the eggs or dried and powdered remains of snakes, lizards, or scorpions into one's food. The "live things" were thought to sap the victim's strength no matter how much food was consumed, to cause mysterious pains as they gnawed at vital organs, and to produce strange tingling sensations as they traveled up and down his or her legs.[12]

As was true of the "Gri-Gri Case" in Louisiana, conjure doctors made their way into official records only when they attempted to harm whites. The earliest known occult practitioner in the English North American colonies was a free black conjurer who in 1712 provided magical powder to a group of slave rebels in New York. Gullah Jack Pritchard, an African-born leader of the 1822 Denmark Vesey rebellion conspiracy in South Carolina, gave courage to his followers by telling them to eat nothing but parched corn and peanuts on the morning of the insurrection, and "when you join us as we pass, put into your mouth this crab-claw and you can't be wounded."[13]

References to charms and conjure doctors also appear in the published narratives of escaped slaves, notably those by Frederick Douglass and Henry Bibb, in which they recall events of the 1830s. The autobiographies of Douglass and Bibb are, of course, primarily antislavery treatises, but they also contain two of the earliest allusions to charms and conjuring actually written by African Americans.

A description of a protective charm is given in the *Life and Times of Frederick Douglass*, published as a short narrative in 1845 and expanded and reissued in 1892. Douglass was born in 1817 on the Eastern Shore of Maryland. During his youth, he lived for a while as the house servant of his master's relatives in Baltimore, where he learned to read and write and caught a glimpse of a larger and more liberated world. In 1833 he became the slave of his master's son-in-law on a farm near St. Michaels, Maryland. After nine months of conflict with this new owner, he was proclaimed "unmanageable" and was sent to a slave-breaker named Covey.

Here Douglass was treated with great cruelty and nearly starved and worked to death. He believed that he would have indeed been "broken" by Covey had it not been for an incident of magical significance. Following a severe beating, Douglass ran away and was found in the woods by Sandy, a slave from a neighboring farm.

> Sandy . . . was not only a religious man, but he professed to believe in a system for which I have no name. He was a genuine African, and had inherited some of the so-called magical powers said to be possessed by the eastern nations. He told me that he could help me, that in those very woods there was an herb . . . possessing all the powers required for my protection. . . . He told me, further, that if I would take that root and wear it on my right side it would be impossible for Covey to strike me a blow, and that, with this root about my person, no white man could whip me. He said he had carried it for years, and that he had fully tested its virtues.

Douglass, who was a Methodist, found "all this talk about the root . . . ridiculous, if not positively sinful." He had an "aversion to all pretenders to divination" and considered it "beneath one of my intelligence to countenance such dealings with the Devil." Sandy, however, reminded Douglass that all his book-learning had not prevented Covey from beating him, and urged him to try the root. The next morning Douglass put the protective charm in his right pocket and walked up bravely to Covey's house as though nothing had happened: "Singularly enough, just as I entered the yard-gate I met [Covey] and his wife on their way to church. . . . He . . . inquired how I was, and seemed an altered man. This extraordinary conduct really made me begin to think that Sandy's herb had more virtue in it than I, in my pride, had been willing to allow, and, had the day been other than Sunday, I should have attributed Covey's . . . manner solely to the power of the root."

On Monday morning Covey had reverted to his former character and attempted to give Douglass another beating, but this time Douglass, with the root still in his pocket, fought back. He was never again mistreated by Covey. This incident, he said, "rekindled in my breast the smoldering embers of liberty . . . and inspired me with a renewed determination to be a free man."[14]

Another early account of charm beliefs appears in the narrative of Henry Bibb. Bibb was born into slavery on a Kentucky plantation in 1815, and, after several failed attempts, escaped to the North. There he joined a group of abolitionists and spent the rest of his life lecturing and writing about the evils of slavery. His autobiography was published in 1849. By this time he had acquired an education and become a devout Christian, so he tended to scoff at belief in conjure.

> There is much superstition among the slaves. Many of them believe in what they call conjuration, tricking, and witchcraft; and some of them pretend to understand the art, and say that by it they can prevent masters from exercising their will over the slaves. . . . At other times they prepare certain kinds of powders, to sprinkle about their masters' dwellings. This is all done for the purpose of defending themselves in some peaceable manner, although I am satisfied that there is no virtue at all in it.
>
> I got myself into a scrape . . . by going off [to visit a neighboring plantation without permission], and I expected to be severely punished for it. I had a strong notion of running off . . . but was advised . . . to go to one of these conjurers, who could prevent my being flogged. After I paid him, he mixed up some alum, salt, and other stuff into a powder, and said I must sprinkle it about my master. . . . He also gave me [a] root to chew, and spit toward [the master]. . . . According to order I used his remedy, and for some cause I was let pass without being flogged that time.

Thinking he was now immune to punishment, Bibb again stayed away all night without permission. When his master approached to whip him, "I commenced talking saucy to him. . . . He became so enraged . . . that he grasped a handful of switches and punished me severely, in spite of all my roots and powders."[15]

In the late nineteenth century, articles about conjure appeared in the *Southern Workman*, a monthly journal of the Hampton Normal and Agricultural Institute in Virginia. Hampton was founded in 1868 by white New Englanders from the American Missionary Association, with support from the Freedmen's Bureau, to provide teacher training and trade and agricultural skills to freed slaves. The school's first director, although he saw no difference between the intellectual capacity of blacks and whites, believed that blacks were ignorant and "morally deficient." To prepare Hampton students to eliminate "superstition" among members of their race, they were directed to record what they had observed or heard about conjure. An 1878 article in the *Southern Workman*, "Conjure Doctors in the South," quotes from some of these student reports. The preface illustrates prevailing attitudes among whites and blacks alike:

> A careful inquiry among the students and graduates of Hampton has elicited a great mass of testimony in regard to the prevalence of superstition among the freedmen, especially of the belief in what is known among them as conjuration or "tricking." From over a hundred letters, we select the following specimens, to throw light upon the mental condition of the masses of this people, and the kind of work that must be done among them if they are to be raised to civilization or even saved from extinction.

The student reports describe sick people being visited by the conjure doctor, who diagnosed the malady as the result of a "trick." After collecting a sizable fee from the victim, the conjurer would locate the concealed charm, destroy it, and "turn the trick" against the perpetrator. It was often implied by the students that the doctor had personally placed the charm there, and that the herbal remedies administered by this practitioner contributed to the patient's sickness. In most cases, the afflicted person eventually got better. If not, the conjure doctor took no responsibility; the failure was blamed on the victim for waiting too long to seek help or for not following instructions. One student said that a conjure doctor could earn more than a white physician—sometimes as much as five hundred dollars a week—and that he or she always demanded payment in cash. Some of the respondents did not doubt that the conjure doctor could do what was claimed, and others were skeptical, but all expressed fear of these individuals.

The writer called "A." relates:

> A dear friend of mine was sick; her parents had all the [medical] doctors come to see her . . . but instead of her getting better, she would get worse. One day her brother said . . . that he was going to a conjuring doctor to ask him to come to see her. . . . That night he brought home . . . the Reverend Mr. H. I can see him now, for we did laugh at him. He had his hair braided like a woman, and rings in his ears. He went to work . . . [saying] "I will dig up what they put down [have buried] for her." . . . He dug up a bottle that had all kinds of things in it, flies, bugs, lizards, and lots of green looking things, and one large frog. . . . He spit in his hand, rubbed it over the bottle . . . [and] put it in running water. . . . [My friend] did get better after a long time.

This writer also describes a love charm. The practice of burying an intimately associated article of the charm user's clothing in the target's path is an example of contagious magic.

> I knew a woman who used to love a man . . . [but he] treated her very cooly. She said she intended to have him if money could get him, so she went to an old woman and told her . . . that she would pay any amount of money to fix him. . . . This old woman told her to bring one of her own underskirts . . . [to] be buried in a place where he would step over it. . . . He commenced to love her after a month or so. He got so he could not stay away from her, and they were married just before I left home.[16]

By the 1890s, attitudes had changed at Hampton, and these beliefs were no longer viewed as "moral deficiencies." Alice Bacon, a white teacher, strongly believed that African American folklore should be preserved before it disappeared altogether. In 1893 she organized the Hampton Folklore Society, and its work continued until Bacon left Hampton in 1900. Between 1893 and 1899 a monthly "Folklore and Ethnology" section, consisting of material provided by Folklore Society members, was published in the *Southern Workman*. Although several white faculty members participated in the Folklore Society, Bacon wisely insisted that the collection of data could only successfully be done by blacks.

In a letter circulated to Hampton graduates and "others who may be interested," Bacon urged: "If this material is to be obtained, it must be gathered soon by intelligent observers . . . who enter into the homes and lives of the more ignorant colored people and who see in their beliefs and customs no occasion for scorn, or contempt, or laughter. . . . The work cannot be done by white people, much as many of them would enjoy the opportunity of doing it, but must be done by the educated and intelligent colored people who are at work all through the South among . . . their own race." Bacon especially asked her respondents to collect animal tales; customs connected with birth, marriage, and death; folk medicine; proverbs; songs; traditions of African ancestry; African words; and conjure beliefs.[17]

Alice Bacon and the Hampton librarian, Leonora Herron, drew upon the 1878 student reports for their article, "Conjuring and Conjure Doctors," which appeared in the *Southern Workman* in 1895 and was reprinted the following year in the *Journal of American Folklore*. Leonora Herron discussed the work and characteristics of conjure doctors:

> The conjure doctor's business was of two kinds: to conjure or "trick" a person, and to cure persons already conjured. . . . They were appealed to upon the least pretext. . . . Jealousy or envy . . . [or] a quarrel between two neighbors . . . would result in a visit to the conjure doctor and the subsequent illness, or death perhaps, of one of the parties. Love affairs gave plenty of employment to the conjure doctors, as they were believed to be able to "work their roots" so to make one person return another's affection. . . . If the affair resulted unhappily, the slighted party sought revenge in having the other "tricked" so that no rival should be more successful. In slavery times . . . the conjure doctor [was] appealed to, to save the slave from punishment.

According to the Hampton students' reports, the source of the conjure doctor's powers was either the Devil or a special revelation from God. Many claimed to be the seventh child of a seventh child and to have been born with a caul. The students described conjure doctors as being tall and very dark, with red eyes. One doctor was said to wear lizards on a string around his neck, to be able to transform his cane into a snake by throwing it down, and to possess the art of turning himself green.

Alice Bacon discussed rituals and charms. She concluded that some cases of conjuration were outright poisonings caused by vegetable substances or dried and powdered toads, scorpions, lizards, snakes, and salamanders being surreptitiously placed in a person's food or drink. She accepted the belief that sickness could also be caused by supernatural means.

Bacon gave examples of some of the charms reported by the Hampton students: a black bottle containing a liquid mixture and nine pins and needles; a bottle filled with roots, stones, and a reddish powder; bottles filled with beans, nails, and powder; a bottle full of snakes; a preserve jar containing a snake and several insects; bags, often made of red flannel, containing various combinations of salt, pepper, silver coins, needles, pins, hair, snake heads, anvil dust, and a "kind of root [possibly John the Conqueror] conjurers always carry in their pockets." These containerized charms were thought by the students to cause illness or insanity when deposited in the vicinity of the intended target: "If you fail to get near enough to your victim to place the spell in his room, his hand, his bed, or his path, you may yet, if you are skillful, succeed in carrying out your fell design by simply burying your charm under his doorstep or in his yard . . . where it can work untold evil."

The conjure doctor sometimes determined the nature of the illness by putting a silver coin into the hand or mouth of the victim. If it turned black, the person had certainly been "tricked." The doctor would then locate the charm and destroy it by throwing it into running water or burning it, and, if requested, would "turn the trick" back upon the one who sent it. Many of the Hampton informants accepted the notion of "live things in the body." It was suggested by Bacon that some unscrupulous practitioners would produce a wriggling creature at the dramatic moment, claiming to have removed it from the victim.

Cures were sometimes accomplished by means of herbal baths, teas, or ointments. One patient was bathed in an infusion of mullein and moss, and the water was thrown toward the sunset with the words, "As the sun sets in the West, so should the works of the Devil end in judgement." In another case a tea was made of roots and leaves, causing the patient to "throw up a variety of reptiles." Another doctor gave a conjured person "some roots to carry in his pocket and something to rub with."[18]

As we saw in the chapter on New Orleans Voodoo, many freedmen began to distance themselves from traditional African magical and religious practices during the late nineteenth century. Ministers and educators, both black and white, attempted to suppress "superstition" and the more exuberant forms of religious expression, believing that these "remnants of heathen Africa" were an impediment to racial progress. The black elite joined Baptist, Methodist, and African Methodist Episcopal churches and denounced anything reminiscent of their slave past. Others organized Pentecostal, Holiness, and Spiritualist congregations and continued their African-based practices. Although conjure was outwardly condemned, it remained a vital tradition among people who found meaning in the beliefs of their ancestors.[19]

Hoodoo and Rootwork: 1900—1940s

Despite the disapproval of those who sought to "uplift the Negro race," magical practices were still plentiful in the American South during the first decades of the twentieth century, as documented by Newbell Niles Puckett, the Federal Writers' Project fieldworkers, Harry Middleton Hyatt, and others. The old-fashioned terms *conjure*, *goofer*, and *tricking*, although still heard, were being replaced by *hoodoo* in the Gulf Coast and Mississippi Delta regions and by *rootwork* in the coastal Low Country of North Florida, Georgia, and the Carolinas. Researchers found that many rituals and charm beliefs had changed little from those described by Frederick Douglass, Henry Bibb, and the members of the Hampton Folklore Society. These practices were fairly consistent throughout the South, having been disseminated through the sale and movement of slaves from the older coastal regions to the newly opened lands of Kentucky, Tennessee, Mississippi, Alabama, Arkansas, and Texas. The presence of similar charm traditions in Louisiana is owed in part to the sale of slaves from the Upper South in New Orleans after the Purchase of 1803. Popular books on the occult, which began to appear in the nineteenth century and were widely circulated by the 1930s, may also account for some similarities. Along the Gulf Coast from Mobile to east Texas and in the Mississippi Delta, hoodoo practice exhibited a strong New Orleans influence. In the Low Country there existed a particularly African form of rootwork that centered on graveyard rituals and the power of the dead.

Traditional hoodoo doctors and rootworkers prepared baths and washes, anointing substances, powders and sweeping compounds, fumigants, substances to be ingested, and charm assemblages. A protective charm was referred to as a *shield* or a *guard*; recall that a similar charm is called *gad* in Haiti. Other charms were called *hands*, *mojos*, or *tobies*. Robert Farris Thompson traces mojo to the word *mooyo*, by which the Kongo people mean the indwelling spirit of a charm, and toby to the *tobe* charms of Kongo, a mixture of palm wine and earth from a grave.[20]

People who suspected that they were being controlled or harmed by occult means said that they had been hoodooed, rooted, fixed, jinxed, given a "dose," or that they were suffering from a "crossed condition" or a "misery." A person might express fear that something had been "put down against me," referring to the common practice of burying a charm or sprinkling a powder in the target's path or yard. In the Low Country, it was said that somebody "put bad mouth on me," or had been "diggin' in the graveyard for me."

Mention of the crossroads often appears in interviews with southern practitioners. Dirt from the crossroads was a common charm ingredient, and charms were deposited at the crossroads to absorb its power. There the believer might also encounter a supernatural being or even the Devil, from whom he or she could learn the art of conjuring or music. Many old-time fiddlers and bluesmen are said to have acquired their skill at the crossroads. These beliefs undoubtedly derive from the symbolism of the Kongo cosmogram, which defines the crossroads, or any site where two lines intersect, as a magical place where the realm of the living touches the realm of the spirits.

Variations on the ritual to obtain the lucky black cat bone have been documented all over the South. As in Zora Neale Hurston's Louisiana description, the procedure was to catch a pure black feline, fling it into a pot of boiling water, slam the lid on, and cook it until the flesh fell off the bones. It was said that the cat would scream horribly, and while it boiled one would see dreadful apparitions—sometimes the Devil himself. The "lucky bone" was variously said to be the one that floated to the top of the pot, the one that floated upstream when the contents of the pot were thrown into running water, or the one that rendered the owner invisible in a mirror or tasted bitter when held in the mouth. If the would-be hoodoo worker could withstand this ordeal, he or she would have a magical bone that enabled its owner to become a master conjurer, control others, and become invisible.[21]

■ ■ ■

In the early 1920s, Newbell Niles Puckett, a white Mississippian, undertook the first systematic study of African American beliefs since the 1893–99 work of the Hampton Folklore Society. *Folk Beliefs of the Southern Negro*, which began as Puckett's doctoral dissertation in sociology at Yale, was published in 1926. For the section called "Voodooism and Conjuration," Puckett drew heavily upon material from the *Southern Workman* and on articles culled from the *Journal of American Folklore* and other publications.

His impressive list of more than four hundred informants includes few actual hoodoo practitioners. Many, in fact, were students and faculty from the Negro colleges to which Puckett sent questionnaires, plus white law enforcement officers and friends of the Puckett family who contributed stories gleaned from their servants.[22]

Most of Puckett's personal fieldwork was done in his hometown of Columbus, Mississippi. His primary informant was the hoodoo doctor Ed Murphy. Like many occult specialists, Murphy was also a devout Christian, and Puckett characterized him as an awe-inspiring preacher at revival meetings. He lived alone, foretold the future by gazing at a clear pebble, and was believed by other blacks to be able to change himself into an animal. Murphy showed Puckett how to make a gambling hand out of the herbs called seed of the earth, Sampson's snake-root, and Devil's shoestring, which were wrapped in black cloth, folded toward the maker, sewed with white thread, and carried in a red flannel bag. The charm was to be periodically "fed" with whiskey and always carried on one's body. Ed Murphy spoke of chewing a root to "soften a person's heart." This charm was efficacious when conducting business deals or when courting a lady. Recall that similar root-charms were mentioned in the 1849 narrative of Henry Bibb and in the 1878 *Southern Workman* article. Puckett learned from Hattie Harris that you may "harm your enemy beyond repair by getting a rabbit's tail, scorching it, mixing with red pepper and graveyard dirt, and putting it where he will come into contact with it."[23]

Puckett noted that certain common charm ingredients were purchased at the drugstore: "Druggists throughout the South report a large sale of snakeroot, sassafras, lodestone, brimstone, asafoetida, resin, and bluestone to the colored people for the purpose of hoodooing."[24] He did not mention the sale or use of manufactured spiritual products in the rural South.

Occasional references to magical practices are sprinkled throughout the Federal Writers' Project interviews with former slaves, but with the exception of the Louisiana, Georgia (Savannah Unit), and Florida Writers' Project material, the Federal Writers' Project interviews contain surprisingly little of substance on conjure, hoodoo, and rootwork. Some people claimed that these practices were unknown during slavery because the masters would not have allowed them: "Never was there anything said 'bout that hoodoo stuff. I never heard of it 'til these later years."[25] Most informants denied confidence in such things, perhaps fearing ridicule by white interviewers. Typical are statements such as, "I ain't never believe in none of them charms . . . and ain't know nothin' 'bout no conjuring."[26] The narratives of those who did tell fieldworkers about their experiences with charms and conjurers strongly resemble the nineteenth-century accounts published in the *Southern Workman*.[27] It is difficult to ascertain whether the speakers are referring to nineteenth-century conjure or to events of the 1930s and 1940s.

Hyatt's *Hoodoo-Conjure-Witchcraft-Rootwork* is an excellent source of information on charm beliefs in the Anglo-Protestant South. In addition to his work in New Orleans, Hyatt interviewed practitioners along the Gulf Coast in Mobile and St. Petersburg; in the Mississippi Delta cities of Vicksburg, Little Rock, and Memphis; in the Atlantic coastal Low Country from Jacksonville, Florida, to Wilmington, North Carolina, and in Virginia, Maryland, and Washington, D.C. He did not venture far into the "interior" of the South, and he never visited Texas.[28] Some of Hyatt's informants used commercial spiritual products, but most were still making charms from traditional materials.

Hyatt found that, in addition to the old-fashioned rural conjurer, hoodoo doctor, or rootworker, a new, more professional and commercially oriented type of practitioner was emerging in the Anglo-Protestant South. Some of these men and women attracted clients from all over the east coast. They were generally less flamboyant than the New Orleans hoodoo workers described in the preceding chapter, and only a few wore a special costume, such as a robe or a turban. The title of "spiritualist" or "Christian reader" was preferred because of the negative perception of hoodoo and rootwork by blacks and whites alike. Hyatt, always interested in nomenclature, asked a Memphis informant in 1938 if "this type of work" was called hoodoo: "Oh, no! No! they call it in this country 'spiritualment.' Hoodoo . . . that's people that don't believe in nothin' but settin' death-candles on you, takin' and puttin' snakes in you, scorpions in you, killin' you, doin' off with you, puttin' you in bad health, messin' you up."[29]

We have noted that magical practices in the Anglo-Protestant South did not incorporate Roman Catholic elements. Areas of the Gulf Coast and Mississippi Delta, with strong cultural ties to New Orleans, are the exception. In Mobile and in the Mississippi Delta cities of Vicksburg and Little Rock, Hyatt found some practitioners using Catholic sacramental objects and combining old-fashioned hoodoo charms with commercial products.[30] But it was in Memphis that Hyatt found the most evidence of Louisiana-style practices and use of commercial products.

Hyatt visited Memphis in May 1938 and again in October 1939, interviewing approximately fifty people. Sixteen complete interviews are included in volumes 2 and 3 of *Hoodoo-Conjure-Witchcraft-Rootwork*, fourteen with women and four with men. Although Memphis was not a predominantly Catholic city, it was closely connected to New Orleans, and many informants spoke of using altars, candles, incense, oils, holy water, and the power of the saints. They described several examples of the beef tongue court-case charm and the miniature-coffin death charm. Van-Van Oil, a New Orleans favorite, was also popular in Memphis. Nowhere else in the Anglo-Protestant South do we find rituals and charm beliefs so nearly resembling those of New Orleans.

Much of this activity centered on Beale Street, which, like New Orleans' South Rampart Street, was once a thriving center of African American commerce and entertainment. From the turn of the century through the 1940s, the Beale Street neighborhood was occupied by clothing stores, groceries, barber shops, theaters, bars, and gambling joints. According to Margaret McKee and Fred Chisenhall's *Beale Black and Blue*, "mojo artists, herb doctors, peddlers of love potions, dealers in dream books, conjure men, and con men" also inhabited Beale Street.[31] Hyatt conducted his interviews at the Eureka Hotel on Mulberry Street, a few blocks off Beale.

Here, Hyatt learned of the "nation sack," a charm unique to Memphis. The nation sack was a cloth bag, worn by a woman tied around her waist inside her clothes, in which she kept her money and "all [her] different little concerns," meaning magical objects and substances. The nation sack was never to be touched by a man: "A man . . . goin' have some serious trouble with that old lady if he try to touch that bag . . . you'll see her every night go and lock it up in her trunk. Next mornin' you see her go there and get it." The great Delta bluesman Robert Johnson, in his classic "Come on in My Kitchen," confesses that he violated hoodoo tradition by rummaging in his woman's nation sack and stealing her last nickel. Hyatt's informant, "Nation Sack Woman," related that her mother-in-law wore such a charm. "I know she did conjuring on Mr. Simpson [her husband] 'cause she been married to him fifty years, and she really kept him too. She had him in that bag."[32]

Many of Hyatt's Memphis informants were professional hoodoo workers who preferred white clients. Madam Collins said that Memphis was overrun with "false pretenders . . . out walkin' the streets knockin' on doors. . . . The real doctors of this city get cooperation from the white business people, because they are the [ones] that needs them." The "Self-Sufficient Doctor" said her customers were exclusively white, upper-class residents who "keep the cooks and maids." Madam Wiley bluntly stated that "my trade is white; I don't need no nigger trade."[33]

Madam Collins, like the New Orleans practitioners, had a special altar room and wore a white satin robe and cap. The cap, she explained, was to protect her hair from turning gray—"This work will age you." She never had to bribe the police (the usual fee was fifty dollars a month) because she was a licensed "spiritual doctor." "I paid for my license . . . an' I have a diploma on it from the White Brotherhood in St. Joe's, California." The White Brotherhood, Hyatt later ascertained, was a branch of the Rosicrucians operating out of San Jose, California. Madam Collins periodically received mailings from this organization advertising various products and charm formulae, for which she paid by money order. Her robe was purchased from the White Brotherhood, and she was told not to wash it herself, but to return it for cleaning because it had been blessed.[34]

Hyatt obtained from Madam Collins a recipe to cure impotence, or "loss of nature." A man could be rendered totally impotent by an enemy's curse. He could also be made selectively impotent with any woman but the user of a controlling charm, which would inhibit his sexuality and keep him faithful. The woman could wipe the semen from her lover's penis after intercourse, tie the cloth in nine knots, and wear it next to her skin or hidden under her mattress. An alternative method was to measure his penis with a string as he slept; the string, like the cloth, was tied in nine knots and worn on her body or put under the mattress. The same purpose could be accomplished by sealing the man's urine or semen in a bottle with pins and needles, or by writing his name on a slip of paper and wearing it in her shoe. Madam Collins, an astute spiritual merchant, revealed that her formula for restoring a man's "nature" cost only sixty cents to make, but she sold it for five dollars. One of the ingredients, Arm and Hammer baking soda, was chosen because its logo—an erect, muscular arm swinging a hammer—symbolizes the desired result of the charm: "In a basin, mix together Arm and Hammer baking soda, saltpeter, and dry mustard. When pouring in the baking soda, say 'In the name of the Father'; pour in the saltpeter, 'In the name of the Son'; and the mustard, 'In the name of the Holy Spirit.' Then say 'Remove these evil spirits from this person's body.'" The client was given a packet containing the dry ingredients. In his own home, he was to mix four tablespoons with a gallon of water, and bathe with it on Mondays, Wednesdays, and Fridays. Madam Collins instructed him to wash from his head downward, then let the water go down the drain and "straight to the river." After three baths he would be cured.[35]

Several Memphis practitioners, in addition to Madam Collins, used commercially produced powders, oils, and other items. These products were readily available in Memphis. One woman spoke of purchasing "a little mixture outa some of these places uptown where you can buy that." Keystone and Lucky Heart, two of the pioneering manufacturers of spiritual products, were located in Memphis and were mentioned by several of Hyatt's informants. The Lucky Heart factory was on Mulberry Street, just a few doors from the Eureka Hotel, where Hyatt conducted his interviews. He was probably referring to this company when he remarked that a particular powder was available "just a stone's throw from where we were sitting."[36] Although not specifically cited, Schwab's Beale Street department store would have been another source of supplies. Schwab's, still in its original location and still operated by the Schwab family, has devoted a section of the store to spiritual products since the 1930s.

Some people ordered spiritual products by mail from New York and Chicago or traveled to New Orleans to buy them—the Cracker Jack and other New Orleans hoodoo drugstores were in their heyday in the late 1930s. One of Hyatt's informants used a special Controlling Powder—"'Course we always sent to New Orleans to get it until they stopped . . . mailin' it. Now, you gotta go there and get it." Another woman used Drawing Powder to attract customers and knew of a special key, favored by burglars and bank robbers, that would open any lock—"Well, you can hardly get them here, but you can get them in New Orleans."[37]

A few years after Hyatt conducted his Memphis fieldwork, a Mississippi hoodoo doctor and healer named Wash "Doc" Harris settled on Mary Angela Street in the Coro Lake Community, an African American neighborhood in Southwest Memphis. Harris established the St. Paul's Spiritual Temple, where he carried out his work for approximately fifty years. He was arrested and fined several times for practicing medicine without a license. Mary Angela Street was populated by Doc's family and followers and came to be known by outsiders as the "Voodoo Village." According to Sharon Bynum, a graduate student at the University of Memphis who is conducting research on Harris, the yard of Harris's temple was decorated with crosses and triangular structures, many of which were painted red and white, and with dolls in glass cases decorated with Christmas lights.[38]

Like Memphis, Houston has cultural ties to Louisiana. In the 1930s and 1940s many black Louisianians migrated to Houston to take jobs in the oil refineries and railroad yards, bringing with them a kind of New Orleans–style hoodoo. Mexican folk beliefs also entered the mix. A series of five articles, entitled "Voodoo in Houston," appeared in the *Houston Press* on March 22–26, 1937, indicating that the practice was rife among

Houston's black population. It was reported that "almost every elderly Negro searched at the police station will have a rabbit's foot in his pocket. . . . Others have lodestones, . . . bottles containing mysterious ointments . . . [or] vials of 'consecrating oil.'" Mexicans were often found to carry a small bag containing coal dust and a coin. Charms such as these were obtained from local practitioners, who also sold roots and herbs and commercial spiritual products. Some people preferred to order directly from New York, Chicago, or New Orleans.[39] Although it is not mentioned in the 1937 article, at least one hoodoo drugstore, Stanley Drug, has operated in Houston since the 1920s.

■ ■ ■

The Atlantic coastal Low Country and Sea Islands, extending from Jacksonville, Florida, through Georgia and South Carolina and into southern North Carolina, has maintained a highly Africanized culture. In the eighteenth and nineteenth centuries, blacks greatly outnumbered whites, and hundreds of slaves worked the large rice, indigo, and cotton plantations with little contact with masters and overseers. Like New Orleans, Savannah and Charleston received white, colored, and black refugees from the Haitian revolution at the turn of the nineteenth century, although they arrived in lesser numbers. The smuggling of slaves directly from Africa continued until the mid-nineteenth century. After the Civil War, some of the plantations were divided into parcels and awarded to newly freed blacks, who, until recently, have continued to live there in relative isolation. Before 1940 the Sea Islands were accessible only by boat. The creole language of the residents, called Gullah in South Carolina and Geechee in Georgia, is a fusion of African languages with English.[40] While similar charm beliefs were found elsewhere in the South, they were particularly intense and concentrated in this region.

The culture was documented in the late 1930s by the Savannah Unit of the Georgia Writers' Project and by Harry Middleton Hyatt. Here we find no trace of Catholicism—no saints, altars, candles, incense, or holy water. Charms of any sort—baths, powders, oils, fumigants, substances to be ingested, or magical ingredients assembled in a container—were known as "roots." Many rituals involved a visit to the cemetery to solicit the aid of the dead and obtain graveyard dirt, the most important ingredient in Low Country charms. This undoubtedly derives from the African (particularly Kongo) belief that a person's grave is infused with his or her spirit. There was very little mention of commercial spiritual products, but the interviews indicate that some local residents worked as sales agents for Memphis and Chicago spiritual supply companies.[41]

The work of the Savannah Unit of the Georgia Writers' Project was published in 1940 as *Drums and Shadows: Survival Studies among the Georgia Coastal Negroes*. In his introduction to the 1986 Brown Thrasher edition of *Drums and Shadows*, historian Charles Joyner called it "the pioneering work in demonstrating the continuing, living influence of African folklore." The fieldworkers, directed by Mary Granger, interviewed 138 people in black communities surrounding Savannah and on the nearby Sea Islands, seeking out the oldest inhabitants, those who had been slaves, and those who remembered African-born "Golla" (Gullah) ancestors. These Africans were said to be able to make a pot boil without fire, cause a hoe to work by itself, navigate the waterways in a boat rowed by buzzards, and fly back to Africa when they became disgusted with slavery. I have been unable to locate the original field reports of the Savannah Unit.

We know from the interviews that some of the African-born slaves were Muslims and that others practiced traditional African religions. Most Low Country blacks eventually became Methodists or Baptists. Their unique form of Protestant Christianity included an African style of circle dancing called the "ring shout," the use of drums at church services and funerals, "settin' up" all night with the dead, and river baptisms at which a special prayer was addressed to the river, asking that their sins be carried away with the ebb tide.[42]

The Georgia Writers' Project fieldworkers found that belief in the supernatural was strong among the residents of black communities near Savannah and on the Georgia Sea Islands. The informants complained of "hags" and "witches" who could shed their skins, slip into the house through the smallest crack, and "ride" the victim at night. Laying a broom across the door, sprinkling salt or benne (sesame) seed around the bed, or placing a Bible under the pillow was thought to keep these evil creatures away. Doors and window frames were painted blue to protect against the "plateye," a hideous spirit-animal. The people also believed in the reality of ghosts. To those who had been born with a caul, there was nothing remarkable about seeing spirits: "I sees 'em all the time. They don't hurt you none, just walk along with you and talk." One man said that he could go into the cemetery at midnight and see the dead standing beside their graves.[43]

Rootwork was common, and, to those who believed, nothing was thought to happen simply by chance. The Savannah fieldworkers observed that several elderly residents always dragged a broom behind themselves so that an enemy could not take up their foot tracks, and that many people burned their hair combings to prevent incorporation of these bodily products into a malevolent charm. One man wore copper wire bracelets strung with charms and a copper wire around his head, to which were attached mirrors that lay flat against his temples—copper is commonly used to prevent or relieve the pain of arthritis and rheumatism. A silver dime tied around the ankle was thought to turn black, warning the wearer to take action against the harmful machinations of an adversary.[44] Many residents carried a "hand." One woman told the fieldworkers that "most of the folks carry something for protection [to] keep other folks from workin' conjure on 'em. They's made of hair, and nails, and graveyard dirt . . . [and] pieces of cloth and string. They tie 'em all up in a li'l bag."[45] Another described a bottle charm containing "some funny oily stuff. . . . The enemy catch the person's spirit in that bottle . . . the man fell sick and had to go to a root doctor."[46]

Hyatt conducted approximately 148 interviews in the coastal cities of Jacksonville, Florida; Brunswick and Savannah, Georgia; Charleston, South Carolina; and Wilmington, North Carolina. He went inland to Waycross, Georgia, and Sumter and Florence, South Carolina. Forty-nine complete interviews were published; thirty-five with men and fourteen with women.

We find that Hyatt's informants considered the power of the dead to be the most important element in rootwork. This necessitated a trip to the cemetery at some specified hour, usually midnight, to negotiate with the spirits. The rootworker chose the appropriate grave for the task at hand, using the grave of a good Christian or an innocent child for beneficent magic and the grave of a sinner or a wicked person—"drunkards, whore mongers, gamblers, and murderers"—for evil intentions.[47] It was sometimes specified that a spoonful of salt should be carried for protection against the spirits. The rootworker would call the name of the person buried there, reverse the wooden headboard and footboard to awaken the deceased, ask his or her assistance in solving the problem, and take slivers from the wooden marker, a bone or a tooth, or a handful of dirt. Graveyard dirt was often called "goofer dust," possibly derived from the Kongo word *kufwa* (to die).[48] It was of utmost importance to pay the dead with pennies or silver coins, or occasionally with rice. These offerings were usually buried, although they sometimes were placed on top of the grave. Nobody would dare remove them.

Almost every person interviewed by Hyatt in the Florida, Georgia, and Carolina Low Country reported some kind of cemetery ritual: graveyard products and the power of the dead were used to bring peace in the home, reunite the separated, assist in court cases, detect criminals, force an enemy to leave town, or to kill. Charms might be left in a grave for a period of time in order to absorb the power of the deceased for doing good or harm.[49]

Most Low Country towns had a resident root doctor. Charleston resident Ben Blair told me of a white practitioner, Doctor Shehorn, who served both black and white clients near Blair's family home of Camden, South Carolina, in the 1930s. "The spirits that he worked with lived in large iron wash pots, and had to be fed regularly with animal blood, rum, tobacco, or money. The money would either be buried in the cemetery or used to hold a party for the spirits."[50] This description, of course, bears a remarkable resemblance to the spirit-containing iron cauldrons called *prendas* in the Cuban Palo tradition. Their presence in South Carolina can perhaps be explained by the strong Kongo influence on both Palo and rootwork.

The most famous of the Low Country root doctors was Doctor Buzzard of St. Helena Island, near Beaufort, South Carolina. Like Marie Laveau of New Orleans, Doctor Buzzard is legendary. Although I could find no mention of him in the nineteenth-century literature on the Georgia and South Carolina Low Country, or in the published or unpublished reports of the South Carolina Writers' Project, someone by that name appears to have been practicing in the 1890s. Albert Jenkins, an elderly Georgia preacher quoted in *Drums and Shadows*, tells of visiting Doctor Buzzard in 1893 to cure his badly swollen foot and leg.[51] Mamie Garvin Fields, a black Charlestonian, mentions Doctor Buzzard in her memoir, *Lemon Swamp and Other Places*. Fields first heard of this "witchdoctor of witchdoctors" in 1909, when she was teaching at the Negro School on John's Island, South Carolina. Doctor Buzzard's reputation was so formidable that "people would say to you if they got mad, 'I'll go to Beaufort on you!'"[52] Hyatt heard fantastic and wildly conflicting stories about Doctor Buzzard. Informants said that clients were rowed across the river to the doctor's place of business by a pair of buzzards, and that Doctor Buzzard could "make a buzzard fly 'round the courthouse and the judge would dismiss the case." He usually was said to have lived near Beaufort, but other informants cited the South Carolina towns of Charleston, Florence, or Orangeburg. One even insisted on Monroe, Louisiana. Most people said he was black, but one swore that he was white.[53]

J. Edwin McTeer, a white man who was high sheriff of Beaufort County from 1926 to 1963, recounted his experiences with rootwork and root doctors in two short works, *High Sheriff of the Low Country* (1970) and *Fifty Years as a Low Country Witch Doctor* (1978). Sheriff McTeer had a good deal of professional contact with root doctors during his years in law enforcement, and was himself a practitioner of beneficent magic, locally known as "The White Prince." The Doctor Buzzard of McTeer's day was a man named Stephney (sometimes spelled Stepney)[54] Robinson, described as very dark skinned, tall, thin, somberly dressed in an expensive black suit, and recognizable by his purple-tinted sunglasses, the traditional badge of the root doctor. He was said to have inherited his powers from his father, possibly the nineteenth-century Doctor Buzzard referred to in *Drums and Shadows*.

Sheriff McTeer's account has been corroborated by the research of Roger Pinckney, published in 1998 as *Blue Roots: African-American Folk Magic of the Gullah People*. Pinckney's father was the coroner of Beaufort County during McTeer's tenure. McTeer and Pinckney both state that Doctor Buzzard had clients all over the Southeast and became wealthy through his rootwork practice. He owned a substantial home on Oaks Road on St. Helena Island near the town of Frogmore, always drove an expensive car, and financed the building of two large churches. For a fee, he prepared "roots," which McTeer describes as small charm packets made of flannel: "The thread of a small root protrudes from the pointed end, and even though the ingredients are secret, its carrier knows that powerful forces are at work for him inside." Out-of-state customers sent postal money orders in exchange for advice on horse races and lucky numbers. Doctor Buzzard specialized in court cases. By "dusting the courtroom" with powder and chewing a special root—possibly John the Conqueror—while glowering at the sheriff, judge, and lawyers through his purple glasses, he was believed by his clients to be able to bring about an acquittal or at least a lighter sentence.[55]

Stephney Robinson first appears in the federal census for 1880, at which time he was a young boy living with his parents, Thomas and Lucy Robinson. Legend has it that Doctor Buzzard's father was an African-born conjurer, but Thomas Robinson is recorded as being a South Carolina native. Stephney Robinson is listed in the 1910 and 1920 census with his wife, Molcey, and their many children. He died in 1947. Census data leads me to believe that Robinson was born in the late 1860s or early 1870s. His death certificate, however, states that he was born in 1885. Both the census and the death certificate give his occupation as self-employed farmer.[56] His "mantle of power" passed to his son-in-law, W. T. Gregory, who continued to practice on St. Helena Island until he died in 1997.

Doctor Buzzard became familiar to the general public with the publication and subsequent motion picture version of John Berendt's best-selling "nonfiction novel," *Midnight in the Garden of Good and Evil*. The title refers to the Beaufort graveyard where a root woman named Minerva, supposedly the common-law wife of Doctor Buzzard and inheritor of his practice, performs rituals to bring about the acquittal of the main character, a Savannah antiques dealer charged with murdering his young male lover. According to a 1994 article in the *Beaufort Gazette*, the character of Minerva is based on an actual person.[57]

Doctor Jim Jordan of Coastal North Carolina exemplifies the transition from the old-time practitioners documented by Hyatt, the Federal Writers' Project fieldworkers, and others, to today's hoodoo workers, root doctors, and spiritual advisors. Doctor Jordan maintained a successful practice in Manley's Neck Township, near the Virginia border, until the early 1960s. Thanks to a remarkable little book, *The Fabled Doctor Jim Jordan: A Story of Conjure* by F. Roy Johnson, we have an accurate biography of Doctor Jordan based on interviews with his family and members of the local community. Doctor Jordan was born in 1871, the son of former slaves. His mother, of African-Indian ancestry, taught him Native American herbal lore, and he learned the art of conjure from one of his uncles. Doctor Jordan's practice began in earnest in 1927 when he opened an office adjacent to his country store on Highway 258. His successful mercantile, farming, and logging operations were overseen by his grown sons while he attended to a growing clientele that came from as far away as New York, Philadelphia, and Washington, D.C., some even arriving by chartered bus. Out-of-state customers paid fees as high as a thousand dollars, while local people in more humble circumstances paid with meat, produce, or services.

At first Doctor Jordan used only roots and herbs gathered in the surrounding woods, but in the 1940s he began to purchase some of his materials from mail-order houses and sales agents. He also bought and studied popular occult texts and dream books: *The Sixth and Seventh Books of Moses*, *Secrets of the Psalms*, *Master Book of Candle Burning*, and *The Lucky Star Dream Book*.

Doctor Jordan was a member of the Baptist Church, the Masonic Lodge, and maintained a good relationship with the community, including white businessmen, medical doctors, and law enforcement officials. Although he did a brisk mail-order business, he was never charged with mail fraud. He was once investigated by the State Board of Health, but was found to have broken no laws. After that he obtained a diploma from the St. John's Science Church of Christ, enabling him to legally call himself a doctor, spiritual advisor, and healer. Doctor Jordan continued his practice until his death, at the age of ninety-one, in 1962.[58]

Hoodoo and Rootwork Today

Unlike the relatively accessible African-based cultural practices of New Orleans, hoodoo and rootwork in the Anglo-Protestant South remain hidden from the outsider. This by no means implies that these traditions are dead, only that they have gone deeply underground.

Signs of the continuing vitality of hoodoo and rootwork are found in the anecdotes of people with knowledge of the tradition, in local newspaper articles about individual practitioners, in advertisements in the personals section of national newspapers with a primarily black readership, and in the presence of old-time religious stores, candle shops, and hoodoo drugstores.

In Memphis, the Mary Angela Street domain of the late Mississippi hoodoo doctor Wash "Doc" Harris, with its crosses and yard shrines, still exists. Harris died in 1995, and his practice is said to be carried on by his granddaughter.[59]

Roger Pinckney, author of *Blue Roots*, verified that root doctors still ply their trade in the Low Country. A new Doctor Buzzard, Arnold Gregory, grandson of Stephney Robinson, is continuing the family tradition. "These folks charge lawyers' rates; it's $250 for a basic case, a thousand if it involves graveyard work because that's so hard on the practitioner's spirit." This was corroborated by Ben Blair of Charleston, who added that many white people patronize root doctors for health concerns, trouble with personal relationships, and legal problems.[60] A firsthand account of Low Country rootwork was related to me by a Washington, D.C., area botánica owner. This woman, a native of the Dominican Republic whose spiritual orientation is toward Vodou and Santería, was troubled by the practices she encountered in South Carolina:

> A client of mine was having trouble in her family and wanted me go with her to South Carolina to do a cleansing. But, oooh, those people down there, the way they do this work, it's *evil!* They go in the graveyard, they dig up dirt, they bury things. I met this root doctor—he just stared in my eyes, and he tells me, "If I was to say you die tomorrow, you'd die." And I asked him how that made him feel, to have power to kill people like that. He said, "It don't bother me at all, it's my work and I make good money by it." And I asked him did he enjoy that money, and he said he sure did. He don't believe in God or nothing![61]

Newspapers like the *Miami Times*, New York's *Amsterdam News*, and the *Chicago Defender* carry advertisements for the services of practitioners and notices of chartered bus excursions to visit well-known spiritual workers. A search of these columns reveals "Reverend James, a southern-born spiritualist," providing "solutions to the mysteries of the Deep South"; organization of a bus trip to visit Fred Moore, a hoodoo worker of Donalsville, Georgia; and "Mrs. Millie, southern spiritual healer and advisor," offering help with "all problems of life: love, marriage, bad luck, loss of nature, and falling hair."[62]

One finds occasional newspaper articles about individual practitioners. Sara Murphy of Maxton, North Carolina, has been in business since the 1930s. Her reputation is widespread, and some clients drive from out of state or arrive by chartered bus. Mrs. Murphy helps with problems and ailments—jinxes, pains and miseries, and snakes and insects in the body. Her special herbal remedy, which sells for forty-five dollars a jar, is believed to cure most sicknesses; she also makes red bags for good luck. Oscar Gilchrist, the "Bone Man" of Nichols, South Carolina, is well known as a healer, advisor, and psychic who says that his ability is a "gift from God," passed on from his Jamaican grandparents. His compound, facing a rural two-lane road, is covered with bleached bones hung on chicken wire. The bones, according to Gilchrist, are used for divination. He collects roots and herbs from the swamp near his home and also uses feathers, beehives, and birds' nests for magic and healing.[63]

The strongest indicator that hoodoo and rootwork are alive in the American South is the presence of spiritual stores oriented toward this tradition. All sell commercial spiritual products, and one occasionally finds traditional charm ingredients like sulfur, ammonia, saltpeter, alum, camphor, turpentine, Reckitt's laundry bluing, and Red Devil lye. Stores of this type are scattered throughout the South. I located hoodoo stores in Florida, Georgia, South Carolina, Mississippi, Tennessee, and Texas (see appendix), and there are undoubtedly many more. Spiritual merchandise can also be found in such unlikely venues as hairdressing salons, barber and beauty supply companies, record stores, gas stations, pawn shops, and neighborhood groceries; in one South Carolina town I even discovered a full range of products at a body-piercing parlor.

PART II

Sold as a Curio Only: The Evolution of the Spiritual Products Industry

CHAPTER 5

The Commodification
of Traditional Charms

*a*s we have seen in the preceding chapters, manufactured spiritual products gradually began to replace traditional charms. The same process has occurred in many aspects of American life: most cooks today use a packaged mix instead of baking a cake from scratch; manufactured apparel has largely replaced hand-sewn clothing; people no longer make soap from fat and lye or churn their own butter. When offered the convenience of a ready-made product, consumers are less inclined to assemble the necessary materials and make it themselves. While old-fashioned charms were—and sometimes still are—made by hand from natural ingredients by a traditional practitioner for a specific client, spiritual products are produced by nonbelievers for a mass market. All who engage in the making and selling of charms are, in a sense, spiritual merchants: the priests and priestesses of Vodou and Santería, Voodoo queens, hoodoo workers, root doctors, spiritual advisors, mail-order dealers, the proprietors of hoodoo drugstores, candle shops, botánicas, and yerberías, and the large-scale manufacturers. The evolution of the spiritual products industry, from the earliest entrepreneurs to the largest manufacturers/wholesalers, will be discussed in the following chapters.

The trend toward the commodification of traditional charms began around the turn of the twentieth century and accelerated in the 1920s. By the 1930s, anything required by the hoodoo worker—roots and herbs, black cat bones and other animal parts, graveyard dirt, lodestones, baths,

floor wash, oils, perfumes, powders, sprays, incense, candles, and prefabricated mojo bags—could be easily obtained from spiritual stores and mail-
order companies.

Traditional practitioners held differing opinions about manufactured
spiritual products, or "curios," as they were called in the early days of the
business. Hyatt's informant Madam Lindsey of Algiers, Louisiana, was skeptical. Hyatt asked her about "those houses that send out catalogs—sell stuff
. . . like the people up there in Memphis," referring to the Keystone and
Lucky Heart companies. Madam Lindsey knew of them, but had no faith in
such innovations—"I notice they say it's only sold as curios, so if you risk
your money, well, then you're just out [the price of the product] if it don't
work."[1] A woman in Jacksonville, Florida, who worked as a sales agent for
Keystone and Lucky Heart, explained to Hyatt that handmade charms were
more powerful, but commercial products were cheaper. "When it's real,
when it's the very best . . . at its highest strength, people get it and they can
pull your mind off anywhere they want. They pays hundreds and hundreds
of dollars for those controlling things." The products that she sold contained "a very little of those [expensive and powerful] ingredients . . . just
enough to make people satisfied."[2] In *High Sheriff of the Low Country*, Sheriff Ed McTeer recalled the comments of Doctor Eagle of Beaufort, South
Carolina. Doctor Eagle wholeheartedly endorsed manufactured products
because they saved him time and labor. He explained to McTeer that he
had more business than ever, but the work was not as arduous as in the old
days, when he had to dig up roots and spend the night in the graveyard
collecting dirt. "We buy direct from the factory . . . now. We buy dolls and
all the powders and oils prepackaged and prepared."[3]

■ ■ ■

Spiritual suppliers provide the plants, animal parts, minerals, and other
raw ingredients necessary for charm making. They also sell manufactured
products that serve as substitutes for traditional handmade charms.

Until the early twentieth century, dried roots, leaves, barks, flowers,
berries, seeds, and resins, referred to as "botanicals," were employed as home
remedies, prescribed by doctors, and used by pharmacists for the formulation of healing preparations. Botanicals were available at the local drugstore and could also be ordered by mail from companies like the Indiana
Botanic Gardens in Hammond, Indiana (founded in 1910); Penn Herb in
Philadelphia (founded in 1924), and Doctor Michael's in Chicago (founded

Fig. 1. 7-11 Curios—Sovereign Products Catalog, Chicago, 1936. Botanicals were attractively packaged for sale as magical "curios."

in 1928). Drugstores and mail-order houses were supplied by larger importers and wholesalers. Practitioners of hoodoo and rootwork purchased certain botanicals for magical, rather than medicinal, purposes. While a few old-time "workers" still harvested fresh plants, many bought dried herbs at the drugstore or ordered them by mail.

This fact was not lost on the early spiritual salesmen. From the beginning, mail-order entrepreneurs and the owners of spiritual stores offered botanicals along with their other wares, no doubt obtaining their supply from the same wholesalers as the drugstores and dealers in medicinal herbs. I suspect that, in the formative years of the spiritual business, some of these commercially available botanicals were substituted for indigenous roots and herbs traditionally used in hoodoo practice, and that some botanicals that had never been used in hoodoo were given evocative names and marketed as charms. Did these spiritual merchants, for example, decide that the phallus-shaped Mexican jalap root, a particularly effective purgative, could be sold as High John the Conqueror? Did it occur to them that galangal, an Asian member of the ginger family used in cooking and to treat coughs, sore throat, and stomach upsets, could be sold as "Chewing John the Conqueror"? Did they notice that salep, an orchid root used medicinally to sooth irritated tissues, looked like a tiny, shriveled, human hand and name it "lucky hand root"?[4] Many wholesalers and mail-order retailers of spiritual products still carry a long list of botanicals, including common culinary and medicinal herbs, as well as those specifically associated with charm beliefs. Some companies give short descriptions of magical uses, and others refer the customer to one of the many herbal spell books that, of course, are sold by the same companies.

In traditional practice, the bones, teeth, claws, hair, internal organs, excreta, and other parts of insects, reptiles, birds, and animals are common charm ingredients because they evoke the particular characteristics of these creatures. Some of these animal parts are obtainable from spiritual merchants, although what is sold is seldom the real thing. The bones, feet, claws, and teeth of opossum, raccoon, bobcat, bear, coyote, and alligator are "leftovers" from the trade in furs and hides, and are often marketed as parts from more exotic animals. The alleged black cat bone and the heart and eyes of wolf, bat, and swallow are actually chicken bones and other offal, by-products of the chicken-processing and fast-food industry. One mail-order company even sells bulldog hair, which may or may not be genuine.[5]

Various minerals have always been thought to have magical properties or to be beneficial for certain conditions. Bluestone (ferrous sulfate, also known as copperas) was used for protective charms because of its blue color. The magnetic ore called lodestone, valued for its ability to attract iron, was a staple of the early spiritual merchants. Lodestones were usually sold with a supply of "magnetic sand" (actually "cast shot," molten iron that has been spewed out through a nozzle to form tiny, round granules). The action of the lodestone in attracting the iron granules symbolizes the ability of the owner of this charm to attract money and win at gambling. Victor Flores Designs, a Los Angeles–based company, currently manufactures bracelets with combinations of gemstones for health, stress and depression, alcoholism and drug

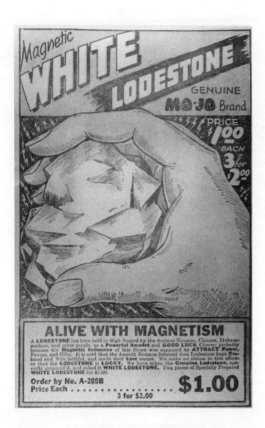

Fig. 2. White Lodestone—King Novelty Curio Catalog, Chicago, 1945. Lodestones were popular money-drawing and gambling charms.

addiction, weight loss, unconditional love, court-case and legal problems, good business, and good luck.

Manufactured spiritual products are made from some combination of water, alcohol, soaps and foaming agents, oil, talc, dyes, and fragrances. There is nothing symbolic about these ingredients. The "magic" resides in the color and scent of the products, their titles, and the highly evocative images on their labels. As we have learned, white is traditionally used for purity, peace, and uncrossing; red or purple for victory; pink or red for love; yellow or green for money; blue for protection; and brown or black for evil. In the early days of the spiritual business, preparations for "bad work" had an offensive odor; now all products, regardless of their purpose, are highly perfumed. Titles and graphics reflect the use for which the product is intended. Often the customer has a choice of the same title in the form of bath-and-floor wash, soap, douche compound, perfume, oil, sachet powder, sprinkling salts, yard dressing granules, floor sweep, room spray, incense, or candles. As one would guess, no rituals are performed during the manufacture of commercial spiritual products. By a leap of faith

The Commodification of Traditional Charms

Fig. 3. Black Cat Bone Emblem—Sovereign Products Catalog, Chicago, 1936. These plastic facsimiles were substituted for actual cat bones. Present-day spiritual merchants sell chicken bones for the same purpose.

Fig. 4. Lodestone Perfume—Oracle Laboratories, Long Island City, New York. The only lodestone here is in the illustration. The zip code on the label indicates that it was manufactured after 1963, but the graphics appear to be from the 1940s. This bottle was part of a large stash of Oracle products purchased at the Seven Powers Garden store in Los Angeles in 1997.

and logic, the users of spiritual products have transferred to these manufactured goods their belief in the properties of traditional charms, rendered magical because they are composed of symbolic ingredients and activated by symbolic rituals. Spiritual products are thus a symbol of a symbol.

Apparently there is perceived to be just as much spiritual value in the names of the magical roots and herbs, animal parts, and minerals as there is in the genuine article. In the case of the ubiquitous John the Conqueror root, the name has been applied to a whole range of products—the multitudinous permutations of John the Conqueror will be examined in chapter 9. I also came across Devil's Shoestring Bath-and-Floor Wash, Five Finger Grass Oil, and Lucky Hand Root Powder. Plastic facsimiles of black cat bones were offered as amulets by an early mail-order company, and a variety of products are emblazoned with the black cat name and image. One company markets a line called Black Cat with Nine Lives. In addition, there are oils and powders called Cat's Eye, Bat's Blood, Wolf's Eye, Wolf's Heart, and Swallow's Heart. Various

Fig. 5. Chinese Wash—Clover Horn Company, Baltimore. Chinese Wash was a popular cleanser used to promote spiritual purity and good luck and to drive out evil influences. Several companies manufactured their own version of Chinese Wash. Although I bought this bottle in 1997, the label design dates from the 1940s.

"lodestone" money-drawing products are sold. Some of the oils and perfumes contain an actual piece of lodestone, but most do not.

Homemade preparations for bathing and scrubbing the floor have metamorphosed into personal hygiene and home care products, made "magical" by the addition of appropriate colors and scents and by their titles and graphics. Early spiritual suppliers, many of whom also manufactured toiletries and household cleansers, promoted the idea that freshness and sanitation were synonymous with spiritual purity, love, financial success, protection, and good luck, and that personal slovenliness and a dirty, foul-smelling home would result in attack by evil spirits, an unfaithful spouse, financial ruin, and general misfortune. Liquid soaps are sold as spiritual baths, and bath crystals, bar soap, and douche compound are offered as spiritual cleansers and bringers of luck. Ordinary cleaning products are currently marketed as magical floor washes.

Anointing substances were traditionally applied to the body to cure minor aliments and attract luck and love, and were also used for "feeding" charm assemblages and "dressing" candles. These homemade herbal preparations have been replaced by highly colored and scented oils and perfumes with names and images denoting their use. Early mail-order companies offered bottles of Van-Van Oil or perfumes like Wish-Bone or Lucky 7-11 for "feeding" their prefabricated mojo bags.[6] A contemporary mail-order spiritual supply catalog, on the page advertising candles for sale, reminds customers, "Don't forget to order the oil!"[7]

Homemade powders have been replaced by "sprinkling sands and salts," "yard dressing granules" (bits of colored Styrofoam), and talcum-based

The Commodification of Traditional Charms

Fig. 6. Van-Van Oil—King Novelty Curio Catalog, Chicago, 1936. Van-Van, New Orleans' favorite good-luck preparation, was originally made from alcohol and oil of lemon grass.

sachets, all scented and dyed appropriately. Sachets are colored pink for Love Powder, red for Hot Foot Powder, and brown for War Powder. Instead of formulating homemade powders for "dusting the courtroom," one can now buy purple Court-Case Powder. A moldy-colored green sachet is sold as Goofer Dust, and a black sachet is now commercially packaged as Graveyard Dirt. In a catalog from the 1970s, the customer could even choose "dirt" from the grave of a suicide, an unbaptized infant, or a murder victim: "Just in! Genuine! Only a few available; practically unobtainable anywhere else!"[8] A product called Friday's Bed Powder comes with instructions to "put the powder between the mattress and box springs on Fridays for controlling . . . make your wish three times to have control over the other person's mind and body."[9] One company, no doubt having found a cheap supply, offers volcanic ash "to sprinkle on an enemy's clothes for fast destruction."[10] Ordinary janitorial floor sweeping compound is sold as magical "floor sweep."

Traditional fumigants—sweet-scented or acrid-smelling substances that were to be burned to attract good influences and drive out evil—have been replaced by commercially produced sprays and incense. Early manufacturers advertised fragrant bottled products that were to be sprayed with an atomizer: "Many people claim it drives away evil spirits and brings good

Sold as a Curio Only

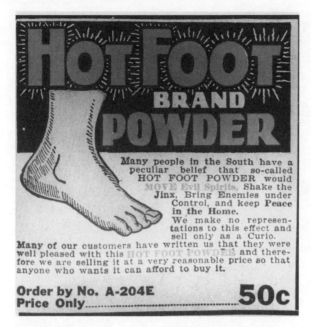

Fig. 7. Hot Foot Powder—King Novelty Curio Catalog, Chicago, 1936. Earlier hoodoo workers formulated hot foot powder from symbolically hot or strong ingredients for the purpose of banishing an enemy. Such homemade powders were replaced by commercial sachets.

Fig. 8. Lucky Mo-Jo Perfumed Room Spray—King Novelty Curio Catalog, Chicago, 1936. Room sprays and aerosols replaced traditional fumigants.

The Commodification of Traditional Charms

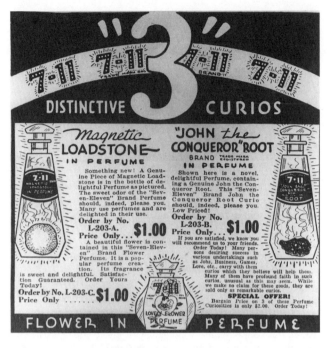

Fig. 9. Magnetic Lodestone and John the Conqueror Root in Perfume—Sovereign Products Catalog, 1936. These products continue the tradition of assembling symbolic ingredients in a bottle.

luck, and some even say that they have brought in big winnings."[11] Aerosol room-freshening sprays became popular in the early 1970s. While incense had always been available to hoodoo practitioners through religious supply houses and the drugstore, spiritual companies began to manufacture incense specifically for the hoodoo trade, using the same titles and graphics found on the labels of other spiritual products.

The type of homemade charm meant to be secreted in a person's food or drink does not exist in the world of commercial spiritual products. Today's manufacturers are very aware of regulations by the Food and Drug Administration, and advertisements specifically state that the products are not to be ingested.

Some of the designations for assembled and containerized charms, like the mojo bag or the lucky hand, are now applied to products. One finds brand names such as Lucky Mo-Jo, Midnight Mojo, and Mystic Mojo.[12] The traditional "hand" has been translated into the labeling of good luck products with the image of a human hand. Old-fashioned bottle charms evolved into bottles of oil or perfume containing a John the Conqueror root or a piece of lodestone. One mail-order company advertises the Jo-Jo Jar—"write your enemy's name on parchment paper, shake it up, and hide it in a dark place"—and the Satan Be Gone Bottle—"bury to keep all evil out of your yard . . . and send it back to the person who put it there."[13] Some mail-order companies also offer prefabricated mojo bags and ritual kits.

Traditional practitioners have always used symbolically colored candles in their rituals. Specific colors are chosen for specific intentions or for the saint or deity whom the charm user wishes to activate. The earliest catalogs featured plain tapers in various colors, or candles with printed images of the saints affixed directly to the wax. By the 1950s, manufacturers were offering "seven-day" glass-encased candles in solid white, red, purple, pink, yellow, green, blue, brown, and black, and "combination" candles in layers of three or seven colors. As one catalog advertisement suggested, "When the candle has burned out, continue to use the blessed glass for drinking water."[14] The 1960s saw the introduction of glass-encased candles bearing images of the saints, High John the Conqueror, and the Seven African Powers, and for special needs like controlling, peaceful home, employment, court case, jinx removing, sending back evil, or fast luck. Some of the early glass-encased candles had the title and image painted on the inside of the glass; others were silk-screened onto the outside. Paper labels are a more recent innovation. Candles are also available in various shapes: naked men and women, representations of the male and female genitals, skulls, witches, Buddhas, cats, goats, snakes, mummies, devils, pyramids, and crosses. One can choose white, red, or black, according to the purpose for which the candle is to be burned.

■ ■ ■

Despite the change from handmade charms to manufactured products, the intentions for which they are used remain the same: the state of one's own body and mind; relationships with others; and the control of external forces like luck, the saints, and the spirits.

Because of Food and Drug Administration regulations, very few manufactured spiritual products are specifically intended for health and healing, although many offer personal well-being. Early catalogs and some present-day mail-order companies offer tonics, laxatives, and "pep tablets," but no magical properties are attributed to these preparations. Today some packaged baths made from dried herbs are sold for "spiritual and bodily purification," and one company offers Radiant Health Oil "to regain or maintain one's natural state of being, sound in body, mind, and spirit." The copper bracelets

Fig. 10. Harry's Love Sachet—
Harry's Occult Shop, Philadelphia;
purchased in 1998. The label was
designed by the original owner,
Harry Seligmann, in the 1920s.

traditionally worn to prevent arthritis and rheumatism are still sold by some spiritual stores and mail-order companies. One catalog advertisement reads: "The story of copper and its alleged powers are well known. Some believe it relieves the pain of arthritis, and it has always been a mythical good luck charm."[15]

As with traditional charms, the largest category of spiritual products is intended for governing relationships with others. Charms promote beneficial interactions with lovers, family, friends, neighbors, customers, and employers; they keep out authority figures and others who intend harm; and they are employed to curse one's enemies.

What are commonly called "love" charms are actually more concerned with control than with romance. One first has to attract the object of one's affection, and then keep him or her faithful and obedient. For this purpose there are products like Love Sachet, Follow Me Boy, Hug and Kiss Me, Love Me Always, Faithful Husband, and I Dominate My Woman. Loudell Snow, in her article "Sorcerers, Saints, and Charlatans," cites an advertisement for Passion Potion, a modern version of the traditional charm for controlling a man's "nature." Instead of rendering her lover impotent with other partners by means of old-fashioned charm rituals of knotting, bottling up, and treading underfoot, the aggrieved woman could order Passion Potion: "If your husband or boyfriend is running around, driving you nuts, please read this! It is possible to end all that foolishness and bring him back under your control. . . . Your loved one will have his mind on you and only you. . . . If he is running from woman to woman, [Passion Potion] will curb that."[16]

For a household free of quarreling and violence, there is Peaceful Home incense. For a good relationship with the community, one can buy bottled Peace Water, appropriately colored a tranquil shade of blue. For business and employment we find Crowd-a-Plenty, Better Business Oil, Loan Approval Powder, Steady Work, Crown of Success, and Boss Fix Oil. Products like Essence of Bend Over, Compelling Soap, and Commanding Pepper are general control charms, effective on lovers, family members, employers, and others.

Protective charms guard against assailants and the curses of one's adversaries. Spiritual products that fortify the user from the machinations of human enemies include Blue Shield Wash, Fear Not to Walk Over Evil, and Fiery Wall of Protection. For uncrossing there is Run Devil Run, Jinx Removal, Uncrossing Power, and Spell Breaker. Reversible Oil, like the traditional concept of "turning the trick," is intended to "turn evil back on the one who sent it."

Repelling charms like Keep Away Trouble prevent the bill collector, the landlord, or the police from entering one's premises. The Law Stay Away talisman is to be hung on the mirror of one's car or truck as protection against traffic violations and parking tickets.[17] Court-case

Fig. 11. Uncrossing Power Incense—Sonny Boy Products, Birmingham. Uncrossing Power is one of many products marketed for the removal of an enemy's curse. This 1988 gift from Erin Loftus was the first item in my collection.

charms influence the judge, the prosecutor, the witnesses, and the jury. Present-day spiritual merchants offer commercial oils, powders, and candles with titles like Jury Winning and Just Judge for trouble with the authorities.

Malefic charms are intended to cause the estrangement of lovers, discord within a family, lack of success, accidents, injuries, physical and mental illness, or chronic depression. A variety of products is available for cursing; some representative titles are Break Up, Revenge, Inflammatory Confusion, Weed of Misfortune, and Black Destroyer. The ultimate curse, of course, is the death charm. For this purpose there is a particularly sinister black candle emblazoned with skulls and the title D.U.M.E.—"Death Unto My Enemy."[18]

Like traditional charms, spiritual products seek to control luck and to summon the powers of the saints, the African deities, the spirit guides of Latin American Espiritismo, and various local heroes.

Luck is the external force that governs general well-being, the accumulation of wealth, and games of chance. Of particular concern in the 1920s–40s was the discovery of a "gig," the winning combination of numbers to bet in the illegal daily lottery called "policy." Several popular brands

The Commodification of Traditional Charms

Fig. 12. St. Barbara Changó Rub-On—Grandpa's Candle Shop, Baltimore; purchased in 1997. This preparation is made "in-house" at an old-time hoodoo store with a mostly African American clientele. The use of Santería imagery in this venue constitutes an interesting blending of traditions.

of incense, such as Old Grandma's Lucky 7-11, revealed an alleged "lucky number" in the ashes,[19] and some items manufactured today contain a lucky number inside the package. The acquisition of money is also governed by luck. Products for luck, money, and gambling have titles like Lady o' Luck, Money Jackpot, Wage Increase, Quick Cash, Money House Blessing, Lucky Lottery, Winning Number, and Race Track. Slots-of-Luck Oil is recommended for anointing the handle of the slot machine; Easy Money Oil, according to a recent catalog, contains "actual U.S. currency."[20]

Spiritual products that invoke the saints are most often named for St. Michael, St. Expedite, St. Barbara, St. Lazarus, St. Anthony, and St. Jude, although dozens of other saints, favored by various ethnic and regional groups, are also represented. The images are adopted from traditional chromolithographs and holy cards. Some of the early spiritual catalogs sold religious pictures and medals, but the names and images of saints on product labels did not become widespread until the 1960s. By the 1970s, depictions of the saints representing the Seven African Powers, as well as the individual orichas of Santería, were applied to candles, aerosol sprays, soaps, perfumes, and incense. Although products named for the orichas are now ubiquitous, the names of the lwa are entirely absent owing to the popularity of Santería in the United States relative to the more submerged character of Haitian Vodou. Other products portray Allan Kardec (the founder of European Spiritism, which became Espiritismo in Latin America), and the spirit guides, which, it will be recalled, are classified as *Madamas, Indios,* and *Congos.*

The names and images of various unofficial saints and folk heroes appear on spiritual products. In cities where many Central and South Americans have settled, we find San Simón Maximón and Dr. José Gregorio Hernández. San Simón, venerated by Guatemalans, is a conflation of a Mayan grandfather spirit called Mam with St. Jude, Judas Iscariot, and a

Fig. 13. Polvo San Simón—Paco's Botanical Products, New York; purchased in 1994 at a Guatemalan-owned botánica.

Fig. 14. Dr. Hernández Bath—La Milagrosa Products, Brooklyn; purchased in 1994.

Fig. 15. Marie Laveau's Magic Mojo Bean—packaged by Marie Laveau's House of Voodoo, a shop in New Orleans' French Quarter that caters to tourists; purchased during the 1997 St. Joseph's holiday. This fava bean is identical to those given out as "lucky beans" at Sicilian-American St. Joseph's altars in New Orleans.

Fig. 16. Oil with Live Lodestone—Lucky Heart Company, Memphis. The label shows typical lucky symbols: hearts, lodestone, wishbone, horseshoe, and four-leafed clover. The swastika indicates that it was manufactured before 1940. All Lucky Heart materials were purchased from Gary Young, present owner of Lucky Heart, in 1997.

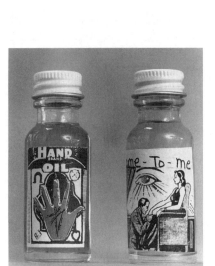

Fig. 17. Hand Oil and Come to Me Perfume—Clover Horn Company, Baltimore. These bottles were purchased at Clover Horn in 1997, but the label designs, with eye and hand symbols, date from the 1940s.

Spanish landowner who gave charity to the local Indians.[21] Dr. Hernández was a beloved physician of Caracas, Venezuela, who lived from 1864 to 1919.[22] Mexican *curanderos* (healers) like Don Pedrito Jaramillo and El Niño Fidencio are popular in the Southwest,[23] as are products named for the Mexican revolutionary general Pancho Villa. The name and image of Marie Laveau is frequently seen on New Orleans products.

Although the appeal of some spiritual products is in their evocative titles, it is the graphic images, found on product labels and in catalog advertisements, that are most compelling. Two hearts pierced by an arrow symbolize love. Dollar signs, a treasure chest, and bags of money represent wealth. The horseshoe, four-leafed clover, and wishbone represent luck, as did the swastika until it became associated with Nazism. Vintage product labels and catalogs can, in fact, be dated by the presence of the swastika, which is never found after 1940. The eye, perhaps inspired by the Masonic symbol of the All-Seeing Eye, is a popular motif on spiritual product labels, as is the hand. The early manufacturers were familiar with the charm

Fig. 18. Come-to-Me Incense—Husco Curio Company (Hussey Distributors), Atlanta. I acquired this can from a dealer in advertising ephemera long after Hussey ceased operations in 1980.

assemblages called "lucky hands" and represented this concept with a conflation of a palmist's symbol with the Most Powerful Hand, a Roman Catholic icon that depicts the hand of Jesus bearing the wounds of the crucifixion.

Intentions are represented by cartoonlike figures. Come-to-Me Incense is illustrated with a 1930s-style couple—a confident-looking woman drags a befuddled man by the arm. The label on a jar of Commanding Pepper delineates a helpless figure held fast by a giant hand. Job Powder is illustrated with a couple in business attire. Get Away Evil Enemies Incense pictures a terrified man chased by a ghost. Uncrossing Power Incense shows a figure holding a lighted candle ascending a staircase while a devil and a black cat lurk in the background. John the Conqueror is symbolized by the figure of a king.

Most of the individuals portrayed in these illustrations are white, and even those that represent people of African descent are depicted as light-skinned mulattos. The image of a dark-skinned man or woman who looks distinctly African American is almost never seen. In contrast, manufacturers of soap, stove polish, coffee, pancake mix, rice, cereal, and other goods marketed to the general public frequently employed images of blacks in their advertising and packaging. While the earliest of these were insultingly grotesque caricatures, the representations of Aunt Jemima, Uncle Ben, and the Cream of Wheat chef, although still portrayed as servants, were less demeaning.[24] The manufacturers of spiritual products evidently assumed that African American customers would be offended by depictions of blacks with Negro features, and such images were therefore not used in advertisements or on product labels.

The exception is a stereotypical "mammy" character, evoking the wise old conjure woman who can predict lottery numbers. This image first appeared on *Aunt Sally's Policy Players Dream Book* in 1889; Aunt

Fig. 19. *Aunt Sally's Policy Players Dream Book,* originally published in 1889 and still in print. Aunt Sally is the only representation of an individual with African features seen on the labels of early spiritual products.

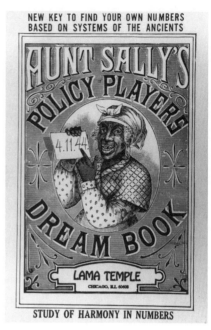

Fig. 20. Good Luck Madam Incense— La Milagrosa Products, Brooklyn, purchased in 1998. La Madama is the black healer and fortune-teller of Espiritismo; her image, somewhat resembling the Aunt Sally figure, only appears in the later twentieth century.

Sally was later depicted on incense labels inspired by this book. In recent years, manufacturers of spiritual products have used the image of La Madama, the black healer and fortune teller of Espiritismo, who, like Aunt Sally, has African features and wears an apron and headcloth.

One of the most common figural images in catalogs and on product labels is the North American Indian, represented by a generic warrior in full feather headdress. Inspired by the persona of the Native American herbalist, nineteenth-century folk healers called themselves "Indian doctors," and the mail-order catalogs of old-time herb dealers such as the Indiana Botanic Gardens were illustrated with Indian imagery. Blacks have historically held a particular reverence for Native Americans, viewing them as people of color who, like themselves, were exploited by Europeans. Some hoodoo doctors claim to have learned herbal medicine from an Indian ancestor. The manufacturers of

Fig. 21. Money House Blessing Indian—
E. Davis Company, Piscataway, New Jersey.
This pink and gold plastic Indian is designed
to sit atop a can of Money House Blessing
aerosol spray. Gift of Rayna Greene, 1998.

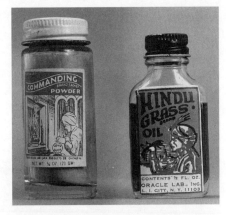

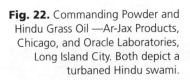

Fig. 22. Commanding Powder and
Hindu Grass Oil —Ar-Jax Products,
Chicago, and Oracle Laboratories,
Long Island City. Both depict a
turbaned Hindu swami.

spiritual products use brand names like Powerful Indian, Indian Grandma, Indian Spirit, Indian Sales Company, and Indio Products.

The Hindu Swami, a ubiquitous image found in early catalog advertisements and on product labels, epitomizes the concept of spiritual authority and occult learning. East Indian spirituality was immensely popular in the 1890s and into the first decades of the twentieth century. Early Chicago spiritual suppliers like Ar-Jax and the DeLaurence Company used the Hindu Swami as their logo. The Swami also appeared on the labels of Mystic Drawing Oil and Hindu Room Spray and Floor Wash, manufactured by Lucky Heart of Memphis, and Hindu Grass Oil by Oracle Laboratories of Long Island City, New York. The Allan Company of Houston still makes Hindu Floor Wash.

During Hyatt's 1938–42 travels throughout the South, he encountered the widespread belief that occult knowledge came from the East and that spiritual products were made by Hindus. One of Hyatt's New Orleans informants said that he had been trained by "a Hindu who came down here from Morris Jahout Palace in Calcutta, India." Hyatt made a note in the transcription that "this so-called palace in Calcutta . . . was surely one of the many diploma mills issuing a paper stating that you are qualified by the institute, brotherhood, fellowship, or whatever it is, to practice or teach so-and-so." Madam Collins of Memphis told Hyatt, "You know, most of the luck oils and things are made by those Hindu people." Hyatt commented in his notes, "Madam Collins probably believes what she has just said, but little or nothing in hoodoo is made by Hindu people; Hindu [titles and graphics] being exotic atmosphere and advertising by hoodoo merchants—like the turbans worn by some doctors, spiritualists, and others."[25] In the 1920s–40s, spiritual supply outlets were sometimes called "Hindu stores,"—seen in the 1943 photograph of the Hindu Mysterious Store of "Alleged Yogi and Professor Phillips" in Harlem.

Spiritual merchants also employ representations of other ethnic types. A medieval scholar or a biblical prophet symbolizes knowledge of the occult. Exoticism is suggested by a harem beauty, a Spanish dancer, or a Chinese.

The graphics described on the preceding pages, although presumably copyrighted by the company with which they originated, have been freely appropriated by other manufacturers. The same image may appear on the labels or catalog advertisements of many different companies. Illustrations range from crude representations, often drawn by the manufacturer himself, to beautiful and sophisticated graphics created by professionals. The outstanding catalog and label illustrations from Valmor Products of Chicago and Keystone and Lucky Heart of Memphis are the work of artists employed by these companies.[26] Some of the businesses that originated in the 1920s–40s continue to use their original label designs. Later companies have either copied these old-style graphics or introduced more contemporary designs. Most of today's catalogs are illustrated with photographic reproductions of the products or generic "clip-art" images, and lack the visual appeal of the vintage catalogs.

Quite by accident I learned that the father of one of my colleagues had been a creator of spiritual product labels for the botánicas of Spanish Harlem and the Bronx. The Puerto Rican artist Manuel Quiles came to New York in about 1925. Quiles was in no way involved in the African-based religions, nor was he even a Catholic; his family had converted to the Baptist church before leaving Puerto Rico. He initially settled on 116th Street in what became known as Spanish Harlem and later moved to the Bronx. His son Mario recalls that Quiles was engaged in a variety of commercial activities, such as painting signs, designing and silk-screening Spanish-language greeting cards, and making cast-plaster statues of the saints. In the early 1950s he turned his talents to designing and producing labels for herbal baths, oils, and perfumes. Unlike the graphics for hoodoo-oriented products, Quiles's designs featured floral motifs or pictures of the saints. To

Fig. 23. (left) A Harlem spiritual store documented in 1943 by the photographer Arthur Fellig, commonly known as "Weegee." Hand-painted signs on the display windows announce: "Hindu Mysterious Store. Hindu Cosmetics and Special Hair Growing Products, Lucky Perfumes and All Kinds of Oils. Spiritual Advisor." A large statue of the Buddha, plus an array of unidentifiable products, can be seen in the window. National Museum of American History, Smithsonian Institution, Photographic History Collection, catalog #71.4.009. Used with permission of International Center of Photography, New York, bequest of Wilma Wilcox, copyright Arthur Fellig 1994.

Fig. 24. Agua San Lozoro and Agua Santa Marta—Chicas-Rendón, New York, purchased in 1998. These labels were designed in the early 1950s by Manuel Quiles and are still used by Botánica Chicas-Rendón.

find prototypes for these images, Mr. Quiles sketched the figures in nearby churches and copied illustrations from library books. The labels were silk-screened by hand, ninety-six to a sheet, using between four and nine separate screens. Sometimes titles were inserted with a small hand press.[27] These beautiful images are still used by the venerable Spanish Harlem botánica of Otto Chicas-Rendón, although they are now reproduced photomechanically.

■ ■ ■

Spiritual stores and mail-order companies not only sell herbs, minerals, animal parts, and spiritual products, they also sell occult books. Customers buy the products and other paraphernalia required to perform the rituals described in the books; they buy books to learn how to use the products they see in the stores and catalogs. Some catalogs, in fact, make statements to the effect that "we cannot give instructions on the use of the herbs and products offered. If interested in learning the occult value of these items, check our book section."[28]

The books carried by spiritual suppliers include English translations of European occult texts, nineteenth-century American spell books based on these European works, books of dream interpretation and lucky numbers, and modern books of magical formulae.

Several German texts were translated into English in the nineteenth and early twentieth centuries and have always been sold through the hoodoo mail-order catalogs and retail stores. *The Egyptian Secrets of Albertus Magnus* was first printed in Germany around 1725, although it probably existed in earlier manuscript versions. An English translation was published in the United States by DeLaurence, Scott and Company of Chicago in 1910. This book has nothing to do with the German philosopher Albert von Böllstadt, known as Albertus Magnus (1206–1280), and has no connection with Egypt. It is, instead, a collection of German folk medicine and protective and good luck charms for humans and livestock, containing cures for worms, colic, fever, bleeding, warts, toothache, convulsions, and other ailments, plus advice on farming, animal husbandry, fishing, and beekeeping. It also gives formulae against witchcraft, theft, fire, injury by sword or firearms, and rituals to promote good luck, employing a combination of Christian prayers, the names of the Trinity, and medicinal and magical herbs.

A German-American spell book called *Lange Verborgene Freund* was first published in Reading, Pennsylvania, in 1820. It was translated into English as *Pow-Wows or Long Lost Friend* in 1855. The book contains rituals and formulae nearly identical to those found in the *Egyptian Secrets of Albertus Magnus*. The author, Johann Georg Hohman, was a member of the Pennsylvania German community, where this sort of magic and healing was called "pow-wowing."[29]

The Sixth and Seventh Books of Moses, said to be based on ancient Hebrew texts, was first published in Germany in the late eighteenth century, and a German version was published in the United States in 1880 by the Vicor Company of Elizabethville, Pennsylvania. The first English translation appeared in 1910; like the *Egyptian Secrets*, it was published by DeLaurence, Scott and Company. Only the first sixteen pages constitute the actual Sixth and Seventh Books of Moses, consisting of magical seals with their accompanying uses: the Seal of Fortune and Long Life; the Seal of Dreams and Visions; the Seal of Good Luck, Play, and Games; the Seal of Shemhamforas, which "brings to light the treasures of the earth." The rest is a conglomeration of various long-winded treatises—heavily larded with Latin and Hebrew phrases and illustrated with more seals—on "The Magic of the Israelites," "Formulas of the Magical Kamala [evidently a variant spelling of kabbalah], an Extract from the Genuine and True Clavicula of Solomon the King of Israel," the "Arcana Magica of Alexander," the "Citation of the Seven Great Princes," the "Magical Cures of the Old Hebrews," and "The Use of the

Psalms for the Physical Welfare of Man." This last section was also published separately as *Secrets of the Psalms*.[30]

It is difficult to see how the old-time hoodoo doctors, some of whom were barely literate, were able to make much sense of the *Sixth and Seventh Books of Moses*, yet it was mentioned by those interviewed by Hyatt and the Federal Writers' Project more frequently than any other text. Most of the mail-order catalogs in my collection contain advertisements for "authentic seals taken from the Sixth and Seventh Books of Moses and from ancient Quabalistic records, reproduced on genuine virgin parchment in dragon's blood red ink," which were to be carried for various purposes and "anointed with a sacred oil once every ten days." Hoodoo charm formulae are full of references to the Psalms, many of which correspond to the uses given in the *Sixth and Seventh Books of Moses*.

The Great Book of Magical Art, Hindu Magic, and East Indian Occultism by Lauren William DeLaurence was published by his own establishment, DeLaurence, Scott and Company, in 1902. *The Great Book of Magical Art* was a massive tome cobbled together from the works of European magicians like Paracelsus, Cornelius Agrippa, and Alibeck the Egyptian, and from elements borrowed from the kabbalah and the doctrines of Hinduism and Spiritualism. A photograph of the author, a handsome, very young-looking white man wearing a huge mustache and the costume of a Hindu swami, appears on the frontispiece.

Upon reading the interviews by Hyatt and the Federal Writers' Project with African American hoodoo workers, it becomes obvious that they were borrowing and reinterpreting charm formulae from *The Egyptian Secrets*, *The Sixth and Seventh Books of Moses*, *Pow-Wows*, and *The Great Book of Magical Art*. While many of the interviewees spoke of using these books, some individuals presented the charm formulae and rituals as their own, meaning that this knowledge had already entered hoodoo lore and was by then being passed from one practitioner to another.

Books of dream interpretation have been known for centuries. *Aunt Sally's Policy Players Dream Book*, published in 1889 by H. J. Wehman of New York and still in print, was one of the earliest to include "lucky numbers" associated with the various dreams. The same format was used in the hundreds of dream books, especially popular with gamblers, that have been published over the years.[31] The pages of dream books are often interspersed with advertisements for spiritual products and other books from the same publisher.

The twentieth century has seen the emergence of magical spell books, issued by the manufacturers and retailers of spiritual products, that call for ingredients provided by the publisher or bookseller. What may have been the first of this genre, a booklet called *The Life and Works of Marie Laveau*, was originally published in New Orleans, possibly by the Cracker Jack Drug Store. According to a Louisiana Writers' Project report, the book had blue covers illustrated with the image of a "Gibson Girl," indicating that it might have been printed around the turn of the twentieth century, when the Gibson Girl was in style. We know that *The Life and Works of Marie Laveau* was in existence by 1927, when it was mentioned in a newspaper article about a crackdown by postal authorities on mail-order hoodoo.[32] The booklet consisted of a series of petitions, each related to a specific problem, followed by instructions for a ritual to alleviate the difficulty. These little vignettes had titles like "The Man Who Lost His Sweetheart," "The Court Scrape," "The Lady Whose House Has Been Crossed," and "The Lucky Hand." The text was written in archaic, stilted, pseudo-biblical language. Clothes were called "raiment"; money was referred to as "shekels" or "the bright gold and jingling silver of the empire"; measurements were given in "hins" (an ancient Hebrew unit of liquid measure) and "drachmas" (a unit of measurement equal to an apothecaries' dram). In order to carry out the instructions, various herbs and commercially produced washes, powders, oils, and candles were required. The book also contained horoscopes, instructions for praying the Novena, a section on the significance of candles, and a short essay on Spiritism, attributed to "Bivens, N.P.D." The identity of Bivens and the significance of the initials N.P.D. remain a mystery. Zora Neale Hurston used the vignettes from *The Life and Works of Marie Laveau* in "Hoodoo in America," claiming to have learned them from her mentor, Samuel Thompson—the man called Luke Turner in *Mules and Men*. Even a misspelled word, "hearken" instead of "harken," has been reproduced in Hurston's text.[33]

    I have been unable to locate an original copy of *The Life and Works of Marie Laveau*, but I do have in my collection two reissued versions. One, called *Marie Laveau's Old and New Black and White Magic*, has no author, date, or publication information. Throughout the book are advertisements for spiritual products and other popular spell books, plus the announcement, "We claim no original procedures but anyone interested in obtaining the items mentioned in this book may request our Occult Curio Catalog. Simply write to Fulton Religious Supply Co. 1304 Fulton Street, Brooklyn, N.Y. 11216." Fulton Religious was, at that time, owned by Dorene Publishing Company, an early printer of occult books and manufacturer of spiritual products. The owner of Dorene, Ed Kay, could only tell me that the original booklet did not identify an author or publisher and had no copyright—"we just reprinted it; we figured it would help sell our products." A later "revised edition," called *Marie Laveau's Original Black and White Magic*, was published by International Imports/Indio Products in 1991. Several mail-order companies now sell kits ranging in price from twenty to thirty-five dollars that provide all items necessary to perform the rituals from Marie Laveau's Original Black and White Magic.

Black Herman's Secrets of Magic, Mystery, and Legerdemain was written by the African American stage magician Herman Rucker. "Black Herman" performed all over the United States, sold herbal medicines, and published a monthly magazine from his Harlem headquarters. In the preface to *Secrets of Magic, Mystery, and Legerdemain*, Black Herman claimed to have been born in Africa and traveled in Egypt, India, China, France, and England, where he learned the "mystical secrets . . . of the magicians and philosophers." Ed Kay of Dorene Publishing scoffed at the notion that Rucker was a native of Africa, recalling that he spoke with no trace of a foreign accent.[34] This preface, dated New York, 1925, may originally have been a pamphlet that Black Herman distributed at his performances. The *Secrets of Magic, Mystery, and Legerdemain* was copyrighted by Dorene Publishing in 1938. It contains parlor tricks, horoscopes, dream interpretations, lucky numbers, and a short section of charm formulae. Like other books of this type, Black Herman's calls for ingredients commonly sold in spiritual stores and mail-order catalogs.

Dorene also publishes the occult standards by Lewis de Claremont and Henri Gamache. Both draw heavily upon European folk and ceremonial magic and spiritualism, with some features culled from other, more "exotic" cultures. De Claremont is credited with *The Ancients Book of Magic; Legends of Incense, Herbs, and Oils; Secrets of Attraction; How to Get Your Winning Number; The Ten Lost Books of the Prophets; The Seven Keys to*

Fig. 25. (right) Book display from the Hindu Mysterious Store, documented in 1943 by "Weegee." Titles include *Pow-Wows; Number Facts for 1943; Aunt Sally's Policy Players Dream Book;* the *Sixth and Seventh Books of Moses; Crystal Gazing;* the *Gypsy Queen Fortune Teller Dream Book; Fortune Telling by Cards; Know Your Numbers;* the *Lucky Star Dream Book; What Your Dream Means; Book of Luck; Solid Gold Dream Book; Egyptian Secrets of Albertus Magnus; Raja Rabo's 5-Star Mutuel Dream Book; National Dream Book;* the *Five in One Dream Book; Seven Keys to Power; Master Book of Candle Burning; Fu Futtams Magical Spiritual Dream Book; Ancients Book of Magic; Sen Chu's Number System; Professor Abdullah's Mystic Square Dream Book; Black Herman's Secrets of Magic, Mystery, and Legerdemain;* and *Imitation of Christ.* National Museum of American History, Smithsonian Institution, Photographic History Collection, catalog #71.4.012. Used with permission of International Center of Photography, New York, bequest of Wilma Wilcox, copyright Arthur Fellig 1994.

Power; and *The Seven Steps to Power*—all published between 1936 and 1940. The frontispieces of these books display an "artist's conception of Lewis de Claremont in tunic and turban with Spirit Guide." Henri Gamache is the supposed author of *The Eighth, Ninth, and Tenth Books of Moses*; *The Master Key to Occult Secrets*; *Master Book of Candle Burning*; *Protection Against Evil and Harm*; and *The Magic of Herbs*, published between 1942 and 1946. According to Ed Kay of Dorene Publishing, the exotic-sounding names de Claremont and Gamache were, in reality, *noms de plume* of a man named Young, about which little else is known.[35]

The 1945 Valmor Products catalog introduced a line of incense named for the popular spell books and dream books. With the purchase of a book of the same title, the customer could receive a free tin of Black Herman Incense, Aunt Sally's Lucky Dream Incense, or Seven Keys to Power Incense. A free John the Conqueror root was offered with an order for Gamache's *Magic of Herbs*, and a free sample of Van-Van Incense with de Claremont's *Legends of Incense, Herbs, and Oils*.

The 1970s and 1980s saw the publication of a new crop of spell books that, like those previously discussed, gives a series of rituals and charm formulae calling for herbs, candles, parchment paper, seals from the *Sixth and Seventh Books of Moses*, and spiritual products, available from the same stores and mail-order companies that sell the books. The best-known of these writers is the extremely prolific Dorothy Spencer, who writes under the name "Anna Riva." This appellation is derived from the names of her mother, Anna, and her daughter, Riva. Spencer is a serious student of the occult, although she is not a follower of any of the African-based religions.[36] She is the author of *Powers of the Psalms*; *Modern Witchcraft Spellbook*; *Modern Herbal Spellbook*; *Secrets of Magical Seals*; *Candle Burning Magic*; *Magic with Incense and Powders*; *Golden Secrets of Mystic Oils*; *Spellcraft, Hexcraft, and Witchcraft*; and *Voodoo Handbook of Cult Secrets*.

Other manufacturers and retailers of spiritual products also write and publish their own spell books. The owner of Mi-World Supplies in Hialeah, Florida, produces manuals similar to the Anna Riva titles under the name "Donna Rose." The Allan Company of Houston issues a series of pamphlets, *The Guidebook to Black and White Magic*, "a collection of special occult set-ups . . . that are being used today by many successful spiritualists, workers, and psychic readers," with instructions for rituals and the requisite products. James Sicafus, owner of Papa Jim's in San Antonio, Texas, is the author of a charmingly ungrammatical series of books on Mexican herbal medicine and magic, including the *Papa Jim Magical Herb Book*; *Medicinal Herbs Commonly Used*; the *Magical Oil Book*; the *Papa Jim Candle Book*; and the *Papa Jim Dream Book*.

■ ■ ■

The availability of "over-the-counter" charms and magical spell books has changed, and in some cases usurped, the role of the spiritual professional. Some clients skip the expensive counsel of the hoodoo doctor or rootworker altogether and rely on advice gleaned from books to prescribe for themselves. While some traditional practitioners still work from their homes, offering consultations and preparation of handmade charms for individual clients, many now own candle shops, botánicas, and yerberías, or are employed by these stores as "readers." These practitioners are more likely to prescribe manufactured products than charms made from natural and household ingredients.

CHAPTER 6

Mail-Order Doctors and Hoodoo Drugstores

The spiritual professional provides consultations for individual clients and prescribes the charms and rituals appropriate to the situation. The entrepreneur produces and markets "magical" substances that are devoid of the symbolism and ritual required in the formulation of traditional charms, and has no personal involvement with his or her customers. As we will see in the following chapters, the distinction between the professional "worker" and the entrepreneur can be vague and sometimes arbitrary. Many individuals, variously engaged in the making and selling of charms and spiritual products, exist along the continuum between these two seemingly opposite poles. All are spiritual merchants.

Entrepreneurship and the merchandising of charms does not necessarily mean deliberate exploitation of the believers. A person who provides spiritual products because he or she believes they benefit others, and in the process makes a decent living, is not an exploiter. A person who engages in the work solely for profit, and who looks upon the customers with contempt, is preying upon the faith of others. While some retailers and manufacturers may have a cynical attitude toward the spiritual business, none of those who agreed to be interviewed ever spoke disrespectfully of the customers or their beliefs.

What has evolved into the spiritual products industry began on a very small scale in the first decades of the twentieth century. Many of the earliest makers and sellers of hoodoo-oriented supplies were African

Americans, who one assumes were at least conversant with the belief system, if not actual practitioners. It did not take long, however, for whites to perceive the demand for spiritual products. Some of the first white entrepreneurs were neighborhood pharmacists who began to concoct baths, oils, and powders in response to the requests of their black customers. As we will see in chapter 8, others entered the business through the manufacture of cosmetics, cleaning products, incense, candles, and the publication of books on the occult. These early companies specialized in the paraphernalia of hoodoo, targeting African American customers. Although a few Latino-owned retail businesses in Florida and New York have catered to the Santería community at least since the 1930s, it was not until the 1970s that manufacturers began to label their products in Spanish and develop Santería-oriented merchandise.

No sooner did entrepreneurs initiate the marketing of spiritual merchandise by mail and through small retail businesses than local, state, and federal authorities began to regulate this endeavor. In the nineteenth century, African American spiritual practices had been outlawed because they were perceived as sinful and threatening. In the twentieth century, hoodoo was proscribed because it was seen as fraudulent. Much of our knowledge of the birth of the spiritual products industry in the early 1900s comes from court records and newspaper accounts of those who ran afoul of various antifraud laws. Most, but not all, of those who encountered these difficulties were African Americans. Cases involving blacks were more widely publicized than those against white spiritual merchants, and black defendants were more severely penalized. Local jurisdictions shut down hoodoo entrepreneurs for operating a business without a permit or violating other ordinances against fraud. State boards of health were concerned with bogus cures and practicing medicine without a license. The Food and Drug Administration and the U.S. Post Office also cast a watchful eye upon the spiritual products business.

The federal Pure Food and Drug Act of 1906 protected consumers against dangerous or adulterated substances, and a 1911 amendment outlawed false statements and therapeutic claims. Although many of the early spiritual merchants professed the ability to cure sickness as well as bring luck and afflict enemies, they do not appear to have had as much trouble with the Food and Drug Administration (FDA) as they did with local and state agencies. Today's manufacturers of spiritual products are careful to make no curative claims and to specify that their wares are for external use only. Even innocuous herbs like cinnamon and mint are marketed with the caution that they are "not sold for therapeutic, medical, or cosmetic use and are not to be consumed." Since spiritual products are technically not food or drugs, they are currently of little concern to the FDA. According to FDA historian John Swann, the agency has its hands full investigating consumer complaints against ineffective treatments and harmful substances. Swann maintained that reports of buyers being injured by spiritual products would certainly be given full attention.[1]

The greatest threat to the spiritual merchant was the U.S. Post Office (now the U.S. Postal Service). In 1909 the Post Office began to prosecute mail fraud cases. The law states that any person "having devised . . . a scheme or artifice to defraud . . . by means of . . . matter . . . sent or delivered by the Post Office . . . shall be fined not more than one thousand dollars or imprisoned for not more than five years, or both." Citing a 1923 case in which the defendant mailed circulars offering "magnetic talismans" for the lifting of evil spells, the court ruled that the scheme, "though absurd and impossible and not capable of deceiving persons of average intelligence," nevertheless constituted mail fraud under the law. But in an unrelated case it was stated that "the fact that a scheme is visionary does not make it fraudulent, if the promoter actually in good faith believes in it."[2] This provided a possible loophole for hoodoo entrepreneurs who could convince the court of their sincerity, even though nonbelievers would consider the claims made for their wares to be clearly "absurd and impossible."

A mail fraud investigation by the Post Office could originate from a consumer complaint, a tip from a disgruntled employee or a competitor, or a local postmaster who noticed that an individual was receiving an inordinate volume of out-of-town mail. Once the probe was set in motion, a Post Office investigator would actually seek to entrap the suspect by posing as a customer and ordering merchandise. Incoming and outgoing mail was held as evidence. If the investigation led to a grand jury indictment, the case was tried in federal court. Conviction carried a fine or a penitentiary sentence, although this could be suspended at the discretion of the judge.[3] A number of early spiritual entrepreneurs were investigated for mail fraud, and some are known to have served federal prison terms.

Dealers in spiritual products eventually learned to avoid prosecution by postal authorities. Almost all spiritual products offered today carry disclaimers such as "sold as a curio only," "alleged," "sold as a novelty," "no claims as to metaphysical qualities are intended or implied," or "gathered from folklore—no claim of supernatural or magical powers is made or inferred." Orders are never sent by the U.S. Postal Service; even the tiniest purchase is shipped by an independent express carrier.

Mail-Order Doctors

By the turn of the twentieth century, spiritual merchants were marketing roots and herbs, lodestones, mojo bags, baths, powders, and oils. While some sold only to a local clientele, most expanded into the mail-order trade, combining hoodoo with the sale of medical cures and hair preparations.

Spiritual advisors and entrepreneurs advertised in the country's leading African American newspaper, the *Chicago Defender*, which was founded in 1905 and had a national circulation. A search of the *Defender*'s back pages revealed advertisements for merchants in small towns and cities all over the country. The first advertisement for spiritual services appeared in 1910, when Professor White, a Chicago "Psychic and Scientific Palmist," offered readings for twenty-five and fifty cents; he also treated corns, bunions, and ingrown toenails.[4] The first announcement specifically oriented toward hoodoo dates to 1919. R. D. Wester of Montgomery, Alabama— probably an individual operating from his home or store—advertised "roots, herbs, lodestones, magnetic sand, the Book of Black Magic, Underground Treasure Book, the Wonderful Pow-Wow, secrets for growing hair, the Key of Solomon, magic finger ring, magic mirror, and herb medicine."[5] In 1925 E. R. Goode of Boynton, Virginia, offered "luck, success, happiness, power over others, spells removed, pains conquered. Valuable root and herb secrets; terms to suit everybody. Satisfaction guaranteed . . . send 10¢ for reply." On the same page, a Chicago resident, D. S. Brown of 4639 South State Street, was selling "Voodoo bags for success in hazard betting, card games, dice, and all games of chance . . . for all undertakings and general luck and against all evil influences . . . and for controlling the opposite sex, man or woman."[6]

In 1935 Doctor E. N. French, residing at 3338 South State Street, Chicago, advertised the Success Seal, said to be helpful "in business, to get work, in love and marriage, to win games, and to gain influence and power over all things." Doctor French also offered a course, "easy to learn; based on the Bible," in the "great art of giving readings, healings, and spiritual advice to others. $500 course for only $55.50. Send me $1.00 and I will send your first lesson at once. You can pay $1.00 weekly." Doctor French furnished testimonials from customers in Cleveland, Philadelphia, Los Angeles, and Jacksonville, Florida. While there is no way of knowing the race of most advertisers, the accompanying picture of Doctor French shows a black man wearing a business suit and a turban.[7]

We have extensive documentation of the hoodoo business in New Orleans because of the aggressiveness with which these merchants were pursued by the authorities. Some of this was undoubtedly motivated by racism. When black entrepreneurs sold to the local trade, they had trouble with the New Orleans police because they lacked the required permit or violated various ordinances against healing, fortune-telling, obtaining money under false pretenses, and having "no visible means of support." When they advertised and sold by mail, especially if they claimed the ability to cure disease, they ran afoul of state and federal agencies. The Louisiana Medical Practice Act of 1894 required that anyone offering therapeutic treatment be a graduate of an accredited medical school and be licensed by the State Board of Medical Examiners. The U.S. Post Office, of course, pursued mail fraud violations. From the early 1900s through the 1940s, dozens of articles regarding arrests for hoodoo-related fraud appeared in New Orleans newspapers. Black hoodoo merchants were arrested, fined, and sentenced to the local jail, and several went to the federal penitentiary for mail fraud. News items dealing with blacks were written in a jeering tone, quotations from the accused were rendered in exaggerated dialect, and the name and address of the defendant was always published. Articles about the investigation of a white New Orleanian for operating a mail-order hoodoo business kept his identity secret, and he does not appear to have been sentenced.[8]

One of the earliest accounts of an arrest for hoodoo-related fraud was the case of Julius P. Caesar, who in 1902 was jailed for violation of city ordinances against healing and the selling of charms. At this early date, his activities were not yet deemed illegal by the Post Office, and he was therefore prosecuted by city authorities and fined fifteen dollars or thirty days.

HUSBANDS AND LOVERS
ARE VOODOO SAGE'S SPECIALITY

Complaints had been received at police headquarters about "Doctor" Julius P. Caesar, and the officers were sent out yesterday to make an investigation. His bureau of information is located at 1960 Lafayette

Street. . . . Letters were found in his room from all parts of the country, asking for remedies to make lovers and husbands return to their sweethearts and wives. The "doctor" claims to be a magnetic healer, and said he had a diploma from a college in Missouri. However, there is an ordinance against healers and fortune-tellers, and the "doctor's" certificate, if he had one, did not deter the officers from placing him where he could do no more harm.[9]

Doctor Caesar's cousin, interviewed by Hyatt in 1938, said that Caesar's place of business had an altar with images of the saints, Jesus Christ, and the Virgin Mary, and that he wore a robe and a Hindu-style turban to receive clients. His cousin called Caesar the "top hoodoo in this city" and said he left $150,000 worth of real estate when he died.[10] He was listed in the city directory for 1902, the year of his arrest, as a cooper.

After the 1909 Post Office ruling against mislabeled, worthless, and dangerous merchandise, postal antifraud laws began to be used against hoodoo merchants. A man who called himself "Doctor Cat," proprietor of the Swift Hair Grower Company, was indicted in New Orleans in 1914:

"DOCTOR CAT" PLEADS GUILTY

Confesses to Judge Foster He Used the Mails to Defraud

James M. McKay, alias Doctor C.C. Cat, indicted by a federal grand jury June 26 for making fraudulent use of the mails, pleaded guilty upon arraignment before Judge Foster on Friday. Sentence was deferred. Defendant ran afoul of the federal authorities through his extensive advertising campaign and "literature" sent through the mails in furtherance of a scheme to get money from gullible persons. Most of his customers were of his own race, Negroes, and he is said to have made considerable money by pretending to be "gifted with the power of remedying any trouble of nature whatever." Following his indictment in this city McKay left for parts unknown. He was found last week in Birmingham, and was returned to New Orleans by Post Office Inspector Perdum.[11]

The grand jury indictment, now in the files of the U.S. District Court, National Archives and Records Administration, states that James M. McKay, alias Doctor C. C. Cat, advertised in various newspapers offering to cure all illnesses and to give luck. In return for a specified amount of money, McKay would send a small bag or a vial of fluid, accompanied by instructions and a request for more money. A letter to F. L. Howk of Waycross, Georgia, was included in the indictment:

> Dear One I got your letter to day and will say you know my rules and that is this. I must have $5.00 if you want me to do any-thing for you. Just as soon as you send the money I will start to doing what you want me to do. Yes! I am a man can do anything . . . if you do as I say. I been in this business for years and I never lost a case yet. . . . Anything you want done I am the man for it. Address all my mail to Swift Hair Grower Co., Box 1190, New Orleans, Louisiana, and I all ways will get it.[12]

On July 14, 1914, the *Times-Picayune* reported that Doctor Cat had been sentenced to two years in the federal penitentiary at Atlanta.[13]

In the 1930s the New Orleans police, the State Board of Health, and federal postal authorities launched an all-out attack on the hoodoo business. As Robert McKinney stated in a Louisiana Writers' Project report, "The queens and doctors (black and white), whose practices net them over $50,000 annually, are between the devil and the deep blue sea."[14] The most publicized of the New Orleans hoodoo-related mail-fraud cases was that of Rockford Lewis, a black man who ran a business at 5100 Royal Street in the Lower Ninth Ward. In 1928 he began to call himself "Doctor" Lewis, president and general manager of the Chemical Labora-tory of Louisiana. By 1932 the Chemical Laboratory had vanished, but Lewis was listed in the city directory as the owner of a drugstore. At about this time he got into the mail-order business, selling sachet bags, lucky beans, medals, and "Save Your Life Rheumatic Oil," through which he became quite prosperous. Lewis in many ways fits the description of Zora Neale Hurston's mentor, "Father Watson." Like this preacher and hoodoo worker, Lewis held church services several nights a week at an auditorium adjacent to his house—might this have been the prototype of Father Watson's "Myrtle Wreath Hall"?

Rockford Lewis soon attracted the attention of the U.S. Post Office. A typed transcript of the mail fraud trial of Lewis and his wife, Helen, exists in the Louisiana Writers' Project files. State's witnesses included officials from the Post Office and the Department of Agriculture. The Lewises were accused of mailing "letters and circulars" that claimed they "fully understood the complaints and desires of those who corresponded with them, and that they could cure their ills and grant their desires for a specified fee." Several of these letters are reproduced in the transcript. One, postmarked July 25, 1933, shows that Lewis was already wary of the Post Office:

> Dear Friend,
>
> I got your message and I understand it well. What you need is what I have. . . . Anything you plan to do or put your hands to got to make a great success. . . . Get busy your order will be sent to you. Look! Look! Don't send money by Post Office Order. Send money by Western Union Telegram or through Express Office . . . not by mail.[15]

Sentencing took place on February 6, 1934. An article in the *New Orleans Item* tells the story in embarrassingly racist language:

> "Doctor" A. Rockford Lewis, coconut-headed, kinky-haired, his brow . . . furrowed with what seemed to be the tedium of the law's delays rather than the worry of a possible impending punishment, took the stand before Judge W. I. Grubb in Federal Court this morning at his trial for using the mails to defraud. . . . Federal Post Office inspectors told the court that Lewis was doing a large business in voodoo charms, thereby defrauding the customers of the U.S. Post Office Department of their rights to expect legitimate return for everything they ordered and paid for. . . . [Lewis's] stenographer testified that the mail order business . . . was entirely concerned with shipments of "Save Your Life Rheumatic Oil," . . . but a Post Office inspector . . . testified that . . . he wrote asking for help in getting a job as a . . . railroad president . . . and received some lucky charms, perfumes, and powders.[16]

Rockford Lewis spent two years in the federal penitentiary at Atlanta for mail fraud. His wife received a suspended sentence.

Louisiana Writers' Project fieldworkers Robert McKinney and Hazel Breaux visited Lewis in 1937, after his release from prison, and filed this report:

> This burly, dark complexioned, uneducated Negro . . . stunned his race . . . with his arrogant and open practice of Voodooism.

. . . Lewis resides in half of a double cottage, in good condition and fairly well furnished. To the right of his home is a large auditorium where his meetings were held and which he rented out for dances . . . to the rear of the auditorium is the laboratory where he manufactured his herb and root concoctions. . . . Prior to his arrest Lewis employed five secretaries to handle his out-of-town correspondence, sported a huge diamond ring, and rode in a Pierce-Arrow driven by a liveried chauffeur. Lewis owns the above mentioned property and some other houses in the vicinity. . . . After serving his sentence, Lewis returned to his haven unheralded and unnoticed.[17]

In 1938 Lewis was in trouble again, this time with the Louisiana Board of Health, because an Ohio woman claimed she had been defrauded of money through his advertisements. Lewis faced another jail sentence, but was able to avoid it through the services of a good lawyer. An article in the *New Orleans Item* stated that "so-called voodoo doctor A. Rockford Lewis . . . pleaded not guilty to violation of the Louisiana health code. . . . Lewis is one of several [Negroes] arrested recently in the campaign by the State Board of Health."[18] McKinney and Breaux paid a second visit to Rockford Lewis shortly after this, but found him understandably reluctant to talk— "I gotta be careful . . . you can't tell who might be the government." Robert McKinney commented in his notes: "Lewis is still making money from the practice of Voodoo, but he is using spiritualism to cover up and thereby keep within the law. . . . We later visited the auditorium which is now used for his church and saw some small altars and other spiritualist paraphernalia. Such as this has, on more than one occasion, shown that spiritualism is nothing but a sham for Voodooism."[19]

Rockford Lewis's hoodoo business survived into the 1950s. He was mentioned in a 1951 *Ebony* magazine article, "The Truth about Voodoo" by Edward T. Clayton, where he was listed as "one of the five biggest names in New Orleans Voodoo." Lewis's prison mug shot is reproduced in the article, above the caption "Wealthy 'doctor' still offers his 'services' in New Orleans."[20] According to city directories, Lewis lived in the same lower Royal Street neighborhood until 1957, still operating his drugstore, auditorium, and nightclub.

There were also black entrepreneurs in New Orleans who escaped the snares of the police, the Board of Health, and the U.S. Post Office. One such business was John Hall's Novelty Shop, which occupied several locations on South Rampart Street between 1937 and 1948. Like others, Hall had a flourishing mail-order trade in addition to local sales. McKinney and Breaux, as part of their documentation of New Orleans hoodoo businesses, visited "Professor" Hall in 1937.

> Hall is very popular on Rampart Street and in the night clubs because of the money he carelessly spends in entertaining his friends. Hall is a brownskin Negro, weighs about 210 lbs. and stands 5'6" tall. He is always neatly groomed with an exceptionally flashy appearance and wears a large diamond ring. . . . He has bought a new automobile every year for the past five years . . . . He is a foremost hoodoo racketeer thought to be a "two-headed man" by ignorant Negroes. He called hoodoo a "junk" but admitted that it is the best legitimate racket to be found. . . . He spoke of beating the government in using the mails, bragging, "I'm no Rockford Lewis."[21]

While the hoodoo trade appears to have been particularly vigorous in New Orleans, spiritual products were sold throughout the South. The U.S. Postal Service inspector's files at the National Archives and Records Administration contains the transcript of a 1924 mail fraud investigation against "Doctor" P. F. Hough, also known as "Prince Huff," of DeSoto, Mississippi: "P. F. Hough . . . is a colored man, about 70 years of age. . . . He is known among ignorant people of his own race as a 'Voodoo' or 'Hoodoo' doctor. In addition to a local 'practice,' he carries on a mail-order business, wherein he represents that he can diagnose any disease . . . by having his patients spit on a piece of cloth and send it to him. . . . The evidence shows that Hough claims he will furnish medicine that will cure syphilis, tuberculosis, and other serious disorders."

The local postmaster reported that Hough was receiving an average of ten letters a day. As part of the investigation, a U.S. Post Office inspector wrote to Hough complaining of a "bad disease." He was instructed to spit on a white cloth and send it to Hough with a fourteen-dollar deposit. The inspector sent the money and a cloth smeared with egg white. Several days later he received an envelope of brown powder, along with the following letter:

> Dear Sir: Yos Receved. Lisen—Emty contents in a pint bot. Fill it with clen water. Take a table spoon three times a day before meals. Shake the bot till all resolve . . . to cure you and make

you luck, never go brok, and get all the work you can do and bor all the money you want to run any busnes you want will cost you 21 dols. A frind, P. F. Hough.

A fraud order was issued against Hough, who was charged with "conducting a scheme for obtaining money through the mails by means of false and fraudulent pretenses." According to an article in the *Chicago Defender*, Hough was subsequently convicted of mail fraud; we do not learn from this report whether or not he received a prison sentence.[22]

■ ■ ■

I was also able to acquire advertising flyers and copies of letters addressed to a hoodoo entrepreneur named D. W. Watson of 217 East Marlboro Street, Florence, South Carolina. A cardboard box of advertising materials and letters, all dated 1925, was found in the basement of the Florence post office when the building was renovated. The flyers and letters, which had been opened and reinserted in their envelopes, apparently had been held at the post office as evidence in a mail fraud investigation and then abandoned. The letters were given to a local pharmacist, who donated them to the Pharmacy Museum at the University of South Carolina.

Hoodoo was evidently a sideline with Watson, a supplement to his income from more conventional employment. He was listed in the Florence city directory for 1924–25 as a railroad brakeman and in 1929–30 as a bricklayer. An asterisk by his name indicates that he was black.

"Do you want to be lucky, happy, and well?" asks Watson's flyer. "Tell your secrets to the right man. Spells of all kinds released and broken. Medical preparations for conjured pains and sufferings. . . . I can deal with you no matter where you are." Having made these claims, Doctor Watson wriggled out of legal responsibility by asking the customer to agree that "no advice has been given by D. Watson as to what I should order or what goods I should use." He offered a full refund if complaint was made in writing within ten days.

The accompanying brochure and price list, which "tells just what to use to deal with persons at long distance or in your own town," was supposedly written by "Professor S. B. Ayapa, Master of Science and the World's Greatest Root Worker." Watson was obviously inspired by Professor S. B. Ajapa, a Harlem entrepreneur whose similarly worded advertisements appeared in the *Chicago Defender* during the 1920s.[23]

Doctor Watson's prices were exceptionally high—most retailers at that time charged between twenty-five and fifty cents for roots and spiritual products. Watson's Adam and Eve root, at five dollars, was the least expensive item on the list. Bring Back Powder, Chase Away Powder, Hard Luck Powder, Break Up Dust, Easy Life Powder, and Boss Fix Dust were fifteen dollars each; the Demanding Bottle, "for influencing a man or a lady," was ten dollars; Goofer Dust, "for throwing or breaking up spells," was twenty-five dollars, as was the Black Cat Ruling Hand and King Solomon's Wisdom Stone. This last item "causes a person to become famous in finance, love, and business. Everybody will respect you white or colored." The Black Cat Wish Bone, which was alleged to make the bearer clairvoyant, rich, and invulnerable to the police, cost a whopping one hundred dollars! One wonders if, for that price, Watson actually boiled a live cat, as required by the classic black cat bone ritual.

The letters came from Texas, Arkansas, Louisiana, Kentucky, North Carolina, and South Carolina. Henry Hall of Leesville, Louisiana, wrote for help in locating buried treasure on his property:

> My grandpapa had alot of gold an silver in his lifetime . . . and it is another old white man he is been ded about ten year and was a tall red face man one eye out and he was good friend to a robber and the robber got kill . . . and they say he had aplenty money berred. . . . Come and we will go get it . . . rite me if you do that kind of business.

Isaac Burton of Fayetteville, Texas, was in love with a married woman. Although he had given her money and clothes, she would not leave her husband, and Burton began to suspect that the husband had her "fixed." Burton was so smitten that he wanted to continue the affair, even if the woman would not go away with him.

> I see in your advertisement the Demanding Bottle will draw influence of a lady . . . and I see Love Me Quick fixed in bag will draw the person you desire. What one of them will do what I want? Please answer me at once.

Arthur Short of Rockport, Kentucky, was troubled by enemies.

> I want the Chasing Away Powder for male and female. Now their is several people after us and they have gave my mother three or four different doses [recall that a "dose" meant a harmful charm].

Now we can't get clost enough to them to sprinkle it on them, so I hope it is so we can fix them, and be miles away . . . some of these parties live on the other side of the river. Can I stay on this side and chase them away? Times are awful hard here, but we will pay you ever penny I promised you. Before long they will move and if it don't work I understand you are to return the money.

Short wrote again three months later. He was not satisfied with the results, and he balked at paying Watson's high fee.

The only instructions you gave me concerning the Leaving Powders was write the names down on a piece of paper and tie them up and throw them in a running stream of water, which I did and no one has left yet. And if there was any thing else to do you should have told me. Now $50.00 is what you said you would charge me to move them. . . . We sure have a hard time trying to get hold of any money. I hope you will not quit me until this is completed. I want all my enemies sent away. I *did* just what you told me to do.[24]

An intriguing tidbit, which may be a reference to Doctor Watson, turns up in Hyatt's *Hoodoo-Conjure-Witchcraft-Rootwork*. Referring to the man he called "Rootworker from Florence," Hyatt commented in his notes that "our informant outwitted the postal laws by sending his hoodoo products through the mail, and instructions for their use a few days later."[25] I found no record of a mail fraud investigation of D. W. Watson in the files at the National Archives and Records Administration.

■ ■ ■

During the Great Migration of 1915 to 1940, thousands of African Americans left the South for the industrial cities of the North in search of better economic opportunities and a less repressive racial climate. The movement of black southerners was determined, in part, by the railroad routes. The Illinois Central and the Louisville and Nashville brought people from Louisiana, Mississippi, and Alabama to Chicago and other midwestern destinations. The Southern Railway, the Seaboard Atlantic Coast Line, and the Airlines Railway transported workers from Florida, Georgia, and the Carolinas to Washington, D.C., Baltimore, Philadelphia, and New York City.

These black southerners brought their culture with them, including the belief in hoodoo and rootwork.[26] Just as individual practitioners and entrepreneurs made a business of formulating and marketing spiritual products in the South, such businesses also developed in Chicago, New York, and other northern cities.

In the late 1930s, the African American sociologists Saint Clair Drake and Horace Cayton compiled a report on Chicago's "Bronzeville," the South Side neighborhood in which black newcomers settled during the Great Migration. This research was later published as *Black Metropolis: A Study of Negro Life in a Northern City* (1945). Drake and Cayton noted that the neighborhood was home to several hundred black "spiritual advisors." As we saw at the beginning of this chapter, some South Side residents advertised such services in the *Chicago Defender*. One of those documented by Drake and Cayton was Professor Edward Lowe, Astro-Numerologist, who had migrated to Chicago from Texas. From his store, he sold "policy" numbers, roots and herbs, lodestones, oils, and occult texts such as the *Sixth and Seventh Books of Moses* and *The Egyptian Secrets of Albertus Magnus*, plus his own book, *Key to Numerology*. Another was Doctor Mason Pryor, who, according to earlier advertisements in the *Chicago Defender*, began his career as a manufacturer of medicines and hair preparations.

In a 1919 notice in the *Defender*, Doctor Pryor promoted his "energy pills—the pill with the pep, a builder of men and women . . . recommended for lost energy, lame back, indigestion, constipation, and run-down condition."[27] In 1921 his Japo Wonder Soap was advertised in the *Defender*:

GOOD NEWS FOR ALL MEN

Simply wash the hair. Oh Boy.

Doctor Pryor's Japo Wonder Soap . . . will straighten the hair without turning it red or injuring the scalp. . . . Big money for agents. For sale by all drug stores or by mail.

Pryor Chemical Company, 3319 State Street, Chicago[28]

By the time of Drake and Cayton's study in the 1930s, Doctor Pryor had metamorphosed into a manufacturer of spiritual products and pastor of a storefront church. From his Japo-Oriental Company, relocated to 5039 South Indiana, he sold his book of dream interpretation and lucky numbers, Jinx-Removal Candles, Sacred and Lucky Powders, Holy Oriental Oil, Controlling

Oil, John the Conqueror Oil, and Doctor Pryor's Holy Floor Wash and House Spray. The floor wash and house spray was guaranteed to "rent houses, draw crowds, and eliminate the evil works of the Devil." He was also pastor of the King Solomon's Temple of Religious Science, located in the same building.[29] In the 1950s Doctor Pryor's Japo-Oriental Company was bought by Lama Temple, a large Chicago manufacturer of spiritual products.

■ ■ ■

New York's Harlem was the East Coast equivalent of Chicago's Bronzeville, and many black southerners settled in Harlem during the years of the Great Migration. At the same time, immigrants from the Caribbean islands were drawn to the neighborhood. Harlem thus was home to a unique combination of African American hoodoo and West Indian obeah. (Obeah is a system of magic and herbal medicine practiced in the British West Indies.)[30] Conjurers, spiritualists, and herb doctors did a thriving business. Some Harlem entrepreneurs proclaimed themselves to be natives of Africa—recall that the Harlem-based magician Black Herman also made this assertion. Advertisements in the *Chicago Defender* include photographs of black men attired in African-style robes. In 1924 a person calling himself S. Indoo, professor of African science, advertised: "Separated people brought together, lost love restored, luck given in anything you wish, medicines guaranteed successful in every kind of sickness, evil spells and undesirable people chased away from the home. . . . Call or write. Delays are almost always fatal."

On the same page, Edet Effiong, supposedly from Nigeria, "begs to announce that he is head of the Nigeria Remedy Company, registered with the Department of Health, New York City." Effiong offered Nigeria Liniment, Stomach Bitters, Rheumatic Remedy, and Building Tonic, as well as Nigeria Herb Incense. In 1925 Professor Domingo, an "Occultist from Karo, West Africa," was selling African Secret Incense to bring "luck and success to your home."[31] The alleged city of Karo may have existed somewhere in West Africa in the 1920s, but it is not listed in the current *Rand McNally Cosmopolitan World Atlas*.

■ ■ ■

These small mail-order operations are not a thing of the past. In 1993, when I began the research for this book, I telephoned the Lucky Starr Incense and

Candle Company of Columbus, Georgia, to request a catalog. I have since received monthly advertising fliers from "Mister Felix" for outrageously expensive spiritual products, talismans, and lucky hands.

THE MASTER HAND
THIS IS IT; LOOK NO FURTHER

> This is the ultimate, the finest, in powerful GOOD LUCK—THE MASTER HAND, made especially for you by Mister Felix. It's the DADDY OF THEM ALL and you will be especially proud when you are working on those Big Time Deals. Filled with genuine ingredients and dressed with powerful MASTER OIL. Lets you think BIG when you need that "special touch" for FANTASTIC RESULTS.

MASTER HAND AND MASTER OIL—$299.00

The State Lottery-Casino-Riverboat Gambling Hand, Dog and Horse Track Hand, Baseball-Bingo-Sweepstakes Hand, or the Master Protection Hand were only ninety-nine dollars. The Egyptian Gold-Silver Master Piece, a "secret artifix in a special gold pouch," came with Powerful Gold-Silver Good Luck Oil and a "dressed" billfold containing "seed money":

> You will receive free with each GOLD-SILVER MASTER PIECE a SPECIALLY DRESSED BILLFOLD which is alleged to attract money and we guarantee this billfold will never be stolen from you. Should you lose it we will replace it absolutely free. Inside this billfold will be placed $5.00 as SEED MONEY for attracting large sums.

GOLD-SILVER MASTER PIECE, BILLFOLD,
AND SEED MONEY—$200.00

Another flyer announced:

WANT TO GET MONEY FROM WELFARE,
SOCIAL SECURITY, AND/OR DISABILITY?

> Obtain some of Mister Felix's Special Money Dust and some Mister Felix Money Herb. Place this in a jar along with the name of the place you are trying

to get the money from, and screw the lid on tightly. Place the jar in a pan of water and let it remain for three days. On the fourth day, bury the jar in your yard.

Complete supplies for the above—$33.00

From time to time Mister Felix sends out the *Alleged Do-It-Yourself Sure Fast Success Guide*. In bold type, he reassures his customers, "In this special issue I have covered some of the everyday problems that we all face. I sincerely pray that you find these articles as helpful as I have." In small type at the bottom of the page is the disclaimer, "The authors of this book wish to have it understood that the statements made are not to be accepted as facts, but only to tell you of the strange things people do and believe. We make no claim that these sayings are of help to anyone."

The December 1995 mailing contained the "Important Notice" that Mister Felix had relocated to Phenix City, Alabama, and had formed a partnership with "Sister Powers, a true and dedicated spiritual advisor." Phenix City, as Mister Felix explained to his customers, is just across the Chattahoochee River from Columbus, and he had only moved six blocks from his previous location. The "Year End Special" was Cast Out Evil Floor Sweep and a Seven Day Garlic Candle to "help you cleanse your home of all evil influences and be ready to thrive in 1995."

In 1996 Mister Felix and Sister Powers returned to 1228 Broadway, Columbus, Georgia, and in 1998 they again relocated to 5949 Veterans Parkway, where they have remained. Their Grand Opening Special included Peace and Prosperity House Dressing, Uncrossing and Evil Removing Wash, and the King Midas Gold Touch Anointing and Bath Oil at twenty-five dollars each or all three for sixty-five dollars.

Hoodoo Drugstores

At roughly the same time that African Americans were engaging in small retail and mail-order operations, white people were also entering the spiritual business, often through ownership of a neighborhood drugstore with a predominantly black clientele. The pharmacy was a common source for the "materia medica" of hoodoo. In the nineteenth and early twentieth centuries, all pharmacies stocked botanicals, oils, essences, and flavorings for the formulation of healing preparations, and they sold common household preservatives and cleansers such as alum, saltpeter, ammonia, laundry bluing, lye, and sulfur. As we have seen in previous chapters, all of these items had been adopted by hoodooists as charm ingredients.

Certain white druggists were willing to make up hoodoo "prescriptions" for customers. These were harmless concoctions, usually containing talc, boric acid, magnesium carbonate, zinc oxide, alcohol, oil, or water, to which coloring and herbal essences had been added. These pharmacists simply responded to the demands of their patrons, and gradually found themselves formulating charms more often than filling medical prescriptions. A 1931 article in the *American Pharmacist* recounts an interview with John Bonne, owner of the Terminal Pharmacy in New Orleans. Bonne used butyric ether, which has a pleasant smell, as the base for good luck concoctions. For bad luck, the base was disulfide of carbon, which has a disagreeable odor. Hot ingredients like ginger and pepper were added to make the mixture seem more powerful. He explained how to make Fast Luck Water: "Into a quart bottle, he poured a couple of tablespoons of butyric ether; added a few drops of wintergreen, lavender, oil of lemon grass, and essence of vertivert; then filled the bottle with water and added a touch of red coloring. . . . 'Fifteen cents worth of material. I'll sell it for eight dollars. Fraud? Not a bit of it. It's what my customers want, and the price is what they want to pay. . . . They are satisfied, and how else can you measure money's worth?'"[32]

These businesses were common in the South, especially in New Orleans, and with the Great Migration of southern blacks to the industrial cities of the North, they also appeared in such places as Chicago, New York, Philadelphia, and Baltimore. Some of the hoodoo drugstores evolved into medium-sized manufacturing and mail-order businesses, while others sold roots and herbs and carried the products of other manufacturers.

■ ■ ■

New Orleans' South Rampart Street, across Canal Street from the French Quarter, was the primary black commercial and entertainment district—from its numerous bars, brothels, and dance halls evolved the music that became jazz. The merchants of hoodoo also flourished on South Rampart. We have already noted John Hall's South Rampart Street establishment, but the most famous and longest-running of these businesses was the Cracker Jack Drug Store. The Cracker Jack, located at 435 South Rampart, was owned by Dr. George A. Thomas, a white physician/pharmacist who began with an ordinary drugstore and eventually became a spiritual merchant. It is not known exactly when this transition took place. His business, George A. Thomas Drugs, was founded in 1897. The store was evidently successful; in 1919 Thomas, his French-born wife, Alice, and their three sons moved from rooms above the store to a large and imposing home in an affluent neighborhood near City Park.[33]

In 1927 both the *New Orleans Morning Tribune* and the *Times-Picayune* carried front-page articles about a white physician who was under investigation for running a mail-order hoodoo business on South Rampart Street.

FEDERAL AGENTS EXPOSE BUSINESS IN GOOFER DUST.

> A Voodoo practice . . . founded on the superstitions of Marie Laveau . . . and carrying on a mail-order business extending from New Jersey to Texas, was exposed by federal post office inspectors on Friday. The inspectors found the organization manipulated by an aged white physician. His practice . . . has been entirely confined to Negroes whose superstitious nature has enabled him to found a drugstore dealing in such articles as "goofer dust," "eagle eyes," and other charms for good and evil. . . . The method . . . was to mail out a catalogue of charms "purchasable at his drugstore only." The list, made up of 250 articles, included black cat bones . . . roots, [and] pictures of [the saints]. Besides the various powders and charms, the drugstore offered for sale a small pamphlet entitled *The Life and Works of Marie Laveau*. In this book were instructions for the use of charms to win husbands, cause bad luck to befall a neighbor, and prevent others from working evil on the reader. Assistant U.S. Attorney Edmond E. Talbot said that he had requested the physician to appear at his office . . . he had not determined what form the prosecution would take.[34]

Although both the *Tribune* and the *Picayune* printed articles about the mail fraud investigation, neither revealed the identity of this merchant. We have a clue in a 1936 report by Louisiana Writers' Project fieldworker

Mail-Order Doctors and Hoodoo Drugstores

Robert McKinney, in which he noted that *The Life and Works of Marie Laveau* was available only at the Cracker Jack,[35] leading one to suspect that the "aged white physician" was Dr. George Thomas. Nothing further appeared in the newspapers regarding this case, and no record of the investigation was found in the U.S. Postal Service inspector's case files, in the records of the U.S. District Court, or in the arrest records of the New Orleans Police Department.

In 1932 the name of Dr. Thomas's business changed from George A. Thomas Drugs to the Cracker Jack Drug Store. Thomas continued to be listed as the owner until 1940. Dr. Thomas died in 1941, and the business was taken over by his widow, Alice. In 1942 Alice Thomas married Morris Karno (originally Karnofsky).[36] It is not known whether Karno, who owned a music business on South Rampart Street, was ever involved in the operation of the Cracker Jack. He died in 1944.

The Cracker Jack Drug Store was mentioned by virtually all of Hyatt's New Orleans and Algiers informants as a source for supplies. One informant did not refer to the Cracker Jack by name, but when Hyatt asked where he had obtained a certain powder used in a fortune-telling ritual, he said, "You buy it at the drugstore. It's hoodoo stuff. Dr. Thomas got it down here . . . yeah, right down here on Rampart Street." A woman interviewed in 1938 indicated that the hoodoo items at the Cracker Jack were no longer displayed prominently for all to see. When asked where to obtain War Powder, she told Hyatt, "You go . . . and ask the drugstore man—it's the [one] they call the Cracker Jack Drug Store." But she cautioned Hyatt that he, as an outsider, could not just "go down and buy it there. . . . You got to have somebody to get it [for you] what's been dealing with the hoodoos."[37] Dr. Thomas would obviously have been reluctant to sell to a white man who might be an undercover policeman or an investigator for some state or federal agency.

Jane "Miss Sister" Jones, an elderly black New Orleans resident, told me that, as a young girl in the late 1930s, she and her friends would stop at the Cracker Jack on their way home from school: "It was so dark in there. They had all kinds of snake powders and insect powders for harming people. It was a white man and wife that owned it, but they had black people working for them. No, we never bought anything—we was just curious—but a lot of the reverend mothers [from the Spiritual churches] would buy their things there."[38]

Edward Clayton's 1951 *Ebony* magazine article, "The Truth about Voodoo," also describes South Rampart Street and the Cracker Jack:

The most commercial evidences of voodoo are to be found on crowded South Rampart Street where at least a half-dozen drug-stores carry full stocks of *gris-gris* for customers seeking money, power, or straying husbands. These druggists fill voodoo pre-scriptions with the same dispatch and attention they would give to a regular medical draft, although most admit they don't know if "the stuff" works or not. One such drugstore is the Cracker Jack, a rather forlorn and dismal looking place that has done a lucrative business dispensing such wares for more than two gen-erations and is still said to be one of the most popular sources of voodoo paraphernalia in New Orleans.

The accompanying illustration shows an unimpressive two-story building with nothing to indicate that it was New Orleans' leading purveyor of hoodoo supplies. A small sign simply says "Cracker Jack," and advertise-ments for Ex-Lax, Hadacol, Stanback, and Gillette can be seen in the dis-play windows. The caption below reads, "Oldtimers say owners once displayed roots, herbs, and other items so prominently and had such brisk trade, that police were dispatched for probe."[39]

The original Cracker Jack building was torn down in 1972. The store was briefly relocated a few blocks away at 183 South Prieur Street. According to a 1973 article in the Sunday magazine of the *Times-Picayune*, it was a slate-gray building bearing only the name "Cracker Jack." Inside, there were a few faded and dusty drugstore items, but it was obvious that spiritual products were the "real" merchandise. In addi-tion to selling the usual commercially produced items, charm prescrip-tions were filled.

A small but steady stream of people are in and out of the Cracker Jack, usually sitting one-at-a-time on a small wooden chair beside the high glass counter at the rear as they wait for their orders to be filled. Behind the counter are shelves lined with all sizes and shapes of bottles, containing colored liquids and powders. Many brown paper sacks, wrapped and tied with string, fill another shelf—two of these were labeled "Cinnamon" and "Wahoo Bark." And on the table nearby . . . are hundreds of tiny glass bottles, waiting to be filled when the formulas are mixed. "Medicine" is the answer given when questions are raised about the activities going on behind this counter.[40]

Alice Thomas Karno continued to own the Cracker Jack for thirty-two years after the death of Dr. George Thomas, but she was not involved in the daily operation of the business. A black man named George Williams acted as manager and buyer,[41] and Mrs. Karno's son, Lucien Thomas, was listed in the city directory as an employee at the Cracker Jack from the 1950s until the store closed in 1974. Mrs. Karno died the following year at the age of 89.[42]

■ ■ ■

John C. Coleman's Ideal Drugstore, at the corner of South Rampart and Thalia Street, was also identified by Louisiana Writers' Project fieldworkers as a source of hoodoo supplies. According to the city directory, Coleman was employed as a pharmacist at various New Orleans drugstores in the 1920s and 1930s. In 1935 he was listed as the manager of the Dixie Drugstore. The Ideal was only in business for one year, 1937. Coleman was interviewed at that time by LWP workers McKinney and Breaux. Their report specified that he was white.

> Mr. Coleman is a registered pharmacist. His drugstore is not of the first class in appearance or stock, but it is clean and seems equipped with sufficient drugs to satisfy the patrons. . . . His wife clerks in the store. . . . Due to his clever method of selling and advertising his Voodoo merchandise he has evaded any arrests; he doesn't use the mails but ships by express. . . . The oils and powders are numbered; people write in and order by number and not by name. . . . In the rear of the store is a printing press and mimeograph machine for turning out his publicity. He cited [his associate] Professor Hubert as an example of how Voodooism may be practiced within the law. . . . Mr. Coleman keeps a supply of Hubert's cards and gives them to prospective clients.[43]

A printed flyer from the Dixie Sales Agency, 2121 Erato Street (Coleman's home address), enumerates the various herbs and products offered for sale—Dixie John the Conqueror root, five finger grass, dragon's blood sticks, High John the Conqueror root, 1000 Strength Oil, Queen Elizabeth root, dragon's blood powder, life everlasting, Dixie Love Perfume, Hot Foot Powder, Devil's shoe string, brimstone, lodestone, and magnetic sand. Each item was followed by a paragraph describing its use, a disclaimer, an order number, and the price.[44] John C. Coleman and the Ideal Drugstore vanished from New Orleans in 1938, and both the store and Coleman's home address were listed in the city directory as vacant.

■ ■ ■

The Dixie Drugstore, formerly managed by John C. Coleman and undoubtedly affiliated with his Dixie Sales Agency, was located at 1240 Simon Bolivar Avenue, a street that runs parallel to South Rampart. The Dixie was the last of New Orleans' old-time hoodoo drugstores. Francis Hendrick, a registered pharmacist with a degree from Tulane University, bought the Dixie in 1963. Hendrick, who was white, was assisted by his wife, Ellen, their teenaged sons, and Joseph "Buddy" Bush, a longtime black employee at the store. Most of the customers were African Americans from the neighborhood and patients from an adjoining Medicaid clinic.

The Dixie was already carrying spiritual products when Hendrick took ownership, and he soon found that the demand for this merchandise exceeded that for prescriptions and other drugstore items. More and more space was appropriated for the display of herbs and products. In the beginning Hendrick ordered from Rondo's Temple in Atlanta, Sonny Boy Products in Miami, and Lama Temple in Chicago. He subsequently formed a business partnership with a black pharmacist, Horace Bynum Jr., and they began to formulate their own baths, powders, and oils. Bynum had previously been a sales agent for Sonny Boy and was therefore well acquainted with the spiritual business.

Francis Hendrick died suddenly in 1979, and Ellen Hendrick continued to operate the Dixie until 1984, when the building was destroyed by fire. During that time she published *The Mystical Secrets of Marie Laveau*, a booklet of charm formulae that also contains a brief history of the Dixie Drugstore. Mrs. Hendrick later opened Marie Laveau's House of Magic at 636 St. Ann Street in the French Quarter. A 1984 *Times-Picayune* article on Voodoo includes a photograph of a motherly, middle-aged Ellen Hendrick posed in front of an arrangement of spiritual products.[45] Marie Laveau's House of Magic closed when Mrs. Hendrick died in 1986.[46]

All of the original hoodoo drugstores in New Orleans have disappeared. South Rampart Street's once-vibrant black commercial district and the surrounding neighborhoods have been devastated by poverty, "urban renewal," and the building of elevated highways. Many building sites have

Mail-Order Doctors and Hoodoo Drugstores

been left vacant, strewn with trash and rubble. The location of the famous Cracker Jack is now occupied by the Cheap Rate Parking Lot.

■ ■ ■

Other southern cities also had their hoodoo drugstores, and, unlike the New Orleans establishments, some of them are (or at least were until recently) still in existence. The Charleston Cut-Rate Drugstore, 567 King Street, supplied herbs and spiritual products to the Low Country for almost fifty years. It was, in fact, at the Cut-Rate that my friend bought the can of Sonny Boy Uncrossing Power Incense that inaugurated my collection of spiritual products and resulted in this research project. When I visited Charleston in March of 1999 and made a beeline for upper King Street, I was devastated to learn that I was six months too late. The Cut-Rate closed in 1998, and the building is currently occupied by a finance company. I was, however, fortunate enough to locate and interview two of the former owners, Ann Epstein and Samuel Rosen, now both retired.

The Cut-Rate was opened in 1936 by David Epstein. In 1945 the business was taken over by Epstein's younger brother, Alex, a trained pharmacist who had just returned from his service in the navy after World War II. Later, when their children were in school, Epstein's wife, Ann, came to work in the store. Mrs. Epstein recalls that the patrons, most of whom were black, "called my husband Doctor Aleck and they called me—it was all one word—MizAleck."

> In about 1955 my husband started to carry some spiritual products at the request of one of our very good customers. This lady used to travel to New York on the train to buy seven-day candles, and she asked if we would order them for her. What began with a few dozen candles developed into a tremendous portion of the store: roots, lodestones, little red flannel bags, incense, sprays, oils, powders, and books. I did the ordering. I bought from Lama Temple in Chicago, from a place in Miami called Sonny Boy, and from Original Products in New York.
>
> People came from all over North Carolina, South Carolina, and Georgia, and from all the Sea Islands around here. They didn't buy a little of this and a little of that—they bought by the box. Sometimes they would just clean us out. These people

were professionals, and they charged a great deal of money for their work. If they ever did anything "ugly" on behalf of their clients, they never told me, and I didn't want to know. The things we sold were meant to help people—for attraction, love, money-drawing, spirituality, purity, health—only good things. No, I didn't advise the customers. Unless it was a very simple question, I would suggest that they read a book.

There was only one time that anyone objected to what we were doing. We had a customer, a fine old black gentleman from out on one of the islands, who was a retired minister. He would come in every few weeks and spend five or six dollars, until one day his daughter came in with him and said she didn't want him wasting his money on these things. She had a representative from the Department of Social Services to visit us and look at what we were selling, but the social worker found nothing wrong with it, and the reverend chose to continue making his little purchases.

After my husband died in 1977, the store was bought by Barry Bloom. He asked me if I would stay on for a few months, just until he got the hang of ordering the spiritual products, and that stretched into three years. I wish now that I had let Barry have the drugstore and that I had kept the spiritual department myself. I enjoyed it and I miss it. I liked the customers and they liked me.

In 1987 Barry Bloom left Charleston and the Cut-Rate was purchased by Sam Rosen. Rosen recalled that during his ownership many people from outside the community sought out the Cut-Rate. Staff from the Medical University of Charleston sometimes came to visit, seeking information on how to treat patients who believed they had been "rooted." The drugstore was featured in several television documentaries on Low Country lore, and even appeared in a music video by the South Carolina rock group "Hootie and the Blowfish."[47]

■ ■ ■

Houston's famous Stanley Drug Company, 2718 Lyons Avenue, was opened by Stanley Hollenbeck in 1923 and operated by the Hollenbeck family until the late 1940s. The store has since had a series of proprietors. I sent one of my questionnaires to the present owners of Stanley Drug and received a hand-written note saying that "the family who owns the store is unwilling to release any information." Subsequent requests for interviews were ignored.

I visited Stanley Drug in November 1998. The original drugstore build-ing is no longer standing. The business, located on the outskirts of Hous-ton, now occupies a modern, corrugated-metal structure about the size of a small supermarket, set in the middle of a parking lot enclosed by chain-link fence and razor wire. Most of the building is devoted to manufacturing and warehouse space and to Stanley's large mail-order business. In the small retail outlet, products are neatly displayed on racks, busy clerks scurry around waiting on customers, and a cashier is stationed at the door. On the front wall, below a framed photograph of a clean-cut, middle-aged white man, is the hand-lettered inscription, "In Loving Memory, Wayne Ford." This, I was told, was the late brother of the present owner. The staff was not inclined to chat, and I got no further with this inquiry.

Even at nine in the morning, the store was crowded and several people were already lined up for consultations with the spiritual advisor. While waiting to pay for my purchases, I eavesdropped on two black women as they discussed the merits of various products and rituals. One, who owned a small business, was buying Van-Van Incense to "untie" her money. The other wanted to get rid of "this Mexican wench who's tryin' to take my man. Just watch me, I'm gonna send her right back to where she came from." When I tried to join the conversation they shut up like clams. The second woman scribbled her phone number on a slip of paper and handed it to the first. "Call me," she whispered. "I'm a worker. I can take care of that money problem for you."[48]

The Stanley Drug Company mail-order catalog is a modest produc-tion. The plain blue cover bears a drawing of a "Lucky Buddha" figure. The text is typewritten, illustrated with simple line drawings and reproduced on a photocopier. An introductory note to customers has an endearingly folksy quality that belies the no-nonsense atmosphere of the store: "We are get-ting new merchandise in all the time, so if you are looking for any item that you cannot find, please ask for it because we probably have it. You will notice that we do not specialize in 'kits' as many other stores do. We strongly believe that there is not a 'one size fits all' solution to your problems. We prepare your order to suit your individual needs."

Although other Houston spiritual stores cater to the Mexican Ameri-can community and the followers of Santería, Stanley's orientation has always been toward hoodoo. Stanley Drug Company carries roots and herbs, the largest inventory of animal parts offered by any mail-order house, and their own brand of baths, oils, perfumes, powders, sprinkling salts, yard dressing granules, and incense. Stanley's also sells Ouija boards, tarot decks, and crystal balls for fortune-telling; an extensive list of occult books in English and Spanish; seals from the *Sixth and Seventh Books of Moses;* holy cards and medals; and statues of the saints "for home, business, or car."

The most interesting offerings are what are categorized as "miscellaneous" products. Special lucky hands and tobies are offered for gambling and protection. The price varies, but the custom toby bag, "prepared just for you," sells for one hundred dollars. A number of old-fashioned drugstore and household items used in traditional charms are available at Stanley's: herbal essences and flavorings, asafetida gum, camphor, benzoin resin, copperas, alum, powdered sulfur, ammonia, saltpeter, turpentine, laundry bluing, and Red Devil lye. Nature Aids and Stimulants include Emotion Lotion, Erection Cream, Korean Ginseng Root Extract Tonic, Ramrods, and Spanish Fly Liquid.

■ ■ ■

Atlanta also has its hoodoo drugstore. Donald "Doc" Miller, a registered pharmacist with a degree from the University of Georgia, opened Miller's Dixie Hills Pharmacy in northwest Atlanta in 1960. In 1965 the business moved to 87 Broad Street S.W., in Atlanta's old predominantly black downtown business district, and the name changed to Miller's Rexall Drug Inc. Doc Miller's nephew, Richard, began helping in the Broad Street store when he was twelve years old, and the two now run the business together. I interviewed both Doc and Richard by telephone:

> This is still a functioning drugstore; we sell vitamins, over-the-counter remedies, and fill prescriptions. We didn't know anything about spiritual products when we started, but people kept asking for these things, so we learned. In the late 1960s we bought a few candles like Money Drawing and High John the Conqueror from Cohen's House of Bargains in Atlanta. Later we ordered wholesale from Lama Temple and E. Davis and from Hussey Distributors, an Atlanta company that marketed cleansers, brushes, roach powder, cosmetics, and other sundries, plus spiritual products, through house-to-house sales agents. We also carried the whole line of Valmor Products.

Mail-Order Doctors and Hoodoo Drugstores

Asked about their clientele, Richard Miller answered that most of their local customers are middle-aged black women who come from a hoodoo tradition. Miller Drug serves mail-order patrons all over the world. According to Richard, "A lot of them are white people who are involved in the New Age movement."

The cover of Miller's extensive mail-order catalog is illustrated with a hand holding a burning candle; green wax drips between the fingers. Inside the catalog is a work sheet for those in need of help. The customer is instructed to check any applicable problems on the "Trouble Sheet." The list includes a variety of health conditions, smoking, alcoholism, drug addiction, overweight, depression, "loss of nature," love, money, job, and legal troubles. For a fee of eighty dollars, Doc Miller will study the problem and pray for solutions, prepare and select the necessary ingredients, and mail the package with full instructions.

Miller's carries roots and herbs, manufactured spiritual products, seals, amulets, and books. The store does not sell holy cards or statues of the saints, and little of the merchandise is oriented toward Santería. Magic Bag Kits sell for eighteen dollars, and the more expensive Ritual Kits cost between twenty-five and forty dollars. Other interesting catalog items are "voodoo dolls" complete with a name tag, pins, a cord, and an instruction booklet, and a "dressed" miniature wooden coffin with instructions for the "dreaded black coffin spell." Miller's "house brand" is called Monkey Paw and is available as soap, spray, incense, candles, oil, and sprinkling sand. These items, according to Richard Miller, are purchased from a wholesaler and repackaged with the Monkey Paw label. One can also order a so-called Monkey Paw Lucky Hand for one hundred dollars— "Limited Supply . . . Extremely Rare." This, like other animal parts sold by spiritual suppliers, is actually the paw of a North American animal obtained as a by-product of the fur trade. The catalog states that "good luck can be obtained by stroking the palms of the hands and soles of the feet with the monkey's paw."

Like Stanley Drug in Houston, Miller's catalog lists some of the preservatives, cleansers, and other household items commonly used in traditional charm formulation. Miller's also carries herbal "dietary supplements" and old-fashioned patent medicines such as Beef Iron and Wine Tonic, Carter's Little Liver Pills, Red Foot Corn Remover, Father John's Cough Syrup, and Lydia Pinkham's Medicine for Women, and one can order the copper bracelets traditionally worn to prevent arthritis and rheumatism.[49]

■ ■ ■

The Corner Drugstore in Vicksburg, Mississippi, is owned by Joseph Gerache and currently managed by his son. The elder Gerache entered both the pharmacy and the spiritual business through family connections. His father was also a pharmacist who, like other early-twentieth-century drugstore owners in the South, sold botanicals and spiritual products. Joseph Gerache attended the School of Pharmacy at Loyola University in New Orleans from 1946 to 1950. During that time he became interested in the folklore of hoodoo, especially as it related to pharmacy, and visited old-time drugstores like New Orleans' Cracker Jack and Dixie. In 1959 Gerache bought the Corner Drugstore, a Vicksburg landmark that has been in existence since 1900, and began to carry manufactured spiritual products from Valmor and Sonny Boy.

Unlike some other druggists, Gerache did not give consultations or offer advice. People in need of spiritual aid would visit one of the local hoodoo doctors, who phoned in the "prescription" and sent the client to the drugstore to pick it up. Gerache particularly remembered "Charlie the Blind Man," a black hoodoo worker who was not only blind but was missing a leg and had a deformed arm. Charlie's prescriptions always began with a dose of calomel (mercurous chloride), a strong purgative that thoroughly cleansed the system and made the client feel deathly ill. The calomel was followed by rituals involving various baths, powders, oils, the burning of candles, and recitation of prayers. According to Gerache, by the time the disagreeable effects of the calomel had worn off, the client's physical and mental state was so much improved that he or she thought the charm had done the work. Charlie the Blind Man died in the 1960s, and other less spectacular workers have taken his place.

I visited the Corner Drugstore in May 1997. There is nothing to suggest the hoodoo drugstore here. It is a clean, modern pharmacy, the only distinguishing feature of which is Gerache's collection of antique medicine containers and, in the middle of the aisle, a "bottle tree" (once a feature of many rural southern yards, created by sticking bottles, preferably blue ones, on the bare limbs of a tree to keep away evil spirits).[50] The spiritual merchandise is in a back room. As I observed while waiting for Mr. Gerache, customers enter the store, whisper to the salesclerk that they need to visit the "chemical room," select the needed merchandise, and emerge with a brown bag. According to Gerache, they prefer the privacy afforded by this system.[51] Other such drugstores in southern cities—Finley's in Mobile; Harmon's in Jackson, Mississippi; and Champion's in Memphis—openly display the spiritual products.[52]

■ ■ ■

Just as there were African American spiritual entrepreneurs in northern cities, there were also white-owned hoodoo drugstores. Nettie Seligmann, now retired and in her nineties, tells a typical story of entry into the spiritual products business in Philadelphia. Mrs. Seligmann's late husband, Harry, was a registered pharmacist. In 1918 the Seligmanns opened a drugstore in the South Street neighborhood, Philadelphia's black business district. They noticed that their customers, newly arrived from the South, frequently asked for various powders and oils. At first Mr. Seligmann had no idea what they meant, but his interest was aroused, and he began to read occult texts and spell books. Soon he was making spiritual products in the back room, designing the labels (see fig. 10), and providing the customers with what they wanted.

In 1929 the Seligmanns purchased a building at 1238 South Street. "It was dirt cheap. We had nothing, but we were able to afford it." They opened Harry's Occult Shop, a store devoted exclusively to spiritual products. They sold occult books, their own line of products, and roots and herbs that were brought in from New Jersey by people who grew or gathered them in the wild. According to Nettie Seligmann, her husband was very scrupulous about using only the purest ingredients, and he sincerely believed that his charm preparations could help people. He enjoyed advising the customers about their problems.

In 1945 the Seligmanns sold Harry's Occult Shop to Mr. Seligmann's brother and moved to Los Angeles. They purchased a small factory, Cross Candle Company, in the South Central neighborhood. The Seligmanns began to import religious statues and medals from Italy and continued the manufacture of their own line of spiritual products. Mrs. Seligmann operated the wholesale business and her husband ran a nearby retail store, also called Harry's Occult Shop. Their customers were a mix of southern blacks who had recently migrated to Los Angeles and priests and nuns from a nearby Catholic church, who bought candles, medals, statues, incense, and oils. The Los Angeles branch of Harry's Occult Shop closed in 1962 when Harry Seligmann died; Nettie Seligmann continued to run the factory, operating the wholesale business and selling retail to local customers.

Cross Candle was destroyed by fire during the Watts riots of 1968. According to Mrs. Seligmann, the smell of incense filled the air for blocks. "The firemen told me it was the nicest fire they'd ever smelled." Mrs. Seligmann insisted that Cross Candle was not the target of the protesters.

"They didn't burn my store deliberately; they loved my store. They were going after the Western Auto next door." Nettie Seligmann never reopened Cross Candle, but continued to operate a small business from her home until she retired completely.[53]

Meanwhile, the original Harry's Occult Shop in Philadelphia lives on, looking much as it did in the days of Harry and Nettie Seligmann. The sign in the window reads,

SPIRITUAL AND OCCULT SUPPLIES
SINCE 1918 OUR AIM IS TO HELP
LIGHT A TORCH FOR THE GOOD
CROSS SWORDS AGAINST EVIL
Essential Oils, Incense
Candles, Roots, Talismans
Herbs, Religious Articles

The store is now owned by Harry Seligmann's nephew, James Seligmann. "Mr. Jim" is seldom in the store, which is run by a manager and a large multiracial staff. On the morning of my visit in May 1998, I was amazed to see eight people working in such a small establishment—the manager, two clerks, a cashier, a reader, and several people in the back room filling orders and mixing baths, powders, oils, and incense. The interior resembles an old-fashioned drugstore, with ornate wooden cabinets. Over the counter hangs a sign, "We Aim to Help." The shelves hold jars of roots and herbs, minerals, and Harry's own line of products with attractive, 1920s-style labels (fig. 10). I bought several items. The bottle of Seven Mystics Fire incense contains layers of pink, yellow, blue, rose, brown, green, and black powder. When I expressed worry about disturbing the layers while carry-ing it home, the young African American clerk assured me that it had been very tightly packed by hand and that "you could even shake it and you wouldn't mess it up." She instructed me to sprinkle the Love Powder in my dresser drawers and on my body to attract a partner, and rub the Lucky Mojo Powder on my hands to draw money.[54]

CHAPTER 7

Candle Shops, Botánicas, Yerberías, and Web Sites

The earliest spiritual entrepreneurs were oriented toward African American magical beliefs and catered primarily to black customers. Today's retailers may offer the accoutrements of hoodoo, Santería, Palo, Espiritismo, Mexican curanderismo and brujería, folk Catholicism, or some combination of these traditions, depending on the ethnicity and magico-religious tradition of the owner and the demographics of the locality. As noted in chapter 2, few stores carry ritual items specifically associated with Haitian Vodou.

I found that the owners of spiritual stores may be black, brown, or white, American-born or foreign-born, Christians, Jews, or followers of the African-based religions. Some of the old-time hoodoo-oriented candle shops and religious stores are owned by African Americans and others are white owned. The white proprietor and his or her family, assisted by black employees, often work in the store and are very knowledgeable about the products and the belief system of the customers. In other cases, the white owner is seldom present, leaving the daily operation to an African American manager and clerks who may or may not be traditional practitioners. Such stores are sometimes acquired by an African American employee or friend of the family when the white owner retires or dies. Botánicas are usually owned by people from Latin America or the Caribbean who are followers of one of the African-based religions; some are initiated priests or priestesses. I have encountered Cuban, Puerto Rican, Dominican, Salvadoran, Columbian, Guatemalan, Haitian, and Brazilian botánica owners. Yerberías are owned by Mexicans or Mexican Americans who are familiar with the traditions of curanderismo and brujería. Since the mid-1990s retailers have also marketed their wares via the World Wide Web.

Some candle shops, botánicas, and yerberías are highly profitable, but many of these establishments appear to be modest affairs. As we will see in the following examples, many store owners are dedicated to their work and are not in business strictly to make money. I felt that questioning proprietors about their income was inexcusably intrusive; but, according to an informant, who for obvious reasons I will not identify, a well-run store with a good customer base can gross between 70 and 90 percent profit before expenses for stock, rent, utilities, insurance, salaries, and taxes. The price charged for ritual supplies and spiritual products varies considerably from store to store, indicating that some retailers are taking a much higher markup than others. In a few stores, the merchandise had no price tag, and I suspected that I was being asked to pay more because I was perceived as an outsider.

Retail stores, mail-order businesses, and even the operators of web sites not only sell merchandise but also provide consultations and spiritual "work" in person or by telephone. In some cases, a high percentage of the store's income is derived from these services. In stores that are owned by spiritual professionals, the proprietor often offers consultation or divination, followed by the requisite rituals, charm formulation, and advice for future action. Other stores employ "readers" or at least display the business cards of community members who provide this assistance.

During the years 1993 to 2000 I observed the gender and ethnicity of spiritual store customers and asked store owners about their clientele. I found that far more women than men buy from such stores. Not surprisingly, the candle shops and religious stores were patronized primarily by African Americans, and the Santería-oriented stores were most often frequented by Latinos who serve the orichas. The education level and economic status of these customers was not easily identified, but they appeared to be poor or working-class people. Some store owners told me that many of their customers are "middle-class white professionals who need help just like everybody else," and white Americans who follow the African-based religions certainly buy their supplies in botánicas. But with the exception of the "tourist voodoo" outlets in New Orleans' French Quarter and on Beale Street in Memphis, I seldom encountered another white shopper in my six years of frequenting spiritual stores. These buyers, perhaps fearful of encountering hostility or crime in the neighborhoods where such stores are often located, may be ordering by mail or by Internet.

There are hundreds, maybe even thousands, of spiritual stores in the United States, located in cities and small towns with large African American or Latino populations. The number and orientation of these merchants in any given locale depends primarily on demographics, but factors such as community attitudes, police interference, and gentrification might explain why some otherwise promising areas have few spiritual stores. I visited approximately sixty retail businesses in New Orleans, Memphis, Vicksburg, Jacksonville, Miami, Savannah, Charleston, Columbia (South Carolina), the Washington, D.C., area (including suburban Maryland and Virginia), Baltimore, Philadelphia, New York, Houston, Phoenix, and Los Angeles. I usually found these shops by looking under "religious goods" or "candles" in the yellow pages of the telephone directory. Candle shops, botánicas, and yerberías are listed along with the Christian bookstores, church supply houses, Hebrew gift shops, and New Age boutiques—the purveyors of Bibles and prayer books, choir robes and ecclesiastical vestments, rosaries and holy cards, yarmulkes and menorahs, crystals and herbal essences. I also learned of spiritual stores through the recommendations of friends, other store owners, and manufacturers. Because these stores tend to cluster together in certain neighborhoods, a trip to one store often led to the discovery of several others nearby.

I offer here a sampling of the stores that I visited in various American cities. I have selected examples that represent the variety of spiritual merchants in the South, the northern industrial cities, and on the West Coast. These businesses serve many different spiritual traditions: some are oriented toward hoodoo, some toward the many permutations of Santería, and some toward the Mexican belief systems. Their owners are of many different ethnic groups and religious persuasions. The stores were also, of necessity, chosen on the basis of the proprietor's willingness to be interviewed and photographed. Each one is unique; each has its own personality.

Religious Stores and Candle Shops

The Keystone Lucky Store, Jacksonville, Florida

Jacksonville, a north Florida coastal city with a large black population, is more related to the Georgia/South Carolina Low Country than to the Latino culture of South Florida. When I visited in 1998, Jacksonville had only one botánica. Hoodoo stores flourish on Broad Street, the main thoroughfare of Jacksonville's old black business district. The white-owned Eureka Novelty Store, a purveyor of herbs and spiritual products documented by the Florida Writers' Project, was in business from 1936 to 1941 at 409 Broad.[1] A more recent arrival, the Starlite, is located a few blocks up the street. The Keystone Lucky Store opened in 1940 and is still in business.

The Keystone, located in a Spanish-style stucco building at 303 Broad Street, advertises itself as "the oldest store of its kind in Jacksonville." Originally called Keystone High Hat Toilet Preparations, this business may have had some relation to Keystone Laboratories of Memphis. Hyatt's Jacksonville informant, "Agent for Curios," said that she worked for "the Keystone . . . and also the Lucky Heart, and then I've recently taken up the High Hat . . . all in Memphis, Tennessee, and probably [all] in the same building."[2] By 1942 the name had changed to Keystone Lucky Store. The Keystone passed through several white owners, the last being Seymour Boardman. Vernon Sands, a former chauffeur who was originally from the Bahamas, went to work for Boardman at the Keystone and inherited the store when Boardman died in the 1970s. Sands himself died in 1992, and in 1997 his daughters asked Deloris Kay, a longtime friend and neighbor, to take over the business. A photograph of Sands is still

Fig. 26. Vernon Sands at the Keystone Lucky Store, Jacksonville, Florida, May 13, 1983. Products from Lama Temple and E. Davis are displayed on the counter. Photograph copyright 1998 *Florida Times-Union*/Florida Publishing Company, used by permission.

taped to the cash register, along with the motto "Credit makes enemies; Let's stay friends."

I visited the Keystone on a very hot summer day in 1998. The square room was dimly lit. This, explained Deloris Kay, was because some of the lights were burnt out, not because she was trying to create a spooky atmosphere. Shelves and display cases lined the walls. There were the usual washes, sprays, and glass-encased candles from Indio Products, Vandi, and E. Davis, but I was most attracted to some oils, perfumes, and powders, apparently decades old, with wonderful graphics but no manufacturer's name on their labels. I eagerly picked out one of each and set them aside on the counter.

The back wall of the store is occupied by a large, multitiered altar covered with candles, crystals, and statues of the saints. According to Ms. Kay, "all those things are for energy and power." They are placed there "to attract positive vibrations to the store," and do not represent offerings or ritual work done on behalf of clients. "Mr. Sands used to set candles for the customers, but I'm afraid of starting a fire." Deloris Kay does not give spiritual advice, but a reader is available on Saturdays. Consultations are held in a back storeroom, where two chairs and a large desk, covered with the multicolored drippings from dozens of candles, are wedged between cartons of merchandise. The reader "might recommend that [the client] burn a candle or incense, or get some oil and anoint with it, or use a bath, but we don't do any type of hexing or voodooing. The people come in, and if we have what they want, we sell it to them." Asked about the race of her customers, Deloris Kay replied that "most are black, but we have a mixture—black, white, Spanish, and some Africans."

When I paid for my stash of vintage spiritual products, Ms. Kay counted out my change and "dressed" one of the dollar bills with a strong perfume. The scent permeated my handbag for days.[3]

Lady Dale's Curio Shop/Ray's New Age Curios, Philadelphia

Philadelphia attracted many African American migrants from the South. Two old-time hoodoo-oriented stores, Lady Dale's and Harry's Occult Shop (Harry's is discussed in chapter 6), existed within a block of each other on South Street, once a thriving center of black- and Jewish-owned businesses. More recently, the city has become home to a large Puerto Rican community, and several botánicas are now located in the Latino neighborhood.

Lady Dale's Curio Shop, at 1356 South Street, was opened in 1945 by Alex Silverberg. The Silverberg family owned extensive property on South

Street. The building that became Lady Dale's was formerly Samuel Silverberg's Meat Market; Alex Silverberg's parents lived upstairs and Alex grew up in the building. The Silverbergs also operated a magazine wholesale and distribution business, through which Alex Silverberg became aware of the market for books of dream interpretation and lucky numbers. He began to publish dream books, including *The Lady Dale Diary, Lucky Thirteen, Policy Pete's, Rajah Rabo's, The National Dream Book,* and *The Original Lucky Dream Book.*

The inspiration for entering the spiritual business came from his association with Joe Kay, owner of Dorene Publishing and the Fulton Religious Store in Brooklyn, to whom he furnished dream books. Alex Silverberg opened Lady Dale's—named for his young daughter—as a retail shop for his wife, Lily. The Silverbergs used *Culpepper's Herbal* as a resource on roots and herbs, and books like *Marie Laveau's Old and New Black and White Magic* and Henri Gamache's *Master Book of Candle Burning* (both published by Joe Kay) for information on charms, rituals, and spiritual products. Customers contributed traditions handed down in their families, and, Dale Silverberg told me, "my parents probably invented some things, too." Because of his chemistry background, Mr. Silverberg was able to formulate the baths, oils, and powders required by the customers. Mr. and Mrs. Silverberg both worked in the store, and when their daughter, Dale, was old enough, she also worked there on Saturdays and during school vacations.

Lady Dale's was more than just a store. It also functioned as a social service agency for the regular customers, who were virtually all black, more women than men. According to Dale Silverberg, "My mother and father loved people. They always encouraged them to develop, to get their education." Dale herself once intervened in a workman's compensation case for a customer—"It had been dragging on for years; the woman was being jerked around by the system. I called her lawyer, I called a judge that I know, and she finally got her money." The Silverbergs did not like to prescribe herbs for medicinal purposes, and they urged customers with medical problems to see a doctor.

"Jinx removal was big in the old days; people were always imagining that their enemies had 'put something on them.'" For protection, Lady Dale's sold a charcoal-based powder called Scat-Away, which was to be sprinkled around the front steps of the house. Women sought help with recalcitrant spouses and lovers. The usual prescription was the daily use of a bath preparation, followed by an oil to be rubbed on the palms of the hands and soles of the feet. Male customers came in for Red Rooster pills and ginseng to increase their sexual potency. Gamblers bought Lady Dale's Most Powerful Money Drawing Oil, a mixture of herbs, oil, water, and glitter. Alex Silverberg, because of his interest in the kabbalah and Hebrew mysticism, was drawn to the *Sixth and Seventh Books of Moses* and sold the associated seals, parchment paper, and Dove's Blood Ink.

Mr. Silverberg made mojo bags for clients, and later his wife started making "power pouches," using semiprecious stones and crystals. Candle burning was popular with Lady Dale's customers. For those who were reluctant to light candles at home, the Silverbergs had an altar in the store where a seven-day candle could be left to burn continuously. Inspired by the instructions in *The Master Book of Candle Burning*, candles of various colors and shapes—man, woman, devil, skull, or cross—symbolizing the intention of the client, were assembled in an aluminum tray, placed on the altar, and burned.[4]

In the 1980s and 1990s, the focus of customers' intentions shifted from jinx removal, love problems, gambling, and "loss of nature" to more grim concerns. Distraught mothers and grandmothers came for help with young family members awaiting trial or already in prison for drug-related crimes. Instead of Scat-Away, Attraction Bath, You-and-Me Lovers' Oil, Money Drawing Perfume, and Red Rooster Pills, they asked for court-case products.

After the death of Lily Silverberg in 1992 and Alex Silverberg in 1994, ownership of Lady Dale's passed to their daughter, Dale. Because she was involved in her own retail business, day-to-day operation of the store was left to longtime employees Ray Minton and Albert Hampton. Lady Dale's closed in 1996. The original store, now vacant, still bears the sign "Lady Dale's Curio Shop, Complete Line of Traditional and New Age Products, Quartz, and Affordable Gems." Ray Minton has opened his own business, Ray's New Age Curio Shop, next door at 1358 South Street. He is assisted by his old friend Albert, now semiretired. I visited the store in the spring of 1998.

Ray, a stocky, mustached, ponytailed white man in his mid-forties, and Albert, a trim, wiry black man in his late fifties, both began work for Alex Silverberg in the 1970s as truck drivers in Silverberg's magazine and dream book business. They later became essential employees at Lady Dale's. They kept the inventory, ordered supplies, formulated products, and served customers. Albert also ran errands and delivered products and dream books to other stores. "I was [Silverberg's] right-hand man. I picked him up every morning and drove him home after work." Ray and Albert had nothing but

Fig. 27. Ray Minton and Albert Hampton at Ray's New Age Curios, Philadelphia, May 29, 1998.

praise for Alex Silverberg: "He was a sweetheart . . . if he liked you, he would give you anything in the world he had. He could be hard on the customers, though; he'd tell 'em off, but they came back. He sold them what he thought was good for them, and he'd always say, 'If you don't believe in it, don't spend your money.'" A framed photograph of Alex Silverberg, a large man with a kindly, intelligent face, hangs behind the counter.

Ray and Albert make baths, oils, powders, and perfumes in a small back room; these are sold under the brand name Ray's New Age Curios. The store also carries packaged roots and herbs, dream books, statues of saints, talismans, and spiritual products from other manufacturers. Lady Dale's tradition of burning candles for customers has continued. In the back of the store is a restaurant stove hood beneath which many candles are burning. On top of this hood I noticed a stack of aluminum trays, evidently for the making of candle assemblages. A spiritual advisor is available on Friday and Saturday afternoons. As I was leaving the store at about 11:00 A.M. on a Friday, several black women had already arrived for their readings. Each was handed a paper cutout of a hand with a number written on it. These were not lucky hand charms as I at first thought, but slips to indicate the customer's position in line. "Yeah, it's about to get real crowded in here," remarked Ray.[5]

Eye of the Cat, Columbia, South Carolina

Columbia, the state capital and home of the University of South Carolina, seems an unlikely venue for an old-time candle shop. This middle-sized city, located in the center of the state, bears little resemblance to coastal Charleston, Beaufort, and Savannah with their traditional rootwork associations. And yet Columbia's Rosewood Avenue, a somewhat seedy strip-commercial thoroughfare, has not one but two purveyors of spiritual products. In addition to Eye of the Cat, there is the Voodoo Garage, a body-piercing parlor that, as a sideline, carries a selection of oils, powders, incense, spell kits, and occult books.

Eye of the Cat, at 1366 Rosewood Avenue, is a one-story cement-block building, possibly a former grocery store, surrounded by a parking lot. A large sign in front, emblazoned with a red Halloween-style cat, announces "Eye of the Cat—Pop's Place—Candles, Oils, Incense, Herbs, Beer, Wine, Hot Dogs." A hand-lettered notice on the plate-glass window advertises "Readings $20.00, Consultations $15.00." On the day of my visit, several men loitered outside, drinking out of bottles hidden in brown paper bags. The interior of the store has a cooler for beer and soft drinks, a small selection of wine and snacks, and shelf after shelf of packaged spiritual products, including an inordinate number of black candles. A back corner, apparently the "laboratory," is filled with large bottles of oils and fragrances and jars of dried herbs. My attention was particularly drawn to two cardboard boxes of dirt: one contained lumps of the red clay soil typically found in the southern midlands, the other a rich black loam.

The proprietor, Thomas "Pop" Williams, agreed to talk to me in his consultation room, which contains a large easy chair, a little table on which a deck of cards is placed, and a straight-backed chair for the client. The walls are hung with pictures of his family—his "sixteen head of children," as he described them. Williams is a middle-aged, powerfully built, dark-skinned man with a dazzling smile. He was plainly dressed in khaki pants, a plaid flannel shirt, and a ball cap; his hands were adorned with a number of elaborate rings. He was vague about his entry into the spiritual business and the means by which he had acquired his powers, simply stating that about fourteen years ago he had "hooked up with some other people he knew and tried to make a go at it." The presence of what appeared to be the raw ingredients of charm formulation in the "laboratory" corner prompted me to ask Williams if he made things for his clients. Again, the answer was evasive: "No, I just sell them the merchandise. The old folks, the ones who

Fig. 28. Thomas "Pop" Williams at Eye of the Cat, Columbia, South Carolina, March 15, 1999.

know what to look for, they still go out in the woods and get their own herbs. They use salt, pepper, sugar, vinegar, eggs, rice—even grits. I use the products—not that I don't know how to use those other things, but I just don't go through all that."

I inquired about the boxes of dirt in the outer room. "That's grave-yard dirt. See, you got three toppings [levels], the first, the second, and the last—the real nitty-gritty." Although Williams did not elaborate further, I assume that the black soil is the first "topping," the red clay is the second, and that the "nitty gritty" is the dead body itself. "Yeah," he answered, "I go out in the graveyard and dig for it. If you gonna use it you gotta go get it." Williams gave a wicked chuckle when I asked if he paid the spirits for the dirt by pouring a drink of whiskey into the hole or leaving a silver dime or a portion of rice:

> I don't think too many root doctors are gonna go through explainin' that part. There's a little secret to everything. It's just like bakin' a cake. You'll say "how come my cake don't turn out like yours?" and it's because I didn't tell you all the ingredients. The main trick is, you have to deal with a spirit

who's willing to communicate with you. No matter how bad they been or how much you pay them, you still have to go from one grave to the next until you find the right one. Some just won't communicate.

While Williams acknowledges that he works with the dead, he warned against calling upon the Devil for assistance: "Lucifer will give you the answer for most everything you want to know, if it's wrong, but he ain't gonna give you no right answer." His ability to see into the minds of others, he said, came to him as he was playing with a deck of cards—"I always had to have 'em in my hands." I asked what sort of work he does for his clients. "People come to me for any little thing that strikes their mind, anything that's botherin' them. They want the pressure off 'em."
As I was gathering my camera and tape recorder to leave, Williams was already busy with the next customer, a heavy-set black woman who, I noticed with surprise, was wearing the necklaces of the orichas. He probed her desires and intentions, and I overheard her whispered answer: "I just want my man to come back."[6]

Botánicas

Botánica Chicas-Rendón, New York

I discovered a high concentration of botánicas in New York's Spanish Harlem, a neighborhood populated by Puerto Ricans, Cubans, and others from the Caribbean and Central and South America. In the area from 103rd Street to 116th Street between First and Fifth Avenues, there is a botánica on practically every block.

Chicas-Rendón was the first botánica in New York City, and possibly the first in the United States. Like many of the businesses discussed in chapter 6, this store was established by a pharmacist. When Alberto Rendón first came to New York from Guatemala, he found employment at a drugstore in what was then called East Harlem. The neighborhood was at that time populated by southern blacks and West Indians, and Rendón noticed that these people came to the pharmacy looking for herbal remedies, baths, oils, powders, and the like. In 1921 he decided to open his own shop, the West Indies Botanical Garden, at 74 East 114th Street. In a small laboratory in the back, he formulated herbal preparations. He also arranged to have daily shipments of fresh plants flown in from Puerto Rico. His business was immediately successful.

Candle Shops, Botánicas, Yerberías, and Web Sites

Beginning in the 1920s and accelerating in the early 1940s, Puerto Ricans settled in the neighborhood, which became known as Spanish Harlem or *El Barrio* (the neighborhood). The new Spanish-speaking customers shortened the store's name from West Indies Botanical Garden to Botánica. The focus of the shop shifted from African American hoodoo and West Indian obeah to Espiritismo. As more Cubans came into Spanish Harlem, Rendón began to carry items for Santería. In 1945, Alberto Rendón's nephew, Otto Chicas, arrived in New York to work with his uncle, and the store was renamed Botánica Chicas-Rendón. When Rendón died in the late 1970s, Chicas took over ownership of the store.

Botánica Chicas-Rendón now occupies two buildings at 56 and 60 East 116th Street. At number 60, the main store, life-sized statues of the saints are located directly inside the door; St. Barbara, St. Lazarus, and Our

Fig. 29. Statue of Santa Barbara/Changó, Botánica Chicas-Rendón, New York, October 3, 1994.

Fig. 30. Otto Chicas at Botánica Chicas-Rendón, July 9, 1998.

Lady of Charity, representing Changó, Babalú Ayé, and Ochún, are draped with satin capes and adorned with metal crowns, necklaces, and artificial flowers. On the floor in front of the saints is a basin for offerings.

Large metal cans and wooden crates of dried plants occupy the center aisle, and on the shelves are white plastic containers of smaller herbs and bottles and packets of herbal preparations. Atop a refrigerator case containing fresh herbs and the succulent leaves of aloes is a homemade wire cage full of cockatoos and parakeets. Next door at *La Casa de Velas* (House of Candles) is a life-sized statue of the Guatemalan folk saint Simón Maximón. The figure is dressed in actual clothes—a dark suit, white shirt, tie, and wide-brimmed hat; in his mouth is a real cigar. The courteous staff, twittering birds, fragrant herbs, statues of the saints, and the air and sunlight streaming through the open doors make both stores uncommonly pleasant.

I first visited Botánica Chicas-Rendón in 1994 and returned in 1998. On my second trip, Mr. Chicas himself was there and graciously showed me around, answered my questions, and gave me a copy of his book on San Simón. I learned that the fresh and dried herbs are imported daily from Central America and the Caribbean. The baths, oils, perfumes, and incense are made on the premises, and no products from other manufacturers are sold. I was delighted to see that some of the beautiful labels designed by

Manuel Quiles in the 1950s are still in use. The business is strictly retail, with no mail order. In addition to herbs and products, Chicas-Rendón sells a full range of ritual supplies for Santería. Store personnel were quick to say that Chicas-Rendón carries nothing for "voodoo." It was unclear whether this term was being used to denote sorcery or the Haitian religion.[7]

Seven Powers Garden Temple Store, Los Angeles

Los Angeles, like New York, has at least a hundred botánicas. The Seven Powers Garden Temple Store is located at 5311 South Broadway in South Central Los Angeles, a mixed African American and Latino neighborhood. Said to be the oldest botánica in Los Angeles, the Seven Powers Garden was founded by Ray Pizzarro. Pizzarro was born in Puerto Rico, attended high school in New York, and graduated from the University of Puerto Rico. He enlisted in the navy during World War II and served at the Brooklyn Navy Yard. In 1947 he joined the Billy Rose Shows as a dancer, performed on Broadway, and toured the United States and Canada with his own dance team, Ray and Charmaine.

Fig. 31. Ray Pizzarro at Botánica Seven Powers, Los Angeles, April 16, 1997.

Pizzarro moved to Los Angeles in 1956. There he undertook the study of religion, astrology, and spiritualism, and was ordained a minister of the Universal Church of the Master and the *Templo de Luz y Verdad* (Temple of Light and Truth). All who know him refer to him as "Reverend" Pizzarro. In 1958 he was initiated as an oloricha in Guanabacoa, Cuba, where he received Yemayá as his ruling oricha. Consultation of the oracle of Ifá at the time of his initiation determined that, rather than serving individual clients, Pizzarro was to "extend the doctrine of Santería to the people in general, as a ministry, and that is why I created the Seven Powers Garden Temple in 1959." In 1980 he underwent a further initiation and received the oricha Ochún.

Between 1959 and 1965 Reverend Pizzarro was the featured attraction and producer of a television show, "You and the Stars," on KLXA Channel 40, Hollywood, and also hosted the Miguelito Valdes Show, which was carried by television stations in Panama and Colombia as well as Los Angeles, New York, and Miami.

In New York, Pizzarro had been friendly with Emanuel Davis, owner of the E. Davis Company, a major manufacturer of spiritual products. After moving to Los Angeles, Pizzarro served as the West Coast sales representative for the company until Davis's death. Pizzarro explained in a letter: "I was [Emanuel Davis's] advisor and mentor. . . . He made me his representative for Los Angeles, Arizona, and New Mexico plus decided to sponsor my TV show. To my misfortune, on one of his trips to see me on business he decided to go to Hawaii and as he returned, he suddenly died of a heart attack. Then his son that was in college didn't want to have nothing to do with the business, and his wife never interfere, so they appoint the son-in-law who never like my personality and took everything away from me."

Martin Mayer, the owner of Indio Products in Los Angeles, took me to Ray Pizzarro's Seven Powers Garden in April 1997. Pizzarro is now in his late seventies, a strong, vigorous man with copper-colored skin and close-cropped white hair. He attributed his rapid recovery from a recent heart attack to herbal medicines and positive attitude. While Mayer and Reverend Pizzarro swapped trade secrets and regaled each other with tales of the spiritual products business, I explored the store, which has the look of a museum. The front display windows and the counters of the tiny salesroom are piled with statues of the saints, religious pictures, glass-encased candles, artificial flowers, dolls, stuffed animals, and the plaster bust of an Indian wearing a mariachi hat. The walls are covered from floor to ceiling with greeting cards, newspaper clippings, old calendars, and pictures of movie stars. Above the counter is a photograph of Reverend Pizzarro posing with Ronald Reagan and George Bush, a souvenir of his service on the Reagan Task Force of the Republican National Committee. Of most interest to me were the rows of bottles, jars, and incense tins that lined the shelves. Many of these were manufactured by the long-defunct Oracle Laboratories in Long Island City, New York. When I attempted to pay for the large accumulation that I had stacked on the counter, Reverend Pizzarro waved me aside: "Just put something in the donation box."[8]

Botánica Solano, New Orleans

I was disappointed to find that, in the city designated by Zora Neale Hurston as the "Hoodoo Capital of America," there have been no genuine hoodoo stores since the demise of South Rampart Street's old-time spiritual merchants. Island of Salvation, the F & F, Divine Light, and Botánica Solano serve customers of all races and religious persuasions. Several French Quarter shops specialize in "tourist voodoo" souvenirs.

Botánica Solano was owned by Cuban-born Frank Rodriguez until his death in late 1998. He was known by most people simply as "Solano," and by his close friends as "Papa Frank." Rodriguez was a short, stocky man with white hair and a flowing beard who was never without a cigar in his hand. Although he had been in the United States for more than forty years, he retained a heavy Cuban accent. Rodriguez explained that his knowledge of Santería came from his grandfather, who was both a babalawo and a master Freemason. "I was supposed to receive Eleguá, but he say to me that I will never be able to leave Cuba—Eleguá don't like to travel—and I want to come to the U.S." He immigrated to Miami in 1955, where he became a devotee of Ochún—"She'll go anywhere with you." Because of the high cost of initiation, Rodriguez never became a priest of Santería.

Frank Rodriguez moved to New Orleans in 1969, where he worked as a waiter before following the command of Ochún to open a botánica in 1972. Botánica Solano is located at 1626 Elysian Fields in a predominately black neighborhood below the French Quarter. The store occupies one side of a typical New Orleans double shotgun house; the other side has been opened up and equipped with a sliding garage door. The Rodriguez family lives in the back.

I visited Botánica Solano on several occasions when Frank Rodriguez was alive. Near the front of the store, three plastic ducks floated in a basin surrounded by three glasses of water, a devotion to the *egun* (ancestral spirits). In the corner was a shrine to Babalú Ayé, the god of disease and healing, represented by a statue of St. Lazarus. A shrine to Ochún, symbolized by a small statue of Our Lady of Charity (*La Virgen de la Caridad de Cobre*) dressed in a gold and white robe, resided on a high shelf behind the counter. An offering of yellow apples (Ochún's preferred color) had been placed before the saint. The store displayed the necklaces of the orichas and other accoutrements of Santería, plus the usual manufactured spiritual products. These were covered with dust and appeared to have been there for years. According to Rodriguez, "it makes them more strong when they get old like that." Most of the botánica's business consisted of the charms and remedies that Rodriguez formulated in his "laboratory" in the back of the shop, which was filled with bottles of essential oils and jars of herbs.

Frank Rodriguez had adopted the New Orleans/Sicilian custom of the St. Joseph's altar and community feast. St. Joseph has no counterpart among the orichas, although he is popular with New Orleanians as the

Fig. 32. Frank Rodriguez in his "laboratory," Botánica Solano, New Orleans, March 16, 1998.

patron of laborers and guardian of the family and the home. On the day of my first visit to Botánica Solano in 1995, the shop was officially closed while Rodriguez prepared for this event. He kindly let me in and stopped his work to answer questions. As I left, he handed me a printed invitation to his St. Joseph's observance for "friends and customers of Botánica Solano."

On the Eve of St. Joseph I returned for the celebration, which was held in the converted left side of the double house. The garage door was open, and the space was brightly lit. People sat on benches along the wall and spilled out onto the sidewalk. Most of the guests were African Americans from the neighborhood, plus some Latinos and a few interested white Americans. An elderly black lady with whom I was chatting pointed out several reverend mothers from the Spiritual churches among the participants. The altar was decorated with a statue of St. Joseph, before which were placed baskets of fruit and vegetables and vases of flowers, rather like the offerings made to the orichas and the egun. It was simple compared to the large and elaborate structures erected by the Sicilian community, which are laden with candles, statues, bottles of wine, traditional pasta dishes, baked fish, cakes, cookies, and special St. Joseph's breads, as well as fresh fruits and vegetables, which often fill an entire room.[9] Visitors to Solano's celebration pinned offerings of money, mostly one-dollar bills, to the yellow cloth drapery behind the altar. After the Catholic priest had completed the blessing, we were invited to take something from the altar for good luck. This again differs from the Sicilian altars, where visitors are given blessed fava beans for luck and bread to avert storms.

The meal, consisting of boiled crawfish, potato salad, dainty finger sandwiches on white bread, noodle casserole, bread pudding, beer, soft drinks, and an assortment of cakes and pies, was served on a long buffet table to the side of the altar. Rodriguez, his Polish-born wife, Sophie, and their teenaged son bustled around, replenishing the food and serving guests. This occasion was strictly a neighborhood celebration honoring a Roman Catholic saint and was completely devoid of Santería overtones.[10]

I returned to Botánica Solano in October 1998 to give Mr. Rodriguez the photographs I had taken on an earlier visit. He shook his head when he saw that I had portrayed him with his ever-present cigar. "I'm all finished with those—the doctor says I can't have them no more." I was saddened to learn that Frank Rodriguez died of lung cancer a few months later. A friend who visited the botánica on the day before his death found Mrs. Rodriguez trying to run the store. "The poor lady didn't know anything about it. She kept calling Solano at the hospital every few minutes to ask him questions.

Because she recognized me, she let me talk to him directly. He told me where all the ingredients were and how to mix them." Botánica Solano has been closed since Rodriguez's death, and its fate is uncertain.[11]

Botánica San Miguel, Silver Spring, Maryland

The Washington, D.C., area has a large black population, many of whom are affluent, well-educated professionals; a core of well-to-do whites; and many Central and South American immigrants. The city has one candle shop and at least seven botánicas. These are not clustered in any one locale; four are found in the predominantly Latin American neighborhoods called Adams-Morgan and Mount Pleasant, and others are scattered throughout the surrounding suburbs of Maryland and Virginia.

Botánica San Miguel is located at 8425 Georgia Avenue, above a nail-sculpting salon and across from a high-rise office building, in the Washington suburb of Silver Spring, Maryland. The shop was opened by Catalina de Guzman, who is originally from the Dominican Republic, when she retired from her job as a custodial worker for the local telephone company in 1994. She is assisted by her husband, also retired from the telephone company.

At least a dozen large statues are arranged in front of the windows, and offerings of candles, fruit, and money are placed in front of the figures of saints and African deities. The small shop had a remarkable array of stock. In addition to packets of dried herbs, baths, powders, oils, incense, sprays, and candles, there are small plaster statues of the various Virgins and saints that represent the orichas, as well as Changó Macho, San Simón Maximón, Doctor Hernández, and the Madamas, Indios, and Congos of Espiritismo. This is one of the few stores where I also saw statues and chromolithographs of saints representing the lwa—the Mater Dolorosa for Ezili-Freda and the Mater Salvatoris for Ezili-Dantò. Behind the counter are paper cups of cascarilla (powdered egg shells used in Santería rituals), cakes of camphor, squares of laundry bluing, jars of gold and silver glitter, a big jar of yellow powder labeled *"asufre"* (sulfur), and popular perfumes such as Florida Water and Hoyt's Cologne.

Catalina is a handsome, dark-skinned woman with large, expressive eyes. Her fingers are covered with rings. I introduced myself by mentioning a mutual friend. She greeted me warmly and directed me to have a seat; she was occupied with a consultation for a young woman in the back room. Periodically she popped out to fetch candles, bottles of spiritual bath for the cleansing, and a pack of incense sticks. Over the noise of a television that blared Spanish soap operas, I could hear ritual music from the tape player. Mr. de Guzman puttered around washing out bottles and going through the receipts. A traveling salesman from Miami arrived with a huge, bulging suitcase and hauled out an assortment of Santería regalia—feather fans, multistranded necklaces, and ruffled checked gingham dresses—blue and white for Yemayá, red and white for Changó, and yellow and white for Ochún. A delivery man brought flowers for Catalina's birthday. Other customers drifted in.

At last Catalina called me into her tiny consulting room, containing two chairs and a table covered with a lace tablecloth on which were arranged stones, sea shells, candles, an egg, goblets of water, and a bell. A deck of cards, which she uses for readings, also lay on the table. The walls are covered with chromolithographs of the saints, and on a high shelf is a statue of St. Michael. Catalina described for me her call to serve the spirits, which is similar to the narratives of other spiritual professionals who resisted until accidents and illnesses drove them to undergo initiation.[12]

> I was nine years old when the spiritual power first came to me. I could see things. People were always asking me to tell their fortunes, to give them a lottery number. I couldn't concentrate in school. My mother [a Pentecostal minister] took me to a lady to have the power taken off. For a while it went away. I grew up, got married, had children. We moved to the United States in 1969. But then things began to happen: I had broken bones, I got sick, I was in and out of the hospital. I went to somebody in New York to help me, and she said the spirits wanted me to be initiated. No, it wasn't like they do it in Haiti and Cuba. I wore a white gown; she cleaned me with two white chickens, but she didn't kill them—there was no blood. I started doing some spiritual work on the side, just to help people. Then my husband and I opened this store.

I asked about her consultations.

> I don't do the coconuts or the cowrie shells. I read cards. The little pictures just go by like a movie, but I don't really need them. The spirits tell me what to do. I want to help people—they have trouble with love, with their jobs, with their health. People come to me who are dying and I pray for them. Some ask me to do things that aren't right, to break up husbands and wives. They offer me good money, but I won't do it. This work takes a *lot* out of you.

Catalina allowed me to photograph her in her consulting room. I was extremely pleased with the result, but when I returned to have her sign the form granting me permission to include the photograph in my book, she refused. "I'm sorry, this is a beautiful picture, but I don't feel comfortable having it published. It shows the spirits I work with [the chromolithographs and statues]. In my country this religion is very private; we don't put it out in the street." Pointing to the photograph, she indicated a shape that, to the casual observer, appeared to be a reflection in the window behind her. "But here's what *really* bothers me—this isn't just in the window, it goes down below the window. It's not a reflection and it's not a shadow. This is my aura." The image was indeed inexplicable. Unnerved, I promised not to use the photograph.[13]

Yerberías

Rosario's Mistic, Houston

Houston's population is an interesting cultural mix of white and black Americans (many of Houston's blacks migrated from Louisiana), Mexicans and Mexican Americans, and other Latinos. As we saw in chapter 6, one of the longest-running of the old-time hoodoo drugstores, Stanley's, still thrives in Houston. So does the Allan Company, a white-owned hoodoo-oriented business that has been in operation since the mid-1970s. In addition, I found sixteen botánicas and yerberías listed under "religious goods" in the yellow pages. Five of these are named for the orichas, indicating the spread of Santería into Texas cities.[14]

Rosario's Mistic, owned by Rosario Garcia and her husband Eloy Nañez, is a well-kept, bright yellow cement-block building in a commercial strip at 5314 Canal Street. The large figures painted on either side of the door, an Aztec warrior on one side and St. Lazarus on the other, signify the duel orientation of this store. Rosario's serves the traditional Mexican community, with its heritage of folk Catholicism, curanderismo (healing), and brujería (magic), as well as the followers of Santería. The magical and medicinal herbs, statues and chromolithographs of Roman Catholic saints, baths and oils from Papa Jim's in San Antonio, and teas, charm packets, and spiritual products from Mexico are typical of a Mexican-style yerbería. The store is festooned with garlic braids, and glass-encased *Ajo Macho* (male garlic) candles are prominently displayed. In the Mexican belief system, garlic is a powerful protector against evil. On the counter are figures of feather-bedecked Indians and life-sized plastic

Fig. 33. Eloy Nañez and Rosario Garcia at Rosario's Mistic, Houston, November 4, 1998.

skulls. Interspersed among the merchandise are photographs—a woman with a baby, a child posing with Santa Claus, a young man in a graduation cap and gown.

But other elements suggest Santería. The space is dominated by a large statue of St. Barbara, draped with necklaces and surrounded by candles, flowers, and offerings of money. Near the door is a smaller statue of St. Lazarus, to which petitioners have taped dollar bills. To those who serve the orichas, St. Barbara represents Changó, the lord of thunder, lightning, and male virility, and St. Lazarus is associated with Babalú Ayé, the oricha of disease and healing. According to Mexican American folklorist Cynthia Vidaurri, neither St. Barbara nor St. Lazarus are especially venerated by Mexicans. In the back corner is a three-tiered altar topped with a figure of the Sacred Heart of Jesus, below which are a bust of Doctor Hernández, candles, holy cards, and potted plants.

Rosario Garcia is a well-known tarot card reader, an art learned from her Mexican grandmother who was both a *curandera* (traditional healer) and a reader. A photograph of this venerable lady guards the front door. Garcia and Nañez have been at their present location since 1984, having previously operated a yerbería in Nuevo Larado, a town on the Texas-Mexican border.[15]

Spiritual Products on the World Wide Web

The number of web sites offering herbs, minerals, animal parts, "voodoo dolls," charm kits, spiritual products, and occult books is proliferating daily. Some present a stereotypical version of African-based magico-religious beliefs, and others are informative and serious. Many of the major wholesalers and mail-order retailers also have web sites.

Lucky Mojo Curio Company

In 1995 Catherine Yronwode (pronounced "Ironwood") established the Lucky W Amulet Archive as an illustrated online museum of "folkloric amulets, talismans, charms, and magical stuff from many cultures and eras." There are entries on South and Central American bottle charms and magical packets, *milagros* and *ex votos*, ancient Egyptian amulets, and Middle Eastern charms to avert the evil eye, but the primary emphasis is on hoodoo—mojo bags, John the Conqueror root, lodestone and magnetic sand, occult books, and hoodoo-oriented spiritual products.

Yronwode was born Catherine Manfredi in San Francisco in 1947; she adopted the name Yronwode as an adult. She describes herself as "the daughter of a left-wing German Jewish refugee librarian mother and an Italian-American abstract expressionist artist father. My parents were Beatniks who owned an antiquarian bookstore in Berkeley; I grew up reading about European witchcraft. I protested the Vietnam War, got arrested for growing marijuana, and became a back-to-the-land hippie." She now lives on two acres near rural Forestville, California, where she is a freelance writer, editor, and graphic designer in the fields of popular culture, comic books, collectibles, folkloric magic, gardening, and herbalism.

I had not yet discovered the Lucky W Amulet Archive when, in 1996, I received a postcard from Catherine Yronwode. She had seen my notice seeking old hoodoo products and catalogs in the *Paper and Advertising Collector's Newsletter* and was interested in trading goods and information. Soon we were corresponding by e-mail and sending each other duplicates of items in our collections and photocopies of vintage product labels, advertisements, and catalogs.

Like me, Yronwode was a young rhythm-and-blues fan. She spent her teenage years (the early 1960s) listening to San Francisco's radio station KDIA ("Lucky-13") and traveling to the black neighborhoods of East Oakland to buy records.

I didn't want to spend money on the bus, so I would walk all the way from Berkeley to Oakland. One day I passed a store that said "Spiritual Supplies—Candles," and I walked in. The owner was a very nice, tall, thin, black man; he let me look around, and I saw this bottle of Essence of Bend Over Floor Wash. I thought it was so funny I almost burst out laughing. I picked this thing up and turned to the man, and I asked, "Why would anybody want Essence of Bend Over Floor Wash?" He was very grave and serious, and he said, "Well, honey, some of the people work for some of the other people," by which he meant that many blacks of that time labored at menial jobs in the employ of whites. "You don't want to buy this. You a young girl—you don't work for nobody. What you want is Magnetic Sand." I bought the sand and he taught me to sprinkle it around the feet of the guys I liked. I went back to that store many times.

In early 1997 Catherine Yronwode began making her own spiritual products under the name Lucky Mojo Curio Company, re-creating the look and spirit of traditional hoodoo charms and products from the 1920s–40s. Two of her first items were Essence of Bend Over and Magnetic Sand, inspired by that visit to the Oakland spiritual store almost forty years earlier. Although her marketing technique fully exploits modern technology, her approach to charm-making is traditional. The online catalog offers herbal baths and washes, bath crystals, anointing oils, sachet powders, and incense. Advertising copy emphasizes that these are "the real thing, made the way they were made in your grandma's day . . . with genuine herbs and botanical fragrances." The products of certain large manufacturers are referred to as "fake spiritual supplies and pseudo-voodoo." One can also order roots and herbs, lodestones and magnetic sand, candles, amulets, custom-made mojo bags, complete spell kits, books, and "zoological curios" including alligator teeth and feet, badger teeth, rabbits' feet, and rattlesnake rattles. The best seller is the authentic raccoon penis bone, known as the Coon Dong.

Yronwode sent me a box of samples: bath crystals, incense, and sachet powders in bright-colored, foil-wrapped packages, and small bottles of oils containing herbal essences, roots, leaves, seeds, berries, and mineral fragments. Each item had a distinctive aroma, unlike the generic fragrance of most commercial products. Titles included such hoodoo favorites as Black Cat, Cast Off Evil, Court Case, Fast Luck, Hot Foot, John the Conqueror, Lucky Hand, and New Orleans Style Van-Van. Lavender Love

Drops, a product invented by Yronwode, is "the gay and lesbian equivalent to Adam and Eve Oil."

Yronwode arrives at the recipes for these products in various ways. Some are culled from books like *Doctor Chase's Last and Complete Work* (1876), the *National Formulary* (1888), Hiscox's *Book of Formulas, Processes, and Trade Secrets* (1907), and Joseph Meyer's *The Herbalist* (1918). Some derive from European herbal magic. Some are re-created from her memory of how the old products smelled. The color is determined by traditional hoodoo color symbolism: a clear oil for purity and uncrossing; purple for victory; red for love; green for money; blue for spirituality and protection; and black for "bad work." To make Chinese Wash, Yronwode enlarged the almost indecipherable label on the Chinese Wash bottle pictured in an old catalog and replicated the "oriental gums and grasses" listed there, combining vetiver, palma rosa, citronella, and lemon grass. The liquid is transparent, with just a hint of sunny yellow to convey the idea of cleanliness.

Yronwode gave a detailed description of the formulation of her products. Bath crystals, sachets, and incense powder are mixed in a stainless steel pan. Herbs, oil, and the appropriate colorant are combined with the crystals or powder, and the products are packaged. For the spiritual oils, small bottles are filled with various symbolic ingredients, as dictated by the name and purpose of the product. Lodestone Oil contains bits of lodestone. John the Conqueror Oil contains small pieces of jalap root, obtained by breaking up the large tubers—"they're very hard—I put them in a Tyvek envelope and smash them on the sidewalk with a section of railroad tie." Pale green Attraction Oil, intended to draw both love and money, contains damiana leaves, orange oil (orange blossoms are worn at weddings), and almond oil to inspire love, calamus root to make another person do one's will, cinnamon oil and bits of cinnamon bark to draw money, and pieces of glittering pyrite to symbolize riches. Vitamin E is added to prevent oxidation. The bottles are shaken by hand and then labeled.

Fig. 34. Attraction Oil—Lucky Mojo Curio Company.

Many of the herbal ingredients come from Yronwode's own garden. Other herbs and essential oils come from

Fig. 35. Essence of Bend-Over, New Orleans Style Van-Van Oil, Southern Style Hot Foot Oil—Lucky Mojo Curio Company, Forestville, California, 1998. These illustrations were inspired by advertising graphics from the 1936 Valmor catalog.

Fig. 36. Stay With Me Sachet Powder— Lucky Mojo Curio Company.

two distributors, Trinity Herbs and Simplers, both located in the town of Forestville. Jalap roots, sold as John the Conqueror, come from Mexico. She uses genuine graveyard dirt, obtained from a rural cemetery near her home— "I dig down in the grave and pay the spirit with a silver dime." The raccoon penis bones are by-products of the fur trade. Lodestone and magnetic sand (cast shot) come from Utah. The lodestone is shipped by the pallet-load; cast shot arrives in fifty pound bags. Pyrite is mined in Peru and purchased from a wholesale mineral dealer in Nevada.

The graphics are recognizably inspired by vintage catalogs and product labels, particularly Valmor/King Novelty, and from other illustrations of the 1920s–40s. Some of the Lucky Mojo labels were reproduced by scanning and enhancing the original graphics on the computer; others were created by professional artists known to Yronwode through her comic book business. Printed instructions on the back of the packets of bath crystals, sachet, and incense are written in the style of the old catalogs and spell books, recommending prayer or the reading of a Psalm as part of the charm ritual, and ending with the classic denial, "We do not make any claims, but sell this [name of product] as a curio only."

Sold as a Curio Only

With the help of two part-time employees, Catherine Yronwode mixes, packages, and ships all the products. She also operates a retail outlet in one of the buildings on her property and has begun to wholesale to some stores that have learned of the Lucky Mojo Curio Company through the web site. The products are remarkably low-priced given the superior ingredients and amount of handwork required to make them. Yronwode explained, "I'm very conscious of people's economic situation; I make enough money to live on, to pay my bills and pay my employees, but I'm not out to get rich off this." She also offers spiritual consultations by telephone, for which there is no charge.

As she explains:

About 75 percent of the people who call are African Americans. Others are white liberals who know about hoodoo through blues music—they want a mojo bag like the one Muddy Waters and Lightning Hopkins sang about, and I make something for them called the Blues Boy Special. I also get calls from Middle Eastern, Eastern European, and Mediterranean people who are attracted by the Evil Eye charms on my web site and want advice on removing a curse. Most of my callers are Christian, both Catholic and Protestant; some are Jewish; and some of the white folks identify themselves as Wiccan or Pagan. Some know exactly what charms and rituals should be performed, and I learn from them. Others don't know anything, and I give them full instructions.

The women usually have love problems. The men want luck for gambling, money, good jobs, and success. Some people want to do "bad work," to get rid of a disagreeable neighbor or coworker. I won't do it myself, but I send them the ingredients with instructions for how to use them. I also get customers who really need serious help; these are people with health problems, court-case problems. I do what I can for them. I try to answer their questions through contacts I have in the medical and legal professions and encourage them to participate in the magic that will get their minds in the right place.[16]

CHAPTER 8

The Manufacturers

a s we have seen, the owners of retail stores and small mail-order operations are multiracial and multicultural. The pioneering manufacturers and wholesalers, on the other hand, were almost exclusively white Americans. Many of the early manufacturers entered the spiritual products business through the publication of books on the occult; the production of toiletries, patent medicines, and household cleaning products; or the manufacture of candles and incense. Some got their start in neighborhood hoodoo drugstores. Family connections have been another means of entry into the spiritual business. Most spiritual supply companies are family owned; spouses and in-laws are involved, and the current owners are often the children and grandchildren, nieces and nephews, of the "founding fathers" who established these companies in the 1920s–40s. Even when they are not related by blood or marriage, most manufacturers of spiritual products know each other, and these associations may also be the means of entry into the business. Interactions between company owners are usually friendly and cooperative, but they may be viciously competitive; one hears of hateful rumors deliberately spread, malicious letters, and mysterious fires.

All of the white manufactures are at least nominal members of one of the mainstream faiths; some are Christian, some Jewish. I know of none who are initiates of the African-based religions or participants in the belief system, although most are highly knowledgeable and sensitive to the beliefs of their customers. They do not use their own wares, but many share my opinion that spiritual products can be effective if the user has faith. Company owners told me that they view their business as providing a commodity and a service to those who want and need them. Only one person, a thirty-year veteran of the industry who asked that I not use his name, expressed doubt about the ethics of capitalizing on people's belief in charms.

There is nothing new about the commercialization of traditional culture by outsiders. American business interests have voraciously absorbed and commodified the music, religion, crafts, clothing styles, foodways, and even the names of many minority groups, using their traditions to promote recordings, movies, cars, athletic teams, patent medicines, fast food, and tourist attractions. The manufacture of spiritual products differs from these endeavors in that the intention has never been mass marketing to the general public. The targeted customers for spiritual products are the ethnic communities from which these charm beliefs originated. These goods are comparable to other commodities that were marketed by whites to a strictly black clientele, such as the early blues recordings called "race records" and the "ethnic cosmetics" specially formulated for African American hair texture and skin color.[1]

The manufacturing and wholesaling of spiritual products can be highly lucrative, although some of those with whom I spoke say they "aren't in it for the money," but because they truly enjoy the business. Just as I did not question retailers about their income, I never asked individual manufacturers how much they earn per year. I did, however, ask about profitability. According to one informant, manufacturers make a profit of between 48 and 75 percent before expenses for raw ingredients and packaging materials, rent/mortgage and maintenance of their factory and showroom, utilities, insurance, employees' salaries, and taxes. Those who charge lower wholesale prices, of course, have a higher volume of sales. The successful entrepreneur puts most of the company's earnings back into the business, maintains an attractive workplace, and endeavors to have a good relationship with employees and customers. Others extract as much profit as possible from the business, let their premises become rundown, exploit their employees, and treat customers badly.

The early spiritual suppliers sold retail, wholesale, by mail order, through sales agents, or some combination of these methods. Most present-day manufacturers are primarily wholesalers who also maintain a showroom/retail outlet (complete with spiritual advisor) for local customers. Some companies that sold wholesale in the past are now strictly mail-order retailers. None of these spiritual suppliers would be classified as large businesses. Of the companies that are still in operation, the largest, Indio Products, has only forty-five employees; most have fewer than twenty employees.

In this chapter I will discuss, in roughly chronological order, the manufacturers of spiritual products about whom I was able to assemble complete histories through some combination of interviews, vintage catalogs and products, and archival research. DeLaurence and Dorene exemplify companies that evolved out of the publication of occult books. The founders of Valmor, Keystone, Lucky Heart, and Amateau became involved through the manufacture of cosmetics and/or cleaning products, and the owner of Lama Temple was a cosmetics manufacturer who bought an existing incense company. One of the owners of Original Products is related by marriage to the Amateau family. Martin Mayer, owner of Indio Products, got his start in his family's hoodoo drugstore. Of the manufacturers considered in this chapter, only the founder of Sonny Boy Products was African American. Like the early mail-order hoodoo doctors discussed in chapter 6, she may or may not have been a genuine practitioner who became an entrepreneur.

Some of the early companies, such as E. Davis of New York and Clover Horn of Baltimore, have passed out of the founding families to other owners who declined to be interviewed; it was also difficult to wrest much information out of the new white proprietors of Sonny Boy. The owner of Vandi Parfums was initially friendly and cooperative, but did not respond to my follow-up letters and telephone calls. Inquiries to smaller manufacturers like La Milagrosa, Rondo's Temple, Old Grandpa Sales, and Mister Lucky were not answered. Other manufacturers are long out of business: the R. C. Adams Company and Sovereign Products of Chicago, Oracle Laboratories of Long Island City, and Hussey Curio Company of Atlanta are known to me only through ephemera purchased from other collectors or discovered on the shelves of old-time spiritual stores. A list of manufacturers, past and present, will be found in the appendix.

The L. W. DeLaurence Company, Chicago

The L. W. DeLaurence Company (formerly DeLaurence, Scott and Company) is the oldest and longest-running of all spiritual suppliers. Originally a publishing house for books on hypnotism, magic, the kabbalah, spiritualism, and Hindu mysticism, DeLaurence soon expanded its offerings to include perfumes, oils, sachets, candles, incense, seals, talismans, and herbal medicines.

The company was founded by Lauren William DeLaurence. A retail catalog from the mid-1990s claims "over one hundred years of service to the Mystic Brotherhood," implying that the business had its beginnings in the late nineteenth century. Nathan Hobley, one of the Louisiana Writers' Project informants, spoke of working as an agent for "Laurence D. Scott, the India Spiritualist," in the 1890s.[2] L. W. DeLaurence did not appear in the Chicago city directory until 1902, when he was listed as a hypnotist. The next year "Doctor" DeLaurence was listed as director of the Delaurence Institute of Hypnotism, and by 1904 the entry appeared in bold type as "The Delaurence Institute of Hypnotism, Hindu Magic, and East Indian Occultism, Lauren W. DeLaurence, President." It was one of the few businesses in Chicago that had a telephone.

In 1907 L. W. DeLaurence and Campbell Scott were recorded as co-owners of a mail-order business, DeLaurence, Scott and Company. Although the company did business under this name until 1929, Campbell Scott seems to have vanished. The year 1907 was the only one in which Scott's name appeared in the city directory, and he was not listed in the census for 1910 or 1920.

DeLaurence, Scott and Company, and later the L. W. DeLaurence Company, published English translations of *The Sacred Magic of Abra-Melin the Mage*, *The Greater Key of Solomon*, *The Lesser Key of Solomon*, *The Philosophy of Natural Magic* by Agrippa von Nettesheim, *The Hermetic and Alchemical Writings of Paracelsus*, plus the work of nineteenth-century French and English writers on magic, alchemy, the tarot, and the kabbalah. He also published his own works on hypnotism and palmistry. DeLaurence's best seller was *The Great Book of Magical Art, Hindu Magic, and East Indian Occultism*, which was enormously popular and has run to many editions. We know from the interviews of Hyatt and the Federal Writers' Project that *The Great Book of Magical Art* served as a handbook to some of the old-time hoodoo workers of the South.[3]

In 1919 DeLaurence, Scott and Company was the subject of a mail fraud investigation for "engaging in a scheme to obtain money through the mails by means of fake and fraudulent pretenses, representations, and promises." The circumstances that led to the investigation are particularly interesting, in that the case was instigated by a disgruntled employee, not by a dissatisfied customer. The 162-page transcript of the mail fraud hearing, now at the National Archives and Records Administration, offered considerable information about this case.

A young Nigerian pharmacy student, Michael Williams, was ambitious to become a master magician. He claimed that he was induced by DeLaurence's writings, which were especially popular in Africa, to come to Chicago for instruction. Upon his arrival, Williams was employed by DeLaurence, but was fired after a few months. DeLaurence testified that "Williams upset the girls in the office. If a girl had to climb up on a stepladder to fetch something, Williams would walk under the ladder and look up her clothes." At one point there was a physical altercation between DeLaurence and Williams, and Williams claimed that DeLaurence hit him with a chair. Williams subsequently contacted an attorney. According to an article in the *Chicago Defender*, "Slick Man Lures Boy from Africa, Beats and Robs Him," DeLaurence was charged with assaulting Williams and cheating him out of $150 in "tuition."[4]

At the mail fraud hearing, DeLaurence testified that he was born in 1868 in Cleveland, Ohio, was of French-Canadian descent, and that DeLaurence was his real name. These statements are supported by DeLaurence's listing in the 1920 census and by his death certificate, in which he is stated to have been born in Ohio of a French-Canadian father and an American mother.[5] After witnessing a stage performance by a hypnotist, DeLaurence determined to go into this line of work himself. He testified that after receiving one lesson in hypnotism, he began to travel around the country giving lectures, exhibitions, and selling books on psychology and hypnotism door to door. He began his writing and publishing career after moving to Chicago.

DeLaurence told U.S. Post Office attorneys that his first book, *Hypnotism: A Complete System of Method, Application, and Use* (1900), was a financial success, but he was cheated out of his royalties by the publisher, the Alhambra Book Company of Chicago. He then established his own business, DeLaurence, Scott and Company. DeLaurence became vague when asked about Campbell Scott, answering that he had simply bought an existing business from him, and that he "couldn't remember exactly who Scott was." I suspect that "Campbell Scott" may have been a fictitious business partner created by DeLaurence to limit his responsibility in the event of lawsuits.

The attorneys for the Post Office seemed determined to prove that DeLaurence was a fake. Asked about the title of "Doctor," DeLaurence confessed that he did not have a medical degree, and had, in fact, completed only two years of high school. He also stated that, although he called

Fig. 37. Black Incense—
L. W. DeLaurence Company,
Chicago; purchased in 1996.
DeLaurence's labels bear the
image of a turbaned swami.

himself an "Adept of the Orient in Hindu Magic, Metaphysics, Alchemy, Cabala, and Occult and Natural Philosophy," he was completely self-taught and had never traveled outside the United States. DeLaurence admitted that the products sold by the DeLaurence Company had no inherent supernatural qualities. The candles came from a maker of church supplies; the amulets from a local jewelry manufacturer; the "100% virgin parchment made from the skins of unborn lambs" was actually paper; and the herbal remedies came from the Parke-Davis Pharmaceutical Company.

One of the attorneys quoted a passage from the *Great Book of Magical Art, Hindu Magic, and East Indian Occultism*: "To make yourself invisible, pierce the right eye of a bat and carry it with you." The attorney then inquired of DeLaurence whether he actually believed "any such damn foolishness." DeLaurence answered that, no, he did not personally believe it, then proceeded to deliver a discourse on the positive influence of faith, stating, "Lots of people say this is a great book and they get results from the things we put down there." DeLaurence was given two weeks to remove all "fraudulent and objectionable" claims from his retail catalog. The final outcome of the case is not stated in the transcript, and I could find no record of DeLaurence's having served a prison sentence.[6]

L. W. DeLaurence died in 1936, and the business was taken over by his son, Velo.[7] For many years the company was located at 180 North Wabash, a large office building in downtown Chicago. In 2000 I received a printed notice stating that DeLaurence had relocated to Michigan City, Indiana. The company is owned and managed by Mickey DeLaurence, a female descendant of the founder. My letters to her were not answered, and when I contacted the company by telephone, I was informed by a receptionist that Ms. DeLaurence does not give interviews.

The DeLaurence Company currently does a large mail-order retail business in Europe, Africa, and the Caribbean, as well as the United States. The catalog gives instructions for paying in "the paper money of your coun-

Sold as a Curio Only

try, British Postal Order, or International Postal Money Orders issued in U.S. dollars." Customers can purchase the inch-thick paper-bound catalog, which costs fifteen dollars "due to rising costs for printing and postage," but the "mini-catalog," a packet of photocopied sheets, is free. The catalog contains material that is essentially the same as that described in the mail fraud hearing: books on magic and the occult, plus candles, talismans, seals, and spiritual products with brand names like Transcendental, Golden Aura, and Obeah. The labels bear the image of a turbaned swami. Unlike other spiritual supply companies, DeLaurence still eschews the customary disclaimers, such as "alleged," and "sold as a curio only," that protect a merchant from mail fraud charges.

Valmor: King Novelty and Famous Products, Chicago

The Valmor Company was founded in 1928 by Morton G. Neumann. Over the years, the business occupied various buildings on South Indiana, South Michigan, Cottage Grove, and East 63rd Street, all in the South Side neighborhood known as "Bronzeville." Morton Neumann was born and raised on the South Side and was trained as a chemist. His name first appeared in the Chicago city directory in 1923, simply followed by the word "soap." In 1928 the Valmor Company was listed in the city directory as a manufacturer of toilet articles. Valmor marketed skin lighteners, hair straighteners, perfumes, soaps, deodorants, tooth powders, douche compounds, tonics, and laxatives under the names Madam Jones and Sweet Georgia Brown for women and Slick Black and Lucky Brown for men. The company also manufactured spiritual products, printed its own dream books, and even produced a line of "race records" on the Valmor label. Like other companies that combined the manufacture of patent medicines, toiletries, and cleansers with the marketing of spiritual products, the Valmor Company promoted a total concept of health, beauty, and hygiene that was synonymous with success and good luck.

Valmor covered all bases: the company sold wholesale to smaller stores, did a retail mail-order business, and recruited sales agents from all over the country through advertisements in its retail catalogs and dream books and in the *Chicago Defender*. Valmor's spiritual supplies were marketed through subsidiary companies called King Novelty and Famous Products. The back cover of the Valmor Dream Book advertises Famous Products incense in seven fragrances—John the Conqueror, Aunt Sally's Lucky Dream, Van-Van, Lodestone, Lucky Mo-Jo, Lucky Spirit, and

Frank-Incense.[8] By placing a notice in an ephemera-collectors' newsletter, I was able to acquire King Novelty Curio Catalogs for 1936 and 1945, and an undated issue that appears to be from about 1950. In the excellence of their graphics and the wildly exuberant hyperbole of their advertising copy, these catalogs exhibit a vitality that has seldom been surpassed.

The cover of the 1936 catalog depicts a scantily clad young lady of indeterminate race, presumably a harem beauty, kneeling before an incense burner and gazing into a crystal ball. A domed palace and a caravan with elephants and camels create an exotic setting. The catalog offered a little of everything—health and beauty products; lingerie; stockings; books of advice on courtship and marriage, such as *How to Make Love* and the *Model Book of Love Letters for Ladies and Gentlemen*; talisman rings and religious medals; and, of course, dream books, occult texts, seals from the *Sixth and Seventh Books of Moses*, and spiritual products. The illustrations depict glamorous people of mixed race with light complexions and lustrous, wavy hair. A variety of Lucky Mo-Jo brand oils and perfumes, some of which contained a lodestone or John the Conqueror root, were advertised. Van-Van, the perennial New Orleans favorite, was available as oil, perfume, sachet powder, or incense. Botanicals could be purchased individually for twenty-five or fifty cents. By far the most interesting items in the King Novelty Curio Catalog were the mojo bags and "curio boxes," inspired by classic lucky hands. The obvious influence of New Orleans hoodoo on Valmor's product line may derive from the community of black Louisianians who settled in Chicago during the Great Migration.

SOUTHERN STYLE HERB BAG
DRESSED WITH SOUTHERN STYLE VAN-VAN OIL

To those of our Customers who might want an ALGIERS Southern Style Herb Curio Bag, we have prepared this remarkable collection of Herbs, Roots, and Lodestones. Certain Voodoos, Witch Doctors, and Fetish Worshippers claim that a Bag of certain herbs, worn on the person, would drive away Evil and bring Good Luck in Games, Business, Love, etc. However, we make no representations to that effect. We are merely stating facts that have come to our attention . . . if you wish this specially prepared Southern Style Herb Bag, we sell only as a curio. Get Yours NOW!

Sold as a Curio Only

Fig. 38. King Novelty Curio Catalog, Chicago, 1936.

Fig. 39. Southern Style Herb Bag—King Novelty Curio Catalog, 1936. In the advertising copy, the Chicago manufacturer demonstrates familiarity with the reputation of Algiers, Louisiana, as "Hoodoos' Town."

Fig. 40. Mo-Jo Brand Curio Box—King Novelty Curio Catalog, 1936.

The Mo-Jo Brand Alleged Curio Luck Box contained a lodestone, a packet of lodestone powder, a pair of Adam and Eve roots, a vial of "special perfumed essence," and a red flannel curio bag.

The cover of the 1945 catalog also features a harem beauty, this time being offered jewels and perfumes by a bearded, turbaned Hindu swami. In addition to the selection of books offered in 1936, the 1945 Curio Catalog advertised *The Master Book of Candle Burning* and *The Magic of Herbs* by Henri Gamache, and *The Seven Keys to Power* and *Legends of Incense, Herb, and Oil Magic* by Lewis de Claremont. New offerings included lodestones colored gold, silver, white, black, red, green, and blue, and even more elaborate charm kits and curio boxes.

BIG HAND CURIO OUTFIT

> This outfit consists of a Big Hand Brand Curio Bag, filled with Lodestone, High John the Conqueror Root, Salep Root sometimes called Hand Root, bottle of Van-Van Oil, and Devil's Shoestrings. We make no claims that these articles are lucky . . . and sell only as curios.

King Novelty also offered Essence of Bend Over, which, as we will remember from the preceding chapter, was the product that first captured the imagination of Catherine Yronwode, creator of the Lucky Mojo Curio Company.

The fascinating career of Morton Neumann is discussed in a 1986 article, "The Valmor Story," by Terry Zwigoff, a San Francisco filmmaker, musician, collector of advertising ephemera, and associate of the underground

Fig. 41. Big Hand Curio Outfit—King Novelty Curio Catalog, 1945.

cartoonist Robert Crumb. Zwigoff found some vintage Valmor products for sale in a flea market in 1972 and was so captivated by the graphics, which somewhat resembled the work of the underground cartoonists, that he launched a search for more Valmor products and the original artwork.

In 1974, on a trip to Chicago with Crumb's band, the Cheap Suit Serenaders, Zwigoff discovered that Valmor was still listed in the telephone directory. Hoping to find a treasure trove of old advertising art and products, he drove to the warehouse, which he described as occupying an entire block in a "bad neighborhood on the South Side." There he encountered Neumann's wife, Rose, who served as the receptionist. As Zwigoff attempted to explain his mission and Mrs. Neumann grew increasingly hostile, "an old guy about eighty appeared out of the recesses of the seemingly deserted back warehouse. Morton Neumann, complete with cigar, reminded me of an extremely cranky George Burns." After considerable pleading by Zwigoff, Neumann finally sent an elderly janitor into the warehouse for a cart full of bottles and cans, which Zwigoff eagerly purchased.

"By the time I met Neumann in 1974," wrote Zwigoff, "Valmor had become a two-person operation. Morton and his wife actually filled all the

mail orders themselves. Morton . . . personally delivered merchandise to local stores. An old woman who ran a tiny candle shop in one of the South Side's most dangerous neighborhoods told me that he'd drive up and double park his Rolls Royce to deliver her monthly order."[9]

But Morton Neumann was not only a manufacturer of toiletries, tonics, and spiritual products. He was widely known and respected as a collector of twentieth century art, particularly the work of Picasso, Klee, Miró, Matisse, Giacometti, Dubuffet, Léger, and Man Ray. His collecting began on a 1948 trip to Paris, when he purchased several paintings and visited the studios of Man Ray and Picasso. A major exhibition of the Neumann Family Collection opened in 1981 at Washington's National Gallery of Art and then traveled to the Art Institute of Chicago. After Neumann's death in 1985, at the age of eighty-seven, much of his art collection was donated to the Art Institute of Chicago.[10]

Neither of Morton Neumann's sons went into the family cosmetic and curio business; according to Neumann's obituary, one became a doctor and one an art dealer. Valmor Products was bought by R & H Cosmetics of New York, which was only interested in marketing the most popular hair-dressing preparations. The Chicago warehouse was cleaned out, and products, original artwork, and printing plates were hauled to the dump.[11]

Keystone Laboratories, Memphis

The Keystone Chemical Company, later called Keystone Laboratories, was established in 1925 by Joseph Menke and Morris Shapiro. Joseph Menke was a chemist with a background in cosmetics. His friend and neighbor Abe Plough, founder of the Plough Chemical Company and manufacturer of Plough's Black and White hair and skin preparations (later the Maybelline Cosmetics Company), inspired Menke to create a line of toiletries especially for African Americans. Like Valmor, Keystone combined the sale of ethnic cosmetics with spiritual products. It is unclear which company first developed this merchandising scheme. Valmor was enthusiastic in its promotion of spiritual products while these items were merely a sideline with Keystone. Therefore I suspect that the concept originated with Valmor and was emulated by Keystone.

Product development and marketing strategy were shared by Menke; his wife, Hilda; Morris Shapiro; and two vice presidents, Lista Wayman and Connie Clark. The products were formulated by a staff of chemists, one of whom, Jackson Green, was African American. Labels and packaging were designed by professional artists, and an advertising manager was in charge of publicity. Lista Wayman is the only surviving member of the original Keystone staff. In its early years the company occupied several different buildings in the Beale Street neighborhood, at that time a flourishing center of retail stores, bars, night clubs, and theaters patronized by African Americans. The factory and offices have now moved to an industrial area on the outskirts of Memphis. I interviewed Lista Wayman in the spring of 1997, along with the current owner of the company, Joseph Menke's granddaughter Melinda Menke Burns.

Valmor and Keystone both emulated the highly successful sales tactics of black-owned cosmetics businesses, such as Madame Annie T. Malone's Poro Company and the Madame C. J. Walker Company, marketing directly to the community through sales agents. For the owners of Keystone, this decision was partially based on the fact that black customers were not welcome in white-owned stores in the South. Agents, both male and female, were recruited through advertisements in the *Chicago Defender* and through the Church of God in Christ, a Memphis-based black Pentecostal denomination. Keystone always maintained a booth at the Church of God in Christ convention, and Lista Wayman recalled that

Fig. 42. Joseph Menke, founder of Keystone Laboratories, in front of the Keystone factory, 154 Calhoun Street, Memphis, early 1930s. Collection of Melinda Menke Burns, Memphis, used by permission.

they would attend services and "shout" right along with the congregation. Keystone had agents all over the United States, in the Virgin Islands, Honduras, and even in Africa. For $3.50 the sales agent purchased a kit containing fifty items—cosmetics, hair-dressing preparations, skin-lightening creams, lotions, perfumes, stockings, personal hygiene products, and curios—which he or she could sell for ten dollars, an arrangement beneficial to Keystone and to the agent. Keystone made fifty thousand mailings to out-of-town agents twice a month; Memphis-based agents could pick up orders at a city sales office.

Both Hyatt and the Savannah Unit of the Georgia Writers' Project interviewed some of these agents in the late 1930s. In Jacksonville, Florida, the woman who Hyatt called "Agent for Curios" was selling Keystone and Lucky Heart products. This informant showed Hyatt her samples and catalogs, saying that her most popular items were High John the Conqueror in Holy Oil and High John the Conqueror Root, which came attractively packaged in a box. Other favored articles were Live Lodestone, Adam and Eve Root in Love Oil, Go Away Powder, and Lucky Candles. She displayed a Curio Box containing Devil's shoestring,

Fig. 43. Keystone and LaJac Beauty Manual, Memphis, 1930s. Collection of Terry Zwigoff, San Francisco, used by permission.

dragon's blood, life everlasting herbs, Devil's stone, and "dead man's bones." Although her employers offered products like Controlling Powder for "bad work," the Jacksonville agent refused to sell them. In *Drums and Shadows*, the fieldworkers noted that one of their informants was selling spiritual products from her home. Mattie Sampson of Brownsville, Georgia, did an active business as sales representative for Keystone, Lucky Heart, and Valmor. Her best sellers were Mystic Mojo Love Sachet, Magnetic Lodestone in Holy Oil, five finger grass, and Black Cat Incense.[12]

All of Keystone's personal care products were manufactured at the factory. Lista Wayman remembers that Joseph Menke would go across the street to the grocery store and buy a bag of cucumbers to make Keystone's famous Cucumber Lotion. The roots and lodestones and such were purchased from another source and packaged at Keystone. According to Mrs. Wayman, the Keystone staff gleaned their knowledge of African American charm beliefs from their sales agents, from customer requests, and by observing what other companies were selling.

In an undated Keystone Laboratories retail catalog that appears to be from the 1930s, we find products for "wooing and winning lady luck with genuine curios"—some of the same items referred to by "Agent for Curios" and Mattie Sampson:

HIGH JOHN THE CONQUEROR ROOT IN HOLY OIL

A remarkable alleged luck token. Owned and cherished by many who want Love, Sweethearts, Power, Popularity, and Leadership. Its possession makes you a sophisticated person who likes to get all the "breaks." We make no supernatural claims, but offer it as a curio only. Double Size Root in Holy Oil—Price 50¢.

HOLY OIL WITH LIVE LODESTONE

An extra large double strength lodestone in alleged Holy Oil is carried by smart folks for its reputed effect. Do you lack confidence in yourself and in your ability to win popularity, hold sweethearts, to be a leader, and to make money? Thousands of such people carry this lodestone when in doubt. We frankly state that we offer it as a curio only and do not make supernatural claims. Extra big, extra strong Lodestone in so-called Holy Oil—Price 50¢.

The Manufacturers

Fig. 44. Page of curios from the Keystone catalog. Collection of Terry Zwigoff, used by permission.

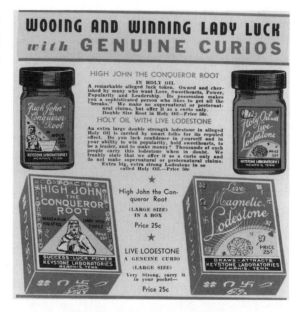

Fig. 45. Two in One Good Luck Perfume and Love Powder—Curio Products Company, a subsidiary of Keystone Laboratories, Memphis, 1930s. The colorful box is illustrated with embracing couples, money, four-leafed clovers, horseshoe, lucky black cat bone, swastika, and a heart pierced by an arrow. Purchased from the collection of Terry Zwigoff.

In my collection are three examples of Keystone's attractive curio packages: Two-in-One Genuine Love Powder and Perfume—"The Siren Lover's Delight"; Two-in-One Triple Strength Lodestone and Adam and Eve Paradise Root—"The Love and Money Maker"; and a Black Cat Brand Moonstone. All are contained in small boxes with colorful graphics. The Love Powder and bottle of Love Perfume are long gone, but the Triple

Sold as a Curio Only

Strength Lodestone and Adam and Eve Paradise Root box still holds a small square of black lodestone and two tiny roots in a cellophane bag, and there is a chip of mica-flecked quartz in the Black Cat Brand Moonstone box.

Joseph Menke died in 1940. His widow, Hilda, continued to run the business even after she remarried and moved to upstate New York. The son of Joseph and Hilda, Hubert Menke, became president of Keystone Laboratories in 1951. Within a few years, the company began to market its line of cosmetics to small beauty and barber shops rather than through agents or retail catalog sales; the spiritual products were discontinued in the late 1960s. Hubert Menke died in 1991 and was succeeded as president by his daughter, Melinda Menke Burns. Keystone's personal care products are now sold through large chain stores.[13]

Lucky Heart Laboratories, Memphis

In 1933 Morris Shapiro left Keystone to found Lucky Heart Laboratories with his business partners Benjamin Spears and I. N. Arnoff. LaRue Marx was the head chemist, chief purchasing agent, and vice president of production, and Bob Thomas was sales manager. The company was located at 388–400 Mulberry in the Beale Street neighborhood, within blocks of Keystone Laboratories and just a few doors from the hotel where Hyatt conducted his interviews in 1938 and 1939. The original Lucky Heart building still houses the manufacturing plant, and the offices are now located around the corner on Huling Avenue.

Like Keystone Laboratories, Lucky Heart marketed its products through sales agents in the black community and recruited through the Church of God in Christ. The agent's "display outfit," which cost $9.72, included a carrying case, the *Agent's Guide to Making Money* with "new proven sales plans and helpful suggestions," a price list and order forms, and a large array of products. Lucky Heart agents were given a certificate from the company authorizing them to sell goods for future delivery and protecting them from harassment by city, county, or state officials. Agents received monthly mailings from sales manager "Lucky" Bob Thomas promoting new products, extolling the merits of self-employment, praising those who had done exceptionally well, and chiding those who had not recently placed an order. Thomas made periodic trips through the South to meet and visit with the agents, describing in one of his mailings "their smiling faces, the beautiful clothes they were wearing, the nice homes they were living in . . . and how glad they were to be Lucky Heart Agents. . . . When

Fig. 46. Letter to agents, 1940, Lucky Heart Company, Memphis. Sales agents received monthly mailings to keep their enthusiasm high.

they joined the Lucky Heart Company, they found prosperity, happiness, success, and the money they needed."

The company manufactured toiletries and spiritual products under the brand names Lucky Heart and Lucky Mon-Gol, and a line of patent medicines under the name Erbru Roots and Herbs Medicine Company. A 1935 wholesale price list includes items very similar to those sold by Keystone: High John the Conqueror Root with Holy Oil in Mystic Bottle, Mystic Curio Box, Magnetic Lodestone in Holy Oil, Hindu Double Mystic Love and Luck Oil, Quick Love Perfume with Genuine Lodestone, and so forth. Like Keystone, Lucky Heart stopped carrying spiritual products in the 1960s.

When Morris Shapiro died in 1961, his share of the company went to his son, Paul Shapiro, who eventually bought out the interests of Spears and Arnoff. Paul Shapiro was one of the original advocates for the establishment of the National Civil Rights Museum at the Lorraine Motel, site of Martin Luther King Jr.'s 1968 assassination. The museum is directly across the street from Lucky Heart's offices. Shapiro gave a sizable donation, and the employees of Lucky Heart also gave what they could.

After Paul Shapiro's death in 1993, his widow, Lucy, took over management responsibilities. Lucy Shapiro's second husband, Gary Young, is the current president of Lucky Heart. When I interviewed Young in 1997, he allowed me to look through three cartons of vintage advertisements, labels, and promotional letters to agents, from which I was able to purchase duplicates. The company, now called Lucky Heart Cosmetics, still sells through agents, but the products are no longer exclusively for African Americans. The cover of the retail catalog features a trio of beautiful women—black, brown, and white. Products include cosmetics, fragrances, jewelry, hair-straightening combs, tonics and salves, spices, household cleaning supplies, and a line of men's toiletries.[14]

Sonny Boy Products, Miami and Birmingham

Sonny Boy Products of Miami was originally owned and operated by an African American woman known only as "Mrs. Mills" to everyone with whom she conducted business. Despite considerable research, I have been unable to discover her first name. The 1997 *Sonny Boy Guide to Success and Power*, a combination mail-order retail catalog and spell book, states that the charm rituals contained therein are reproduced from the first edition of 1926. The present owners support 1926 as the date of Sonny Boy's founding, although they claim to have no information on the history of the company. Nobody else with whom I spoke can remember the business existing before 1960.

Pharmacist Horace Bynum Jr., later a partner in New Orleans' famous Dixie Drugstore, told me of being hired by Mrs. Mills to solicit and deliver orders to stores in Mississippi, Alabama, Louisiana, and Texas in the early 1960s. I also recorded accounts from Doc Miller of Miller's Rexall Drug in Atlanta and a Miami spiritual supplier who asked that I not use his name. Both routinely picked up wholesale orders from Mrs. Mills in the 1960s and 1970s. Elliot Schwab of Schwab's Department Store in Memphis also bought from Sonny Boy during this period. According to these sources, Mrs. Mills, assisted by family members, manufactured the products and ran a wholesale and mail-order retail business out of a trailer and some adjoining buildings. Doc Miller remembers visiting Mrs. Mills, who was at that time much advanced in age, at the Sonny Boy factory, located outside Miami in an area of open fields and light industry. Ann Epstein of the Charleston Cut-Rate Drugstore had the impression that Mrs. Mills was Jamaican because she spoke with a Caribbean accent.[15] Although Sonny Boy never appeared in the Miami city directory, it was listed in the telephone directory as Sonny Boy Products, religious goods, first at 3007 NW 44th Street and later at 8701 NW 24th Street.

The Manufacturers

Mrs. Mills is said to have written the original *Sonny Boy Dream Book* and the *Sonny Boy Guide to Success and Power*. Some of the charm formulae appear in a format similar to those found in *Marie Laveau's Old and New Black and White Magic*, the spell book originally published by a New Orleans drugstore in the early 1900s as *The Life and Works of Marie Laveau*. The *Sonny Boy Guide to Success and Power* gives little anecdotes with titles like "Can You Attract a Lover?" "Can You Be Successful in Business?" "Can You Make a Court Case Go Your Way?" "Do You Know How to Protect Your Home and Loved Ones from Evil?" and, for "bad work," "Do You Know How to Cross Someone through a Spell?" A course of action is prescribed, and the distressed person, having bought the requisite Sonny Boy products and performed the ritual, presumably lives happily ever after.

The language of these charm formulae indicates that the writer was familiar with traditional beliefs. The old-fashioned term *hurt* is used to describe the condition of a person harmed by an "evil woman"; a whole family is said to be "suffering from strange and unnatural pain" caused by someone "putting something down" to harm them. A gambling charm, identical to those collected by Hyatt, involves boring a hole in a nutmeg, filling it with "quicksilver," sealing it with wax from a green candle, and fumigating the "dressed" nutmeg with Lucky Hand Incense. "Can You Run a Person out of Town?" includes instructions to "Dress a Black Doom Candle with red pepper, black pepper, and Crossing Oil. As the candle burns to each line, write your enemies' names. Burn the candle once a day. To make sure the enemy is gone forever, write their names on brown paper, put the paper in Four Thieves Vinegar, and bury. Read Psalm 118."[16]

Throughout the booklet are messages such as "Use only Sonny Boy Products—the power of psalms and prayer cannot be denied"; "The alleged powers of Sonny Boy Products are limited only by your personal faith—through spiritual strength, all things are possible"; and "Sonny Boy original recipe formulas have been handed generation to generation—many items are Triple Strength XXX and should be used under the guidance of your spiritual advisor." According to one of these notices, "all products are made by Indian Grandma."

Following the retirement or death of Mrs. Mills around 1980, Sonny Boy Products was taken over by an unidentified party in Birmingham, Alabama. Barry Bloom, owner of the Charleston Cut-Rate Drugstore at the time, tried unsuccessfully to buy the business from this person. In 1984 the company was purchased by Johnnie Praytor, a white Birmingham businessman.

My communications with Sonny Boy were answered by Mr. Praytor's business partner, who has asked that I not use her name. Although she allowed me to interview her by telephone, the draft of my section on Sonny Boy was returned with all information about the ownership and operation of the business deleted and marked "confidential." She requested that I append a "registered trademark" symbol to every use of the Sonny Boy name.

The address given in the *Sonny Boy Guide to Success and Power*, 1811 4th Avenue North, Birmingham, Alabama, along with the names of both owners, appeared in city directories of the early 1990s. Sonny Boy is not listed in the 1998 city or telephone directories (the latest available to me at the time of this writing), even though the company is definitely still in business. In 2000, because I am on Sonny Boy's customer mailing list, I received notice that the company has moved to 1715 3rd Avenue North. Included with the notice was a certificate for a free bottle of oil with my next order over twenty dollars—cash only.

Sonny Boy currently sells some of the most commonly used roots and herbs and the Sonny Boy brand of bath-and-floor wash, soaps, anointing oil, sprinkling salts, aerosol sprays, incense, and candles, most of which are manufactured at the factory in Birmingham. None are labeled in Spanish or have any association with Santería. Although Sonny Boy is now primarily a mail-order retail company, it has retained some wholesale accounts with old-time businesses like Schwab's Department Store in Memphis, Miller's Rexall Drug in Atlanta, the Corner Drugstore in Vicksburg, Sheftall's Barber Supply in Savannah, Eye of the Cat in Columbia, South Carolina, and, until it closed in 1998, the Cut-Rate in Charleston.[17] According to former Cut-Rate owner Sam Rosen, Sonny Boy Products are considered by black southerners to have the most potency.

Lama Temple Products, Chicago

The Lama Products Company first appeared in the Chicago telephone directory in 1932, listed as manufacturers of incense. The name was later changed to Lama Temple Incense Company, possibly inspired by the Chinese Lama Temple that was exhibited at Chicago's Century of Progress Exposition in 1933. The identity of the original owner is unknown.[18]

In 1948 Lama Temple was purchased by a cosmetics manufacturer, Max Kanovsky. He learned incense formulae, sources of raw materials, and packaging from the former owner. It is unclear whether hoodoo-related products were introduced by Kanovsky or whether this aspect of the business was already in place. When Max Kanovsky retired in 1957 the business was taken over by his son Marvin, who had shortened the family name to Kayne. According to longtime employees, it was Kayne who emphasized the spiritual business. At that time the company was listed in the telephone directory as Lama Temple Products, manufacturers of "religious equipment," and was located at its present address, 141 West 62nd Street.

Lama Temple bought out several small Chicago-based manufacturers of spiritual products. Doctor Pryor's was acquired in the early 1950s. This company was owned by the black "spiritual advisor" and manufacturer of Japo-Oriental products already discussed in chapter 6. Lama Temple still markets Doctor Pryor's *Lucky Number Master Dream Book* and his Seven Holy Spirits Hyssop Bath Oil, Japo-Oriental Sacred Oils, Hot Foot Powder, and House Dressing Floor Wash. Lama Temple later purchased Ar-Jax, another small manufacturer of spiritual products. Ar-Jax Chinese Buddah wash, oils, and incense are still sold by Lama Temple. Under the leadership of Marvin Kayne, the parent company became Candle Corporation of America and expanded into the manufacture of candles for homes, restaurants, and churches. The spiritual products division retained the name Lama Temple. Candle Corporation of America was acquired by a New York investment group in 1977 and opened branches in Brooklyn, Miami, and Los Angeles, in addition to the home office in Chicago. The Lama Temple division is now an affiliate of Indio Products of Los Angeles, owned by Martin Mayer, a former Lama Temple employee.

Martin Mayer, who was hired as an assistant manager of Lama Temple in 1969, remembers working at the West 62nd Street building in the Bronzeville section of Chicago. At that time there were fourteen factory workers and two people in sales, plus the senior manager. All the employees, excepting Mayer and the senior manager, were black southerners— "They believed in hoodoo and they used the products."

Mayer described the daily routine at Lama Temple. Oils, perfumes, and Chinese Wash were mixed in twenty-five-gallon tanks. Incense powders were made in a bakery dough mixer in 250-pound batches and put into small cans, called "tubes," for retail, and into 25-pound boxes for wholesale to stores that repackaged it with their own label. Incense cakes were made by cooking starch in a fifty-gallon kettle and adding charcoal powder, saltpeter, and fragrance to form a dough. "We had this big, black fellow, he was over six feet tall, weighed about three hundred pounds, and he would take this stuff and roll it with a huge rolling pin—that's all he did all day long—and take a big knife and cut it in one inch squares." The incense cakes, called Doctor Pryor's

Lucky Number Incense, received an application of "invisible ink" that, when burned, would reveal a lucky number. Jinx Sticks were made from starch and wood flour, colored green, red, or purple, hand rolled into three-inch, carrot-shaped sticks, dried, and coated with perfume oil. "We sold hundreds of thousands of these." Seven-day glass-encased candles also required several steps: the labels were silk-screened onto the glass containers and dried on wooden racks; the glasses were filled by hand with wax, and the finished candles were packed in cardboard boxes. The wholesale and retail outlet, located on the third floor, was patronized by local store owners and retail customers from the neighborhood, all of whom were black. Mayer recalls that people were sometimes lined up on the rickety wooden stairs, and that the elderly ladies were often so out of breath that he would have to bring them water.[19]

Lama Temple currently manufactures and wholesales a full line of spiritual products under the brand names Powerful Indian, Ar-Jax, River Jordan, and Doctor Pryor's. Most products are labeled in English on one side and Spanish on the other, but Lama Temple has not yet incorporated Santería into its repertoire. The company continues to manufacture only traditional hoodoo supplies: bath-and-floor wash, oils, sprinkling salt, and incense, with familiar titles like Fast Luck, Glory Water, High John the Conqueror, Money Drawing, Has-No-Hanna, Peaceful Home, Van-Van, Jinx Removing, and Love Me. Lama Temple also sells candles, Four Thieves Vinegar, red flannel bags, "voodoo dolls," five-pound bags of saltpeter, rabbit's foot charms, genuine sheepskin parchment, seals from the *Sixth and Seventh Books of Moses*, spell books, and dream books.

Dorene Publishing, New York
Mysteria Products, Arlington, Texas

Dorene Publishing was founded in New York City in 1937 by Joe Kay (originally Joseph Spitalnick). According to his son Ed Kay, now in his late seventies, the family fell into the spiritual business entirely by accident. Joe and his brother Max, the sons of Russian immigrants, were jazz musicians, each leading his own orchestra. In order to avoid confusion—"they couldn't have two Spitalniks out there"—Joseph took the name Joe Kay and Max adopted the name Joe Martin. A man named Young (Ed Kay cannot remember Young's first name) owed Joe Kay a debt, and in lieu of money offered him the publishing rights to a manuscript on the occult. Kay had the book printed and peddled it door-to-door to Gypsies with storefront fortune-telling parlors. Joe Kay originally called his company Empire Publishing and later used the names Dorene Publishing and Raymond Publishing. Over the years, Joe Kay published more books by the enigmatic Mr. Young, under the pen names Lewis de Claremont and Henri Gamache, including standards like *Legends of Incense, Herbs, and Oils; The Seven Keys to Power;* and *Master Book of Candle Burning.*

In 1938 Joe Kay met the Harlem magician Black Herman and became the distributor of his book, *Secrets of Magic, Mystery, and Legerdemain.* It was at this time that Kay realized the tremendous potential of the African American market. In addition to the publication of occult books, he began to market a line of baths, oils, powders, incense, and candles called Dorene Products. In the late 1940s Joe Kay's brother Max (Joe Martin) also got into the spiritual business, opening a company called Ineeda Incense. Kay and Martin did not formulate the products themselves—"it wasn't worth it"—but bought baths, oils, perfumes, and powders in bulk from other manufacturers and repackaged them with their own labels.

In 1948 Joe Kay opened Fulton Religious Supply at 1304 Fulton Street in Brooklyn as a retail outlet for Dorene's books and products. The store was managed by Kay's longtime associate Moe Trugmann, while Joe and Ed Kay were on the road taking wholesale orders from stores all over the country. One of their best sellers, Young's Chinese Wash, was named for the writer of occult books. The label on the bottle reads, "Clear Away that Evil Mess with Young's Chinese Wash . . . leaving in its place the delightful odor of Oriental gums and grasses," and depicts little horned devils fleeing the moral authority of this powerful cleanser. As we noted in chapter 7, it was this label that inspired Catherine Yronwode's present-day version of Chinese Wash, now produced by her Lucky Mojo Curio Company.

After the death of Joe Kay in 1967, ownership of Fulton Religious Supply passed to Moe Trugmann and later to Trugmann's widow, Mitzi. Mrs. Trugmann spends much of her time in Florida, leaving the day-to-day operation of the store to an African American manager. In the same year, Ed Kay and his wife, Mary, moved to Arlington, Texas, a suburb of the Dallas–Fort Worth area, where they continue publication of the Dorene line of books. The Kay family also operates Mysteria, a wholesale and mail-order retail company. Ed Kay's daughter is now president of Dorene and Mysteria, and his granddaughter is the general manager. There are twenty employees.

The Mysteria mail-order retail catalog includes baths and washes, oils, powders, incense, and sprinkling salts (all manufactured on the premises), candles, herbs, minerals, "voodoo dolls," ritual kits, fortune-telling cards, and books, plus a small selection of dietary supplements and even some of Valmor's old-time hair-dressing preparations. None of the spiritual products is labeled in Spanish and there are no references to Santería. The name of Ed Kay appears nowhere in this catalog; the merchandise is offered by a person called "Shana Maidela." In an introductory letter, Shana states that "many of the products you will find within these pages are handmade by me personally and some of the other products I have brought back from my travels around the world." Ed Kay broke up laughing when I asked about the name. "It's Yiddish for 'pretty lady.' That's what I call my lovely wife, Mary." Shortly after requesting the Mysteria catalog, I began to receive monthly flyers. Included in these advertisements were testimonial letters, with photographs, from black and Hispanic women in Louisiana and Texas. One stated that she had won $25,250 playing the slot machine after burning the Golden Lamp of Luck; another reported that she had won $5,383 in the lottery after using the Lucky Gambler's Gold Piece; and a third said that, thanks to the African Mojo Beads and Lover's Amulet, her boyfriend had returned and she had gotten a better job.

A few years ago, Ed and Mary Kay sold their house in Texas, bought a fully equipped motor home, and now spend much of their time traveling. During 1997 and 1998 I had several telephone conversations with Ed Kay; because he was on the road, I had to dial his beeper and wait for him to return the call. On one occasion he telephoned me from a booth along the highway—he and Mary were headed for Las Vegas. Reminiscing about the evolution of the spiritual products industry, Kay noted, "It's a crazy business—so many people look at this and laugh, but I'm gonna tell ya, sweetheart, this laughing business has supported an awful lot of us over the years. No, we don't think it's funny—and neither do the people who buy from us."[20]

Nidia/M & A Amateau, New York

In Nidia/M & A Amateau we again find the manufacture of toiletries merging with the spiritual business. The company was founded by Morris Amateau, who arrived in New York from Spain in 1942 and opened the Nidia Botanical Garden at 70 East 114th Street in Spanish Harlem, two doors away from Alberto Rendón's West Indies Botanical Garden (now Botánica Chicas-Rendón). Morris Amateau was later joined in the business by his son Albert. The company specialized in Spanish perfumes, soaps, and lotions such as Jabon de Patchuli and Locion Sándalo, using genuine floral essences. Seeing the market for spiritual products, the Amateaus expanded

Fig. 47. Robert and Steve Amateau in their showroom at M & A Amateau, New York, July 9, 1998.

in that direction. Their first customers were African Americans and Puerto Ricans, and the products reflected the beliefs of these people. Santería-oriented products were introduced only when large numbers of Cubans settled in New York in the 1960s and 1970s. In 1969 the store moved to its present location, a narrow, three-story building at 73 East 115th Street. The name was changed to Nidia/M & A Amateau Incorporated.

The Amateau family is well represented in the spiritual products business. One of the owners of Original Products is the brother-in-law of Albert Amateau. Jack and Michael Amato (a variant spelling), owners of Rondo's Temple Sales in Atlanta since 1944, are cousins of the New York Amateaus.

Albert's son Robert Amateau began working for the company in 1971, and after the death of both his grandfather and his father in 1984, Robert inherited the business. He and his younger brother Steve now own M & A Amateau as equal partners. The Amateaus are primarily manufacturers and wholesalers of their own products and distributors for the products of other companies. On the day of my first visit in 1994, the area behind the counter was a bustle of activity, where a multiracial staff were bantering in English and Spanish, packing orders, and serving the long line of wholesale patrons picking up their Monday morning orders. I returned to interview Robert and Steve Amateau in 1998.

Amateau's wholesale catalog lists baths, floor wash, waters, perfumes, soaps, aerosol sprays, salts, rubbing alcohols, incense, oils, and candles; all but the soaps, sprays, and candles are manufactured in the back and upstairs rooms of the 114th Street building. A small retail outlet is located in the basement. Instead of producing large quantities to keep in stock, Robert and Steve, assisted by several employees, fill each order as it is received. They also sell roots and herbs, books, talismans, religious pictures, fortune telling cards, sheepskin parchment, copper bracelets, saltpeter, lodestone and magnetic sand, camphor tablets, powdered sulfur, mercury, turpentine, ammonia, benzine, and coal tar. According to Robert Amateau, they service "Europe, South America, the Caribbean, Texas, California, Atlanta, and the streets of New York."[21]

Original Products, the Bronx

Original Products, located at 2486 Webster Avenue in the Bronx, was founded in 1969 by Milton Benezra and Jack Mizrahi. I visited Original Products in the summer of 1998. Jack Mizrahi declined to be interviewed, protesting that he was "tired of answering questions," but Milton Benezra suggested that we go to a nearby coffee shop, where we talked over the din of shouting waitresses, clanking plates, a screaming infant, and a constantly ringing telephone.

According to Benezra, he and Jack Mizrahi met when they were both working for Macy's Department Store in the early 1950s. When Mizrahi left to work for his brother-in-law, Albert Amateau, Benezra saw an opportunity in the spiritual products business and joined his friend Jack at M & A Amateau. In 1959 Benezra opened his own store, the Magi Botanical Garden on Bathgate Avenue in the Bronx, and began to formulate baths, oils, and powders. When his store burned ten years later, he and Mizrahi formed a partnership that evolved into Original Products, also located on Bathgate Avenue. At first they manufactured a limited line of spiritual products and sold by direct retail and mail order. The merchandise was oriented toward African American hoodoo. Articles for Santería were introduced later as more Latinos moved into the neighborhood.

In 1975 Original Products relocated to its present address on Webster Avenue, a large, one-story corner building. The outside wall is decorated with a mural depicting Christ on the cross surrounded by seven Eleguá heads. While Original Products now wholesales to stores all over the United States and in the Caribbean, the business is still primarily retail. The sales area is stocked with ritual implements for Santería, occult books, and products from Original and other manufacturers. I even discovered some oils from the Ineeda Incense Company, the business founded by Joe Martin (brother of Joe Kay of Dorene Publications) and purchased by Original in 1985. Some of the old-style graphics used on Original Products labels originated with Ineeda. In the back of the store are offices and a private room for spiritual consultations by a reader. The rest of the first floor and the basement are devoted to manufacturing, storage, and packing. Only the baths, oils, perfumes, powders, and incense are mixed on the premises. There are ten employees, including Jack Mizrahi's son, Jason. The customers are black Americans, a few white Americans, West Indians, and Latinos—"we have whatever they need, no matter who they are." Milton Benezra and Jack Mizrahi both speak fluent Spanish, enabling them to converse with their Spanish-speaking patrons.

In 1984 Mizrahi and Benezra entered the book business as Original Publications, a separate company now owned by Milton's son, Marc. Their first book was Migene González-Wippler's *Santería: African Magic in Latin America*. When the first edition by Doubleday went out of print, Benezra bought the remainders, contacted the author, and obtained the rights. They now publish and distribute an extensive catalog of titles on Santería and the Yoruba religion, the kabbalah, dreams and numerology, Wicca, astrology, and Spiritism, as well as the classic hoodoo spell books. While most are reissues of out-of-print books, the company also publishes original manuscripts.

As we walked back to Original Products from the coffee shop, Milton Benezra summed up the philosophy of many of the manufacturers with whom I have spoken: "We aren't believers, we aren't practitioners; we don't do readings or perform rituals; we try to give people what they need, and we can advise them on how to use it. But basically, this is a business, and everything in that store is a unit of merchandise."[22]

Indio Products, Los Angeles

Indio Products, "The World's Most Complete Manufacturer and Distributor of Spiritual, Religious, and New Age Items," was founded in 1991 by Martin Mayer. I first contacted Mayer in 1994 while sending inquiries to a number of spiritual companies. He responded promptly, and soon we were exchanging letters and telephone calls. Over the years, "Marty" has been my most generous and cooperative informant, and it is due to him that I have had access to most of the other manufacturers interviewed for this chapter.

Mayer entered the spiritual business by way of a family-owned hoodoo drugstore. His aunt and uncle, Eleanor and Theodore Blum, were the proprietors of the Hy-Test at the corner of East 47th Street and Calumet, the heart of Chicago's black South Side. The Hy-Test opened in the 1920s and, like most drugstores in the neighborhood, sold patent medicines, toiletries, liquor, and spiritual products. The baths, oils, and powders were purchased from Doctor Pryor's Japo-Oriental Company and later from Lama Temple. Unlike some drugstore owners, the Blums never formulated their own spiritual products.

Mr. and Mrs. Blum and their two sons worked in the store and were well acquainted with the merchandise. They also employed black clerks who were knowledgeable about hoodoo and advised the customers on their purchases. Eleanor Blum related a humorous incident about the accidental "invention" of a new item: once a five-pound sack of incense broke on the floor, and her son Steve swept it up and packaged it in individual plastic bags, labeling it "Steve's Big Hit." A customer bought a bag and that night won a considerable sum of money in the local policy game. For weeks afterward, Steve's Big Hit was much in demand.[23]

Theodore Blum died suddenly in 1967. Mrs. Blum took over the management of the Hy-Test, and Marty Mayer, at age twenty-one, came to help his Aunt Eleanor in the store. It was there that he was introduced to the spiritual business and became acquainted with the manufacturers, particularly Lama Temple/Candle Corporation of America.

A year later, Mayer left the Hy-Test Drugstore to take a job at Candle Corporation of America and was employed there for the next seventeen years. Mayer became assistant manager of the Lama Temple Division at the Chicago office in 1969 and was promoted to manager in 1971. In 1972 he transferred to the Los Angeles office of Candle Corporation of America, overseeing the wholesale and retail operations. He left Candle Corporation in 1984 and entered a partnership with David Adler in the Skippy Candle Company, also manufacturers of spiritual products. In 1987 Mayer and Adler purchased International Imports, a mail-order retail company specializing in occult books and spiritual supplies. The partnership with David Adler was severed in 1991, and Mayer changed the name of the company to Indio Products, Incorporated. David Adler moved to Detroit and continued to operate Skippy Candle until the company went out of business in 1997.

International Imports was founded by Dorothy Spencer, author of the well-known "Anna Riva" series, including *The Modern Witchcraft Spellbook; The Modern Herbal Spellbook;* and *Voodoo Handbook of Cult Secrets.* Her mail-order retail catalog, the "Occult Digest—New Dimensions in the Field of Psychic Phenomena," was oriented toward European magical traditions and astrology as well as hoodoo. International Imports sold "witchcraft kits," semiprecious stones, botanicals, amulets, seals from the *Sixth and Seventh Books of Moses,* animal parts, jewelry, sound recordings, a large selection of books, and spiritual products, some of which had traditional hoodoo titles like John the Conqueror, Mojo, Van-Van, War Water, Hot Foot, and Jockey Club. Spencer also formulated several hundred oils, baths, and powders, which are sold under the Anna Riva brand name. The recipes, neatly typed on index cards, are now housed in file drawers at the Indio Products factory and are still used to formulate the Anna Riva line of products. Dorothy Spencer is now quite elderly and, unfortunately, suffers from Alzheimer's disease, so I was unable to interview her.

Starting with the business established by Dorothy Spencer, Martin Mayer built International Imports/Indio Products into the largest manufacturer and wholesaler of spiritual supplies in the world. From the beginning, he introduced products oriented toward Santería and titled them in Spanish. In 1992 he acquired the Seven Sisters of New Orleans Company, and in 1994 he purchased the Lama Temple Division of Candle Corporation of America, his former employers. Mayer continues to buy up small businesses across the country. Indio Products maintains a nationwide network of distributors from whom wholesale customers can pick up orders and avoid shipping charges, although some prefer to order directly from the Los Angeles factory. Mayer has expanded into the foreign market, with accounts in Mexico, Canada, the Caribbean, Australia, Europe, and Asia.

The current wholesale catalog features more than sixty-five hundred items: Mayer's "house brands"—Indio, Anna Riva, Seven Sisters of New Orleans, and Orishas; the Lama Temple line of products—Powerful Indian, River Jordan, Doctor Pryor's, and Ar-Jax; products by other American and foreign manufacturers; four hundred kinds of herbs and minerals; miscellaneous items like frankincense, myrrh, lodestones, saltpeter, camphor, alum, and sulfur; books, fortune-telling cards, crystal balls, Ouija boards, incense burners, talismans, holy cards, rosaries, religious medals, statues, and ritual items for Santería.

In the spring of 1997 I finally got to meet Marty Mayer. In a note informing me that he and his family were coming to Washington, D.C., on

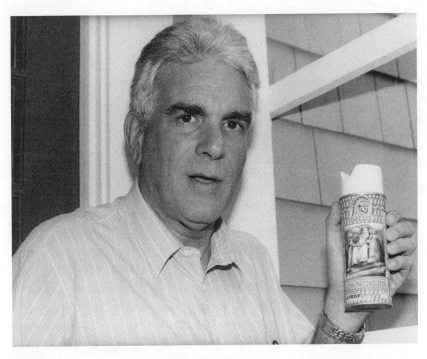

Fig. 48. Martin Mayer, Indio Products, displays a can of John the Conqueror aerosol spray, Washington, D.C., June 19, 1998.

vacation, he added, "Let's get together and talk shop!" One day, while his wife and teenaged daughters went shopping, Mayer and I visited his wholesale customers, and he regaled me with stories of the spiritual business. I had already planned a trip to Los Angeles for the following week, and Mayer offered me a tour of Indio Products.

The Indio Products factory, warehouse, and showroom were originally located in South Central Los Angeles, near Watts. During the 1992 riots that followed the acquittal of four white police officers charged with brutally beating black motorist Rodney King, the building came, as Mayer said, "within an eyelash of being burned to the ground." As a result of that near-disaster, Mayer thought it prudent to move the factory and warehouse thirty miles away to the suburb of Pacoima, leaving only the office and showroom in downtown Los Angeles.

The factory/warehouse is a large, open, one-story structure with work-stations around the walls and floor-to-ceiling racks in the center. The space is clean, well ventilated, and cheerful; on that day, the spring sunshine poured through large rolling doors, and upbeat music played on the sound system. Fifteen people work at the factory. The manager, Hank Solny, is the only white employee. With the exception of one African American woman, all of the factory workers are Mexican, mostly female. Only a few speak English. Mayer requires that they have legal immigration status and green cards. Most are paid minimum wage (the foreman and some who have worked there longer are paid more), and receive vacation, health and dental insurance, and a pension plan. When asked if the employees believe in and use the products they make, Mayer said he has no idea—"it's just a good job for them." I questioned the one black woman, who is originally from South Georgia: "No-no, I'm a born-again Christian. I don't have anything to do with hoodoo."

Heavy racks in the center of the building hold raw materials: herbs in burlap bales and metal drums, bags of wood flour, containers of fragrances and essential oils, powdered pigments, bottles of dye, cartons of jars for the glass-encased candles. Although Mayer has introduced some equipment for mixing the baths, oils, powders, and incense, the products are still essentially made and packaged by hand. This is not a highly mechanized, assembly-line process. Bath-and-floor wash is mixed in a 200-gallon tank, and the oils and perfumes are blended in separate fifty-gallon tanks. Incense powder is made in 250-pound batches in a dough mixer, combining wood flour (a by-product of the Oregon timber industry), mineral oil, fragrances, ground pigments for color, and saltpeter for combustibility. On the day of my visit, the candle department was making red candles shaped like naked women. Several large electric vats were filled with molten wax; a young woman was inserting wicks and pouring hot wax into the molds while another trimmed excess wax from the seams. At a long worktable against the wall, women filled bottles and containers and applied the labels by hand. Using a hammer, a man broke up large rocks of benzoin and myrrh into smaller chunks to be packaged for sale. All workers who handle the raw materials or the products wear protective aprons, rubber gloves, and dust masks. This factory produces the entire line of Indio, Anna Riva, Seven Sisters of New Orleans, and Orishas products, with the exception of the aerosol sprays and soaps, which are purchased from another source and labeled at the Indio factory. The neatly packed wholesale orders are stacked near the door, ready to be sent out by truck or UPS.

Leaving the green hills of Pacoima, we drove into South Central Los Angeles to visit the showroom. The nondescript cement-block building is located at 236 West Manchester between a Mexican restaurant and a drug treatment center. Nothing about the place denotes exoticism or the occult. The sign simply reads, "Indio Products: Candles, Books, Incense, Jewelry." The inside resembles a small supermarket. The merchandise is displayed on racks, and customers, most of whom are local store owners, stroll the aisles, filling their shopping carts with merchandise. At the front are several checkout lines. In a side room, a spiritual advisor is available for consultations. In the back are offices for Mayer, his secretary, several clerks who handle the orders, and Raúl González, the graphic designer. González creates labels, flyers, and the wholesale catalog on the computer.

Mayer is the consummate spiritual merchant, finding the business challenging and exciting. While some companies have carried the same items since their beginnings in the 1920s–40s, Mayer enjoys innovation, creating new products and packaging, and exploring new markets. A recent incense packet bears a graphic image that appears to be a group of amorphous shapes; if one stares at it for thirty seconds and then looks away, the shapes resolve themselves into the face of Jesus. Mayer was particularly pleased with his recently introduced "Orishas" line of candles, made in the appropriate color combination for each deity, and is contemplating something similar for the Vodou lwa, with titles in French. Getting into the spirit of things, I offered my own suggestions for product development. "What about some old-fashioned hoodoo—Doctor Buzzard's South Carolina Court-Case Powder—make it purple, like the purple sunglasses he used to wear. I'll design the labels for you." Mayer immediately perked up. "Yeah, we could make a whole line of Doctor Buzzard products—sell them down South!" "And while you're at it," I added, "Why not make product labels showing the *real* John the Conqueror—a big, strong black man?"[24]

CHAPTER 9

John the Conqueror: From Magical Root to Manufactured Product

*I*n this final chapter we will examine the most famous of African American charms, the spirit-embodying root called John the Conqueror. The name John the Conqueror is known even to those outside the community of believers; it is alluded to in the rhythm-and-blues classics that first sparked my curiosity in the 1950s, and is often exploited by outsiders to lend an element of hoodoo veracity to novels and films set in the American South. In its African derivation, its symbolic name and appearance, its indwelling spirit, its transmutation in the New World by slaves and their descendants, its later adoption by Spanish-speaking immigrants, and its commercialization by the manufacturers and retailers of spiritual products, John the Conqueror exemplifies all of the themes addressed by this book.

The "King Root of the Forest": Traditional Uses and Sources

The root known as High John the Conqueror is carried in the pocket and rubbed when needed; kept in the house as an amulet; "fed" or "dressed" with various substances; boiled to make baths and floor wash; soaked in whiskey, oils, and perfumes for an anointing substance; or incorporated into mojo bags and lucky hands. One also hears of Little John, Low John, Running John, Southern John, and other members of the "John" family.

These are used in the same manner as High John, but are not considered to be as potent. Another root, Chewing John the Conqueror, is chewed and the juice is spit in the vicinity of the person or situation that one wishes to influence. All of the John the Conqueror roots are used for protection from enemies and malevolent spirits; for luck in gambling, business, and money matters; to get a job; to obtain a favorable outcome in court cases; and for success with women. In traditional hoodoo practice, John the Conqueror is seldom employed for "bad work." None of the "John" roots is ingested for medicinal purposes.

In the chapter on African origins we noted the use of root-charms by the Kongo people. Twisted, swollen, phallus-shaped roots representing power and masculinity were incorporated into the charm-assemblages called minkisi. Such roots represent Funza, the Kongo personification of power and masculinity. The rhizomes of munkwiza, a member of the ginger family, embodied chiefly power; the chief's soul was believed to reside in the munkwiza root, which was chewed and spit to ward off enemies and detect sorcerers. Wyatt MacGaffey, the foremost expert on Kongo culture, describes munkwiza root as being "the size and color of a very large parsnip." According to MacGaffey, the BaKongo chew and spit spirit-embodying substances, referred to as medicine, "to put the nkisi or the patient [the target of the charm] in touch with the virtues contained by the medication." He was cautious about declaring munkwiza root to be the prototype for Chewing John, calling it an "interesting possibility."[1]

We also know, from the nineteenth-century accounts of former slaves and from reports submitted by black students at the Hampton Institute, that enslaved people of African descent carried root-charms as amulets or chewed them and spit the juice. The narratives of Frederick Douglass and Henry Bibb, in which they recount events of the 1830s, are quoted in chapter 4. The reader will recall that Douglass spoke of a root, given to him by a slave conjurer who was a "genuine African," to be carried in his pocket for protection against a brutal slave-breaker. Bibb said that an old conjurer on his home plantation gave him "some kind of bitter root to chew and spit toward [the master]" to protect himself from being flogged.[2] One of the 1878 Hampton Institute reports published in the *Southern Workman* told of a "kind of root conjurers always carry in their pockets." Another said: "This old [conjurer] was a slave on a large plantation. His fellow servants would pay him whatever he charged; then he would give them some kind of root to chew, telling them that they could . . . do anything they wanted to and their masters would not find it out."[3] None of these early accounts calls the roots by name, but the one carried in the pocket for protection sounds like High John the Conqueror, and the one that was chewed and spit was probably Chewing John.

In 1891 a root called "Conjure John" or "Indian turnip" was mentioned by Mary Alicia Owen, a white woman from Missouri, in a presentation before the International Folklore Congress. In her paper, "Among the Voodoos," Owen described the beliefs of a group of former slaves, some of whom remembered African parents, who had come to Missouri from the Deep South after the Civil War. They taught her "the value of certain vegetable remedies and poisons, among them Indian turnip or Conjure John." The white root of Conjure John was to be combined with alum, sulfur, and salt to make a "lucky jack," and the red seeds were to be used for a "bad trick."[4] Conjure John might have been the same as John the Conqueror.

The first specific published reference to John the Conqueror root appeared in 1899. A short article called "Remedies to Cure Conjuration" was contributed by an anonymous member of the Hampton Folklore Society and published in the Folklore and Ethnology section of the *Southern Workman*. Without identifying the plant source, the writer specified that "The king root of all the forest is called 'High John the Conqueror.' All believers in conjuring quake when they see a bit of it in the hand of anyone."[5]

This description was quoted by Newbell Niles Puckett in *Folk Beliefs of the Southern Negro* (1926), and is repeated in a 1930 article, "Fern Seed—For Peace" by Ruth Bass: "The king root of all the forest is High John the Conqueror. It will ward off any disease that has been brought on by conjure and all witches quake when they see a bit of it in a person's hand."[6] Bass, a white Mississippian, gathered her information from elderly blacks who worked on her family's plantation and taught her about the healing and magical properties of plants.

I had assumed that "the king root of the forest" was a phrase coined by the writer of the *Southern Workman* article and repeated by Puckett and Bass, until I discovered the identical words in Hyatt's *Hoodoo-Conjure-Witchcraft-Rootwork*. A Brunswick, Georgia, man related that his grandfather, a root doctor who died at the age of 104, "used John the Conker all the time . . . he said that was the king root of the forest."[7] "The king root of the forest" must have been a common designation by black southerners for High John the Conqueror root.

Nineteenth-century examples emphasize the use of John the Conqueror root as a protective charm to "conquer" human enemies and evil spirits. In the 1920s–40s, Zora Neale Hurston, Harry Middleton Hyatt, and the Federal Writers' Project fieldworkers documented a greater variety of uses for John the Conqueror, probably the most frequently mentioned natural ingredient in the charm formulae collected by these researchers. Some of their informants referred to a root that was to be carried or incorporated into charm assemblages, bath-and-floor wash, and anointing substances, and others spoke of a root to be chewed and spit. In addition to its protective function, the root was employed for love, business and employment, court cases, and luck—to "conqueror" others and make them do the will of the charm user. Like the examples seen in previous chapters, these John the Conqueror charms adhere to the principles of imitative and contagious magic while reflecting the improvisational character of African American folklore. There was no significant difference between John the Conqueror charms in New Orleans, the Gulf Coast and Mississippi Delta, the Low Country, or the Upper South.

John the Conqueror roots were still popular as protective charms. Hyatt's "Laughing Doctor" of Waycross, Georgia, used High John in a mojo bag to be hung on the head of the bed. "It conquers anything that come inside that house in the way of . . . devilments—that's why it's called High John the Conker." Doctor England of Norfolk spoke of making a "shield" to guard against evil conjure. In a little bag he combined "High John the Conker, the Devil's shoestring, buckeye, white corime seed, and the gall of the earth. . . . Every Friday morning, wet [it] with your urine." In Richmond, "First Doctor" said that before approaching the house of someone who might be an enemy, "I got a little piece of [John the Conqueror root] in my mouth chewin' on it. Spit in my hand before I [touch] his door knob."[8]

Reports from the Louisiana Writers' Project are primarily concerned with the use of High John the Conqueror in sexual matters. The symbolism of the phallus-shaped root is obvious. In 1936 Madame Ducoyielle, the elderly hoodoo practitioner with whom fieldworker Robert McKinney had established a friendship, took McKinney to a hoodoo drugstore to buy some John the Conqueror roots:

What humdingers they is! Look at old Johnny, he wants to do something already. Boy, I could fix 'em up. . . . Mix [the John the Conqueror root] with some cayenne pepper and sugar and take it to your woman's house. If she is not treatin' you right just put the Johnny Conqueror root under her bed, and child, I mean she is going to function from then on. She is a conquered fool but doesn't know it. . . . Yes sir, Johnny Conqueror is the best stuff for women.

You got a girl that you want bad and she with somebody else? Well, we'll fix that. . . . Get a grapefruit, pie pan, five cents colored candles, cayenne pepper, epsom salts, sugar, and salt. Cut the grapefruit in half. Write the man and the girl's name on a piece of brown paper. Cross the names well so no one can make 'em out. Put the brown paper in the middle of the grapefruit . . . put it in the pie pan, sprinkle the epsom salts, pepper, sugar, and salt. . . . Light the five colored candles 'round the grapefruit. Put this stuff under a fig tree every morning at 6:00 and pray to your Johnny Conqueror to part 'em. . . . On the tenth day they will be good and parted. The girl will get in touch with you.[9]

Although the use of this second charm would supposedly result in separating the young lady from her current lover, its ultimate intention was to draw her to the charm user. Thus this is primarily an attraction charm, not to be classified as "bad work."

Researchers documented a number of John the Conqueror charms for success in business, employment, and money matters. In *Mules and Men*, Hurston reported that to rent out rooms, one must scrub the house with a floor wash made by boiling John the Conqueror root, rice, sycamore bark, and fig leaves.[10] A man interviewed by Hyatt in Brunswick, Georgia, placed a John the Conqueror root over all the doors in his house to bring in customers. In St. Petersburg, Florida, Hyatt was told that John the Conqueror root grows in the swamp—"it got joints in it like your finger." When conducting a business deal, "you bite off a piece 'for you get there . . . and you chew it up and be spittin' as you talk to 'em . . . and he comin' your way." A Vicksburg, Mississippi, informant advised Hyatt that John the Conqueror should be chewed and spit when asking a white man for a favor or a loan. The "Hustling Woman" of Memphis added that, when seeking a job, one must "get [the potential employer] so he'll walk across there where you spit. . . . And then . . . he'll give you the job."[11]

The use of John the Conqueror roots to influence the outcome of a court case was ubiquitous. Hurston advised that the user should soak High John the Conqueror root in whiskey, mix that with Jockey Club perfume, and rub it on the body before going to court.[12] A Waycross, Georgia, informant told Hyatt that one should soak John the Conqueror root in Heart's (Hoyt's) Cologne until it gets soft, then "put it in your pants pocket, and while you be talkin' to the judge, be rubbin' it . . . it conquers anything you up to." A man in Memphis told him to chew the root and spit in the court-house cuspidor and "they be done turn you loose."[13]

Luck, especially luck in gambling, was possibly the most popular use of John the Conqueror root. It was a frequent ingredient in the assembly of "lucky hands." Hyatt's informant, Madam Lindsey of Algiers, Louisiana, gave one such formula: "For the luck bag you just put . . . wishin' beans and powdered John the Conker root, powdered Wonder of the World root, love powder, and five finger grass . . . and dried parsley root. Sew that up. It'll bring you luck." In Fayetteville, North Carolina, Hyatt heard that, "You . . . sleep with that [John the Conqueror root] under your head nine nights and you put that in your pocket . . . when you go to a skin game [game of cards or dice]. You just rub your hand over it . . . and make your wishes, and . . . you'll win like anything." John the Conqueror root was also chewed and spit as a gambling charm. "Hoodoo Book Man" of New Orleans said, "You put that [John the Conqueror root] in your mouth and you chew it, and you spit it all aroun' the table where you're gamblin'. . . . That's to make . . . everything come your way."[14]

In the early years of his conjure practice, the famous Dr. Jim Jordan of North Carolina gathered his own roots and herbs. John the Conqueror, he said, was the root of a climbing vine. Roots that grew on high ground were called High John or Mo Jo, and those that grew on low ground were Low John or Lo Jo. Another root was called Running John: "Jim diced the roots into small wheels and dropped the sections into bottles of perfume. When the Mo Jo had swelled . . . a courting man needed only to put the liquid on his necktie to become irresistible to his lady fair. . . . Lo Jo was prepared like Mo Jo. The potion, however, possessed negative power: [it] 'drove folks from you' [and could] turn friends into enemies. . . . Jim sold the Running John root as a charm . . . to be carried in the pocket to bring good luck."[15] Doctor Jordan's use of Lo Jo for antisocial purposes is inconsistent with tradition.

■ ■ ■

What was the original plant source of the "John roots" used during the time of slavery and in the late nineteenth and early twentieth centuries? Were they all the same plant, were specific plants used for specific intentions, or were a number of different plants used interchangeably, depending on avail-ability and the preference of the practitioner? One assumes that these plants produced large, fleshy taproots, rhizomes, or tubers, and that the bitter "chewing" root contained no pharmacologically active substances that would produce an unpleasant physical reaction. We can conjecture that memories of African roots, like the swollen and twisted formations incorporated into minkisi and the munkwiza root that was chewed and spit, were combined with Native American knowledge of local plants, and that roots with the requisite properties were found in the southeastern United States.

Ruth Bass was the first writer to assign a botanical identity to High John the Conqueror root. In her 1930 article, "Fern Seed—For Peace," she declared that "This magic plant [High John the Conqueror] is the marsh St. John's-wort, a member of the same family which in Europe has been credited with the power of preserving people against lightning. . . . [High John the Conqueror] is commonly placed under the doorsteps to prevent the nightly visitations of ghosts, witches, and nightmares. It is a cure-all for any kind of wounds, and the dew that gathers upon its leaves is excellent for strengthening the eyesight."[16]

Bass's identification is problematic because St. John's wort roots are a branching, fibrous mass, not the fleshy, swollen taproots, tubers, and rhizomes that we associate with John the Conqueror. While there is no record of any part of the St. John's wort plant being employed by African Americans for magical or medicinal purposes, books on European herbalism and folk medicine state that the flowers, leaves, and stems, but not the root, of St. John's wort (*Hypericum perforatum*) were used to protect against lightning, drive away devils and evil spirits, and heal wounds—functions that Bass assigns to High John the Conqueror. St. John's wort was considered to be most potent if gathered on June 24, Midsummer's Day, the feast day of St. John the Baptist.[17] Clarence Meyer, former owner of the Indiana Botanic Garden and author of many books on herbalism, confirmed that "the roots of St. John's wort do not remotely resemble so-called John the Conqueror."[18] It is my opinion that Bass confused European traditions regarding the magical properties of St. John's wort with African American beliefs about High John the Conqueror root. Nevertheless, this misidentification continues to be repeated in such respected publications as *The Dictionary of Folklore, Mythology, and Legend* and *The Encyclopedia of Southern Culture*.

Varro Tyler, professor of pharmacognosy at Purdue University, agrees. In his article "The Elusive History of High John the Conqueror Root" in the *Journal of the History of Pharmacy* (1991), Tyler says: "More than a score of different *Hypericum* [Saint John's wort] species, varieties, and hybrids grow in this country. Many of them grow in low, moist areas, and the roots of most are similar in appearance. For this reason it is not possible to identify with certainty the species of *Hypericum* said to yield High John the Conqueror. Probably several different species are involved, but none appears to yield the root that is commercially available at present."[19]

We have already explored the possibility that the root called Indian turnip or Conjure John was the same as John the Conqueror. This native woodland plant is more commonly known as Jack-in-the-pulpit (*Arisaema triphyllum*). It has an acrid root, and the phallus-shaped spadix, or "Jack," produces bright red seeds in the fall. Jack-in-the-pulpit roots, although very bitter, are not poisonous and were used medicinally as an expectorant and diaphoretic. They could have been chewed without ill effect. Jack-in-the-pulpit grows in the moist forests of the Southeast.[20]

The well-known Appalachian herbalist Tommie Bass identifies Solomon's seal root as John the Conqueror.[21] Solomon's seal (*Polygonatum odoratum*) is a native plant with white, fleshy, jointed rhizomes; the new shoots, when they first emerge in the spring, are flesh-colored and have a startlingly phallic appearance. All parts of the plant are poisonous, so Solomon's seal could not have been the root called Chewing John. It could, however, have been carried as an amulet or incorporated into charm assemblages. According to George Hocking's *Dictionary of Terms in Pharmacognosy* (1955), Solomon's seal was sometimes known as Low John the Conqueror.[22]

Several species of wild morning glory (*Ipomoea*) are also candidates. *Cunningham's Encyclopedia of Magical Herbs*, in fact, says that "the roots of the morning glory may be substituted for High John the Conqueror root."[23] Several species of *Ipomoea* (*macrorrhiza* and *violacea*) grow along the Gulf Coast of the United States. Some *Ipomoea* roots have purgative qualities, rendering them undesirable for chewing, but none is poisonous. The climbing vine used by Doctor Jim Jordan might have been a morning glory. Pam Chavers, a Tennessee herbalist, related that she had observed an elderly black couple harvesting the roots of wild purple morning glories, known to them as High John the Conqueror. They later gave Chavers a dried root, instructing her that it could be used to make floor wash, anointing oil, amulets, or candles.[24] Wild morning glory roots can reach formidable proportions in the semitropical climate of coastal Florida, Alabama, Mississippi, Louisiana, and Texas, where they live from year to year. But in regions of the Upper South where the plants freeze and die in winter, the roots can never achieve the size and fleshiness associated with John the Conqueror.

Jim Haskins, in *Voodoo and Hoodoo* (1978), stated that, according to the "old folks" in his Alabama hometown, the source of High John the Conqueror root was tormentil.[25] The plant usually known as tormentil, *Potentilla tormentilla*, is not native to the United States. Its astringent, red-fleshed roots were used in European folk magic for protection against spirits and to draw a lover. The roots were boiled to make an infusion, and the plant was hung up in the home to drive away evil.[26] Varro Tyler believes that Haskins must be referring to the American tormentil (*Geranium maculatum*) commonly called wood geranium or cranesbill, rather than the European tormentil. Wood geranium grows abundantly in the southeastern United States and its red roots were used as a folk remedy.[27] Outside of Haskins's work, I have never heard of wood geranium being associated with John the Conqueror.

The Identity of John the Conqueror

In the African traditional religions, European folk Christianity and popular magic, and the African-based New World belief systems, magical objects are believed to be endowed with an indwelling spirit or to enable the user to contact an external spirit. While many of the traditional hoodoo roots and herbs have evocative names suggesting their appearance or their use, the title John the Conqueror suggests a real presence behind the charm. Who is John the Conqueror and what is the origin of his name?

John the Conqueror appears to be an African American hoodoo spirit not encountered elsewhere in the New World. The concept of John the Conqueror as the indwelling spirit of a magical root may have Kongo antecedents, introduced into the English colonies of Virginia and Maryland by the predominantly Kongo slaves. In *Flash of the Spirit*, Robert Farris Thompson equates John the Conqueror with Funza, the spirit of power and masculinity also embodied in a root that was incorporated into Kongo minkisi.[28] An alternative theory suggests a Fon/Yoruba origin in Louisiana, where John the Conqueror may have derived from West African deities and been associated with John the Baptist. Either of these possibilities also allows for the conflation of John the Conqueror with the personality of some powerful leader within the African American community.

The prototype of John the Conqueror could have been a historic person, possibly a famous conjurer, who became associated in the minds of believers with this African spirit. I am particularly intrigued by the title "High John." The word *high* connotes authority, as in high sheriff or high court, as well as strength and potency, as in a "high-smelling" perfume. In coastal Maryland and Virginia a conjurer was called a "high man." Hyatt, in fact, met a conjure doctor on Deal Island, Maryland, who called himself "High John the Conqueror, the Root Man, the Gall of the Earth."[29] This, coupled with the fact that the first recorded use of the name High John the Conqueror comes from the newsletter of the Hampton Institute in Virginia, leads me to suspect that the name originated in the earliest English colonies and has its source in English folklore. This topic invites further research: was "high man" synonymous with "cunning man" and "wise man" in England during the time of the slave trade, and was there an English folk character called John the Conqueror?

I have searched in vain for any reference to John the Conqueror in European popular Christianity, magical lore, and hero tales. He does not appear in classic occult texts like *The Egyptian Secrets of Albertus Magnus*, *The Sixth and Seventh Books of Moses*, or *Pow-Wows*, long popular with African American hoodoo workers. I was excited to find an advertisement in the 1929 catalog of the R. C. Adams Company (an early Chicago spiritual supplier), stating that John the Conqueror root was "named after the great British leader." A search of the literature was disappointing. It was William I of England (1066–1087) who was called "The Conqueror," not King John (1199–1216), one of the most unpopular monarchs in English history. Nor was there a famous military commander called John the Conqueror.

One also thinks of Prester John as a possible prototype for John the Conqueror. Prester (or Presbyter) John was the legendary medieval Christian priest-king of a mysterious Asian or African realm. Tales of Prester John first appeared in the mid-twelfth century. He was said to be descended from the Magi, to rule over a kind of earthly paradise where strife and poverty were unknown, and to be the conqueror of the Muslim infidels. Europeans fastened their imagination and their hopes upon this supposed ally against Islam. At first they sought Prester John among the Christianized rulers of Asia, but by the fourteenth century he had become identified with the king of Abyssinia (the present-day country of Ethiopia), where a variant of Coptic Christianity had been practiced since the fourth century. The Portuguese eventually formed an alliance with Ethiopia against the Muslim nations, and during the sixteenth century Portuguese Jesuit missionaries attempted to convert the Ethiopians to Roman Catholicism— an effort that ultimately failed.[30] At approximately the same time, the Portuguese were establishing contact with the Kongo people, and Jesuit missionaries also made intensive efforts to convert the BaKongo to Christianity.[31] The Prester John legend persisted throughout the centuries of the slave trade, and enslaved BaKongo brought to the North American colonies by the English could conceivably have heard of Prester John from Portuguese missionaries.

There is also a possibility that the name comes out of the New Orleans Voodoo tradition. John the Conqueror might be a manifestation of one or more of the Fon/Yoruba deities introduced into Louisiana by slaves imported during the Spanish period. In his role as a protector against human enemies, authority figures, and malevolent spirits, John the Conqueror resembles Gu (Ogou in Vodou, Ogún in Santería), the warrior spirit of iron and warfare. His function as a bringer of luck in gambling, business, and money matters relates him to Eshu (Legba in Vodou, Eleguá in Santería), the trickster spirit who governs chance and the crossroads. In his role as a "conqueror" of women, he is related to Shangó (Changó in Santería), the handsome and virile spirit of thunder and lightning.[32] Although John the Conqueror has parallels among the lwa and the orichas, he plays no role in Vodou or Santería.[33]

In *The Spiritual Churches of New Orleans*, Claude Jacobs and Andrew Kaslow suggest that John the Conqueror might have been Doctor John, the famous nineteenth-century New Orleans Voodoo priest.[34] This notion is reflected in the lyrics of New Orleans musician Mac Rebennack, who uses the stage name Doctor John. In Rebennack's composition "Black John the Conqueror," John the Conqueror is conflated with Doctor John the Conjurer.[35]

French *grimoires*, such as *La Poule Noire* (The Black Pullet) and *Les Secrets Merveilleux de la Magie Naturelle du Petit Albert* (Little Albert's Marvelous Secrets of Natural Magic), commonly called the *'Tit Albert*, were popular with French-speaking blacks in Louisiana and were cited as cherished reference books by some of the people interviewed by Hyatt and the Louisiana Writers' Project. But these books, like the English translations of German manuals favored by hoodoo workers in the other southern states, contain no mention of John the Conqueror.

The same folklore reference books that incorrectly identify John the Conqueror root as St. John's wort, a plant associated with St. John the Baptist, assert that the character of John the Conqueror is synonymous with this saint. None of the people interviewed by Hurston, Hyatt, or the Federal Writers' Project fieldworkers mentioned John the Baptist in conjunction with John the Conqueror. On the other hand, St. John is particularly important in Haitian Vodou, where the patron of Freemasonry is treated as a minor lwa. As we learned in chapter 3, the Eve of St. John the Baptist was the date of important annual Voodoo ceremonies in nineteenth-century New Orleans. This custom could have been introduced by Haitian immigrants. Might St. John, the man who baptized Jesus, preached in the wilderness, was tempted, and conquered Satan, have also been known as John the Conqueror?

Zora Neale Hurston, in her 1943 article "High John de Conker," published in the *American Mercury* magazine, advanced yet another theory. Hurston associated the indwelling spirit of John the Conqueror root with the African American slave trickster hero Old John, a man of great strength and cunning. Stories of Old John and his adversary Old Marster constitute a cycle of folk narratives that parallel the better-known tales of Brer Rabbit.[36] After the abolition of slavery, according to Hurston's article, High John the Conqueror "went back to Africa, but he left his power here, and placed his American dwelling in the root of a certain plant. Only possess that root, and he can be summoned at any time . . . thousands of humble people who still believe in him . . . do John reverence by 'dressing' [the root] with perfume and keeping it on their person, or in their houses in a secret place. It is there to help them overcome things they feel they could not beat otherwise, and to bring them the laugh of the day."[37]

Prior to Hurston's 1943 interpretation, John the Conqueror is not known to have been equated with Old John, although the connection may have existed in the oral tradition. When Hurston's article was reprinted in Alan Dundes's *Mother Wit from the Laughing Barrel* (1973), Dundes stated that "Most accounts of the root make no mention of a related trickster figure, and none of the various collections of "John and Marster" folktales refer to the root. It is just possible that Zora Neale Hurston, who one must remember was both creative writer and folklorist, simply decided to combine the root and the trickster figure for esthetic reasons."[38]

John the Conqueror, the indwelling spirit of a magical root, would appear to be a mélange of African deities, possibly combined with one or more powerful conjurers, a saint who is honored as a lwa, and a legendary slave trickster. In all of these aspects, John the Conqueror personifies a strong, dark, virile, masculine spirit who protects his devotees and brings them success, wealth, and luck. He represents the resiliency and empowerment of black people in surviving slavery and its aftermath of poverty and racism.

The Commodification of John the Conqueror

By the 1920s–40s, few people gathered plants in the wild, preferring the convenience of the hoodoo drugstores and the mail-order dealers in spiritual supplies and medicinal herbs. Hyatt noted that "the meaning of [John the Conqueror] has varied with place and time and individuals—especially in hoodoo shops, where . . . anything available is handed to the customer."[39] Retailers and mail-order houses offered the whole family of John roots, some with names that may never have existed in traditional hoodoo practice: High John, Low John, Little John, Chewing John, European John, Southern John, and Dixie John. A 1940s advertising card from Billon's Pharmacy in Gonzales, Louisiana, lists, among other roots, herbs, and spiritual products, something called "Johnson's Conqueror Root."[40]

The illustrations from early mail-order catalogs and product labels are drawn with such accuracy that pharmacognosist Varro Tyler of Purdue University could easily identify the roots by their botanical names.[41] Tyler's identifications were confirmed by Hocking's *Dictionary of Terms in Pharmacognosy*. Few of the roots sold by these spiritual entrepreneurs were native to the southeastern United States, although some may have resembled the indigenous John the Conqueror roots.

An advertisement (circa 1930s) from the Algiers Company of Port Washington, Wisconsin, depicts High John the Conqueror root as something resembling a dried yam. The message reads:

HIGH JOHN ROOT

Said to contain wonderful lucky properties when carried on one's person. Carry one with you all the time. We make no such claims, but sell only as genuine John the Conqueror. Handy carrying bag FREE with every root.[42]

Sovereign Products of Chicago advertised attractively boxed "root curios," including John the Conqueror, in their 1936 catalog (fig. 1). The Lucky Heart Company of Memphis sold High John the Conqueror roots neatly packaged in a little box. The label featured a tuberous root, lucky symbols, and the words "love, luck, power, fortune." King Novelty, a subsidiary of Chicago's Valmor Company, offered High John in its 1936 Curio Catalog. The advertising copy for High John the Conqueror is consistent with its traditional usage.

A person carrying one of these HIGH JOHN ROOTS in his pocket or on his person will never be without Money and will be very Lucky and Successful in his undertakings. Many . . . think that this strange root acts as a powerful LUCK CHARM for Winning Games, Drawing Lucky Numbers, and that it helps in Love Affairs and Drives Away Evil influences. However, we make no claims to this effect and sell only as a curio.

John the Conqueror

Fig. 49. High John the Conqueror Root label—Lucky Heart Company, Memphis, 1930s.

Fig. 50. High John the Conqueror (jalap root)—King Novelty Curio Catalog, Chicago, 1936.

The High John the Conqueror roots depicted in these vintage advertisements, labels, and catalogs have been identified as jalap (*Ipomoea jalapa*). Jalap is a member of the morning glory family native to Jalapa, in the state of Vera Cruz, Mexico. The root is a hard, dark brown, wrinkled tuber. Immature jalap roots are usually about two inches long and an inch in diameter, sometimes bulbous, sometimes slender and twisted, although they can reach a much greater size. Jalap is a strong purgative that was introduced into the American pharmacopoeia in 1827, and was still used medicinally until about the 1950s.[43] Jalap might have been chosen because other *Ipomoea* species native to the Gulf Coast were traditionally used as High John the Conqueror.

While many of the early spiritual supply companies sold High John roots, only King Novelty offered Little John to Chew and Southern John. The twisted rhizome sold by King Novelty as Little John to Chew is galangal *(Alpinia galanga)*, a member of the ginger family that is not native to the United States. Galangal is used medicinally for coughs, sore throat, and stomach upsets, and as a flavoring in Asian cooking.[44] Recall that the Kongo munkwiza root is also a type of ginger. The advertisement for Little John to Chew states that "Some folks like to chew this root and believe it to be a powerful luck bringer for Money, Love, and Driving Away Evil." Spitting the juice is not mentioned, nor is its use as a court-case charm. The advertisement emphasized that the roots are "fresh and clean . . . and come packed in a sanitary box."

The root advertised in the King Novelty catalog as Southern John is beth root *(Trillium* sp.), an indigenous North American plant used as an astringent and to control hemorrhages during childbirth. Southern John, according to the catalog, was to be carried in the pocket to feel "Strong and Powerful . . . and never be without Luck." Southern John was never mentioned in the 1920s–40s interviews with traditional practitioners, and I suspect that the name was coined by Valmor's owner, Morton Neumann.

I have found that jalap, galangal, and beth root are still sold, somewhat interchangeably, as the various John the Conqueror roots. These medicinal roots were undoubtedly chosen for sale by the spiritual merchants of the 1920s–40s because they were in plentiful supply, would keep indefinitely when dried, and because they more or less resembled the originals. Since most retailers obtain their roots from the same distributors, there are no significant regional variations; the choice of roots depends more on availability and the

Fig. 51. Little John to Chew (galangal root)—King Novelty Curio Catalog, Chicago, 1936.

Fig. 52. Southern John the Conqueror Root (beth root)—King Novelty Curio Catalog, Chicago, 1936.

whim of the store owner. While most of the roots sold as High John the Conqueror are jalap, some stores and mail-order companies are selling beth root or galangal as High John. Galangal is most often sold as Chewing John, but it is also called Little John and Low John. Beth root is sold as Southern John, Low John, and Chewing John. The instructions given by present-day store owners are fairly consistent with traditional usage. I was told to carry the High John and Southern John roots for luck and protection. The Chewing John roots were to be chewed and spit, or simply held in my mouth, should I ever have to appear in court as a defendant.

An intriguing bit of contemporary folklore about John the Conqueror root came to my attention while collecting for this project. In the 1990s, when jalap roots were becoming difficult to obtain from Mexico, I heard from store owners at the Miracle Workshop in Brooklyn, the New Orleans Historic Voodoo Museum, and House of Power in Houston that High John the Conqueror root, presumably jalap, was becoming very scarce because it was being used to treat AIDS.[45] While this sounds like a fabrication calculated to make the product more desirable, there turns out to be a slender connection between AIDS research and John the Conqueror. The pharmacologically active constituents of St. John's wort, hypericin and pseudohypericin, actually *are* being used in AIDS research; however, these substances are not extracted from the plant, but are prepared synthetically.[46]

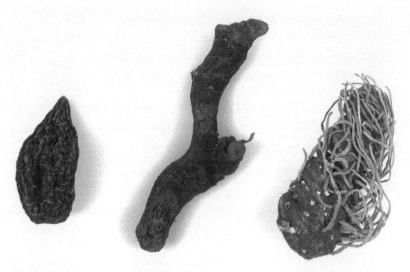

Fig. 53. Jalap, galangal, and beth roots. Compare these roots, purchased from spiritual stores in the 1990s, with the King Novelty Curio Catalog illustrations from 1936.

Although any number of roots have been used and sold as John the Conqueror, I feel quite certain that none of them is Saint John's wort.

■ ■ ■

The early manufacturers and mail-order retailers of spiritual products not only sold individual John the Conqueror roots, they also offered prefabricated mojo bags and lucky hands containing John the Conqueror roots and other allegedly magical ingredients. The 1929 catalog of the R. C. Adams Company of Chicago advertised the John the Conqueror Root Bag, containing "an assortment of roots which in ancient days were believed to bring good luck in love, business, and games." King Novelty sold High John the Conqueror Fixed in Bag with Van-Van Oil and Five Finger Grass:

> Some folks in the South visit the Voodoo man, who often charges big fees such as $5.00 or even $25.00 for his services. Worried and troubled men and women have gone away HAPPY when the Voodoo priest prescribed this fetish which consisted of High John the Conqueror Root fixed in red flannel bag with Lodestone and Five Finger Grass. This bag was to be worn around the neck and sprinkled every morning with Van-Van Oil. The

superstition was that this acted as a Luck Charm and would Drive Away Evil and would Attract much Good Luck and Money and would bring about the thing desired. We of course make no claims to this effect and sell only as a Curio.

The Sovereign Products catalog, also from 1936, sold the Three Snake Head Curio Bag, embellished with a picture of three snakes.

This attractive Bag contains John the Conqueror Root, Real Magnetic Lodestone, Lodestone Powder, Hand Roots, Black Cat Bone Emblems, and Incense. . . . Many persons desiring success in Jobs, Business, Games, and Love carry with them such curios. We make no claim for these goods and sell them only as remarkable curios.

We have already noted that, in the world of spiritual products, the name of John the Conqueror is apparently perceived to be as powerful as the actual root. Vintage catalogs, advertisements, and labels from King Novelty, Famous Products, Sovereign, Keystone, Lucky Heart, and Clover

Fig. 54. High John the Conqueror Fixed in Bag—King Novelty Curio Catalog, Chicago, 1936. This commercially produced item emulated hand-made mojo bags and lucky hands, even providing Van-Van Oil for "feeding" the charm.

Sold as a Curio Only

Horn demonstrate that John the Conqueror tonic, floor wash, oils, perfumes, sprinkling salts, and incense were among the first to be offered by the pioneering manufacturers of spiritual products. The oils and perfumes often contained an actual root, as did traditional anointing substances. In the 1930s, Keystone Laboratories sold High John the Conqueror Root in Holy Oil, and Sovereign Products and King Novelty sold John the Conqueror Root in Perfume—"This is our latest perfume creation—a Genuine John the Conqueror Root in each bottle" (figs. 9 and 44).

To reinforce the concept of power and royalty, John the Conqueror product labels and advertisements carry images of strong, authoritative men—most often a bearded European king with royal robes, crown, and a scepter or sword. This king may have been inspired by the figures on early playing cards.

The image of John the Conqueror as a white medieval king appears to have originated with the Valmor subsidiaries, King Novelty Company and Famous Products. Could the designer of these graphics possibly have known that High John was called "the king root of the forest" or was this simply his

Fig. 55. Playing card, king of swords. National Museum of American History, Smithsonian Institution, Department of Cultural History, Vidal Collection, accession #1997.0097.0173, used by permission.

Fig. 56. Tonic bottle—Famous Products, Chicago, 1937. Gift of Martin Mayer, Indio Products. Photo by Richard Strauss.

interpretation of a "conqueror"? The same king appears in the 1936 and 1945 King Novelty catalogs, advertising John the Conqueror roots, floor wash, perfume, incense, and mojo bags. It was also used on the label on a 1937 bottle of Famous Products John the Conqueror Great Herb Compound, a laxative that contained cascara bark, buckthorn bark, berberis, mandrake root, senna leaves, capsicum, aloes, and juniper berries. Note that it did not contain jalap, the purgative root most often sold as High John.

The King Novelty and Famous Products graphics set the precedent for future images of John the Conqueror. A Lucky Heart label from the 1930s features the same king surrounded by a border of good-luck symbols: heart, horseshoe, four-leaf clover, and swastika (fig. 49). Crude reinterpretations of this king are used on product labels to this day. Examples from my collection include Clover Horn's High John the Conqueror Floor Wash and Old Grandpa's High John the Conqueror Bath, both made by Baltimore spiritual suppliers; a bottle of oil from Paco's Botanical Products in New York; and Hi-John the Conqueror Perfume from Stanley Drug in Houston. Other manufacturers of spiritual products—Lama Temple, E. Davis, Amateau, Vandi, La Milagrosa, and Indio—have their own version of the white king. Martin Mayer of Indio Products has pulled off the ultimate insider joke. The bearded king, dressed in a white robe and seated on a throne resembling an overstuffed chair, has Mayer's own face!

During the course of this research I have collected thirty-two John the Conqueror products—washes, soaps, bath crystals, oils, perfumes, sachets, floor sweep, yard sprinkling granules, incense, sprays, and candles. The labels of twenty-five of these products are illustrated with some sort of figural representation of John the Conqueror, and all but four portray him as a European king. The other John the Conqueror product labels are illustrated with alternative images of powerful men. Mister Lucky's Juan el Conquistador incense features an armored knight, adapted from the painting of

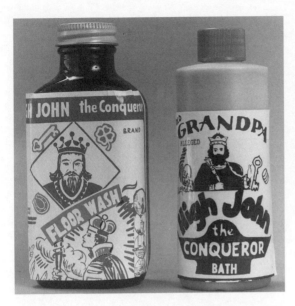

Fig. 57. High John the Conqueror Floor Wash from Clover Horn Company, Baltimore, and High John the Conqueror Bath from Grandpa's Candle Shop, Baltimore. Notice the similarity between the king portrayed on labels and advertisements from Lucky Heart, King Novelty, Famous Products, Clover Horn, and Grandpa's; compare these with the representation of the king on the playing card.

St. George and the Dragon by Raphael. Sonny Boy's John the Conqueror incense is illustrated with a Roman gladiator. A bottle of John the Conqueror Triple Strength Oil from Rondo's Temple Sales bears a biblical prophet copied from Henri Gamache's *Master Book of Candle Burning*. Chicas-Rendón's *Juan el Conquistador* incense packet is illustrated with a handsome youth, presumably Mercury, sporting a winged helmet. Any copyright that might apply to these graphics is disregarded; identical kings, knights, gladiators, and so forth appear on the labels of many different companies. Catherine Yronwode of Lucky Mojo Curio Company has rejected these images of white male supremacy; the labels of her John the Conqueror products are illustrated with a drawing of the root.

Why would African American customers of the 1920s–40s have bought products bearing an image so alien to the traditional personification

Fig. 58. High John the Conqueror Bath-and-Floor Wash—Lama Temple, Chicago, purchased 1996. This king resembles the earlier versions, but the figure is seen in three-quarter view.

Fig. 59. High John the Conqueror Incense— La Milagrosa Products, Brooklyn, purchased 1998. This illustration is particularly interesting because it depicts the traditional white king on horseback in a pose undoubtedly inspired by the chromolithograph of St. James the Great, the warrior saint who represents Ogún in Santería and Ogou in Haitian Vodou.

Fig. 60. John the Conqueror Spray— Indio Products, Los Angeles, purchased 1998. The figure of John the Conqueror has Martin Mayer's own face.

of John the Conqueror? The answer undoubtedly lies in the devastating psychological legacy of slavery, which persisted at least into the first half of the twentieth century. Many blacks of that time lacked self-esteem and tended to perceive anything associated with white people as being "superior." When Hortense Powdermaker conducted her fieldwork among the African American residents of Sunflower County, Mississippi, in the early 1930s, she encountered the belief that blacks are inferior to whites. This attitude was especially prevalent among the older generation, who were accustomed to depending upon whites for help and advice, but many of the poor and less educated young people also held these views.[47] Hyatt's informant, Dr. Ira Wands of Florence, South Carolina, expressed the same opinion: "You see, seventy-five years ago, it was slavery. The people down here was under bondage and the white man turnt 'em loose . . . without bein' a self-experienced man. . . . [The Negro] will believe what the white man say."[48] I asked Martin Mayer why even today John the Conqueror is represented by the white king. "In the 1930s customers would not have put their trust in a black spirit. Now, people are accustomed to the white king. They might not buy the product if we put some other picture on the label."[49]

The packaging of John the Conqueror products is usually purple, signifying royalty, and often the product itself is purple. Bottles, packets, and incense tins have purple labels. Lama Temple's John the Conqueror aerosol house blessing spray comes in a purple can, and Amateau's John the Conqueror soap has a purple wrapper. I have in my collection a purple John the Conqueror candle from Mission Candle Company of San Antonio, Lama Temple's purple "triple strength" bath-and-floor wash, purple oil from Paco's Botanical Products, purple sachet powder from Stanley Drug, and Skippy's purple bath crystals. My Yard Sprinkling Granules from Stanley Drug, packaged in a plain plastic bag with a typed label, appear to be bits of Styrofoam dyed purple.

■ ■ ■

The spell books carried by spiritual stores and mail-order companies include instructions for the use of John the Conqueror roots and products. These books are seldom written by traditional practitioners, but are published by the manufacturers of spiritual products in order to promote sales. Within their pages, John the Conqueror becomes an all-purpose charm. Not only are the root and its derivative products prescribed for protection, love, business and employment, court cases, and luck, but also for negative intentions like controlling and cursing. One suspects that these charm formulae are concocted at random, with little understanding of the principles of imitative and contagious magic or the symbolic ingredients and rituals required in traditional charm preparation.

One of the earliest such spell books was *The Life and Works of Marie Laveau*, printed in the early twentieth century by one of New Orleans' hoodoo drugstores, possibly the famous Cracker Jack, and reissued by Joe Kay's Dorene Publishing Company as *Marie Laveau's Old and New Black and White Magic*. The required ingredients would have been available at Fulton Religious Supply, Dorene's Brooklyn retail outlet, and at other stores that carried Dorene Products. "The Man Whose Business Is Poor" is instructed to "put three drops of Lucky Lodestone Perfume on a John the Conqueror root so it will attract money." "The Person Who Is Going to Trial" is instructed to "sprinkle a John the Conqueror root with Protection from Harm Perfume, wrap it in red flannel, keep it behind the bed for nine days, and then carry it to the courthouse and drop it on the floor." To counteract bad luck, "fill a chamois bag with lodestone, John the Conqueror root, a pair of Adam and Eve roots, and a piece of Devil's shoestring; anoint with Holy Oil and say the 23rd Psalm." To make a gambling hand, one is to "put into a small bag made of red flannel the following worshipful and holy articles: John the Conqueror root, magnetic lodestone powder, steel dust, and a green lodestone . . . [anoint with] three drops of Fast Luck Perfume." In addition to these prescriptions, almost every formula in *Black and White Magic*, regardless of purpose, includes the burning of John the Conqueror incense.[50]

Dorene also published *Black Herman's Secrets of Magic, Mystery, and Legerdemain*, which advises that, for uncrossing, one should "Wear a charm bag for three months, consisting of Devil's shoe string, John the Conqueror root, deer's horn shaving, dragon's blood, and wahoo bark, dressed with holy oil. . . . On rising say the 23rd Psalm and before going to bed the 104th Psalm."[51] Another Dorene publication, *Legends of Incense, Herb, and Oil Magic* by Lewis de Claremont, recommends anointing one's feet and forehead with High Conquering Oil and putting a few drops on the four corners of legal documents before going to court. High John the Conqueror root, according to de Claremont, is to be "carried in the pocket for good luck . . . some people wrap a dollar bill around it." His interpretation of Chewing John (probably galangal root) differs from tradition in that one is instructed to chew the root, spit it out, and swallow the juice: "this is considered an excellent aid in stomach conditions . . . and takes away a crossed condition."[52]

The Sonny Boy Guide to Success and Power gives many uses for John the Conqueror products—all, of course, manufactured by Sonny Boy. "Can High John the Conqueror Help You?" tells the story of "Brenda," who was cheated out of a well-deserved promotion when the job went to her employer's sister. Note that punishment of enemies, the intention of this ritual, is not consistent with the traditional uses of John the Conqueror. Brenda is instructed to obtain a silver coin from her employer and put it in a jar between a Crossing Candle and a High John Candle, anoint the candles with oil, burn them for seven days, and repeat, "I am worthy of my revenge for he has done wrong to me. Make his greedy soul suffer for all the world to see." She was to "write on a piece of parchment paper the boss's name, the name, address and telephone number of the company, and draw his image," roll the paper and seal it with wax from the High John the Conqueror candle, placing it in the jar with the coin. For nine days she was to burn High John the Conqueror incense before going to work and add the ashes to the jar. After Brenda completed this ritual, "Customers began to complain. Business dropped off so much the boss had to fire his sister. The boss and his wife got a divorce and she took most of his money."[53]

Anna Riva's *Modern Witchcraft Spellbook*, published by her own International Imports Company, recommends that gamblers wash their hands with water in which John the conqueror root has been boiled before going out to play, and in her *Modern Herbal Spellbook*, she advises: "For a man to win the love of a woman, he should get a lock of hair from the head of the one he desires, place it in a red bag with a High John root, and sleep with it under the pillow. Each morning anoint the bag with Attraction Oil.[54]

Mister Felix of Columbus, Georgia, publishes the *Alleged Do-It-Yourself Sure Fast Success Guide*, modeled after the *Sonny Boy Guide to Success and Power*, in which he gives two formulae for John the Conqueror:

To Improve Your Business

After business hours burn one-half box of Business Builder Incense and one-half box of Hi John the Conqueror Incense allowing the fumes to penetrate every corner. Do this for eight days. Before opening your business, anoint a Hi John the Conqueror root with Money Drawing Oil and place on your person, never allowing any one to see or touch the root so that it will work for you alone.

For Luck in Gambling

Carry one Wonder of the World Root, one Lodestone
sprinkled well with lodestone dust, one Master Root,
and Five Finger Grass in a small chamois bag anointed
with Double Luck Oil carried close to your person
allowing NO ONE to touch it. Before playing with
the dice or cards, rub your hands with Mister Felix Hi
John the Conqueror Oil and in your house burn the
incense of Hi John the Conqueror.[55]

In the 1970s, when manufacturers began to label their products in
Spanish, they also started to offer Juan el Conquistador baths, floor wash,
soaps, oils, perfumes, sachet powders, incense, aerosol sprays, and glass-
encased candles. I asked Cuban, Puerto Rican, Dominican, Guatemalan,
Haitian, and Brazilian botánica owners from Florida to New York, as well
as Mexican American yerbería owners in Houston, about Juan el Conquistador. None of them seemed to have a clear idea about his identity—
"he's just a great big strong man who can help you with your problems."[56]
Latinos, who appear to have adopted John the Conqueror after having
seen the products for sale in botánicas, are vague about his identity because
he is not part of their own tradition. They use the root and the products for
the same intentions as African Americans: protection, love, jobs, court
cases, and gambling.

When Martin Mayer took me to visit Ray Pizzarro's Seven Powers
Garden Temple in Los Angeles, we brought up our long-running argument
about John the Conqueror—is he white or black? Puerto-Rican born Pizzarro
gave an insightful answer: "John the Conqueror is a spirit—he has no race.
He is for everybody."[57]

Conclusion

piritual Merchants is structured like the Kongo cosmogram, a cross within a circle, where the spirit makes the journey from birth to death to rebirth, and the realm of the supernatural intersects with the ordinary world of human beings. The book begins with the artifacts—the spiritual products—and places them within their cultural context. We have sought their origins in African, European, and New World traditional charms, traced the evolution of these handmade substances and objects into commercial products, and ended, once again, with a very particular artifact, John the Conqueror root. Part I deals with the supernatural, introducing the magico-religious beliefs of traditional practitioners who serve the spirits, lead religious societies, and perform "work" for individual clients. In the middle chapter, "The Commodification of Traditional Charms," religion and magic intersect with commerce and popular culture. Part II takes us to the everyday world of the entrepreneur, the merchant, and the manufacturer. As I was told again and again by traditional practitioners, retailers, and the manufacturers of spiritual products, "this is religion, but it's business too."

Throughout the text runs the motif of ritual exchange between the seekers and holders of spiritual power. The devotee who fails to provide the obligatory ceremonies and offerings can expect no aid from the lwa, the orichas, the saints, or the dead. Traditional practitioners require payment. The priests and priestesses of African traditional religion, the cunning men and wise women of European folk magic, the oungan, mambo, and olorichas of the Afro-Caribbean religions, and the queens, doctors, and workers of Voodoo and hoodoo all charge for their services. Charm assemblages, believed to be inhabited by an indwelling spirit, must be "fed" or "dressed" in order to work. A trip to the candle shop, the botánica, or the yerbería for the purchase of spiritual products and ritual items can be very expensive.

African and European concepts of magic and religion converged in the Americas. Haitian Vodou, Cuban Santería and Palo, New Orleans Voodoo, and southern hoodoo all, to a greater or lesser degree, combine Fon, Yoruba, or Kongo practices with European folk Christianity and popular magic. In all of these belief systems, the making of charms is based upon the rules of imitative and contagious magic, within which the practitioner may employ almost limitless creativity in the choice of symbolic actions and ingredients.

The trend toward commodification of traditional charms and the evolution of the spiritual products business began in the twentieth century, with a gradual move away from the home-based practitioner and toward the entrepreneur who marketed mass-produced spiritual products. The makers of these products were fully cognizant of the principles by which charms operate, the various forms that they took, and the intentions for which they were used. Customers' faith in traditional charms expanded to include bath-and-floor washes, soaps, oils, perfumes, sachet powders, yard-dressing granules, sprinkling salts, aerosol sprays, incense, and candles. Spiritual products are firmly rooted in tradition, even though manufacturers constantly invent new variations on old themes.

In the early years of the spiritual products business the targeted customers were African Americans, and the merchandise was oriented toward southern hoodoo. Manufacturers used titles, advertising copy, and imagery intended to appeal to black Americans. Mail-order entrepreneurs promoted their wares in publications with a primarily black readership. Candle shops and religious stores were located in black neighborhoods. In the 1970s, when large numbers of Spanish-speaking Latino immigrants began to enter the United States, this orientation changed. Manufacturers began to label their products in both English and Spanish and introduced a line of Santería-oriented items. Botánicas sprang up in Latin American and Caribbean neighborhoods. Haitians also patronize these stores, and some botánicas are even Haitian owned, but products oriented toward Haitian Vodou are virtually nonexistent. Martin Mayer of Indio Products, sensing an untapped market, has recently inaugurated a line of Vodou products named for the lwa, featuring images of their associated saints and labeled in French. White customers are rare. With some exceptions, this merchandise has little cultural relevance for white Americans and is basically unknown to them. Those with an interest in the occult are likely to buy their herbs, crystals, aromatherapy products, oils, incense, and candles at stores specializing in European folk magic, healing, and astrology, or to purchase such products via the Internet.

A few spiritual suppliers, such as Lama Temple, Sonny Boy Products, and the Allan Company of Houston, remain true to their origins and continue to sell hoodoo-oriented products by mail order and through old-time religious stores and candle shops. Catherine Yronwode of Lucky Mojo Products, although she makes use of that most modern of technologies, the Internet, markets a line of handmade herbal products inspired by traditional hoodoo. Her only concession to today's lifestyle is Lavender Love Drops "to attract, enrapture, and hold a lover of the same sex."

Other manufacturers offer new merchandise that, although grounded in tradition, is relevant to the anxieties and aspirations of modern life. Miller's Rexall Drug offers an updated version of the charm intended to repel authority figures: the Law Stay Away talisman is alleged to protect one's car against traffic citations and parking tickets. Mysteria Products, operating within the tradition of charms for luck and gambling, now advertises Easy Money Oil containing shredded U.S. currency, and Slots-of-Luck Oil for anointing the handle of the slot machine. A recently introduced sachet powder from Indio Products, titled Tied Up and Nailed (*Amarrado y Claveteado*), recalls traditional charm rituals that involve tying and nailing. The label shows a man helplessly bound and nailed to the floor; a woman in high-heeled shoes stands on his chest. Indio's Martin Mayer is also welcoming the twenty-first century with the presentation of some very old-fashioned products: Doctor Buzzard's oil, powder, and floor wash for court-case work. These, of course, are named for the Low Country root doctor whose fame dates to the 1800s. The writers of magical spell books (often spiritual merchants themselves) not only reproduce traditional rituals and charm formulae, they invent new ones that, of course, require the latest spiritual products.

The spiritual products industry is evolving and expanding. Manufacturers employ the same up-to-date techniques as other businesses, with an 800 number, a fax machine, and a web site, by means of which anything required for the practice of the traditional belief systems can be ordered by credit card. Existing companies are buying out smaller suppliers. It is unlikely,

Conclusion

however, that the family-owned businesses cited in this book will grow into giant conglomerates. Even Indio Products, the largest manufacturer/wholesaler of spiritual products in the world, is small by contemporary business standards. The temporary status of Lama Temple as a division of the larger and more mainstream Candle Corporation of America was an exceptional case, and Lama Temple is now affiliated with Indio. Ownership of most companies has stayed within the same family. As the founders retire or die, control is passed to younger family members. One cannot envision DeLaurence, M & A Amateau, or Original Products being swallowed up by Bristol-Myers, Revlon, or Proctor and Gamble. New companies are also being created as people of color, some of them initiates of the African-based religions, move from ownership of small retail stores into manufacturing and wholesaling. This trend is exemplified by the career of the Puerto Rican–born oloricha and palero known as Ricardo Obatala, who began as the owner of two Philadelphia botánicas and has moved into manufacturing and marketing his own line of products and ritual items, La Milagrosa Incorporated, via catalog and Internet.[1]

The practice of the African-based religions in the United States is also growing and changing. Vodou and Santería communities have become multiethnic. Some well-educated, middle-class African Americans who would dismiss hoodoo as ignorant superstition find these African-based religions to be an affirmation of their cultural heritage, and white Americans are also becoming initiates. New Orleans Voodoo is experiencing a revival. Some old-time hoodoo practitioners are adopting new traditions.

The proliferation of spiritual stores, selling a wide assortment of herbs, animal parts, minerals, manufactured spiritual products, ritual objects, and magical spell books, has been an important agent of change, leading to considerable cross-fertilization among the various African-based religious and magical traditions. The customers of candle shops, botánicas, and yerberías are reinterpreting and adapting the products for their own uses. Some black Americans who come out of a hoodoo tradition are buying the accoutrements of the orichas. Latinos are buying John the Conqueror roots and products. In some yerberías, once devoted exclusively to the sale of herbs and products for Mexican curanderismo, brujería, and folk Catholicism, one can now purchase an eclectic mix of goods from African American, Latin American, and Caribbean traditions.

But Vodou, Santería, Voodoo, and hoodoo have yet to enter the American mainstream, and the general public is not ready to embrace the use of spiritual products. In the mid-1990s the E. Davis Company attempted to market Money House Blessing Spray in supermarkets and drugstores, where it was displayed along with the other air-fresheners. Within a few months the product disappeared from the shelves due to lack of sales. This experiment failed because the Money House Blessing Spray was not only priced considerably higher than "ordinary" sprays, the customers simply did not know what it was.[2]

Most Americans still have little knowledge of the African-based belief systems. Vodou, Santería, New Orleans Voodoo, and southern hoodoo continue to seem exotic when viewed within the larger context of religion and spirituality in the United States. Candle shops, botánicas, and yerberías occupy a very small and specialized niche in the religious marketplace. It is my hope that the reader, having explored the topic of charms and spiritual products with me, will have gained a greater understanding of the world of the spiritual merchants and the rich culture represented by the artifacts sold in these stores.

Appendix

Retailers

I have not attempted to name every spiritual store in every city. The following is a list of those I have visited in person or from which I have ordered by mail. All of these stores were in business when I conducted my research in the mid to late 1990s. If known, I have given the years of operation and the name and ethnicity of the founder and the present owner.

ARIZONA

Guadalupe Imports
15 West Baseline Rd., Phoenix 85041
602-243-0266
Owner, Jane Soza, Mexican American

Yerbería Gonzalez
695 West Baseline Rd., Phoenix 85041
602-254-8123
Owner, Magdalena Gonzalez, Mexican American

CALIFORNIA

Lucky Mojo Curio Company, 1997–present
6632 Covey Rd., Forestville 95436
707-887-1524
Owner, Catherine Yronwode (originally Manfredi), White American

Seven Powers Garden Temple Store, 1959–present
5311 South Broadway, Los Angeles 90037
213-231-6538
Owner, Ray Pizzarro, Puerto Rican

FLORIDA

Botánica Mística
1512 S.W. 8th St., Miami 33135
305-631-0888
Owner, Cuban

Keystone Lucky Store, 1940–present
303 Broad St., Jacksonville 32202
904-354-2557
Founder, Carl Brimhall, White American
Subsequent owner, Vernon Sands, Bahamian
Present owner, Deloris Kay, African American

Meri Jo Inc./Indian Sales Company, c. 1949–present
(Black Cat with Nine Lives)
P.O. Box 15416, Tampa 33684
813-876-4536
Original owner, African American
Present owner, Martin Mayer (Indio Products), White American

Mi-World Supplies
P.O. Box 8237, Hialeah 33012
305-558-5021
Owner, White American

Nature's Boutique Botánica, c. 1990–present
5853 University Blvd. West, Jacksonville 32216
904-730-7080
Owner, Lisa Bisel, Brazilian

Starlite, c. 1997–present
704 Broad St., Jacksonville 32202
904-353-3738
Owner, African American

GEORGIA

Ben Sheftall Beauty and Barber Supply
346 Martin Luther King Jr. Blvd., Savannah
912-232-1687
Manager, Michael Jenkins

Master Spiritual Supply International
5405 Waters Ave., Savannah
912-355-9995
Owner, Rev. Calvin Samuel

Miller's Rexall Drug, 1960–present
87 Broad St. S.W., Atlanta 30303
404-523-8481
Founder, Donald Miller
Present owners, Donald and Richard Miller, White American

Mister Felix and Sister Powers, c. 1970–present
5946 Veterans Parkway, Columbus 31901
(formerly 1228 Broadway)
706-321-9933
Owner, African American

Rondo's Temple Sales, 1944–present
171 Mitchell St. S.W., Atlanta 30303
404-522-4379
Founder, Jack Amato, White American
Present owner, Michael Amato, White American

LOUISIANA

Botánica Solano, 1972–99
1626 Elysian Fields, New Orlean 70117
504-943-6538
Owner, Frank Rodriguez, Cuban

Divine Light, 1975–present
3316 Magazine St., New Orleans 70115
504-899-6617
Owner, Mark Tillman, White American

F & F Candle Shop, 1976–present
801 N. Broad Ave., New Orleans 70119
504-347-4274
Founder, Enrique Cortez, Cuban
Present owner, Felix Figueroa, Puerto Rican

Island of Salvation, 1995–present
835 Piety, New Orleans 70117
504-948-9961
Owners, Sallie Ann Glassman and Shane Norris, White American

Marie Laveau's House of Voodoo, 1990–present
739 Bourbon St., New Orleans 70116
504-581-3751
Owner, Andy Antippas, White American

New Orleans Historic Voodoo Museum, 1972–present
724 Dumaine, New Orleans 70116
504-523-7685
Owner, Charles Gandolfo, White American

New Orleans Voodoo Spiritual Temple, 1990–present
828 North Rampart, New Orleans 70116
504-522-9627
Owner, Miriam Williams Chamani, African American

Reverend Zombie's House of Voodoo, 1994–present
723 St. Peter St., New Orleans 70116
504-486-6366
Owner, Andy Antippas, White American

The Witches Closet
521 St. Philip St., New Orleans 70116
504-593-9222
Owner, Russell George (Religious Order of Witchcraft), White American

MARYLAND

Clover Horn Company, 1943–present
529 West Lexington, Baltimore 21201
410-539-2456
Founder, Marcus Menke, White American
Present owner, name withheld by request, Native American

Grandma's Candle Shop
113 West Saratoga, Baltimore
410-685-4289
Owner, Linda Frangioni, White American

Grandpa's Candle Shop
West Saratoga, Baltimore
(Old Grandpa Sales, P.O. Box 22056), Baltimore 21203
Owner, Mr. Perry, White American

MINNESOTA

The Tyrad Company, 1959–present
P.O. Box 17006, Minneapolis 55417
Owner, Elbee Wright, White American

MISSISSIPPI

The Corner Drugstore, 1959–present
1123 Washington St., Vicksburg 39180
601-636-2757
Founder, Joseph Gerache, White American
Present owner, Joseph Gerache Jr., White American

Harmon's Drug Store
540 North Farish, Jackson
601-355-2309
Founder, George A. Harmon, White American

NEW YORK

Almacen y Botánica Ochun
95 East 116th St., New York 10029
212-831-9228
Owner, Odalis Tavarez

Botánica Chicas-Rendón and Casa de Velas, 1921–present
56 and 60 East 116th, New York 10029
212-289-0378
Founder, Alberto Rendón, Guatemalan
Present owner, Otto Chicas-Rendón, Guatemalan

Botánica Don Jorge
374 5th Ave., Brooklyn 11215
718-499-0041
Owner, Dominican

Botánica Feraille
616 Flatbush Ave., Brooklyn 11225
718-282-6018
Owner, Haitian

Botánica Illa Quere
74 East 116th St., New York 10029
212-828-8804

Botanique Saint Jacques Majeur
277 Flatbush Ave., Brooklyn 11217
718-638-7689
Owner, Haitian

Botánica San Miguel y San Pedro
645 Fifth Ave., Brooklyn
718-965-1488
Owner, Noel Pedrasa, Puerto Rican

El Congo Real
1789 Lexington Ave., New York 10029
212-860-3921
Owner, Ernesto Arenas, Cuban

Fulton Religious Supply Company, 1948–present
1304 Fulton St., Brooklyn 11216
718-783-7777
Founder, Moe Trugmann, White American
Present owner, Mitzi Trugmann
Manager, Roger, African American

Miracle Warehouse 1997–present
841 Flatbush Ave., Brooklyn 11226
718-941-2400
Owner, Randy Brismann, White American

Paco's Botanical Products
1864 Lexington Ave., New York 10029
212-427-0820
Owner, Guatemalan

Reyes y Reyes
340 Audubon, corner 182d St., New York 10033
212-927-2133
Owner, Dominican

PENNSYLVANIA

Lady Dale's Curio Shop, 1945–96
1356 South St., Philadelphia 19147
Founder, Alex Silverberg, White American
Subsequent owner, Dale Silverberg, White American

Harry's Occult Shop, 1917–present
1238 South St., Philadelphia 19147
215-735-8262
Founder, Harry and Nettie Seligmann, White American
Present owner, James Seligmann, White American

Ray's New Age Curio Shop, 1996–present
1358 South St., Philadelphia 19147
215-545-3135
Founder, Ray Minton, White American

Rick's Spiritual Supplies
1310 South St., Philadelphia 19147
215-545-8160
Founder, Ricardo Obatala, Puerto Rican

SOUTH CAROLINA

Charleston Cut-Rate Drugstore, 1936–98
567 King St., Charleston
Original owner, David Epstein, White American
Subsequent owners, Alex Epstein, Barry Bloom, Samuel Rosen,
    White American

Eye of the Cat/Pop's Academy, 1985–present
1366 Rosewood Drive, Columbia 29205
803-256-6904
Owner, Thomas "Pop" Williams, African American

Voodoo Garage Body Piercing and Jewelry
2769 Rosewood Ave., Columbia 21205
803-933-9350
Owner, Karen Metcalf, White American

TENNESSEE

A. Schwab's Department Store, 1876–present
163 Beale St., Memphis 38103
901-523-9782
Founder, Abraham Schwab, White American
Present owner, Elliot Schwab, White American

Champion's Pharmacy and Herb Store
2369 Elvis Presley Blvd., Memphis 38106
901-948-6622

Tater Red's, 1995–present
153 Beale St., Memphis 38103
901-578-7234
Owner, Leo "Tater Red" Alfred, White American

TEXAS

Allan Family Store, 1978–present
1803 McGowen St., Houston 77004
800-362-3018
Owners, Richard and Bill Allan, White American

Botánica Hijo de Changó
4416 Washington Ave., Houston 77007
713-861-4507

House of Power, c. 1970–present
Canal St., Houston 77003
713-229-8532
Owner, Luz Vara, Mexican American

Mysteria Products, 1967–present
P.O. Box 1466, Dept. B119, Arlington
817-447-3477
Owner, Ed Kay, White American

Papa Jim's
5630 South Flores, San Antonio 78214
210-922-6665
Owner, James Sicafus, White American

Rosario's Mistic, 1984–present
5314 Canal St., Houston 77011
713-928-2948
Owners, Rosario Garcia and Eloy Nañez, Mexican American

Stanley Drug Company, 1923–present
2718 Lyons Ave., Houston 77020
713-222-0800
Founder, Thomas S. Hollenbeck
Present owners, Ford Family, White American

WASHINGTON, D.C., AND SUBURBS

Botánica Gran Poder
1835 East University Blvd., Hyattsville, MD 20783
301-445-0894
Owner, Maggie Velazquez, Puerto Rican

Botánica San Elias y Marta
2617 Mount Vernon Ave., Alexandria, VA
703-519-6129
Owner, Dominican

Botánica San Francisco de Assis, 1998–present
2311 Calvert St. NW, Washington, DC 20008
202-332-8228
Owner, Cuban

Botánica San Lazero, c. 1970–present
1760 Columbia Rd., Washington, DC 20008
202-234-0777
Owner, Cuban

Botánica San Miguel, 1994–present
8425 Georgia Ave., Silver Spring, MD 20912
301-585-2540
Owner, Catalina de Guzman, Dominican

Botánica Santa Barbara, 1998–present
1458 Park Rd. NW, Washington, DC 20008
202-387-2026

Botánica Yemayá y Changó, 1995–present
2441 18th St. NW, Washington, DC 20036
202-462-1803
Owner, Jose Chavarria, Salvadoran

Clover Horn, 1976–present
2543 14th St. NW, Washington, DC 20008
202-483-5112
Owner, Native American

Manufacturers and Wholesalers

Many present-day manufacturers/wholesalers also maintain a retail shop that is open to the public.

R. C. Adams Company, 1920s
3105 Sheffield Ave., Chicago, IL

M & A Amateau, 1942–present
73 E. 115th St., New York, NY 10029
212-369-7390
Founder, Morris and Albert Amateau
Present owners, Robert and Steve Amateau, White American

Cross Candle, 1945–68
East Vernon Ave., Los Angeles, CA
Founders, Harry and Nettie Seligmann, White American

Crusader Candle Company
327 Nevins Ave., Brooklyn, NY
718-625-0005

The L. W. DeLaurence Company, 1903–present
P.O. Box 8988, Michigan City, IN 46360
219-878-8712
Founder, L. W. DeLaurence, White American
Present owner, Mickey DeLaurence, White American

Doctor Pryor, 1919–50
3319 State St., 5039 South Indiana, Chicago, IL
Founder, Mason Pryor, African American

E. Davis
7 Turner Place, Piscataway, NJ 08854
Founder, Emmanuel Davis
Subsequent owner, Warren Bronsnick
Present owner unknown, White American

Hussey Distributing Company, c. 1962–80
115 Broad St. S.W., Atlanta, GA
Founder, Ivan Hussey, White American

Indio Products, 1987–present
236 W. Manchester, Los Angeles, CA 90003
800-944-1414
Founder, Martin Mayer, White American

Keystone Laboratories, 1925–present
1103 Kansas, Memphis, TN 38103
901-774-8860
Founders, Joseph Menke and Morris Shapiro
Present owner, Melinda Menke Burns, White American

La Milagrosa Incorporated
1310 South St., Philadelphia, PA 19147
215-634-7866
Founder, Ricardo Obatala, Puerto Rican

La Milagrosa Products
537 Court St., Brooklyn, NY 11231
718-834-8506

Lama Temple Products, 1933–present
141 West 62nd, Chicago, IL 60621
312-753-8900
Founder, Max Kanovsky
Present owner, Martin Mayer (Indio Products), White American

Lucky Heart Laboratories, 1935–present
138 Huling, Memphis, TN 38103
901-526-7658
Founder, Morris Shapiro
Present owner, Gary Young, White American

Miracle Candle Company, 1956–present
3100 Guadelaupe St., Laredo, TX 78044

Mission Candle Company
San Antonio, TX

Mister Lucky
64 East 116th St., New York, NY 10029
212-987-4482
Owner, Hannibal Moya, Puerto Rican

Nite-Glo Candle Company
7909 Carr St., Dallas, TX
421-381-0918
Owner, Richard Fava, White American

Original Products, 1959–present
Webster Ave., Bronx, NY 10458
718-367-9589
Owners, Milton Benezra and Jack Mizrahi, White American

Skippy Candle Corporation, 1967–97
8031 West McNichols, Detroit, MI 48221
313-862-0725
Founder, David Adler, White American

Sonny Boy Products, 1926–present
3007 NW 44th St., Miami, FL (1976)
8701 NW 24th Ave., Miami, FL (1984–91)
1715 3rd Ave. North, Birmingham, AL 35203
205-251-4209
Founder, Mrs. Mills, African American
Present owner, Johnnie Praytor, White American

Sovereign Products, 1930s
3716-18-20 North Cicero Ave., Chicago, IL
Valmor Products Company, 1927–86
2449 South Michigan, Chicago, IL
Founder, Morton Neumann, White American

Vandi Parfums
64 East 116th St., New York, NY 10029
212-289-4480
Founder, Herbert Brismann, White American
Present owner, Randy Brismann, White American

WEB SITES

Angel Hakim
www.angelmindbodyspirit.com

Aunt Agatha's Occult Emporium
www.newageinfo.com/prod/257

Ava Kay Jones
www.nawlins.com/others/ovpoooo

Botánica Eleguá
www.botelegua.com/home

Branwen's Pantry
www.tiac.net/users/bpantry

Indio Products
www.indioproducts.com
Island of Salvation
www.mindspring.com/~cfeldman/bot2

Louisiana Catalog
www.bayoufolk.com.lacat/

Lucky Mojo Curio Products
www.luckymojo.com/luckymojocatalogue

M & A Amateau
www.amateau.com/prod

Marie-Louise's Lucky Voodoo Boutique
members.aol.com/vaudou/voodoo

Miller Rexall Drugs
www.mindspring.com/~millersrexall/products

New Orleans Voodoo Spiritual Temple
gnofn.org/~voodoo/flyer

Rick's Spiritual Supplies
members.aol.com/rickspirit/

Rondo's Temple Sales
www.lgdesign.com/pic17

Satchmo the Cosmic Dog
www.spellmaker.com/satchmo

Stanley Drug
drugco@aol.com

The Voodoo Shoppe
www.icorp.net/lamall/voodoo

Notes

Unless otherwise indicated, all interviews are by the author.

Introduction

1. This is a composite description. No one store carries all of these items, and the merchandise displayed in any particular store depends on the belief system of the owner and the customers. Similar merchandise is sold by New Age stores oriented toward European folk magic and Native American spirituality. New Age businesses market herbs, crystals, aromatherapy products, personal care items, oils, incense, candles, and books to a predominately white clientele and will not be dealt with in the present work.
2. Throughout this text, the names of religions like Vodou, Santería, and Voodoo are capitalized; hoodoo, conjure, and rootwork are systems of magic and are therefore not capitalized. I have used *hoodoo* as a generic term for any African American magical practice other than New Orleans Voodoo.
3. Michael E. Bell, "Pattern, Structure, and Logic in Afro-American Hoodoo Performance" (Ph.D. diss., Indiana University, 1980).
4. James G. Frazer, *The Golden Bough: A Study in Magic and Religion* (1922; re-print, New York: Macmillan, 1951), 12–52.
5. Julie Yvonne Webb, "Louisiana Voodoo and Superstitions Related to Health," *Health Services and Mental Health Association Reports* 86 (Apr. 1971): 294; Michael Michaelson, "Can a 'Root Doctor' Actually Put a Hex On or Is It All a Great Put-On?" *Today's Health* (Mar. 1972): 39.
6. Gustav Jahoda, *The Psychology of Superstition* (Harmondsworth, England: Penguin Books, 1969), 87–97; Harry Middleton Hyatt, *Hoodoo-Conjuration-Witchcraft-Rootwork* (Hannibal, Mo.: Western Publishing Co., 1970–78), vol. 5: viii.
7. The term *ritual economy* was coined by Karen McCarthy Brown in her essay "Serving the Spirits: The Ritual Economy of Haitian Vodou," in *Sacred Arts of Haitian Vodou*, ed. Donald Cosentino (Los Angeles: Univ. of California Fowler Museum of Cultural History, 1995), 205–23.
8. Jules David Prown, "The Truth of Material Culture: History or Fiction?" in *History from Things: Essays on Material Culture*, ed. Steven Lubar and W. David Kingery (Washington D.C.: Smithsonian Institution Press, 1993), 1.
9. For a history of the FWP, see Jerre Mangione, *The Dream and the Deal: The Federal Writers' Project 1935–1943* (New York: Avon Books, 1972). Many of the interviews with former slaves were published in the late 1970s in *The American Slave: A Composite Biography*, edited by George Rawick (Westport, Conn.: Greenwood Publishing, 1972). Some of the Louisiana interviews were

published by Ronnie Clayton as *Mother Wit: The Ex-Slave Narratives of the Louisiana Writers' Project* (New York: Peter Lang, 1990). The Virginia material has been published as *Weevils in the Wheat: Interviews with Virginia Ex-Slaves*, edited by Charles Perdue, Thomas Barden, and Robert Phillips (Charlottesville: Univ. of Virginia Press, 1992).

10. See Ronnie Clayton, "The Federal Writers' Project for Blacks in Louisiana," *Louisiana History* 9, no. 3 (summer 1978): 327–35; Jerah Johnson, "Marcus B. Christian and the WPA History of Black People in Louisiana," *Louisiana History* 10, no. 1 (winter 1979): 113–15.

Chapter 1. African Origins and European Influences

1. James A. Rawley, *The Transatlantic Slave Trade: A History* (New York: W. W. Norton and Co., 1981), 419–22.

2. See John Thornton, *Africa and Africans in the Making of the Atlantic World, 1400–1680* (Cambridge: Cambridge Univ. Press, 1992); and Ira Berlin, *Many Thousands Gone: The First Two Centuries of Slavery in North America* (Cambridge: Harvard Univ. Press, 1998), 15–77.

3. Albert Raboteau, *Slave Religion: The "Invisible Institution" in the Antebellum South* (Oxford: Oxford Univ. Press, 1978), 8–16; T. Adeoye Lembo, "Traditional African Cultures and Western Medicine," in *Medicine and Culture, Proceedings of a Symposium Organized by the Wellcome Institute of the History of Medicine, London, and the Wenner-Gren Foundation for Anthropological Research, New York*, ed. Lynn Payer (London: Wellcome Institute, 1989); Maurice Mmaduakolam Iwu, *Symbols and Selectivity in Traditional African Medicine* (Nsukka, Nigeria: Univ. of Nigeria, 1990).

4. See Roger Bastide, *African Religions of Brazil* (Baltimore: Johns Hopkins Univ. Press, 1978); Joseph M. Murphy, *Ritual Systems in Cuban Santería* (Ann Arbor, Mich.: University Microfilms, 1981); Robert Farris Thompson, *Flash of the Spirit: African and Afro-American Art and Philosophy* (New York: Vintage Books, 1983).

5. Wyatt MacGaffey, "The Eyes of Understanding: Kongo Minkisi," in *Astonishment and Power: Kongo Minkisi and the Art of Reneé Stout* (Washington, D.C.: Smithsonian Institution, National Museum of African Art, 1993), 21–103; quote from Kavuna Simon translated from Cahier 58.

6. Melville Herskovits, *The Myth of the Negro Past* (Boston: Beacon Press, 1990), 63, 197–206.

7. Melville Herskovits, *Dahomey: An Ancient West African Kingdom* (New York: J. J. Augustin, 1938), vol. 2: 256–88.

8. Suzanne Preston Blier, "Vodun: West African Roots of Vodou," in *Sacred Arts*, ed. Cosentino, 73–76.

9. David H. Brown, *Garden in the Machine: Afro-Cuban Sacred Art and Performance in Urban New Jersey and New York* (Ann Arbor: University Microfilms, 1989), 514; George Brandon, *Santería from Africa to the New World: The Dead Sell Memories* (Bloomington: Indiana Univ. Press, 1993), 12.

10. MacGaffey, "Eyes of Understanding," 49; Robert Farris Thompson, "The World in a Bag," in *Sacred Arts*, ed. Cosentino, 111. According to Wyatt MacGaffey (letter, Aug. 12, 1998): "In West and Central Africa, red is the color of transition, hence potent and dangerous."

11. Thompson, *Flash of the Spirit*, 117–31; Wyatt MacGaffey, *Religion and Society in Central Africa: The BaKongo of Lower Zaire* (Chicago: Univ. of Chicago Press, 1986), 135–68; MacGaffey, *Art and Healing of the Bakongo* (Stolkholm: Folkens Museum-Ethnografiska, 1991), 6, 28; MacGaffey, "Eyes of Understanding," 62–68; Elizabeth McAlister, "A Sorcerer's Bottle: The Visual Art of Magic in Haiti," in *Sacred Arts*, ed. Cosentino, 319.

12. Robert Farris Thompson, *The Four Moments of the Sun: Kongo Art in Two Worlds* (Washington, D.C.: National Gallery of Art, 1981), 44; Thompson, *Flash of the Spirit*, 108–17.

13. Wooden nkisi from the Afrika Museum, Berg en Dal, the Netherlands, in MacGaffey, "Eyes of Understanding," 96–97, fig. 61; ivory scepter and wooden staff from the Belgian Royal Museum for Central Africa, Tervuren, Belgium, in Gustaf Verswijver et al., ed., *Treasures from Tervuren: Selections from the Belgian Royal Museum for Central Africa* (New York: Prestel-Verlag, 1996), 142, fig. 2 (RG43708); 149, fig. 19 (RG43720).

14. Robert Hughes, *Heaven and Hell in Western Art* (New York: Stein and Day, 1968), 237–40.

15. Keith Thomas, *Religion and the Decline of Magic: Studies in Popular Beliefs in Sixteenth and Seventeenth Century England* (London: Weidenfeld and Nicolson, 1971), 588–606.

16. Ibid., 514–26.

17. Ibid., 29–36, 179–80.

18. See Patrick J. Geary, *Furta Sacra: Thefts of Relics in the Central Middle Ages* (1978).

19. For European medicinal and magical herbs, see Joseph Meyer, *The Herbalist* (New York: Rand McNally, 1960), and Scott Cunningham, *Encyclopedia of Magical Herbs* (St. Paul, Minn.: Llewellyn Publications, 1993).

20. Richard Cavendish, *The Black Arts* (New York: Putnam Publishing Group, 1967), bodily products, images, witches' ladder, reversal of normal order, 17–29; hand of glory, 278–79. Newbell Niles Puckett, *Folk Beliefs of the Southern Negro* (Montclair, N.J.: Patterson Smith Reprint Series, 1968), charm bag to cause the ague, 241 n. 5. Carlo Ginzburg, *Night Battles: Witchcraft and Agrarian Cults in the Sixteenth and Seventeenth Centuries* (Baltimore: Johns Hopkins Univ. Press, 1983), bed-charms, 83.

21. Cavendish, *Black Arts*, law of return, 36. Ralph Merrifield, "Witch Bottles and Magical Jugs," *Folk-Lore* 66 (Mar. 1955), 195–207; Ralph Merrifield, "The Use of Bellarmines as Witch-Bottles," *Guildhall Miscellany* (1954): 2–15; for the beef heart charm, see p. 4. Merrifield states that the use of the witch-bottle as a charm against witchcraft was first described by Joseph Blagrave in his *Astrological Practice of Physick*, published in 1671.

22. Thomas, *Religion and Decline*, 51–77.

23. Ibid., 222–31.

24. Cavendish, *Black Arts*, 31–42.

25. Rayna Green, director of the American Indian Program, National Museum of American History, Smithsonian Institution, interview Feb. 26, 1997.

Chapter 2. African-Based Religions in the Latin-Catholic Colonies

1. Africans of many nations were enslaved in the colonies of the New World, but the Fon, the Yoruba, and the Kongo were the most influential. See Gwendolyn Midlo Hall, *Africans in Colonial Louisiana: The Development of Afro-Creole Culture in the Eighteenth Century* (Baton Rouge: Louisiana State Univ. Press, 1992), 286–88.

2 Kimberly Hanger, *Bounded Lives, Bounded Places: Free Black Society in Colonial New Orleans, 1769–1803* (Durham, N.C.: Duke Univ. Press, 1997), 3–4. Hanger bases her statements about the status of slaves in the Latin-Catholic versus the Anglo-Protestant colonies on Frank Tannenbaum, *Slave and Citizen: The Negro in the Americas* (1947), and Stanley Elkins, *Slavery: A Problem in American Institutional and Intellectual Life* (1959).

3. George Brandon, *Santería from Africa to the New World* (Bloomington: Indiana Univ. Press, 1993), 45–52; Bastide, *The African Religions of Brazil*, 40–42; Patricia Rickles, "The Folklore of Sacraments and Sacramentals in South Louisiana," *Louisiana Folklore Miscellany* 2 (Apr. 1965), 27–43.

4 Thompson, *Flash of the Spirit*, 17–18.

5. Alfred Métraux, *Voodoo in Haiti* (New York: Schocken Books, 1972), 15–23, 41–57; James Ferguson, *Papa Doc, Baby Doc: Haiti and the Duvaliers* (Cambridge, Mass.: Basil Blackwell, 1987), 1–29; Selden Rodman and Carol Cleaver, *Spirits of the Night: The Vaudun Gods of Haiti* (Dallas: Spring Publications, 1993), 28.

6. Blier, "Vodun," 61.

7. I have used the standardized phonetic Kreyòl spellings introduced in 1975 by the Institut Pedagogique National. Readers may be more familiar with the spellings "Vodun" and "loa." The names of the deities have many orthographical variations.

8. Métraux, *Voodoo in Haiti*, 192–212.

9. Wade Davis, *Passage of Darkness: The Ethnobotany of the Haitian Zombie* (Chapel Hill: Univ. of North Carolina Press, 1988), 43–45.

10. Brown, "Serving the Spirits," 218–23, 236–39.

11. McAlister, "A Sorcerer's Bottle," 305–15.

12. Karen McCarthy Brown, *Mama Lola: A Vodou Priestess in Brooklyn* (Berkeley and Los Angeles: Univ. of California Press, 1991), 302, 342; Brown, "Serving the Spirits," 213, 220–21.

13. For many illustrations of these elegant artifacts, see Robert Farris Thompson, "From the Isle Beneath the Sea: Haiti's Africanizing Vodou Art," in *Sacred Arts*, ed. Cosentino, 111–18.

14. See MacGaffey, *Art and Healing of the Bakongo*, 51, fig. 19.1.569.

15. Brown, *Garden in the Machine*, 10–11.

16. For an account of the status of Santería under the Castro government, see Brandon, *Santería from Africa to the New World*, 100–103.

17. Murphy, *Ritual Systems in Cuban Santería*, 210; Brown, *Garden in the Machine*, 68–69, 76; Ysamur Flores-Peña and Roberta Evanchuk, *Santería Garments and Altars: Speaking without a Voice* (Jackson: Univ. Press of Mississippi, 1994), 7.

18. The variation in the spelling of the names of the deities is due to the difference between the Yoruba language and Cuban Spanish. Writers who wish to emphasize the Yoruba roots of the religion use the "sh" spelling for orisha, Shangó, Oshún, and ashé. The Cuban spelling is oricha, Changó, Ochún, and aché. Since this section deals with Santería as a New World religion, I will use the Cuban spelling except when specifically referring to the original Yoruba tradition.

19. See Flores-Peña and Evanchuk, *Santería Garments and Altars*.

20. Murphy, *Ritual Systems*, 277–307.

21. Brown, *Garden in the Machine*, 290, 533.

22. Thompson, *Flash of the Spirit*, 121–27; Migene González-Wippler, *Santería, The Religion: A Legacy of Faith, Rites, and Magic* (New York: Harmony Books, 1989), 21; Brown, *Garden in the Machine*, 292–93, 296–310, 371–76; Robert Farris Thompson, *Face of the Gods: Art and Altars of Africa and the African Americas* (New York: Museum for African Art, 1993), 60–69.

23. González-Wippler, *Santería*, 280–81; Raul Canizares, *Walking with the Night: The Afro-Cuban World of Santería* (Rochester, Vt.: Destiny Books, 1993), 74–76; Brandon, *Santería from Africa to the New World*, 85–90, 107–9.

24. See Laënnec Hurbon, "American Fantasy and Haitian Vodou," in *Sacred Arts*, ed. Cosentino, 181–97.

25. Brown, *Mama Lola*, 4, 109–11, 295, 341; Karen McCarthy Brown, "Staying Grounded in a High-Rise Building," in Robert A. Orsi, ed., *Gods of the City: Religion and the American Urban Landscape* (Bloomington: Indiana Univ. Press, 1999), 93–94. This statement is also based upon conversations and personal observation in Brooklyn's multiracial Flatbush Avenue neighborhood during the 1980s and 1990s.

26. Florida Writers' Project, "Hillsboro County, Florida: Negro Superstitions," n.d., #1986-033; "Hillsboro County, Florida: Voodooism," n.d., #1986-005; Manuel Marrero, "Ñañigo Cult in Ybor City," Dec. 14, 1936, #1986-010; "Witchcraft in Ybor City," n.d., #1986-034. Also see Stetson Kennedy, *Palmetto Country* (Tallahassee: Florida A & M Univ., 1989), 175–79.

27. O. H. Hauptmann, "Spanish Folklore from Tampa, Florida: Witchcraft," *Southern Folklore Quarterly* (1939): 197–200.

28. Steven Gregory, *Santería in New York City: A Study in Cultural Resistance* (Ph.D. diss., New School for Social Research, New York, 1986), 55–65.

29. Brandon, *Santería from Africa to the New World*, 104–7; Brown, *Garden in the Machine*, 110–19.

30. Roberta Evanchuk, *When the Curtain Goes Up, the Gods Come Down: Aspects of Performance in Public Ceremonies of Orisha Worship* (Ph.D. diss., Univ. of California at Los Angeles, 1996), 5.

31. Brown, *Garden in the Machine*, 106–9; Brandon, *Santería from Africa to the New World*, 114–20; Rod Davis, *American Voudou* (Denton, Tex.: Univ. of North Texas Press, 1998), 177–241; Anthony Pinn, *Varieties of African American Spiritual Experience* (Minneapolis: Fortress Press, 1998), 82–99.

32. "Where the Best Defense Is a Good Hex," *St. Petersburg Times*, Apr. 10, 1995, B1, B5.

33. Brown, *Garden in the Machine*, 317–25, 362–70; David H. Brown, "Altared Spaces," in Orsi, *Gods of the City*, ed. Orsi, 207–13.

34. Animal rights activist Chris Costello, television presentation, KNBC Los Angeles, Nov. 9, 1988, qtd. in Evanchuk, *When the Curtain Goes Up*, 163.

35. Paul Anderson, Rachel Swarns, and Betty Cortina, "A Triumph for Santeria," *Miami Herald*, June 12, 1993, A1, A24; Linda Greenhouse, "Court, Citing Religious Freedom, Voids a Ban on Animal Sacrifice," *New York Times*, June 12, 1993, A1, A9, and "Excerpts from Supreme Court Opinions on the Ritual Sacrifice of Animals," A9. See also Canizares, *Walking with the Night*, 85–90.

36. Brown, *Mama Lola*; Brown, "Staying Grounded in a High-Rise Building"; Flores-Peña and Evanchuk, *Santería Garments and Altars*.

37. Jake Tapper, "The Witch Doctor Is In," *Washington City Paper*, June 26, 1998, 22–33. Note the title of this article, a perfect example of the disrespect shown the African-based religions by the popular press.

38. The Vodou botánicas of Miami's Little Haiti were documented by Rod Davis, *American Voudou*, 285–93.

39. Sacred Saints, Phoenix, Arizona. It should be noted that Sacred Saints is not one of the major manufacturers of spiritual products.

Chapter 3. New Orleans Voodoo

1. Rickles, "The Folklore of Sacraments and Sacramentals in South Louisiana."

2. Raboteau, *Slave Religion*, 90.

3. Gwendolyn Midlo Hall, *Africans in Colonial Louisiana: The Development of Afro-Creole Culture in the Eighteenth Century* (Baton Rouge: Louisiana State Univ. Press, 1992), 29–55, 291–302; Rawley, *The Transatlantic Slave Trade*, 328.

4. Le Page du Pratz, *The History of Louisiana, with an Account of the Settlements, Inhabitants, Soil, Climate, and Products* (London: Beckett, 1774), 387, 377.

5. Hall, *Africans in Colonial Louisiana*, 163.

6. Ibid., 302.

7. Laura Porteous, "The Gri-Gri Case: A Criminal Trial in Louisiana during the Spanish Regime, 1773," *Louisiana Historical Quarterly* 17 (1934): 48–63; Hall, *Africans in Colonial Louisiana*, 163, 302.

8. Charles Barthelemy Rousséve, *The Negro in Louisiana: Aspects of His History and His Literature* (New Orleans: Xavier Univ. Press, 1937); Mary Gehman, *The Free People of Color of New Orleans* (New Orleans: Margaret Media, 1994); Ina Fandrich, "The Mysterious Voodoo Queen Marie Laveaux: A Study of Spiritual Power and Female Leadership in Nineteenth Century New Orleans"

(Ph.D. diss., Temple University, 1994), 162–63; Kimberly Hanger, *Bounded Lives, Bounded Places*.

9. Christian Schultz Jr., *Travels on an Inland Voyage . . . in the Years 1807 and 1808* (1810), 197, qtd. in Jerah Johnson, "New Orleans' Congo Square: An Urban Setting for Early Afro-American Culture Formation," *Louisiana History* 32, no. 2 (spring 1991): 140–47.

10. Benjamin Latrobe, *Impressions Respecting New Orleans: Diary and Sketches 1818–1820*, ed. Samuel Wilson Jr. (New York: Columbia Press, 1951), 49–51. This facsimile of Latrobe's notebooks includes his sketches of some of the African instruments.

11. Reuben Gold Thwaites, ed. *Early Western Travels 1784–1846*; Pierre Forest, *Voyage aux États-Unis de l'Amérique*, qtd. in Samuel Kinser, *Carnival, American Style: Mardi Gras at New Orleans and Mobile* (1990), 32–34.

12. Ivor Spencer, *A Civilization That Perished: The Last Years of White Colonial Rule in Haiti* (Lanham, Md.: Univ. Press of America, 1985), 1–7; abridged translation of Moreau de Saint-Méry's *Description Topographique, Physique, Civile, Politique, et Historic de la Partie Francaise de l'Isle Saint-Domingue* (1797). Moreau's description of a Vodou ceremony is found in volume 1, pages 45–51, of the original.

13. Hélène d'Aquin Allain, *Souvenirs d'Amerique et de France par une Créole* (Paris: Perisse Frères, 1883), 144–56; George Washington Cable, "Creole Slave Songs," *Century Magazine* 31 (Apr. 1886): 818–19; Henry Castellanos, *New Orleans As It Was* (Gretna, La.: Pelican Publishing Co., 1990), 91–96; Lyle Saxon, *Fabulous New Orleans* (Gretna, La.: Pelican Publishing Co., 1988), 240–41; Puckett, *Folk Beliefs of the Southern Negro*, 178–83; Marcus Christian, "Voodooism and Mumbo Jumbo," Louisiana Writers' Project, Archives and Manuscripts Division, Earl K. Long Library, University of New Orleans, 9–11; Robert Tallant, *Voodoo in New Orleans* (Gretna, La.: Pelican Publishing Co., 1983), 13–14. The origin of this description was also noted by Violet Harrington Bryan in *The Myth of New Orleans in Literature: Dialogues of Race and Gender* (Knoxville: Univ. of Tennessee Press, 1993).

14. Paul Lachance, "The Foreign French," in *Creole New Orleans: Race and Americanization*, ed. Arnold Hirsch and Joseph Logsdon (Baton Rouge: Louisiana State Univ. Press, 1992), 104–5.

15. Hall, "The Formation of Afro-Creole Culture," 85–86.

16. "Idolatry and Quackery," *Louisiana Gazette*, Aug. 16, 1820, p. 2, col. 3. The Tremé neighborhood referred to in this article is behind the French Quarter and was home to a thriving community of free people of color. The number of articles about Voodoo greatly accelerated in the 1850s.

17. Marcus Christian, "Voodooism and Mumbo Jumbo," 11–13, quoting from the *Daily Crescent*, Oct. 4, 1849 and July 31, 1850; the *Daily True Delta*, Apr. 28 and July 25, 1850; July 25, 1851; Nov. 3, 1854. Catherine Dillon, in her unpublished "Voodoo" manuscript, documents fourteen instances of Voodoo arrests between 1847 and 1860; "The Law's Long Arm," 1–14, LWP folder 118d. See also Fandrich, "Mysterious Voodoo Queen," 214–26.

18. *New Orleans Daily Picayune*, July 31, 1850, p. 2, col. 2.
19. Blake Touchstone, "Voodoo in New Orleans," *Louisiana History* 13 (1978): 381, 386.
20. J. W. Buel, *Metropolitan Life Unveiled* (St. Louis: Historical Publishing Company, 1882), 546–47.
21. Castellanos, *New Orleans As It Was*, 90.
22. Cable, "Creole Slave Songs," 815.
23. A Voodoo ceremony lead by Sanité Dédé was supposedly observed in 1822 by a young white boy; the story is recounted in Marie B. Williams, "A Night with the Voudous," *Appleton's Journal* (Mar. 27, 1875) and repeated in Buel, *Metropolitan Life Unveiled*. Marie Saloppé is mentioned in a Louisiana Writers' Project interview with Alexander Augustin. Marie Comtesse appears in interviews with Marie Dédé (LWP folder 25) and Laura Hopkins (LWP folder 43). Doctor Jim Alexander is mentioned in interviews with John Smith and Nathan Hobley (LWP folder 25); Doctor Jim also appears in Charles Dudley Warner's article, "A Voodoo Dance," *Harper's Weekly*, June 25, 1887; in a newspaper report, "A Voudou Orgie—Sensational Disclosure in the Third District," *Times-Democrat*, May 29, 1889; and his death is noted in the *New Orleans Times-Picayune*, Aug. 20, 1890, "The Voudou Doctor: Death of a Notorious Negro Who Throve on the Superstitions of His Kind." Doctor Jim's real name was Charles Lafontaine (death certificate, Aug. 19, 1890, [microfilm, New Orleans Public Library], succession record [typed copy LWP folder 511]). Malvina Latour is mentioned as the successor of Marie Laveau in Cable's "Creole Slave Songs, 818"; in Buel's *Metropolitan Life Unveiled*, 536; and in Asbury's *The French Quarter*, 276–78.
24. Lafcadio Hearn, "The Last of the Voudoos," *Harper's Weekly*, Nov. 7, 1885.
25. U.S. Census for 1850, New Orleans, ward 6, sheet 364, line 33, microfilm roll 236; for 1860, ward 6, sheet 186, line 21, microfilm roll 419; for 1870, ward 6, sheet 263, line 33, microfilm roll 522; for 1880, enumeration district 46, sheet 90, line 39, microfilm roll 461, National Archives and Records Administration, Washington, D.C. Death certificate for John Montancé, vol. 87: 914, microfilm, New Orleans Public Library.
26. Marie's birth date is controversial. Her death certificate (microfilm New Orleans Public Library) states that she was ninety-eight when she died in 1881, which would make her birth date 1783. Ina Fandrich accepts this as the correct date ("Mysterious Voodoo Queen," 242, 302 n. 8). But Marie's father, Charles Laveaux, would only have been eight years old in 1783; Marie would have been thirty-six when she married Jacques Paris, forty-four when her first child, Heloïse, was born in 1827, and fifty-five when her last child, Archange, was born in 1838. The year 1794 is cited by most authors, although this is not supported by archival evidence. Other documents lead me to believe that Marie was born in 1801. Her 1819 marriage contract characterizes her as a minor (July 27, 1819, Notary Hughes Lavergne, vol. 1:5, Notarial Archives cited in Fandrich, "Mysterious Voodoo Queen," 305 n. 21; typed copy in Dillon, "Voodoo/Marie the Great," LWP folder 319, 4–6); her daughter Philomene's

1836 birth certificate states that Marie was thirty-five at the time (Births, Orleans Parish, vol. 4: 159, Louisiana Division of Archives, Records Management, and History; typed copy LWP folder 24).

27. Succession of Catherine Henry, June 28, 1831, Orleans Parish, Court of Probate, Probate and Succession Records: 1805–48, 107 H 1831–32, vol. 4: 317 (between marker 0005 and 00011), microfilm, New Orleans Public Library.

28. The suggestion that the free colored businessman Charles Laveaux was the father of Marie Laveau is found in Roulhac Toledano, Sally Evans, and Mary Louise Christovich, *New Orleans Architecture*, vol. 4: *The Creole Faubourgs* (New Orleans: Friends of the Cabildo, 1974), 117, 152; and in Fandrich's "Mysterious Voodoo Queen," 243 and 304 n. 16. This is confirmed by the marriage contract between Marie Laveau and Jacques Paris, in which Charles Laveaux gave to his daughter a lot at 207 Rue Amour—later North Rampart (Notary Hughes Lavergne, vol. 1: 5, Notarial Archives; typed translation in Dillon, "Voodoo/Marie the Great," LWP folder 319, 4–6; cited in Fandrich, "Mysterious Voodoo Queen," 305 n. 21); and the marriage certificate of Marie Laveau and Jacques Paris, Aug. 4, 1819 (St. Louis Cathedral Marriages, vol. 2: p. 59, act 256, Archdiocesan Archives; typed translation, LWP folder 586; cited in Fandrich, "Mysterious Voodoo Queen," 305 n. 20.)

29. Susheel Bibbs, *Heritage of Power* (San Francisco: MEP Publications, 1998), 13–15, quoting from interviews with Liga Foley, San Francisco, by Helen Holdredge, 1930 (Helen Holdredge Estate, Los Angeles). Thanks to Susheel Bibbs for providing me with an advance copy of this work.

30. Death certificate of Christophe Glapion, June 26, 1855, vol. 17: 42, microfilm, New Orleans Public Library; typed copy LWP folder 202; succession of Widow Duminil de Glapion (Christophe's mother), Feb. 16, 1835; succession of Christophe Glapion #9168, Feb. 4, 1856, microfilm, New Orleans Public Library; typed translation, LWP folder 511; Stanley C. Arthur, *Old Families of Louisiana* (1931), 68; Laura Porteous, "Renunciation made by Daniel Fagot of his office of Regidor and receiver of fines forfeited to the Royal Treasury of this city to Don Cristoval de Glapion, 1776, translated from the original in the Cabildo at New Orleans," *Louisiana Historical Quarterly* 14 (July 1931): 372-82. Fandrich cites many of these sources in her documentation of Glapion's ethnicity ("Mysterious Voodoo Queen," 245–47, 306 n. 26.)

31. Baptism of Marie Heloïse, Aug. 19, 1828, St. Louis Cathedral Baptisms, vol. 21: p. 220, act 1232; baptism and funeral of Marie Louise Caroline, SLC Baptisms, Sept. 10, 1829, vol. 22: p. 56, act 317; SLC Funerals vol. 9: p. 2, act 8; baptism of François, May 13, 1834, SLC Baptisms vol. 23: p. 403, act 2715, Archdiocesan Archives; burial of François, May 18, 1834, LWP file of tomb inscriptions for St. Louis Cemetery No. 2, Louisiana State Museum Historical Center; birth certificate for Marie Philomene, Births, Orleans Parish, vol. 4: 159, Louisiana Division of Archives, Records Management, and History; baptism of Philomene, Apr. 1, 1836, SLC Baptisms, vol. 25: p. 35, act 100, Archdiocesan Archives; death certificate for Archange, Jan. 8, 1845, vol. 10: 297, microfilm, New Orleans Public Library. Using some of the same archival sources,

Ina Fandrich found the same five children ("Mysterious Voodoo Queen," 248 n. 40–43, 308). Fandrich believes, and I agree, that Marie Heloïse and Eloise Euchariste (the name also appears as Eucharis and Epicaris in civil records) were almost certainly the same person (249).

32. U.S. Census for 1850, sheet 131, line 3, New Orleans, microfilm roll 235; for 1860, ward 4, sheet 99, line 24, microfilm roll 421, National Archives and Records Administration, Washington, D.C. In 1850 the two little girls are called Malvina, age four, and Henieta, age one; in 1860 they are identified as Alzonia Crocker, age twelve, and Amazone Crocker, age nine. (The microfilm is nearly illegible, and these names may be incorrect.) The surname Crocker indicates that they are the daughters of Heloïse by Pierre Crocker, a prosperous free man of color and friend of the Laveau-Glapion family. Heloïse/Eloise Euchariste did, in fact, give birth to two girls, Adelai and Marie, who would have been about the right ages (baptism of Adelai, Feb. 3, 1848, SLC Baptisms, vol. 32, part 2, p. 353; baptism of Marie, July 9, 1850, SLC Baptisms, vol. 32, part 3, p. 454, Arch–diocesan Archives). Given the tendency of nineteenth-century New Orleanians to call themselves and their children by a variety of names, plus the inaccuracy with which ages were recorded, Malvina/Alzonia/Adelai and Henieta/Amazone/Marie could have been the same two girls. The Laveau-Glapion family also appears in the U.S. Census for 1880 (Patricia Fenerty and Patricia Fernandez, *1880 Census of New Orleans*, vol. 5, Ward 5, enumeration districts 33–42 [New Orleans: Padraigeen Publications, 1997], 140).

33. Castellanos, *New Orleans As It Was*, 97; James Pelletier (white New Orleans antiques dealer), interview by Newbell Niles Puckett, *Folk Beliefs of the Southern Negro*, 180; Louisiana Writers' Project informant Theresa Kavanaugh said that Marie Laveau was a hairdresser, and "that's how she got in the good graces of the fine people" (Theresa Kavanaugh, interview by Zoe Posey, n.d.); Mary Washington said that "she was some kind of a hairdresser and seamster. . . . Her associating with the white people made her know how to fool them" (Mary Washington, interview by Robert McKinney, n.d.), LWP folder 25.

34. Vieux Carré Survey, Historic New Orleans Collection. Fandrich verified this information through extensive research in the Notarial Archives ("Mysterious Voodoo Queen," 247–48, 307n. 34 and 35).

35. "The Condemned: Decorations of the Altar," *New Orleans Daily Picayune*, May 10, 1871, p. 2, col. 6. For a listing of newspaper stories about Marie Laveau, see Betty Morrison, *A Guide to Voodoo in New Orleans, 1820–1940* (Gretna, La.: Her Publishing, 1970). Louisiana Writers' Project worker Catherine Dillon also compiled a bibliography of newspaper articles in conjunction with her "Voodoo" manuscript (LWP folder 118e), and Marcus Christian cited numerous articles in the "Voodooism and Mumbo Jumbo" chapter of his "History of the Negro in Louisiana" (Archives and Manuscripts Division, Earl K. Long Library, University of New Orleans). These unpublished works include many articles not listed by Morrison.

36. "Death of Marie Laveau: Woman with a Wonderful History Almost a Century Old, Carried to the Tomb Yesterday Evening," *New Orleans Daily Picayune*,

June 17, 1881, p. 8, col. 4; "Marie Laveau—Death of the Queen of the Voudous Just before St. John's Eve," *New Orleans Democrat*, June 17, 1881, p. 8, col. 2; "A Sainted Woman—Another Story About Marie Laveau," *New Orleans Democrat*, June 18, 1881, p. 2, col. 1; "Recollections of a Visit on New Year's Eve to Marie Laveau," *Daily States*, June 17, 1881, p. 3, col. 3. The burial record states that "Dame Christophe Glapion, died June 15, 1881 . . . was buried in the family tomb of Widow Paris, middle vault, opening ordered by Philomene Laveau" (New Orleans Archdiocesan Cemeteries; typed copy LWP folder 24).

37. Dillon, "Voodoo/St. John's Eve," cites the *New Orleans Times*, June 25, 1870; the *New Orleans Daily Picayune* and the *New Orleans Herald*, June 24, 1873; the *New Orleans Bee*, June 25, 1873 and June 24, 1874; the *New Orleans Bulletin*, June 25, 1874; and the *New Orleans Times-Democrat*, June 24, 1884 (LWP folder 118b). Cable, "Creole Slave Songs," *Century Magazine* (1886): 818.

38. Saxon, *Fabulous New Orleans*, 243; Dillon, "Marie the Mysterious"; Robert Tallant, *Voodoo in New Orleans*, 73–76.

39. Fandrich, "Mysterious Voodoo Queen," 268. The house mentioned in the *New Orleans Daily Picayune* article was said to be "in the neighborhood of Rampart, Bagatelle, and Union." This is the location of the property given to Heloïse/Eloise Euchariste by Marie Laveau.

40. Marie Heloïse/Eloise Euchariste Glapion had five children by Pierre Crocker. Their baptisms are noted in the records of St. Louis Cathedral and St. Augustin Church (Archdiocesan Archives). Two children, Joseph Eugene Crocker and Esmeralda Crocker, are buried in the Widow Paris tomb. On Nov. 28, 1881, Victor Pierre Duminy Dieudonné de Glapion (also known as Victor Pierre Crocker) petitioned for possession of the house of his deceased mother at 207 North Rampart. This document unequivocally states that Eloise Euchariste died in June 1862 (Judgment #4597; Civil District Court; H. Miester, clerk; F. A. Monroe, judge; typed copy LWP folder 499). Although listed in the index of successions, the petition is missing from the microfilm (New Orleans Public Library). No death certificate or burial record could be located. New Orleans was occupied by Union troops in 1862, and municipal and archdiocesan record keeping was in disarray; it is also possible that Eloise Euchariste did not die in Orleans Parish.

41. Fandrich did not have access to the typed copy of Victor Pierre's petition, and therefore concluded that Heloïse/Eloise Euchariste Glapion was the second Marie Laveau, and that she died in 1881, a few months after her mother ("Mysterious Voodoo Queen," 249, 255, 268–71, 298).

42. Anita Fonvergne, interview by Hazel Breaux Apr. 13, 1939; Alice Zeno, interview by Hazel Breaux, n.d., LWP folder 25.

43. *The Picayune's Guide to New Orleans* for 1900, 66–67.

44. Martha Grey, interview by Henriette Michinard, 1940, LWP folder 25.

45. Marie Dédé, interview by Robert McKinney, n.d., LWP folder 25. The 1880 census lists Marie Glapion (the Widow Paris), her daughter Philomene, and grandchildren Fidelia, Noémie (known as Memie) and Alexandre. Philomene is the only woman known to have lived in the house at that time who fits the description of "Marie Laveau."

46. Charles Raphael, interview by Jacques Villere and Hazel Breaux, n.d.; Raymond Rivaros, interview by Hazel Breaux, n.d., LWP folder 25.

47. Charles Raphael, interview by Jacques Villere and Hazel Breaux, n.d.; Raymond Rivaros, interview by Hazel Breaux, n.d.; Oscar Felix, interview by Edmund Burke, Mar. 14, 1940, LWP folder 25.

48. Mathilda Mendoza, interview by Maude Wallace, Jan. 1940, LWP folder 25. Mendoza quoted a song about "swimming in St. John's Lake" in reference to the St. John's Eve ceremonies.

49. Pontchartrain Railroad, Dillon, "Voodoo/St. John's Eve" (LWP folder 118b, 8a), citing an advertisement in the *New Orleans Bee*, June 23, 1835. The first newspaper articles about the St. John's Eve celebrations appeared in the *New Orleans Commercial Bulletin* and the *New Orleans Bee*, June 25, 1869; the "antebellum" quote is from the *New Orleans Daily Picayune*, June 25, 1877.

50. Donald Cosentino, "Imagine Heaven," in *Sacred Arts*, ed. Cosentino, 47–52.

51. Touchstone, "Voodoo in New Orleans," 371–86.

52. Oscar Felix, interview by Edmond Burke, Mar. 14, 1940, LWP folder 25.

53. The precarious financial status of Marie Laveau is noted in Fandrich, "Mysterious Voodoo Queen." Fandrich suggests that Laveau might have been confused with her half-sister, Marie de los Dolores, the legitimate daughter of Charles Laveaux and his wife, Françoise Dupart, who was indeed wealthy (246–47, 251). Neither Fandrich nor I found evidence that Laveau ever owned anything of value.

54. Marie Dédé, interview by Robert McKinney, n.d., LWP folder 25.

55. Lafcadio Hearn, "New Orleans Superstitions," *Harper's Weekly*, Dec. 25, 1886, 843.

56. New Orleans city ordinances banned disorderly conduct, exposing the body, and loitering in public places, and were used to break up Voodoo assemblies (#3046 passed May 7, 1879; #7085 passed May 17, 1881; cited in Dillon, "Voodoo/The Law's Long Arm," LWP folder 118d, 29–30.)

57. Mail Fraud Act, Lisa Martin, staff attorney for the U.S. Postal Service, Enforcement Division of the General Counsel's Office, telephone interview, Feb. 9, 1998. Medical Practice Act, Delmar Rorison, executive director, Louisiana Board of Medical Examiners, telephone interview, Oct. 7, 1998. New Orleans ordinances against fortune-telling and obtaining money under false pretenses are cited in Dillon, "Voodoo/The Law's Long Arm," LWP folder 118d, 40, 42, 52 (Council Series #13,347, passed May 12, 1897; #3107, passed Feb. 2, 1916; #7876, passed May 14, 1924). Dillon documents forty newspaper articles about hoodoo-related arrests between 1901 and 1939.

58. Touchstone, "Voodoo in New Orleans," 371–86; Joseph G. Tregle Jr., "Creoles and Americans," in Hirsch and Logsdon, eds. *Creole New Orleans*, 131–85.

59. Mary Washington, interview by Robert McKinney, n.d., LWP folder 25.

60. Claude Jacobs and Andrew Kaslow, *The Spiritual Churches of New Orleans* (Knoxville: Univ. of Tennessee Press, 1991), 28, 74.

61. Louisiana Writers' Project fieldworkers interviewed many of the reverend mothers in the late 1930s (folders 29 and 36) and the Spiritual churches have more recently been documented by New Orleans photographer and historian Michael P. Smith in *Spirit World—Photographs and Journal: Pattern in the Expressive Folk*

Culture of Afro-American New Orleans (Gretna, La.: Pelican Publishing Co., 1984), by anthropologists Claude Jacobs and Andrew Kaslow in *The Spiritual Churches of New Orleans*, and by freelance writer Jason Berry in *The Spirit of Black Hawk: A Mystery of Africans and Indians* (Jackson: Univ. Press of Mississippi, 1995).

62. Mother Dora Tyson, interview by Hazel Breaux, May 4, 1937, LWP folder 36; Bishop Edmonia Caldwell, interview by the author, May 27, 1996, at Black Hawk altar, New Orleans Jazz and Heritage Festival.

63. "Joe Feraille," Harold Courlander, *The Drum and the Hoe: Life and Lore of the Haitian People* (Berkeley: Univ. of California Press, 1960), 321. "La Bas" and "Blanc Dani," Mary Washington, interview by Robert McKinney, n.d., LWP folder 25; Madame Ducoyielle, interview by Hazel Breaux and Robert McKinney, 1936, LWP folder 44. Song for Legba, Métraux, *Voodoo in Haiti*, 101. An early recording by Kid Ory and his New Orleans Jazz Band is called "Eh La Bas," and the phrase can be heard in the Meters' late 1960s recording of "Audubon Zoo."

64. The role of the saints is documented by Hurston, the Louisiana Writers' Project, and Hyatt; Hyatt's New Orleans informant "Beer for St. Peter" (vol. 2: 1220–36) gives a particularly detailed account.

65. These dates come from the chronology of Hurston's collecting trips, written in her own hand, filed with the manuscript "Negro Folktales from the Gulf States," now housed at the National Anthropological Archives, National Museum of Natural History, Smithsonian Institution. This collection of stories became *Mules and Men*. It does not include notes from Hurston's trips to New Orleans.

66. Zora Neale Hurston, review of Robert Tallant's *Voodoo in New Orleans*, *Journal of American Folklore* 60 (1947): 437.

67. Hurston, *Mules and Men*, initiations by Luke Turner, 198–202; Anatol Pierre, 207–8; Father Watson, 216–17. Hyatt questioned whether Hurston's account was "literature or a scientific investigation" (*Hoodoo* 2: 1649). He wondered if Hurston might have been duped by unscrupulous practitioners who "just fixed something for the occasion." He quizzed Madam Murray of Algiers, who denied the existence of such rituals: "We don't do stuff like that . . . I don't know what that is" (2: 1282–83).

68. Hurston, *Mules and Men*, Kitty Brown: controlling charm, 245; Father Watson: "sweet" jar and "break-up" jar, 215; jail charm, 218, black cat bone, 220–21; Doctor Duke: court-case charm, 224; beef tongue charm, 225; Anatol Pierre: death ritual, 209–11; paraphernalia of conjure 183–246, 273–80. Four Thieves Vinegar was originally a preparation used during the London plague of 1665 by a band of four thieves, who, believing themselves protected by this herbal mixture, stole from the corpses of plague victims. The recipe included red wine vinegar, rue, sage, mint, wormwood, rosemary, lavender, camphor, garlic, and sweet spices (Claire Kowalchik and William Hylton, eds., *Rodale's Illustrated Encyclopedia of Herbs* [Emmaus, Pa.: Rodale Press, 1987], 434).

69. LWP fieldworkers Robert McKinney and Edmund Burke were African American, as were Marcus Christian and others from the Dillard University "Negro Writers' Project."

70. Mrs. Dereco, Madame Ducoyielle (Mrs. Robinson), and "Nom" (Oscar Felix), interviews by Hazel Breaux and Robert McKinney, Oct. 22, Dec. 5 and 9, 1936 (others undated), LWP folder 44. In these interviews, Felix's name is given as "Edward," but his address, 1220 South Prieur, is the same as Oscar Felix's in the 1940 interviews by Edmund Burke. Oscar Felix is listed in the city directory at that address. Robert Tallant made extensive use of the McKinney-Breaux interviews in *Voodoo in New Orleans* (155–61), where Mrs. Dereco, Madame Ducoyielle, and Nom are called Mrs. Lombardo, Madame Cazaunoux, and Rooster.

71. Thompson, *Flash of the Spirit*, 108–11; Leland Ferguson, *Uncommon Ground: Archeology and Early African America* (Washington, D.C.: Smithsonian Institution Press, 1992), 26, 110–16; Max Beauvoir, personal communication, Sept. 13, 1997.

72. Hoodoo Book Man, Hyatt, *Hoodoo* 2: 1757–58.

73. Gifted Medium, Hyatt, *Hoodoo* 2: 948. The practice of using different colored ingredients in accordance with the race of the client or the target is also documented in Hyatt's interviews with "Boss of Algiers," vol. 2: 1354, 1356; and "Algiers Atmosphere," vol. 3: 1903.

74. Custodian of a Shrine, Hyatt, *Hoodoo* 2: 1142.

75. Ibid., 1142–43.

76. Beer for St. Peter, Hyatt, *Hoodoo* 2: 1222.

77. Madam Lindsey, Hyatt, *Hoodoo* 2: 1512.

78. Minta Owens, Hyatt, *Hoodoo* 2: 1087.

79. Liza Moore, Hyatt, *Hoodoo* 3: 2210–20.

80. Leslie Williams, "Chicken Man's Remains in Limbo," *New Orleans Times-Picayune*, Jan. 25, 1999, B1, B2; Leslie Williams, "Chicken Man to Get Voodoo Burial," *New Orleans Times-Picayune*, Jan. 25, 1999.

81. Cari Roy, New Orleans, interview Apr. 25, 1996; Jane Jones, New Orleans, telephone interview Nov. 12, 1998.

82. Ava Kay Jones, interview Apr. 28, 1996 at New Orleans Jazz and Heritage Festival; Ron Bodin, *Voodoo Past and Present* (Lafayette: Center for Louisiana Studies, Univ. of Southwestern Louisiana, 1990), 74–82; Rod Davis, *American Voudou*, 299–312; video, "New Orleans Voodoo from the Inside," directed by David M. Jones, DMJ Productions; web site www.nawlins.com/others/vopoooo.

83. Shane Norris, Island of Salvation, interview Apr. 29, 1996; Sallie Ann Glassman, interview May 22, 1997; Rick Bragg, "New Orleans Conjures Old Spirits against Modern Woes," *New York Times*, Aug. 18, 1995, A10; Christopher Rose, "Hurricane Gris-Gris," *Times-Picayune*, July 17, 1998, E1, E2; ceremony for Dambala Mar. 13, 1998; ceremony for Gédé Nov. 1, 1998; web site www.mindspring.com/~cfeldman/bot2.

84. New Orleans Voodoo Spiritual Temple, interview with Temple staff, May 22, 1997; interview with Priestess Miriam Williams Chamani, Mar. 20 and Nov. 1, 1998; *Voodoo Realist Newsletter*; web site gnofn.org/~voodoo/flyer; Leslie Williams, "Priestess to Teach Voodoo in Russia," *Times-Picayune*, Sept. 6, 1999,

B1, B2 (thanks to David Estes for this article). See also Pinn, *Varieties of African American Spiritual Experience*, 44–55.

85. Tour guide's spiel overheard at the tomb of Marie Laveau, May 22, 1997.

Chapter 4. Conjure, Hoodoo, and Rootwork in the Anglo-Protestant South

1. See Herskovits, *The Myth of the Negro Past* (Boston: Beacon Press, 1990); Sobel, *The World They Made Together*; Elliot Gorn, "Black Magic: Folk Beliefs of the Slave Community," in *Science and Medicine in the Old South*, ed. Ronald Numbers and Todd Savitt (Baton Rouge: Louisiana State Univ. Press, 1989); Chireau, "Conjuring: An Analysis of African American Folk Beliefs and Practices" (Ph.D. diss., Princeton, 1994); Berlin, *Many Thousands Gone*.

2. Sobel, *The World They Made Together*, 5, 244 n. 6; Peter H. Wood, *Black Majority: Negroes in Colonial South Carolina from 1670 Through the Stono Rebellion* (New York: W. W. Norton & Co., 1974), 59–60; Thompson, *Four Moments of the Sun*, 32; Charles Joyner, *Down by the Riverside: A South Carolina Slave Community* (Urbana: Univ. of Illinois Press, 1984), 1, 14–15; Margaret Washington Creel, *"A Peculiar People": Slave Religion and Community-Culture among the Gullahs* (New York: New York Univ. Press, 1988), 29–44, 329–34.

3. See Sobel, *The World They Made Together*; Edward D. C. Campbell and Kym Rice, eds., *Before Freedom Came: African-American Life in the Antebellum South* (Richmond: Museum of the Confederacy and Univ. of Virginia Press, 1991); Berlin, *Many Thousands Gone*.

4. Chireau, "Conjuring," 35; Raboteau, *Slave Religion*, 89–92.

5. Charles Colcock Jones, *The Religious Instruction of the Negroes in the United States* (Freeport, N.Y.: Books for Libraries Press, 1971), 127.

6. Ibid., 8–12, 21.

7. Raboteau, *Slave Religion*; Hortense Powdermaker, *After Freedom: A Cultural Study in the Deep South* (Madison: Univ. of Wisconsin Press, 1993), 223–31.

8. Grace Sherwood, a white woman, was tried for witchcraft in Princess Anne County, Virginia, in the early eighteenth century. At the Great Neck Archeological Site, near the former home of Grace Sherwood, a pin-filled medicine phial, dating from the same time period, was found buried upside down. (Floyd Painter, "An Early Eighteenth Century Witch Bottle," *The Chesopiean: A Journal of North American Archeology* 18, no. 3–6 [1980]: 62–71.) For reference to occult books in the libraries of Virginia planters, see Sobel, *The World They Made Together*, 80–83.

9. In 1878 a letter from a graduate of the Hampton Institute, published in *The Southern Workman*, stated that "[The Negroes] all believe in witchcraft and cunning. When one of them gets sick they send for a cunning doctor" (*Southern Workman* 7, no. 4 [Apr. 1878]: 28, rpt. in Donald Waters, *Strange Ways and Sweet Dreams: Afro-American Folklore from the Hampton Institute* [Boston: G. K. Hall, 1983]).

10. Raboteau, *Slave Religion*, 275–88; also see Chireau, "Conjuring."

11. "Wise man or woman," Doctor Heard, Waycross, Ga., Hyatt, *Hoodoo* 3: 1954–55; Requires Secrecy, Brunswick, Ga., vol. 2: 1132; Raggedy Man, Florence,

S.C., vol. 3: 2192; Cautious Healer, Sumter, S.C., vol. 2: 1348; Wise Woman, Wilmington, N.C., vol. 2: 1294–95. "High man," vol. 1: 240, 284, 293, 336; vol. 2: 942.

12. For the health-related folklore of African Americans, see Snow, *Walkin' Over Medicine*. For occult causes of sickness, especially "live things in the body," see Puckett, *Folk Beliefs*, and Michael E. Bell, "Pattern, Structure, and Logic in Afro-American Hoodoo Performance." Wyatt MacGaffey ascribes a Kongo origin to the idea of "live things in the body," quoting K. E. Laman, *The Kongo* 3: 96–100 (letter Oct. 13, 1998).

13. For the eighteenth-century New York conjurer, see Kenneth Scott, "The Slave Insurrection in New York in 1712," *New York Historical Quarterly* (Jan. 1961): 47. For Gullah Jack, see Creel, *A Peculiar People*, 150–59.

14. Frederick Douglass, *The Life and Times of Frederick Douglass, Written by Himself* (New York: Collier Books, 1962), 27–143.

15. Henry Bibb, in *Puttin' On Ole Massa: The Slave Narratives of Henry Bibb, William Wells Brown, and Solomon Northrup*, ed. Gilbert Osofsky (New York: Harper and Row, 1969), 70–71. William Wells Brown also describes a plantation conjurer, but does not elaborate on charms.

16. *Southern Workman* 7, no. 4 (Apr. 1878): 30–31; in Waters, *Strange Ways*, 131–39.

17. Alice Bacon's circular letter was published in *Southern Workman* 22, no. 12 (Dec. 1893): 180–81. The introduction to Waters's *Strange Ways* describes the history and philosophy of Hampton and the founding of the Folklore Society.

18. Leonora Herron and Alice Bacon, "Conjuring and Conjure Doctors," *Southern Workman* 4, no. 7 (July 1895): 117–18; no. 11 (Nov. 1895): 193–94; no. 12 (Dec. 1895): 209–11; in Waters, *Strange Ways*, 235–42.

19. Chireau, "Conjuring," 183–206, 239–86.

20. Thompson, *Flash of the Spirit*, 105, 117; MacGaffey, *Religion and Society in Central Africa*, 157. Wyatt MacGaffey cautions that the attribution of an African origin to "mojo" and "toby" is only a possibility, not a fact (letter, Oct. 13, 1998.)

21. Puckett, *Folk Beliefs*, 256–58; references to the black cat bone in Hyatt's *Hoodoo* are too numerous to mention.

22. Puckett assigned each informant a number and identified him or her in the appendix by name and location. Whites are distinguished from blacks by the use of the titles Mr., Mrs., or Miss.

23. Puckett, *Folk Beliefs*, 205, 234, 248, 266.

24. Ibid., 237.

25. Cull Taylor, Mobile, Ala., interview by Ila B. Prine, July 30, 1937, *Alabama and Indiana Narratives*, ed. George A. Rawick (Westport, Conn.: Greenwood Publishing, 1972), vol. 6: 365.

26. Hector Godbold, Marion, S.C., interview by Annie Ruth Davis June 28, 1937, in *The American Slave: A Composite Biography*, vol. 14 of *South Carolina Narratives*, ed. George A. Rawick (Westport, Conn.: Greenwood Publishing, 1972), pt. 2, 146.

27. See Charles Perdue, Thomas Barden, and Robert Phillips, eds., *Weevils in the Wheat: Interviews with Virginia Ex-Slaves* (Virginia Writers' Project) (Charlottesville: Univ. of Virginia Press, 1992), especially John Spencer, inter-

view by Bernice Lewis, n.d., 278; and Virginia Hayes Shepard, interview by Emmy Wilson and Claude W. Anderson, May 18, 1937, 263.

28. The interviews published in volumes 2 and 3 of *Hoodoo-Conjure-Witchcraft-Rootwork* are arranged in random order, bouncing back and forth in time and location in a most disconcerting fashion. It was only possible to perceive regional variations in rituals and charm beliefs by rearranging the interviews in chronological order by informant number.

29. Mojo Expert, Memphis, 1938, Hyatt, *Hoodoo* 2: 1262.

30. Root-Seller of Mobile, Hyatt, *Hoodoo* 1: 12; informant, 651, Mobile, vol. 1: 872–73; informant 667, Mobile, vol. 1: 275; Rich Man Poor Man, Vicksburg, vol. 3: 2322–39; Divine Healer, Little Rock, vol. 2: 1044–48; Doctor Cunningham, Little Rock, vol. 2: 1315–25.

31. Margaret McKee and Fred Chisenhall, *Beale Black and Blue* (Baton Rouge: Louisiana State Univ. Press, 1981), 16.

32. Nation Sack Woman, Memphis, Hyatt, *Hoodoo* 2: 1458. "Come On in My Kitchen," *Robert Johnson: The Complete Recordings;* thanks to Catherine Yronwode for bringing this to my attention.

33. Madam Collins, Hyatt, *Hoodoo* 2: 996; Self-Sufficient Doctor, vol. 3: 1870; Madam Wiley, vol. 2: 1567.

34. Madam Collins, Hyatt, *Hoodoo* 2: 1001, 1003, 1005, 1009.

35. Ibid., 1006.

36. Eureka, Hyatt, *Hoodoo* 3: 1860.

37. Ibid., 1878; Guinea Pig and Toadfrog, vol. 2: 1730.

38. Thanks to Sharon Bynum, Southhaven, Miss., for bringing the "Voodoo Village" to my attention, telephone interview, Oct. 25, 1999. Bynum cites articles in the *Memphis Press-Scimitar* of May 13, 1947, and Aug. 13, 1975.

39. Paul Hochuli, "Voodoo in Houston," *Houston Press*, Mar. 22–26, 1937.

40. Wood, *Black Majority;* Creel, *A Peculiar People;* Joyner, *Down by the Riverside;* Joyner, *Remember Me: Slave Life in Coastal Georgia* (Atlanta: Georgia Humanities Council, 1989); Berlin, *Many Thousands Gone*, 64–76, 142–76, 290–324.

41. Mattie Sampson, Brownsville, Ga., Georgia Writers' Project, *Drums and Shadows: Survival Studies among the Georgia Coastal Negroes* (Athens: Univ. of Georgia Press and Brown Thrasher Books, 1986), 55–56; Agent for Curios, Jacksonville, Fla., Hyatt, *Hoodoo* 2: 1075–88. The sale of spiritual products by agents will be discussed in chapter 8.

42. Georgia Writers' Project, *Drums and Shadows;* Raboteau, *Slave Religion*, 70–73.

43. Hag and plat-eye, Joyner, *Down by the Riverside*, 150–53. Ghosts, Georgia Writers' Project, *Drums and Shadows*, Elizabeth Roberts, Sunbury, 114; Paul Singleton, Tin City, 17.

44. Georgia Writers' Project, *Drums and Shadows*, foot tracks, 2, 135, 148; burning of hair, 135; copper wire, 21; silver dime, 92, 125, 136.

45. Ibid., Liza Basden, Harris Neck, 124–25.

46. Ibid., Elizabeth Roberts, Sunbury, 114.

47. Doctor Washington, Charleston, Hyatt, *Hoodoo* 3: 2254.

48. Thompson, *Flash of the Spirit*, 105; again, MacGaffey cautions that the derivation of "goofer dust" from the word *kufwa* is only a possibility (letter Oct. 13, 1998).

49. Peace, Tomb of the Babe, Brunswick, Hyatt, *Hoodoo* 2: 1331; reunite couples, Doctor Glover, Charleston, vol. 3: 2258–59; protection, Marcus Brown, Charleston, vol. 2: 1292; court case, Doctor Wands, Florence, vol. 2: 1530; banish enemies, Patient Doctor, Waycross, vol. 2: 973–74, 977; force out competitor, Requires Secrecy, Brunswick, vol. 2: 1130–33; detect criminals, Three Highest Names, Florence, vol. 3: 2085–86; death, Cautious Healer, Sumter, vol. 2: 1350.

50. Ben Blair, Charleston, telephone interview Oct. 25, 1998.

51. Albert Jenkins, Brownsville, Georgia Writers' Project, *Drums and Shadows*, 60.

52. Mamie Garvin Fields, with Karen Fields, *Lemon Swamp and Other Places* (New York: Free Press, 1983), 121. In the chapter "The Teacher and the Root Man," Fields describes the root doctors of John's Island.

53. Hyatt, *Hoodoo* 1: 892–97, 904; 2: 1107, 1416–17. Several Georgia Writers' Project informants also told of court proceedings being disrupted by a buzzard perching atop the courthouse, although this act was not attributed to Doctor Buzzard (Georgia Writers' Project, *Drums and Shadows*, 28, 109–10, 184).

54. According to a 1926 article on the Gullah language, *Stepney* is a word of possible African origin personifying hunger or want; the Gullahs spoke of "keeping Stepney from the door" (Reed Smith, "Gullah," *Bulletin of the University of South Carolina* 190 [Nov. 1, 1926]: 28–29). Thanks to Roger Pinckney for this article.

55. J. Edwin McTeer, *High Sheriff of the Low Country* (Beaufort, S.C.: JEM Co., 1970), 19–38; idem, *Fifty Years as a Low Country Witch Doctor* (Beaufort, S.C.: JEM Co., 1970), 21–25; Roger Pinckney, *Blue Roots: African-American Folk Magic of the Gullah People* (St. Paul: Llewellyn Publications, 1998), 101–20; telephone interview, Oct. 13, 1998.

56. Death certificate #05616, South Carolina Board of Health, Bureau of Vital Statistics. U.S. Census for 1880, enumeration district 50, sheet 87, line 48, St. Helena Township, microfilm roll 1221; U.S. Census for 1910, enumeration district 69, sheet 17A, line 21, St. Helena Township, microfilm roll 1450, National Archives and Records Administration, Washington, D.C. In 1920 Robinson's father, Tom Robinson, age ninety, lived on the adjoining farm (Tom Robinson, U.S. Census for 1920, enumeration district 75, sheet 8, line 38; Stephney Robinson, sheet 17A, line 17, St. Helena Township, microfilm roll 1686, National Archives and Records Administration, Washington, D.C.). Stephney Robinson's children were William, Edward, Victoria, Lucille, John, Lyvania, Florence, Maria, and Stephney Jr.

57. John Berendt, *Midnight in the Garden of Good and Evil* (1994), 241–55; Lolita Huckaby, "Author Revives Interest in Low Country Cult," *Beaufort Gazette*, June 26, 1994, Section D, Focus.

58. F. Roy Johnson, *The Fabled Doctor Jim Jordan: A Story of Conjure* (Murphreesboro, N.C.: Johnson Publishing, 1963).

59. Sharon Bynum, telephone interview, Nov. 1, 1999.

60. Roger Pinckney, telephone interview, Oct. 13, 1998; Ben Blair, telephone interview, Oct. 25, 1998.

61. Catalina de Guzman, Botánica San Miguel, Silver Spring, Md., interview, Sept. 25, 1996.
62. *Amsterdam News*, Nov. 19, 1994, 49; *Chicago Defender*, Nov. 17, 1994, 27.
63. Doug Miller, "Hexed Customers Believe in Root Worker's Powers, *Fayetteville [N.C.] Observer-Times*, Jan. 18, 1997, A1, A4. Craig Whitlock, "Conjure Man," *Raleigh [N.C.] News and Observer*, Mar. 24, 1996, A1, A12. Thanks to Claude Rosser and Cornelia Loftus for these articles.

Chapter 5. The Commodification of Traditional Charms

1. Madam Lindsey, Algiers, Hyatt, *Hoodoo* 2: 1512–13.
2. Agent for Curios, Jacksonville, Hyatt, *Hoodoo* 2: 1097.
3. McTeer, *High Sheriff of the Low Country*, 35.
4. Scott Cunningham, *Cunningham's Encyclopedia of Magical Herbs* (St. Paul, Minn.: Llewellyn Publications, 1993), High John the Conqueror/jalap, 123; chewing John the Conqueror/galangal, 108; lucky hand/salep, 145.
5. Catherine Yronwode, telephone interview, June 12, 1998; Martin Mayer, interview, June 19, 1998. The Allan Company of Houston is the only known supplier of bulldog hair.
6. Valmor/King Novelty and Sovereign 1936 catalogs.
7. F & F Candle Shop catalog 1993.
8. International Imports catalog 1972.
9. Allan Company catalog 1989.
10. Miller Drug catalog 1997.
11. Valmor/King Novelty catalog 1936.
12. Lucky Mo-Jo was manufactured by Valmor, Midnight Mojo by Clover Horn, and Mystic Mojo by Lucky Heart.
13. Allan Company catalog 1989.
14. Clover Horn catalog 1951.
15. Herbal baths, La Milagrosa Products; Radiant Health Oil, Miller Drug catalog 1997; copper bracelet, International Imports catalog 1972.
16. Snow, "Sorcerers, Saints, and Charlatans," 79.
17. Miller Drug catalog 1997.
18. Nite-Glow Candles.
19. Sovereign Products catalog 1936.
20. Mysteria catalog 1998.
21. Dennis Tedlock, *Breath on the Mirror: Mythic Voices and Visions of the Living Maya* (San Francisco: Harper, 1993), 213–27, 249–50. Otto Chicas-Rendón and Héctor Gaitán Alfaro, *Recetario y Oraciones Secretas de Maximón* (New York: Casa de Velas, 1995).
22. Luise Margolies, "José Gregorio Hernández: The Historical Development of a Venezuelan Popular Saint," *Studies in Latin American Popular Culture* 3 (1984): 28–46.
23. For Don Pedrito, see Wilson Mathis Hudson, *The Healer of Los Olmos* (Dallas: Southern Methodist Univ. Press, 1951). For El Niño Fidencio, see Dore

Gardner and Kay F. Turner, *Niño Fidencio: A Heart Thrown Open* (Santa Fe: Museum of New Mexico Press, 1992). Also see Bill Minutaglio, "Los Grandes," *Dallas Life Magazine*, Jan. 23, 1994, 6–10, 19.

24. Douglas Congdon-Martin, *Images in Black: 150 Years of Black Collectibles* (West Chester, Pa.: Schiffer Publishing, 1990), 55–57.

25. Cousin of Julius P. Caesar, New Orleans, 1938, Hyatt, *Hoodoo* 2: 1649–50; Madam Collins, Memphis, 1939, vol. 2: 1019.

26. Morton Neumann, Valmor Products, interview by Terry Zwigoff 1975, in Zwigoff, "The Valmor Story," *Wierdo* 18 (fall 1986); Lista Wayman, Keystone Laboratories, interview by the author May 16, 1997.

27. Between 1994 and 1999 I had many discussions with my colleague Priscilla Quiles Wood, daughter of Manuel Quiles, about her father's work. She also suggested that I contact her older brother Mario, who had a better recollection of the business; Mario Quiles, Santa Fe, N.M., telephone interview, Apr. 26, 1998.

28. International Imports catalog 1972.

29. See A. Monroe Aurand, *The "Pow-Wow" Book: A Treatise on the Art of "Healing by Prayer" and "Laying on of Hands," Etc.* (Harrisburg, Pa.: Aurand Press, 1929); identical charms and rituals were documented among German settlers in central South Carolina, where the practice was called "using" (John Hawkins, "Magical Medical Practice in South Carolina," *Popular Science Monthly* 70, no. 2 [Feb. 1907], 165–74).

30. See the entry for "Secrets of the Psalms: Kabalist Influence on Hoodoo" in Catherine Yrodwode's Lucky W Amulet Archive web site www.luckymojo.com/luckyw.

31. Harry B. Weiss, "Oneirocritica Americana," *Bulletin of the New York Public Library* 48 (June 1944): 519–41; "Preliminary Check List of Dream Books Published in America" (July 1944): 642–53.

32. The original version of *The Life and Works of Marie Laveau* was described by Catherine Dillon, "Voodoo/Stuff and Nonsense," LWP folder 118c, 13–14; The Gibson Girl image was made popular in the late nineteenth century by the American illustrator Charles Dana Gibson. The booklet was cited as evidence of mail fraud in "Federal Agents Expose Business in Goofer Dust," *New Orleans Morning Tribune*, May 14, 1927, p. 1, col. 3.

33. Hurston, "Hoodoo in America," 328–57; the misspelled word *hearken* is found on page 333 of "Hoodoo in America" and on page 7 of *Original Black and White Magic*.

34. Herman Rucker, *Black Herman's Secrets of Magic, Mystery, and Legerdemain* (New York: Dorene Publishing, 1938), 8–29; Ed Kay, Arlington, Tex., telephone interview, Apr. 23, 1998.

35. Ed Kay, telephone interview, Mar. 29, 1997.

36. Martin Mayer, interview, Apr. 5, 1997

Chapter 6. Mail-Order Doctors and Hoodoo Drugstores

1. John Swann, historian, U.S. Food and Drug Administration, telephone interview, Feb. 9, 1998.

2. U.S. Criminal Code Annotated, Title 18, Crimes and Criminal Procedure, Section 1341 (formerly section 338), Frauds and Swindles, 258; note 75,

298–99. The law was revised in 1948 to eliminate obsolete language, but is essentially the same as that enacted in 1909.

3. Lisa Martin, staff attorney for the U.S. Postal Service, Enforcement Division of the General Counsel's Office, telephone interview, Feb. 9, 1998.

4. *Chicago Defender*, Dec. 10, 1910, p. 5, col. 5.

5. Ibid., Mar. 22, 1919, p. 3, col. 7.

6. Ibid., Mar. 7, 1925, p. 15, col. 8.

7. Ibid., June 8, 1935, p. 3, col. 8.

8. A listing of articles about hoodoo-related arrests and mail fraud investigations can be found in Betty Morrison's *Guide to Voodoo in New Orleans, 1820–1940*, and in Catherine Dillon's unpublished manuscript, "Voodoo/The Law's Long Arm," LWP folder 118d.

9. "Husbands and Lovers are Voodoo Sage's Specialty," *New Orleans Times-Democrat*, Oct. 29, 1902, p. 10, col. 4.

10. Cousin of Julius P. Caesar, New Orleans, Hyatt, *Hoodoo* 2: 1642.

11. "Doctor Cat Pleads Guilty," *New Orleans Times-Picayune*, July 11, 1914, p. 4, col. 4.

12. Criminal case files of the U.S. District Court, Eastern District of Louisiana, New Orleans Division, National Archives and Records Administration, Southwestern Region, Fort Worth, Tex.

13. "Dr. Cat in Prison: Wife Seeks Divorce—Voodoo Artist Unable to Save Himself or Hold His Wife," *New Orleans Times-Picayune*, July 14, 1914, p. 4, col. 2.

14. Robert McKinney, "Rockford Lewis Jailed: Gloom Seems Certain for Voodooism," n.d., LWP folder 44.

15. Transcript of mail-fraud trial, U.S. District Court, Nov. 23, 1933–Feb. 16, 1934, LWP folder 374.

16. "Voodoo Charm Doctor Makes Court Defense," *New Orleans Item*, Feb. 6, 1934, p. 1, col. 1.

17. Rockford Lewis, interview by Robert McKinney and Hazel Breaux, Apr. 6, 1937, LWP folder 44.

18. "Innocence Plea in Voodoo Case," *New Orleans Item*, Sept. 15, 1938, p. 8, col. 5.

19. Rockford Lewis, interview by Robert McKinney, n.d., LWP folder 44. Robert Tallant, in *Voodoo in New Orleans*, devoted several pages (211–13) to the story of Rockford Lewis.

20. Edward T. Clayton, "The Truth About Voodoo, *Ebony*, Apr. 1951, 56, 60.

21. John Hall, New Orleans, interview by Robert McKinney and Hazel Breaux, Apr. 13, 1937, LWP folder 44. In Tallant's *Voodoo in New Orleans*, John Hall is represented by the character called "Doctor Freddie Moses" (213–14).

22. U.S. Post Office, Postal Service Inspector's fraud order case files, #4437, Nov. 18, 1924, box 72, National Archives and Records Administration, Washington, D.C.; "U.S. Interrupts Work of Voodoo Mail Order Doctor," *Chicago Defender*, Jan. 10, 1925, p. 1, col. 7.

23. *Chicago Defender*, Jan. 2, 1925, p. 4, col. 8.

24. Dr. Julian Fincher, Dean of the School of Pharmacy at the University of South Carolina, kindly sent me originals of Watson's advertising flyer and price list

and photocopies of the letters. Claude Rosser, the pharmacist to whom the letters were first given, also provided information, telephone interviews, June 9 and Sept. 7, 1996.

25. Hyatt, *Hoodoo* 3: 2092, 2101.

26. James Weldon Johnson, *Black Manhattan* (New York: Arno Press, 1968), 151; Allan H. Spear, *Black Chicago: The Making of a Negro Ghetto, 1890–1920* (Chicago: Univ. of Chicago Press, 1967), 140; Chireau, "Conjuring," 277–86.

27. *Chicago Defender*, Oct. 4, 1919, p. 19, col. 4.

28. Ibid., Apr. 2, 1921, p. 2, col. 8.

29. Saint Clair Drake and Horace Cayton, *Black Metropolis: A Study of Negro Life in a Northern City* (New York: Harcourt, Brace and World, 1945), 474–81.

30. For more on obeah in the West Indies, see Frederic Cassidy, *Jamaica Talk* (New York: Macmillan, 1961), 253–54.

31. Professor Indoo and Edet Effiong, *Chicago Defender*, Dec. 27, 1924, p. 7, cols. 6, 7, and 8; Professor Domingo, *Chicago Defender*, Feb. 28, 1925, p. 13, col. 7. A character similar to these alleged Africans is the subject of Rudolph Fisher's 1932 novel, *The Conjure-Man Dies: A Mystery Tale of Dark Harlem*.

32. Thomas Ewing Dabney, "Witchcraft Medicine," *American Pharmacist* (Sept. 1931): 22–24, 78, 80, 82.

33. The 1920 census lists Dr. George A. Thomas, his wife, Alice (a native of France), and their sons, Lucien, George B., and Andre J.; sheet 13, line 64, Enumeration District 75, New Orleans, microfilm roll 620, National Archives and Records Administration, Washington, D.C.

34. "Federal Agents Expose Business in Goofer Dust," *New Orleans Morning Tribune*, May 14, 1927; p. 1, col. 3.

35. Robert McKinney, n.d., LWP folder 44.

36. The Karnofksys, Russian Jewish immigrants who operated a junk and coal business, were friends and employers of the young Louis Armstrong; they advanced him the money with which to purchase his first cornet (Louis Armstrong, "Storyville—Where the Blues Were Born," *True* 21, no. 126 [1947]: 32, 100–105); Louis Armstrong, manuscript page reproduced in Gary Giddons, *Satchmo* [1988], 63).

37. Informant 823, New Orleans, Hyatt, *Hoodoo* 4: 3224; First Informant in New Orleans, vol. 2: 1625–26.

38. Jane Jones, New Orleans, telephone interview, Nov. 12, 1998.

39. Clayton, "The Truth About Voodoo," 56.

40. Stella Pitts, "Marie Laveau, the Voodoo Queen," *Dixie*, Sunday Magazine, *New Orleans Times-Picayune*, Oct. 28, 1970, 39–41.

41. George Williams, interview by Bobby Joe Neeley, in "Contemporary Afro-American Voodooism: The Retention and Adaptation of the Ancient African-Egyptian Mystery System" (Ph.D. diss., University of California at Berkeley, 1988), vol. 2: 752.

42. The death notice of Alice Vibert Thomas Karno states that she was a native of Bordeaux, France, a resident of New Orleans since 1905, and a member of St. Anthony of Padua Catholic Church. She was survived by her sons Lucien

Thomas, Dr. George Thomas, and Dr. Andre Thomas (*New Orleans Times-Picayune*, June 11, 1975, section 1, p. 1., col. 6).

43. John C. Coleman, New Orleans, interview by Hazel Breaux and Robert McKinney, Apr. 7, 1937, LWP folder 44.

44. Robert Tallant Papers, New Orleans Public Library, Louisiana Division, box 3, folder 17; John C. Coleman was probably the "large and florid-faced druggist" described by Tallant on pages 216–18 of *Voodoo in New Orleans*. Coleman's associate, Professor Hubert, is probably the character called "Professor Graham" by Tallant.

45. Kathleen Mulvihill, "Voodoo: Alive and Well in the '80s," *New Orleans Times-Picayune*, June 24, 1984. See also Angela Carll, "Voodoo Puts Magic in Her Life," *Dixie*, Sunday Magazine, *Times-Picayune*, Apr. 8, 1979.

46. Francis Hendrick Jr., son of Francis and Ellen Hendrick, New Orleans, telephone interview, Mar. 24, 1995; Horace Bynum Jr., New Orleans, telephone interview, Apr. 27, 1995.

47. Ann Epstein and Samuel Rosen, Charleston, interview Mar. 12, 1999.

48. Visit to Stanley Drug, Houston, Nov. 4, 1998.

49. Richard Miller, Atlanta, telephone interview, Sept. 18, 1998; Doc Miller, telephone interview, Oct. 14, 1998.

50. Thompson, *Four Moments of the Sun*, 178–81.

51. Visit to Corner Drugstore, Vicksburg, May 19, 1997; Joseph Gerache, telephone interview, Feb. 12, 1998.

52. This list was compiled from information provided by Joseph Gerache of the Corner Drugstore and by Martin Mayer of Indio Products.

53. Nettie Seligmann, Los Angeles, telephone interview, May 27, 1995.

54. Visit to Harry's Occult Shop, Philadelphia, May 29, 1998.

Chapter 7. Candle Shops, Botánicas, Yerberías, and Web Sites

1. Florida Writers' Project, "Duval County, Florida, Negro Superstitions," n.d., #1986-004. GG; see also Stetson Kennedy, *Palmetto Country*, 166–68.

2. Agent for Curios, Jacksonville, Fla., Hyatt, *Hoodoo* 2: 1075.

3. Visit to Keystone Store, Jacksonville, Fla., and interview with Deloris Kay, June 25, 1998; telephone interview, Sept. 19, 1998. Don Meltin, "Friday the Thirteenth," *Florida Times-Union*, May 13, 1983, D1, D8.

4. See Henri Gamache, *Master Book of Candle Burning* (New York: Dorene Publishing, 1942), 42–46.

5. Dale Silverberg, Philadelphia, interview, May 29, 1998; visit to Ray's New Age Curios and interview with Ray Minton and Albert Hampton, May 29, 1998.

6. Visit to Eye of the Cat, Columbia, S.C., and interview with Thomas Williams, Mar. 15, 1999.

7. Visit to Botánica Chicas-Rendón, New York, and interview with Alex Wer, manager, Oct. 3, 1994; Otto Chicas, interview July 9, 1998; González-Wippler, *Santería, the Religion*, 283–84; John Schwartz, "The Superstition Trade," *Newsweek*, June 13, 1988, 13.

8. Visit to Seven Powers Garden, Los Angeles, and interview with Ray Pizzarro, Apr. 16, 1997; letters Oct. 13 and Nov. 7, 1998. Caesar C. Cantu, "Speaking of the Reverend Ray Pizzarro," *Comercio* 21 (Nov. 1979): 6.

9. See Ethelyn Orso, *The St. Joseph's Altar Traditions of South Louisiana* (Lafayette: Center for Louisiana Studies, Univ. of Southwestern Louisiana, 1990); also see David Estes, "Across Ethnic Boundaries: St. Joseph's Day in a New Orleans Afro-American Spiritual Church," *Mississippi Folklore Register* 21 (1987): 9–22; and David Estes, "St. Joseph's Day in New Orleans: Contemporary Urban Varieties of an Ethnic Festival," *Louisiana Folklore Miscellany* 6, no. 2 (1987): 35–43.

10. Visit to Botánica Solano, New Orleans, and interviews with Frank Rodriguez Mar. 16 and 18, 1995; Mar. 16 and 18, 1998; Oct. 31, 1998.

11. Cari Roy, New Orleans, telephone interview, Nov. 5, 1999.

12. See Brown, *Mama Lola,* 70–78.

13. Visit to Botánica San Miguel, Silver Spring, Md., and interview with Catalina de Guzman, Sept. 25, 1996, Oct. 14, 1998. Thanks to Denise Boswell for acquainting me with Catalina.

14. Gary McKay, "Saints, Spirits, and Spells"; Macario Ramirez, a Houston dealer in Mexican folk art and expert on Mexican culture, provided information on the spread of Santería into Texas and Mexico, interview Nov. 4, 1998. For Santería in the Dallas–Fort Worth area, see J. D. Arnold, "Of Saints and Sacrifice," *FW Weekly*, Dec. 25, 1997–Jan. 1, 1998, 8, 9, 11, 12. Cynthia Vidaurri, Latino Project Coordinator at the Smithsonian's Center for Folklife Programs and Cultural Studies, provided information on traditional Mexican yerberías, interview Dec. 11, 1998.

15. Visit to Rosario's Mistic, Houston, and interview with Rosario Garcia and Eloy Nañez, Nov. 4, 1998.

16. Catherine Yronwode, Forestville, Calif., telephone interviews June 11 and 12, 1998. Additional biographical information from Catherine Yronwode's Home Page www.luckymojo.com/cat.

Chapter 8. The Manufacturers

1. For information on race records, see Jeff Todd Titan, *Early Downhome Blues: A Musical and Cultural Analysis* (Urbana: Univ. of Illinois Press, 1977), and Paul Oliver, *Blues Fell This Morning* (Cambridge, England: Cambridge Univ. Press, Canto Edition, 1994). For information about the ethnic cosmetics industry, see A'Lelia Bundles, *Madam C. J. Walker, Entrepreneur* (New York: Chelsea House Publishers, 1991); Noliwe Rooks, *Hair Raising: Beauty, Culture, and African American Women* (New Brunswick, N.J.: Rutgers Univ. Press, 1996); and Kathy Peiss, *Hope in a Jar: The Making of America's Beauty Culture* (New York: Henry Holt and Co., 1998).

2. Nathan Hobley, New Orleans, interview by Zoe Posey, Jan., 1941, in Clayton, *Mother Wit,* 116–17.

3. Nathaniel Lewis, Tin City, Ga., Georgia Writers' Project, *Drums and Shadows,* 15–16; The Unkus Man, New Orleans, Hyatt, *Hoodoo* 2: 1308; Nathan Hobley, New Orleans, interview by Zoe Posey, Nov. 25, 1940, LWP folder 25.

4. "Slick Man Lures Boy from Africa, Beats and Robs Him," *Chicago Defender*, June 13, 1914, p. 3, col. 1. It is unclear why five years elapsed between this incident and the mail fraud investigation. Thanks to Bradford Verter for providing a copy of this article.

5. The 1920 census lists Loren [*sic*] W. DeLaurence, publisher and book dealer, his wife, Pauline, and their thirteen-year-old son, Velo, living at 4634 Drexel Blvd; sheet 7, line 38, Enumeration District 166, Chicago, microfilm roll 313, National Archives and Records Administration, Washington, D.C. L. W. DeLaurence was not enumerated in the 1910 census, although he lived in Chicago at the time. Death certificate #26763, Illinois Department of Public Health, Division of Vital Records.

6. U.S. Post Office, Office of the Postmaster General, transcript of mail fraud hearing, box 29, folder 77, National Archives and Records Administration, Washington, D.C.

7. See W. F. Elkins, "Lauren William DeLaurence and Jamaican Folk Religion," *Folklore* 97 (1986): 215–18. Again, thanks to Bradford Verter.

8. Thanks to Anthony Shafton of Chicago for providing photocopies of his Valmor Dream Book.

9. Terry Zwigoff, "The Valmor Story," *Wierdo* 18 (1993); Zwigoff, telephone interview, Mar. 25, 1995.

10. Elizabeth Tamny, Art Institute of Chicago, telephone interview, June 27, 1997; Alan G. Artner, "Morton Neumann Knows Great Art When He Sees It," *Chicago Tribune Magazine*, Mar. 15, 1981; Suzy Shultz, "Morton G. Neumann, 87, Chicago Art Connoisseur," obituaries, *Chicago Sun-Times*, Apr. 9, 1985.

11. Zwigoff, "The Valmor Story."

12. Agent for Curios, Jacksonville, Fla., Hyatt, *Hoodoo* 2: 1075–88; Mattie Sampson, Brownsville, Ga., *Drums and Shadows*, 55–56.

13. Melinda Menke Burns, Memphis, telephone interview, Nov. 1, 1996; interview with Lista Wayman and Melinda Menke Burns at Keystone Laboratories, Memphis, May 16, 1997.

14. "A Brief History of Lucky Heart Cosmetics," in-house publication, n.d.; Gary Young, letter, Oct. 28, 1996; interview at Lucky Heart Cosmetics, Memphis, May 16, 1997.

15. Horace Bynum Jr., New Orleans, telephone interview, May 27, 1995; anonymous informant, Miami, telephone interview, Sept. 19, 1996; Doc Miller, Atlanta, telephone interview, Oct. 14, 1998; Elliot Schwab, Memphis, telephone interview, Oct. 15, 1998; Ann Epstein, Charleston, interview Mar. 12, 1999.

16. *Sonny Boy Guide to Success and Power*, catalog, 2nd ed. (1990), 11, 13, 25.

17. Owner, Sonny Boy's Products, Birmingham, name withheld by request; answer to questionnaire 1994; telephone interview Oct. 1, 1998. I was told by Sam Rosen, Charleston, that Barry Bloom had tried to buy Sonny Boy in the early 1980s, interview Mar. 12, 1999.

18. Chicago research is hampered by the fact that city directories only appeared sporadically after 1917 and ceased altogether in 1929. Telephone directories

can be used to determine when a particular company opened and where it was located, but they provide no information on ownership. Former Lama Temple employees did not know the name of the original owner.

19. Martin Mayer, letters Mar. 14 and Nov. 1, 1994; telephone interviews Nov. 16 and Jan. 17, 1995; personal interview, Washington, D.C., June 19, 1998; Si Rosenstein (general manager of Candle Corporation of America 1959–77), letters Sept. 15, 1996, Nov. 10, 1996.

20. Ed Kay, Arlington, Tex., telephone interviews Mar. 29, 1997; Apr. 23 and Oct. 1, 1998. Advertisement for Young's Chinese Wash, 1951 Clover Horn catalog, 18.

21. Robert Amateau, answer to questionnaire, Mar. 18 and Mar. 28, 1994; visit to M & A Amateau Oct. 3, 1994; Robert and Steve Amateau, New York, interview July 9, 1998.

22. Milton Benezra, Original Products, the Bronx, interview July 10, 1998; telephone interviews Sept. 4 and Oct. 2, 1998.

23. Eleanor Blum, Chicago, telephone interview, Apr. 7, 1995.

24. Martin Mayer, letters Mar. 14 and Nov. 1, 1994; telephone interviews Nov. 16, 1995, and June 17, 1996; interview, Washington, D.C., Apr. 5, 1997; visit to Indio Products Apr. 16, 1997; interview, Washington, D.C., June 19, 1998; telephone interviews July 3 and Oct. 9, 1998.

Chapter 9. John the Conqueror: From Magical Root to Manufactured Product

1. Wyatt MacGaffey, letter, Aug. 12, 1998.
2. Douglass, *Life and Times*, 134–41; Bibb, in Osofsky, ed. *Puttin' On Ole Massa*, 70–71.
3. *Southern Workman* 7, no. 4 (Apr. 1878): 30–31; in Waters, *Strange Ways*, 131–39.
4. Mary Alicia Owen, "Among the Voodoos," in *Proceedings of the International Folklore Congress*, ed. J. Jacobs and A. Nutt (London, 1892), 232, 243.
5. Hampton Folklore Society, "Remedies to Cure Conjuration," *Southern Workman* 28, no. 3 (1899): 112–13; in Waters, *Strange Ways*, 326.
6. Puckett, *Folk Beliefs*, 299; Ruth Bass, "Fern Seed—For Peace," in *Folk-Say; A Regional Miscellany*, ed. Benjamin A. Botkin (Norman: Univ. of Oklahoma Press, 1930), 150.
7. Grandson Talks about Doctor Jones, Brunswick, Ga., Hyatt, *Hoodoo* 2: 1750.
8. Laughing Doctor, Waycross, Ga., Hyatt, *Hoodoo* 2: 1484; Doctor England, Norfolk, Va., vol. 2: 1396; First Doctor, Richmond, vol. 2: 935.
9. Madame Ducoyielle, New Orleans, interview by Robert McKinney, 1936, LWP folder 44.
10. Hurston, *Mules and Men*, 274.
11. Toothache-Tree, Brunswick, Ga., Hyatt, *Hoodoo* 3: 2034; Informant 995, St. Petersburg, vol. 1: 593; Informant 674, Vicksburg, Miss., vol. 1: 594; Hustling Woman, Memphis, vol. 2: 1338.
12. Hurston, *Mules and Men*, 275.

13. Informant 1171, Waycross, Ga., Hyatt, *Hoodoo* 1: 594; Informant 1544, Memphis, vol. 1: 593.

14. Madam Lindsey, Algiers, Hyatt, *Hoodoo* 2: 1514–15; Informant 1396, Fayetteville, N.C., vol. 1: 595; Hoodoo Book Man, New Orleans, vol. 2: 1755–56.

15. F. Roy Johnson, *The Fabled Doctor Jim Jordan*, 50–51.

16. Ruth Bass, "Fern Seed—For Peace," 150.

17. Cunningham, *Encyclopedia of Magical Herbs*, 195; Sarah Bunney, ed., *The Illustrated Book of Herbs: Their Medical and Culinary Uses* (New York: Gallery Books, 1985), 169; Claire Kowalchik and William Hylton, eds., *Rodale's Illustrated Encyclopedia of Herbs* (Emmaus, Pa.: Rodale Press, 1987), 447.

18. Clarence Meyer, letter, Feb. 10, 1994.

19. Varro Tyler, "The Elusive History of High John the Conqueror Root," *Journal of the History of Pharmacy* 33, no. 4 (1991): 164–66.

20. Samuel Touchstone, *Herbal and Folk Medicine of Louisiana and Adjacent States* (Princeton, La.: Folk-Life Books, 1983), 77; Norman Taylor, *The Garden Dictionary* (New York: Houghton Mifflin, 1938), 40.

21. James Brown, Samford University, Birmingham, Ala., letter describing a conversation with Tommie Bass, Mar. 6, 1995.

22. George M. Hocking, *Dictionary of Terms in Pharmacognosy* (Springfield, Ill.: C. C. Thomas, 1955), 116.

23. Cunningham, *Encyclopedia*, 156.

24. Pam Chavers, e-mail, Sept. 27, 1995.

25. Jim Haskins, *Voodoo and Hoodoo* (Chelsea, Mich.: Scarborough House Publishers, 1978), 152.

26. Cunningham, *Encyclopedia*, 213.

27. Tyler, "Elusive History," 165.

28. Thompson, *Flash of the Spirit*, 131.

29. Hyatt, *Hoodoo* 1: 293. Unfortunately, this man is only mentioned in passing and his complete interview is not included.

30. *Encyclopedia Britannica*, 11th ed., vol. 22 (1910), 304. For an account of the search for Prester John in Asia, see L. N. Gumilev, *Searches for an Imaginary Kingdom: The Legend of the Kingdom of Prester John* (New York: Cambridge Univ. Press, 1987); for Ethiopia, see Elaine Sanceau, *The Land of Prester John: A Chronicle of Portuguese Exploration* (New York: Knopf, 1944).

31. MacGaffey, *Religion and Society in Central Africa*, 198–200.

32. Thompson, *Flash of the Spirit*, 166–67.

33. Haitian oungan Max Beauvoir, Washington, D.C., telephone interview, Feb. 1997; oloricha and anthropologist Michael Atwood Mason, Washington, D.C., interview 1994; confirmed by New Orleans Voodoo priestess Ava Kay Jones, interview Apr. 28, 1996.

34. Jacobs and Kaslow, *Spiritual Churches of New Orleans*, 91.

35. Mac Rebennack, *Under a Hoodoo Moon: The Life of Doctor John the Night Tripper* (New York: St. Martin's Press, 1994), 140–41.

36. John and Old Marster stories were first recorded in 1888 by Rev. Charles C. Jones in *Negro Myths from the Georgia Coast Told in the Vernacular*, and are

also found in Arthur Huff Fauset's article "Negro Folk Tales from the South," published in the *Journal of American Folklore* in 1927.

37. Zora Neale Hurston, "High John de Conker," *American Mercury* 57 (1943): 450–58.

38. Alan Dundes, ed. *Mother Wit from the Laughing Barrel: Readings in the Interpretation of Afro-American Folklore* (Jackson: Univ. Press of Mississippi, 1973), 542.

39. Hyatt, *Hoodoo* 4: 3678.

40. Elve Louise Newman, *The Ramifications of Voodoo and Gris-Gris into Some New Orleans Drugstores* (undergraduate thesis, Loyola University School of Pharmacy, 1943), illustration facing page 31.

41. Varro Tyler, Purdue University, letter, Feb. 14, 1995.

42. Reproduced in Oliver, *Blues Fell This Morning*, 124. Fort Washington, Wisconsin, was also the home of Paramount, one of the best-known producers of "race records." I suspect that the Algiers Company was a subsidiary of Paramount.

43. George B. Wood and Franklin Bache, *Dispensatory of the United States of America* (Philadelphia: J. B. Lippincott, 1865), 487–91.

44. Hocking, *Dictionary*, 116; Cunningham, *Encyclopedia*, 108–9, 123–24; Touchstone, *Herbal and Folk Medicine*, 109.

45. Miracle Workshop, Brooklyn, Oct. 1, 1994; New Orleans Historic Voodoo Museum, Mar. 20, 1995; House of Power, Houston, Nov. 4, 1998.

46. Tyler, letter Feb. 14, 1995.

47. Powdermaker, *After Freedom*, 325–26.

48. Ira Wands, Florence, S.C., Apr. 6, 1939, Hyatt, *Hoodoo* 2: 1935.

49. Martin Mayer, Los Angeles, letter Nov. 1, 1994.

50. *Marie Laveau's Old and New Black and White Magic* (n.p., n.d.), 12, 17, 23, 29.

51. Rucker, *Black Herman*, 125.

52. Lewis de Claremont, *Legends of Incense, Herb, and Oil Magic* (New York: Dorene Publishing, 1938), 24, 84.

53. *Sonny Boy Guide to Success and Power*, 7, 10.

54. Anna Riva, *Modern Witchcraft Spellbook* (Los Angeles: International Imports, 1972), 51; *Modern Herbal Spellbook* (Los Angeles: International Imports, 1974), 36.

55. Mister Felix, *Alleged Do-It-Yourself Sure Fast Success Guide* (1994).

56. Luz Vara, House of Power, Houston, interview, Nov. 4, 1998.

57. Ray Pizzaro, Los Angeles, interview, Apr. 16, 1997.

Conclusion

1. Ricardo Obatala's Philadelphia-based La Milagrosa Incorporated is not the same company as La Milagrosa Products of Brooklyn.

2. Martin Mayer, Indio Products, interview, July 3, 1998.

Bibliography

Allain, Hélène d'Aquin. *Souvenirs d'Amerique et de France par une Créole*. Paris: Perisse Frères, 1883.

Armstrong, Louis. "Storyville—Where the Blues Were Born." *True* 21, no. 126 (1947): 32, 100–105.

Arnold, J. D. "Of Saints and Sacrifice." *FW (Fort Worth) Weekly* (Dec. 25, 1997–Jan. 1, 1998): 8, 9, 11, 12.

Arthur, Stanley Clisby. *Old Families of Louisiana*. 1931. Rpt. Baton Rouge, La.: Claitor's Publishing Division, 1971.

Asbury, Herbert. *The French Quarter: An Informal History of the New Orleans Underworld*. New York: Garden City Publishing, 1938.

Aurand, A. Monroe. *The "Pow-Wow" Book: A Treatise on the Art of "Healing by Prayer" and "Laying on of Hands," Etc., Practiced by the Pennsylvania-Germans and Others*. Harrisburg, Pa.: Aurand Press, 1929.

Bacon, Alice M., and Leonora Herron. "Conjuring and Conjure Doctors in the Southern United States." *Southern Workman* 24, no. 7 (July 1895); no. 11, 117–18; (Nov. 1895): 193–94; (Dec. 1895): 209–11. Rpt. in Waters, *Strange Ways, 227–29, 235–42*.

Bass, Ruth. "Fern Seed—For Peace." In *Folk-Say: A Regional Miscellany*. Ed. Benjamin A. Botkin. Norman: Univ. of Oklahoma Press, 1930.

Bastide, Roger. *The African Religions of Brazil: Toward a Sociology of the Interpretation of Civilizations*. 1960. English translation, Baltimore: Johns Hopkins Univ. Press, 1978.

Bell, Michael E. "Harry Middleton Hyatt's Quest for the Essence of Human Spirit." *Journal of the Folklore Institute* 1, no. 1–2 (1979): 1–27.

———. "Pattern, Structure, and Logic in Afro-American Hoodoo Performance." Ph.D. diss., Indiana Univ., 1980.

Berendt, John. *Midnight in the Garden of Good and Evil: A Savannah Story*. New York: Random House, 1994.

Berlin, Ira. *Many Thousands Gone: The First Two Centuries of Slavery in North America*. Cambridge: Harvard Univ. Press, 1998.

Berry, Jason. *The Spirit of Black Hawk: A Mystery of Africans and Indians*. Jackson: Univ. Press of Mississippi, 1995.

Bibb, Henry. *Narrative of the Life and Adventures of Henry Bibb, an American Slave*. 1849. Rpt. in *Puttin' on Ole Massa*, ed. Osofsky, 1969.

Bibbs, Susheel. *Heritage of Power*. San Francisco: MEP Publications, 1998.

Bodin, Ron. *Voodoo Past and Present*. Lafayette: Center for Louisiana Studies, Univ. of Southwestern Louisiana, 1990.

Brandon, George. *Santería from Africa to the New World: The Dead Sell Memories*. Bloomington: Indiana Univ. Press, 1993.

Brown, David H. "Conjure/Doctors: An Explanation of a Black Discourse in America, Antebellum to 1940." *Folklore Forum: Folk Religions of the African Diaspora* 23, no. 1–2 (1990): 3–46.

———. *The Garden in the Machine: Afro-Cuban Sacred Art and Performance in Urban New Jersey and New York.* Ann Arbor: University Microfilms, 1989.

———. "Altared Spaces: Afro-Cuban Religions and the Urban Landscape in Cuba and the United States." In *Gods of the City: Religion and the American Urban Landscape.* Ed. Robert A. Orsi. Bloomington: Indiana Univ. Press, 1999.

Brown, Karen McCarthy. *Mama Lola: A Vodou Priestess in Brooklyn.* Berkeley and Los Angeles: Univ. of California Press, 1991.

———. "Staying Grounded in a High-Rise Building: Ecological Dissonance and Ritual Accommodation in Haitian Vodou." In *Gods of the City: Religion and the American Urban Landscape.* Ed. Robert A. Orsi. Bloomington: Indiana Univ. Press, 1999.

Brown, William Wells. *My Southern Home; or, The South and Its People.* 1880. Rpt. Upper Saddle River, N.J.: Gregg Press, 1968.

Bryan, Violet Harrington. *The Myth of New Orleans in Literature: Dialogues of Race and Gender.* Knoxville: Univ. of Tennessee Press, 1993.

Buel, James William. *Metropolitan Life Unveiled; or the Mysteries and Miseries of America's Great Cities, Embracing New York, Washington City, San Francisco, Salt Lake City, and New Orleans.* St. Louis: Historical Publishing Company, 1882.

Bundles, A'Lelia Perry. *Madam C. J. Walker, Entrepreneur.* New York: Chelsea House Publishers, 1991.

Bunney, Sarah, ed. *The Illustrated Book of Herbs: Their Medical and Culinary Uses.* New York: Gallery Books, 1985.

Cable, George Washington. "Creole Slave Songs." *Century Magazine* 31, no. 6 (Apr. 1886): 807–28.

Campbell, Edward D. C. Jr., and Kym Rice, eds. *Before Freedom Came: African-American Life in the Antebellum South.* Richmond: Museum of the Confederacy and Univ. of Virginia Press, 1991.

Canizares, Raul. *Walking with the Night: The Afro-Cuban World of Santería.* Rochester, Vt.: Destiny Books, 1993.

Castellanos, Henry. *New Orleans As It Was.* 1895. Rpt. Gretna, La.: Pelican Publishing Co., 1990.

Cassidy, Frederic. *Jamaica Talk: Three Hundred Years of the English Language in Jamaica.* New York: Macmillan, 1961.

Cavendish, Richard. *The Black Arts.* New York: Putnam Publishing Group, 1967.

Chicas-Rendón, Otto, and Héctor Gaitán Alfaro. *Recetario y Oraciones Secretas de Maximón.* New York: Casa de Velas, 1995.

Chireau, Yvonne Patricia. "Conjuring: An Analysis of African American Folk Beliefs and Practices." Ph.D. diss., Princeton, 1994.

Christian, Marcus. "Voodooism and Mumbo Jumbo." In "A History of the Negro in Louisiana." Louisiana Writers' Project, Archives and Manuscripts Division, Earl K. Long Library, Univ. of New Orleans.

Clayton, Edward T. "The Truth About Voodoo." *Ebony*, Apr. 1951, 54–61.

Clayton, Ronnie. "The Federal Writers' Project for Blacks in Louisiana." *Louisiana History* 9, no. 3 (summer 1978): 327–35.

———. *Mother Wit: The Ex-Slave Narratives of the Louisiana Writers' Project*. New York: Peter Lang, 1990.

Congdon-Martin, Douglas. *Images in Black: 150 Years of Black Collectibles*. West Chester, Pa.: Schiffer Publishing, 1990.

Cosentino, Donald L., ed. *Sacred Arts of Haitian Vodou*. Los Angeles: Univ. of California Fowler Museum of Cultural History, 1995.

Courlander, Harold. *The Drum and the Hoe: Life and Lore of the Haitian People*. Berkeley: Univ. of California Press, 1960.

Creel, Margaret Washington. *"A Peculiar People": Slave Religion and Community-Culture among the Gullahs*. New York: New York Univ. Press, 1988.

Cunningham, Scott. *Cunningham's Encyclopedia of Magical Herbs*. St. Paul, Minn.: Llewellyn Publications, 1993.

Curtain, Philip D. *The Atlantic Slave Trade: A Census*. Madison: Univ. of Wisconsin Press, 1969.

Dabney, Thomas Ewing. "Witchcraft Medicine and Voodoo Superstitions." *American Pharmacist* (Sept. 1931): 22–24, 78, 80, 82.

Davis, Rod. *American Voudou: Journey into a Hidden World*. Denton, Tex.: Univ. of North Texas Press, 1998.

Davis, Wade. *Passage of Darkness: The Ethnobiology of the Haitian Zombie*. Chapel Hill: Univ. of North Carolina Press, 1988.

de Claremont, Lewis. *Legends of Incense, Herb, and Oil Magic*. New York: Dorene Publishing, 1938.

Dillon, Catherine. "Voodoo." Louisiana Writers' Project, folders 118, 317, and 319. Natchitoches, La.: Northwestern State Univ., Watson Memorial Library, Cammie G. Henry Research Center, Federal Writers' Collection, 1937–41.

Douglass, Frederick. *The Life and Times of Frederick Douglass, Written by Himself*. 1892. Rpt. New York: Collier Books, 1962.

Drake, Saint Clair, and Horace R. Cayton. *Black Metropolis: A Study of Negro Life in a Northern City*. 1945. Rpt. New York: Harcourt, Brace and World, 1970.

Dundes, Alan, ed. *Mother Wit from the Laughing Barrel: Readings in the Interpretation of Afro-American Folklore*. Jackson: Univ. Press of Mississippi, 1973.

Estes, David. "Across Ethnic Boundaries: St. Joseph's Day in a New Orleans Afro-American Spiritual Church." *Mississippi Folklore Register* 21 (1987).

———. "St. Joseph's Day in New Orleans: Contemporary Urban Varieties of an Ethnic Festival." *Louisiana Folklore Miscellany* 6, no. 2 (1987).

———. "Assessing Zora Neale Hurston's Accounts of Hoodoo in New Orleans." Paper presented at the annual meeting of the American Folklore Society, Jacksonville, Fla., 1992.

———. "The Neo-African Vatican: Zora Neale Hurston's New Orleans." n.p., n.d.

Evanchuk, Roberta J. "When the Curtain Goes Up, the Gods Come Down: Aspects of Performance in Public Ceremonies of Orisha Worship." Ph.D. diss., Univ. of California at Los Angeles, 1996.

Fandrich, Ina Johanna. "The Mysterious Voodoo Queen Marie Laveaux: A Study of Spiritual Power and Female Leadership in Nineteenth Century New Orleans." Ph.D diss., Temple Univ., 1994.

Farmer, David Hugh. *The Oxford Dictionary of Saints*. Oxford, England: Oxford Univ. Press, 1992.

Fenerty, Patricia, and Patricia Fernandez. *1880 Census of New Orleans*. New Orleans: Padraigeen Publications, 1997.

Ferguson, James. *Papa Doc, Baby Doc: Haiti and the Duvaliers*. Cambridge, Mass.: Basil Blackwell, 1987.

Ferguson, Leland. *Uncommon Ground: Archeology and Early African America*. Washington, D.C.: Smithsonian Institution Press, 1992.

Fields, Mamie Garvin, with Karen Fields. *Lemon Swamp and Other Places: A Carolina Memoir*. New York: Free Press, 1983.

Flores-Peña, Ysamur. "Fit for a Queen: Analysis of a Consecration Outfit in the Cult of Yemayà." *Folklore Forum: Folk Religions of the African Diaspora* 23, no. 1–2 (1990): 47–56.

Flores-Peña, Ysamur, and Roberta Evanchuk. *Santería Garments and Altars: Speaking without a Voice*. Jackson: Univ. Press of Mississippi, 1994.

Florida Writers' Project (FWP). Florida Folklore Archives, Bureau of Florida Folklife Programs, White Springs, Fla., 1935–45.

Frazer, James George. *The Golden Bough: A Study in Magic and Religion*. 1922. Rpt. New York: Macmillan, 1951.

Gardner, Dore, and Kay F. Turner. *Niño Fidencio: A Heart Thrown Open*. Santa Fe: Museum of New Mexico Press, 1992.

Geary, Patrick J. *Furta Sacra: Thefts of Relics in the Central Middle Ages*. Princeton: Princeton Univ. Press, 1978.

Gehman, Mary. *The Free People of Color of New Orleans*. New Orleans: Margaret Media, 1994.

Gamache, Henri. *Master Book of Candle Burning*. New York: Dorene Publishing, 1942.

Georgia Writers' Project. *Drums and Shadows: Survival Studies among the Georgia Coastal Negroes*. 1940. Rpt. Athens: Univ. of Georgia Press and Brown Thrasher Books, 1986.

Ginzburg, Carlo. *The Night Battles: Witchcraft and Agrarian Cults in the Sixteenth and Seventeenth Centuries*. 1966. Translation, Baltimore: Johns Hopkins Univ. Press, 1983.

González-Wippler, Migene. *Santería, the Religion: A Legacy of Faith, Rites, and Magic*. New York: Harmony Books, 1989.

Gorn, Elliot J. "Black Magic: Folk Beliefs of the Slave Community." In *Science and Medicine in the Old South*. Eds. Ronald L. Numbers and Todd L. Savitt. Baton Rouge: Louisiana State Univ. Press, 1989.

Gregory, Steven. *Santería in New York City: A Study in Cultural Resistance*. Ph.D. diss., New School for Social Research, New York, 1986.

Gumilev, L. N. *Searches for an Imaginary Kingdom: The Legend of the Kingdom of Prester John*. New York: Cambridge Univ. Press, 1987.

Hall, Gwendolyn Midlo. *Africans in Colonial Louisiana: The Development of Afro-Creole Culture in the Eighteenth Century*. Baton Rouge: Louisiana State Univ. Press, 1992.

Hampton Folklore Society. "Remedies to Cure Conjuration." *Southern Workman* 28, no. 3 (Mar. 1899): 112–13. Rpt. in Waters, *Strange Ways*, 326.

Hanger, Kimberly S. *Bounded Lives, Bounded Places: Free Black Society in Colonial New Orleans, 1769–1803*. Durham, N.C.: Duke Univ. Press, 1997.

Haskins, Jim. *Voodoo and Hoodoo*. Chelsea, Mich.: Scarborough House Publishers, 1978.

Hauptmann, O. H. "Spanish Folklore from Tampa, Florida: Witchcraft." *Southern Folklore Quarterly* (1939): 3–4.

Hawkins, John. "Magical Medical Practice in South Carolina." *Popular Science Monthly* 70, no. 2 (Feb. 1907): 165–74.

Hearn, Lafcadio. "The Last of the Voudoos." *Harper's Weekly Magazine*, Nov. 7, 1885.

———. "New Orleans Superstitions." *Harper's Weekly Magazine*, Dec. 25, 1886, 843.

Herskovits, Melville. *Dahomey: An Ancient West African Kingdom*. Vol. 2. New York: J. J. Augustin, 1938.

———. *The Myth of the Negro Past*. 1941. Rpt. Boston: Beacon Press, 1990.

Hirsch, Arnold, and Joseph Logsdon, eds. *Creole New Orleans: Race and Americanization*. Baton Rouge: Louisiana State Univ. Press, 1992.

Hochuli, Paul. "Voodoo in Houston." *Houston Press*, Mar. 22–26, 1937.

Hocking, George M. *Dictionary of Terms in Pharmacognosy*. Springfield, Ill.: C. C. Thomas, 1955.

Hudson, Wilson Mathis. *The Healer of Los Olmos, and Other Mexican Lore*. Dallas: Southern Methodist Univ. Press, 1951.

Hughes, Robert. *Heaven and Hell in Western Art*. New York: Stein and Day, 1968.

Hurston, Zora Neale. "Hoodoo in America." *Journal of American Folklore* 44 (Oct.–Dec. 1931): 320–417.

———. *Mules and Men*. 1935. Rpt. New York: Harper Perennial Library, 1990.

———. "High John de Conker." *American Mercury* 57 (1943): 450–58.

———. Review of Robert Tallant's *Voodoo in New Orleans*. *Journal of American Folklore* 60, no. 238 (1947): 436–38.

Hyatt, Harry Middleton. *Hoodoo-Conjuration-Witchcraft-Rootwork*. 5 vols. Hannibal, Mo.: Western Publishing Co., 1970–78.

Iwu, Maurice Mmaduakolam. *Symbols and Selectivity in Traditional African Medicine*. Nsukka, Nigeria: Univ. of Nigeria, 1990.

Jacobs, Claude F., and Andrew Kaslow. *The Spiritual Churches of New Orleans: Origins, Beliefs, and Rituals of an African-American Religion*. Knoxville: Univ. of Tennessee Press, 1991.

Jahoda, Gustav. *The Psychology of Superstition*. Harmondsworth, England: Penguin Books, 1969.

Johnson, F. Roy. *The Fabled Doctor Jim Jordan: A Story of Conjure*. Murphreesboro, N.C.: Johnson Publishing, 1963.

Johnson, James Weldon. *Black Manhattan*. 1930. Rpt. New York: Arno Press, 1968.

Johnson, Jerah. "Marcus B. Christian and the WPA History of Black People in Louisiana." *Louisiana History* 10, no. 1 (winter 1979): 113–15.

————. "New Orleans' Congo Square: An Urban Setting for Early Afro-American Culture Formation." *Louisiana History* 32, no. 2 (spring 1991): 140–47.

Jones, Charles Colcock. *The Religious Instruction of the Negroes in the United States.* 1842. Rpt. Freeport, N.Y.: Books for Libraries Press, 1971.

Joyner, Charles. *Down by the Riverside: A Slave Community in South Carolina.* Urbana: Univ. of Illinois Press, 1984.

————. *Remember Me: Slave Life in Coastal Georgia.* Atlanta: Georgia Humanities Council, 1989.

————. Forward. Patricia Jones-Jackson, *When Roots Die: Endangered Traditions on the Sea Islands.* Athens: Univ. of Georgia Press, 1987.

Kennedy, Stetson. *Palmetto Country.* 1942. Rpt. Tallahassee: Florida A & M Univ., 1989.

Kinser, Samuel. *Carnival, American Style: Mardi Gras at New Orleans and Mobile.* Chicago: Univ. of Chicago Press, 1990.

Kowalchik, Claire, and William Hylton, eds. *Rodale's Illustrated Encyclopedia of Herbs.* Emmaus, Pa.: Rodale Press, 1987.

Lambo, T. Adeoye. "Traditional African Cultures and Western Medicine." In *Medicine and Culture, Proceedings of a Symposium Organized by the Wellcome Institute of the History of Medicine, London, and the Wenner-Gren Foundation for Anthropological Research, New York.* Ed. Lynn Payer. London: Wellcome Institute, 1989.

Latrobe, Benjamin. *Impressions Respecting New Orleans: Diary and Sketches 1818– 1820.* Ed. Samuel Wilson Jr. New York: Columbia Univ. Press, 1951.

Le Page du Pratz, Antoine. *The History of Louisiana or of the Western Parts of Virginia and Carolina, with an Account of the Settlements, Inhabitants, Soil, Climate, and Products.* 1758. English translation, London: Beckett, 1774.

Louisiana Writers' Project (LWP). Northwestern State Univ., Natchitoches, Louisiana, Watson Memorial Library, Cammie G. Henry Research Center, Federal Writers' Collection, 1937–1941. Duplicate copies of some of this material also located in the Robert Tallant Papers, Louisiana Division, New Orleans Public Library.

Lubar, Steven, and W. David Kingery, eds. *History from Things: Essays on Material Culture.* Washington D.C.: Smithsonian Institution Press, 1993.

MacGaffey, Wyatt. *Religion and Society in Central Africa: The BaKongo of Lower Zaire.* Chicago: Univ. of Chicago Press, 1986.

————. *Art and Healing of the Bakongo Commented by Themselves: Minkisi from the Laman Collection.* Stolkholm: Folkens Museum-Ethnografiska, 1991.

————. The Eyes of Understanding: Kongo Minkisi. In *Astonishment and Power: Kongo Minkisi and the Art of Reneé Stout.* Washington, D.C.: Smithsonian Institution, National Museum of African Art, 1993.

Mangione, Jerre. *The Dream and the Deal: The Federal Writers' Project, 1935–1943.* New York: Avon Books, 1972.

Margolies, Luise. "José Gregorio Hernández: The Historical Development of a Venezuelan Popular Saint." *Studies in Latin American Popular Culture* 3 (1984): 28–46.

McKay, Gary. "Saints, Spells, and Spirits." *Houston Metropolitan Magazine*, Apr. 1991, 50–54.

McKee, Margaret, and Fred Chisenhall. *Beale Black and Blue*. Baton Rouge: Louisiana State Univ. Press, 1981.

McTeer, J. Edwin. *High Sheriff of the Low Country*. Beaufort, S.C.: JEM Co., 1970.

———. *Fifty Years as a Low Country Witch Doctor*. Beaufort, S.C.: JEM Co., 1976.

Merrifield, Ralph. "Witch Bottles and Magical Jugs." *Folk-Lore* 66 (Mar. 1955): 195–207.

Métraux, Alfred. *Voodoo in Haiti*. 1959. Translation, New York: Schocken Books, 1972.

Meyer, Joseph. *The Herbalist*. 1918. Revised and enlarged edition. New York: Rand McNally, 1960.

Michaelson, Michael. 1972. "Can a 'Root Doctor' Actually Put a Hex On or Is It All a Great Put-On?" *Today's Health* (Mar. 1972): 39–41.

Minutaglio, Bill. "Los Grandes." *Dallas Life Magazine*, Sunday Magazine of the *Dallas Morning News*, Jan. 23, 1994, 6–10, 19.

Morrison, Betty L. *A Guide to Voodoo in New Orleans, 1820–1940*. Gretna, La.: Her Publishing, 1970. Newspaper citations listed in this bibliography were accessed on microfilm at the Library of Congress Newspapers and Current Periodicals Reading Room, and the New Orleans Public Library Louisiana Division.

Murphy, Joseph M. *Ritual Systems in Cuban Santería*. Ann Arbor, Mich.: University Microfilms, 1981.

———. *Santería: African Spirits in America*. Boston: Beacon Press, 1993.

Neeley, Bobby Joe. "Contemporary Afro-American Voodooism (Black Religion): The Retention and Adaptation of the Ancient African-Egyptian Mystery System." Ph.D. diss., Univ. of California at Berkeley, 1988.

Newman, Elve Louise. "The Ramifications of Voodoo and Gris-Gris into Some New Orleans Drugstores." Undergraduate thesis, Loyola Univ. School of Pharmacy, 1943.

Oliver, Paul. *Blues Fell This Morning*. 1960. Rpt. Cambridge, England: Cambridge Univ. Press, Canto Edition, 1994.

Orso, Ethelyn. *The St. Joseph Altar Traditions of South Louisiana*. Lafayette: Center for Louisiana Studies, Univ. of Southwestern Louisiana, 1990.

Osofsky, Gilbert, ed. *Puttin' On Ole Massa: The Slave Narratives of Henry Bibb, William Wells Brown, and Solomon Northrup*. New York: Harper and Row, 1969.

Owen, Mary Alicia. "Among the Voodoos." In *Proceedings of the 1891 International Folklore Congress*. Ed. J. Jacobs and A. Nutt (London, 1892), 230–48.

Painter, Floyd. "An Early Eighteenth-Century Witch Bottle." *Chesopiean: A Journal of North American Archeology* 18, no. 3–6 (1980): 62–71.

Peiss, Kathy. *Hope in a Jar: The Making of America's Beauty Culture*. New York: Henry Holt and Co., 1998.

Perdue, Charles L., Jr., Thomas E. Barden, and Robert K. Phillips, eds. *Weevils in the Wheat: Interviews with Virginia Ex-Slaves*. Charlottesville: Univ. of Virginia Press, 1976.

Pinckney, Roger. *Blue Roots: African-American Folk Magic of the Gullah People*. St. Paul: Llewellyn Publications, 1998.

Pinn, Anthony B. *Varieties of African American Religious Experience*. Minneapolis: Fortress Press, 1998.

Pitkin, Helen. *An Angel by Brevet*. Philadelphia: J. B. Lippincott Co., 1904.

Pitts, Stella. "Marie Laveau, the Voodoo Queen." *Dixie*, Sunday Magazine of the *New Orleans Times-Picayune*, Oct. 28, 1973, 26–28, 38–41.

Porteous, Laura. "Renunciation made by Daniel Fagot of his office of Regidor and receiver of fines forfeited to the Royal Treasury of this city to Don Cristoval de Glapion, 1776, translated from the original in the Cabildo at New Orleans." *Louisiana Historical Quarterly* 14 (1931): 372–82.

———. "The Gri-Gri Case: A Criminal Trial in Louisiana during the Spanish Regime, 1773." *Louisiana Historical Quarterly* 17 (1934): 48–63.

Post Office Dept., Office of the Postmaster General, Office of the Solicitor. Transcripts of Hearings on Fraud Cases, 1913–1945. "Prince Huff" case, #86957-E, box 72; DeLaurence case, box 29, folder 77. National Archives and Records Administration, Washington, D.C.

Powdermaker, Hortense. *After Freedom: A Cultural Study in the Deep South*. 1939. Rpt. Madison: Univ. of Wisconsin Press, 1993.

Prown, Jules David. "The Truth of Material Culture: History or Fiction?" In *History from Things: Essays on Material Culture*. Ed. Steven Lubar and W. David Kingery. Washington D.C.: Smithsonian Institution Press, 1993.

Puckett, Newbell Niles. *Folk Beliefs of the Southern Negro*. 1926. Rpt. Montclair, N.J.: Patterson Smith Reprint Series, 1968.

Raboteau, Albert. *Slave Religion: The "Invisible Institution" in the Antebellum South*. Oxford: Oxford Univ. Press, 1978.

Rawick, George P., ed. *The American Slave: A Composite Biography*. Westport, Conn.: Greenwood Publishing, 1972.

Rawley, James A. *The Transatlantic Slave Trade: A History*. New York: W. W. Norton and Co., 1981.

Rebennack, Mac. *Under a Hoodoo Moon: The Life of Doctor John the Night Tripper*. New York: St. Martin's Press, 1994.

Rickles, Patricia K. "The Folklore of Sacraments and Sacramentals in South Louisiana." *Louisiana Folklore Miscellany* 2, no. 2 (Apr. 1965): 27–43.

Riva, Anna. *Modern Witchcraft Spellbook*. Los Angeles: International Imports, 1972.

———. *Modern Herbal Spellbook*. Los Angeles: International Imports, 1974.

Rodman, Selden, and Carole Cleaver. *Spirits of the Night: The Vaudun Gods of Haiti*. Dallas: Spring Publications, 1993.

Rooks, Noliwe M. *Hair Raising: Beauty, Culture, and African American Women*. New Brunswick, N.J.: Rutgers Univ. Press, 1996.

Roussève, Charles Barthelemy. *The Negro in Louisiana: Aspects of His History and His Literature*. New Orleans: Xavier Univ. Press, 1937.

Rucker, Herman. *Black Herman's Secrets of Magic, Mystery, and Legerdemain*. New York: Dorene Publishing, 1938.

Sanceau, Elaine. *The Land of Prester John: A Chronicle of Portuguese Exploration*. New York: Knopf, 1944.

Saxon, Lyle. *Fabulous New Orleans*. 1928. Rpt. Gretna, La.: Pelican Publishing Co., 1988.

Saxon, Lyle, Edward Dreyer, and Robert Tallant. *Gumbo Ya-Ya: Folk Tales of Louisiana*. Louisiana Library Commission for the W.P.A. Louisiana Writers' Project, 1945. Reprint Gretna, La.: Pelican Publishing Co., 1987.

Smith, Michael P. *Spirit World—Photographs and Journal: Pattern in the Expressive Folk Culture of Afro-American New Orleans*. Gretna, La.: Pelican Publishing Co., 1984.

Smith, Reed. "Gullah." *Bulletin of the Univ. of South Carolina*, no. 190 (Nov. 1, 1926): 1–34.

Snow, Loudell F. "'I Was Born Just Exactly with the Gift': An Interview with a Voodoo Practitioner." *Journal of American Folklore* 86, no. 341 (1973): 272–81.

———. "Popular Medicine in a Black Neighborhood." In *Ethnic Medicine in the Southwest*. Ed. Edward H. Spicer. Tucson: Univ. of Arizona Press, 1977.

———. "Sorcerers, Saints, and Charlatans: Black Folk Healers in Urban America." *Culture, Medicine, and Psychiatry* 2 (1978): 69–106.

———. "Mail Order Magic: The Commercial Exploitation of Folk Belief." *Journal of the Folklore Institute* 1, no. 1–2 (1979): 44–74.

———. *Walkin' Over Medicine*. Boulder, Colo.: Westview Press, 1993.

Sobel, Mechel. *The World They Made Together: Black and White Values in Eighteenth-Century Virginia*. Princeton: Princeton Univ. Press, 1987.

South Carolina Writers' Project (SCWP). South Caroliniana Library, Univ. of South Carolina, Columbia, S.C.

Spear, Allan H. *Black Chicago: The Making of a Negro Ghetto, 1890–1920*. Chicago: Univ. of Chicago Press, 1967.

Spencer, Ivor D. *A Civilization That Perished: The Last Years of White Colonial Rule in Haiti*. Lanham, Md.: Univ. Press of America, 1985. Abridged translation of *Description Topographique, Physique, Civile, Politique, et Historic de la Partie Française de l'Isle Saint-Domingue* by Medric Louis Moreau de Saint-Méry, 1797.

Schultes, Richard Evans, and Albert Hofman. *Plants of the Gods: Their Sacred, Healing, and Hallucinogenic Powers*. Rochester, Vt.: Healing Arts Press, 1992.

Schwartz, John. "The Superstition Trade." *Newsweek*, June 13, 1988, 13.

Tallant, Robert. *Voodoo in New Orleans*. 1946. Rpt. Gretna, La.: Pelican Publishing Co., 1983.

Tapper, Jake. "The Witch Doctor Is In." *Washington City Paper*, June 26, 1998, 22–33.

Taylor, Norman, ed. *The Garden Dictionary*. New York: Houghton Mifflin, 1938.

Tedlock, Dennis. *Breath on the Mirror: Mythic Voices and Visions of the Living Maya*. San Francisco: Harper, 1993.

Thomas, Keith. *Religion and the Decline of Magic: Studies in Popular Beliefs in Sixteenth and Seventeenth Century England*. London: Weidenfeld and Nicolson, 1971.

Thompson, Robert Farris. *The Four Moments of the Sun: Kongo Art in Two Worlds*. Washington, D.C.: National Gallery of Art, 1981.

———. *Flash of the Spirit: African and Afro-American Art and Philosophy*. New York: Vintage Books, 1983.

———. *Face of the Gods: Art and Altars of Africa and the African Americas*. New York: Museum for African Art, 1993.

Thornton, John. *Africa and Africans in the Making of the Atlantic World, 1400–1680*. Cambridge: Cambridge Univ. Press, 1992.

Titan, Jeff Todd. *Early Downhome Blues: A Musical and Cultural Analysis*. Urbana: Univ. of Illinois Press, 1977.

Toledano, Roulhac, Sally Kitteridge Evans, and Mary Louise Christovich, comp. *New Orleans Architecture*. Vol. 4, *The Creole Faubourgs*. New Orleans: Friends of the Cabildo, 1974.

Touchstone, Blake. "Voodoo in New Orleans." *Louisiana History* 13 (1978): 371–86.

Touchstone, Samuel. *Herbal and Folk Medicine of Louisiana and Adjacent States*. Princeton, La.: Folk-Life Books, 1983.

Tyler, Varro. "The Elusive History of High John the Conqueror Root." *Journal of the History of Pharmacy* 33, no. 4 (1991): 164–66.

Verswijver, Gustaf et al., eds. *Treasures from Tervuren: Selections from the Belgian Royal Museum for Central Africa*. New York: Prestel-Verlag, 1996.

Warner, Charles Dudley. "A Voodoo Dance." *Harper's Weekly Magazine*, June 25, 1887, 454–55.

Waters, Donald J. *Strange Ways and Sweet Dreams: Afro-American Folklore from the Hampton Institute*. Boston: G. K. Hall, 1983.

Webb, Julie Yvonne. "Louisiana Voodoo and Superstitions Related to Health." *Health Services and Mental Health Association Reports* 86, no. 4 (Apr. 1971): 291–301.

Weiss, Harry B. "Oneirocritica Americana." *Bulletin of the New York Public Library* 48 (June 1944): 519–41.

———. "Preliminary Check List of Dream Books Published in America." *Bulletin of the New York Public Library* 48 (July 1944): 642–53.

Wood, George B., and Franklin Bache. *The Dispensatory of the United States of America*. Philadelphia: J. B. Lippincott, 1865.

Wood, Peter H. *Black Majority: Negroes in Colonial South Carolina from 1670 Through the Stono Rebellion*. New York: W. W. Norton & Co., 1974.

Zwigoff, Terry. "The Valmor Story." *Wierdo*, no. 18 (1993).

Index